The Gypsies

The Peoples of Europe

General Editors
James Campbell and Barry Cunliffe

This series is about the European tribes and peoples from their origins in prehistory to the present day. Drawing upon a wide range of archaeological and historical evidence, each volume presents a fresh and absorbing account of a group's culture, society and sometimes turbulent history.

Already published

The Mongols
David Morgan

The Basques
Roger Collins

The Franks
Edward James

The Bretons
Patrick Galliou and Michael Jones

The Early Germans
Malcolm Todd

The Illyrians
John Wilkes

The Gypsies
Angus Fraser

The English
Geoffrey Elton

In preparation

The Picts
Charles Thomas

The Armenians
Elizabeth Redgate

The Celts
David Dumville

The Normans
Marjorie Chibnall

The Russians
Robin Milner-Gulland

The Huns
E. A. Thompson

The Spanish
Roger Collins

The Turks
C. J. Heywood

The Sicilians
David Abulafia

The Goths
Peter Heather

The Early English
Sonia Chadwick Hawkes

The Irish
Francis John Byrne and Michael Herity

The Etruscans
Graeme Barker and Thomas Rasmussen

The Lombards
Neil Christie

The Hungarians
Michael Hurst

The Norsemen
John Haywood

The Gypsies

Angus Fraser

BLACKWELL
Oxford UK & Cambridge USA

First published 1992

Blackwell Publishers
108 Cowley Road
Oxford OX4 1JF
UK

238 Main Street, Suite 501
Cambridge, Massachusetts 02142
USA

British Library Cataloguing in Publication Data
A CIP catalogue record for this book is available from the British Library.

Library of Congress Cataloging-in-Publication Data
Fraser, Angus M.
    The Gypsies/Angus Fraser.
        p.   cm. – (The Peoples of Europe)
    ISBN 0-631-15967-3 (alk. paper)
    1. Gypsies. I. Title. II. Series.
DX115.F72   1993
940'.0491497 – dc20   92-5452
                                                    CIP

Typeset in 11 on 12½ pt Sabon by Best-set Typesetter Ltd., Hong Kong
Printed in Great Britain by TJ Press (Padstow) Ltd., Padstow, Cornwall

This book is printed on acid-free paper

Contents

List of Illustrations

Front cover: Kalderash Gypsy women, 1911
Back cover: A cavalcade of 'open-lot' living-waggons

Acknowledgements

I am indebted to James Campbell of Worcester College, Oxford, for the very sharp eye he brought to bear on the draft of this book, to John Davey of Blackwell for his forbearance over the time it took to complete it, and to my son Simon for keeping my computer on the road in times of crisis during the process of writing it.

Introduction

This is the story of a wandering people which arrived in the Balkans in medieval times and gradually spread over the entire continent of Europe and beyond. When they knocked at the gates of western Europe in the guise of pilgrims, they aroused intense curiosity, and theories proliferated about their origins. Only much later did it become possible to deduce from their language where the diaspora had begun. Over the centuries, despite constant exposure to a multitude of influences and pressures, they managed to preserve a distinct identity and to show remarkable powers of adaptation and survival. Indeed, when one considers the vicissitudes they have encountered – for the story now to be related will in large measure be a history of what has been done by others to destroy their separateness – one has to conclude that their main achievement is to have survived at all.

Since, however, it may not be a truth universally acknowledged that the Gypsies are 'a people of Europe', it seems best to begin by considering their eligibility for inclusion in the present series.

If a people is a group of men, women and children with a common language, a common culture and a common racial type, who can be readily distinguished from their neighbours, it is a long time since the Gypsies were that. They have, over the centuries, become remarkably diversified. So too have the meanings attached to the term 'Gypsy' itself – a semantic problem not of the Gypsies' making. The word is the name (or, rather, one of many names) given to them by outsiders.

Confusion in nomenclature has become particularly acute in the twentieth century. At one time the word 'Gypsy' had an essentially racial connotation. The primary definition still given in *The Oxford English Dictionary* (2nd edn, 1989) is:

gipsy, gypsy . . . A member of a wandering race (by themselves called *Romany*), of Hindu origin, which first appeared in England about the beginning of the 16th c. and was then believed to have come from Egypt.
  They have a dark tawny skin and black hair. They make a living by basket-making, horse-dealing, fortune-telling, etc.; and have been usually objects of suspicion from their nomadic life and habits. Their language (called Romany) is a greatly corrupted dialect of Hindi, with large admixture of words from various European lang[uage]s.[1]

Alongside this meaning, the word has acquired a looser significance. Nowadays it is often applied indiscriminately to any itinerant member of the population who is not obviously a tramp. Other descriptions, perhaps more neutral in meaning (since 'Gypsy' soon took on derogatory overtones), have come into favour, both inside and outside the community concerned: the most current of these is 'Traveller', and its equivalent in other languages. The whole issue has become coloured by modern sensitivities in regard to discrimination on grounds of race, and none of the terms used by outsiders is a satisfactory description free from ambiguities.

The pitfalls are amply illustrated in the evolution of the word 'Gypsy' in English law since the late 1950s. It was stripped of all racial or ethnic meaning – first accidentally, then deliberately – in its only two statutory uses during this period. The Highways Act of 1959, in consolidating previous legislation, omitted the old sweeping-up phrase 'or other person travelling' when it specified the group of people who would be committing an offence if they encamped or pitched a booth, stall or stand on a highway (which includes pavement, grassy verge and lay-by). The list of potential offenders was

---

[1] Of the four possible modern spellings – *Gypsy*, *Gipsy*, *gypsy*, *gipsy* – the one used in this book is *Gypsy*, except in quotations incorporating a variant. As for *Romany*, it is convenient to use the alternative *Romani* when referring to the language.

thus reduced to 'a hawker or other itinerant trader or a gipsy'. There was no evidence that the legislators gave much thought to the implications of this highlighting of the word 'gipsy' which meant it was no longer possible to get away from having to interpret it. At a stroke they had created a tricky problem of semantics which – predictably enough[2] – was going to have to be settled in the courts. When the question did eventually come before the High Court in 1967, the judges concluded that, in its context, the word could not be given its primary dictionary meaning of 'member of the Romany race' – not least because it was to them unthinkable that Parliament could have intended to subject someone to a penalty merely by reason of race. They therefore ruled that 'gipsy' should be taken to mean no more than 'a person leading a nomadic life with no fixed employment and with no fixed abode'. A man might, they said, be a 'gipsy' on one day but not on another.[3]

This concept was renewed the following year when the Caravan Sites Act 1968 was passed to regulate the provision of 'gipsy encampments'. The Act defined Gypsies as 'persons of nomadic habit of life, whatever their race or origin', other than travelling showmen or persons engaged in travelling circuses. Thus, whether or not someone was to be considered a Gypsy was to depend expressly on way of life, and not on cultural or ethnic origins. That definition is today the only one extant in English statute law, since the phrase 'or a gipsy' was finally expunged from the highways legislation as being discriminatory.

An ethnic meaning has, however, recently been reaffirmed in a different legal context where precedents created in regard to highways and caravan sites are not necessarily relevant. This came about by virtue of a judgement arising from the 1976 Race Relations Act, which gives protection in Great Britain against discrimination on racial grounds, defined as meaning 'colour, race, nationality, or ethnic or national origins'. Arguments about whether Gypsies were protected by the race rela-

---

[2] Cf. A. M. Fraser, 'References to Gypsies in British highway law', *Journal of the Gypsy Lore Society* (third series), 40 (1961), pp. 137–9. This journal, which will be frequently cited, is hereafter abbreviated to *JGLS*(1), (2), (3), (4) or (5), according to the series.

[3] *Mills v Cooper*, High Court, 1967 (2 Q.B. 459).

Plate 1   Pub sign in Kent. 12 December 1966, © *Frank Martin /* The Guardian; *photograph, The Bodleian Library, Oxford.*

tions legislation had increased steadily over the years, ever since the first Act of 1965, and much effort had been expended over 'No Gypsies' signs put up by some publicans. These were not unlawful in themselves under the first Act but became so subsequently. Some publicans, however, sought safer ground by resorting to notices saying 'No Travellers', a description which gave rise to trickier legal issues, so much so that, when the Commission for Racial Equality contested the display of such a sign in an east London pub named *The Cat and Mutton*, the implications had to engage the judicial attention of, first, Westminster County Court in 1987 and then, in 1988, the Court of Appeal.

The question was whether such a denial of access to goods and services was discrimination 'on racial grounds'. The County Court judge refused to accept the CRE's case that 'Traveller' was synonymous and interchangeable with 'Gypsy' and that Gypsies were an ethnic group: he concluded that notices like the one in *The Cat and Mutton* were not unlawful, and he dismissed the action. The Court of Appeal[4] upheld this finding to the extent that the three judges agreed that 'Traveller' was not synonymous with 'Gypsy' and that the class of persons excluded by the sign was not confined to Gypsies: there had therefore been no direct discrimination. However, they went on to confirm that Gypsies *were* a racial group for the purposes of the Act. A notice saying 'No Gypsies' would therefore be unlawful; moreover, a 'No Travellers' sign constituted indirect discrimination, to the detriment of Gypsies, by imposing a condition (of not being a Traveller) which fell more heavily on them than on people of other racial groups.

If excuse is needed for having plunged here into such legal niceties, it lies in the fact that we shall find that the question of Gypsy identity has attended their passage through Europe ever since they first arrived, and these legal debates in English courts serve very well to illustrate an important dilemma which refuses to go away in any discussion of Gypsies. Is it the way of life that is the paramount factor in definition? That may be sufficient identification in cases like some of those just mentioned, but it is far from being a complete answer, for where does it leave the many Gypsies who have adopted a settled way of life and do not 'travel', but who nevertheless feel themselves to be Gypsies? On the other hand, to attach prime importance to biological or genealogical criteria quickly leads to absurd demarcations: Gypsy populations, like others, have a mixture of ancestral strains. A pause for a mathematical calculation indicates that, over the period during

---

[4] *Commission for Racial Equality v Dutton*, Court of Appeal, 1988.

which Gypsies have been in Europe, an average of no more than four marriages in every hundred being with non-Gypsies would have produced a proportion of some 70 per cent non-Gypsy ancestry among their present population in Europe. Three in every hundred would still make it 60 per cent. (In the Third Reich the conceptual and practical difficulties in the racial approach were addressed by creating an extensive state apparatus for investigating Gypsy genealogy and by drawing up rules on the degree of Gypsy ancestry that would be enough to lead to classification as a Gypsy – and, eventually, to the death camps.)

One comes back in the end to 'ethnic' criteria, in the sense in which the term was used by the Court of Appeal in England in July 1988, and it is helpful to dwell a little longer on the reasoning set out, very germanely, in that judgement. It was found that 'there are many people who travel around the country in caravans, vans, converted buses, trailers, lorries and motor vehicles, leading a peripatetic or nomadic way of life. . . . They may all be loosely referred to as "gipsies", but as a group they do not have the characteristics requisite of a racial group within the Act.' A previous judgement in the House of Lords[5] had determined that 'ethnic' in the Race Relations Act was not being used in a strictly biological or racial sense, and had laid down two essential characteristics possessed by an ethnic group within that context: one was 'a long shared history, of which the group is conscious as distinguishing it from other groups, and the memory of which it keeps alive'; the second was 'a cultural tradition of its own, including family and social customs and manners, often but not necessarily associated with religious observance'. Other characteristics which, without being essential, could help to distinguish an ethnic group were: a common geographical origin, or descent from a number of common ancestors; a common language; a common literature peculiar to the group; a common religion different from that of the neighbouring groups or the general community; and being a minority or being an oppressed group within a larger community.

---

[5] *Mandla (Sewa Singh) v Dowell Lee*, House of Lords, 1983 (2 A.C. 548).

In applying these criteria to Gypsies, the aspect of the situation in England which caused most difficulty to one of the three Court of Appeal judges in July 1988 was:

Gipsies prefer to be called 'travellers' as they think that term is less derogatory. This might suggest a wish to lose their separate, distinctive identity so far as the general public is concerned. Half or more of them now live in houses, like most other people. Have gipsies now lost their separate, group identity, so that they are no longer a community recognizable by ethnic origins within the meaning of the Act?

He answered his question by accepting that the fact that some Gypsies had become indistinguishable from other members of the public was not enough to establish loss of a historically determined social identity in the group's own eyes and in the eyes of those outside it. 'Despite their long presence in England, gipsies have not merged wholly in the population, as have the Saxons and the Danes, and altogether lost their separate identity. They, or many of them, have retained a separateness, a self-awareness, of still being gipsies.'

No doubt this argument will continue to rumble on. The problems of definition are in fact particularly acute in Britain, because of the very considerable non-Romany element in the ancestry of the British Gypsy population and the long history of other travelling groups which were in existence well before the Gypsies came and which overlapped with them in many aspects of their social life and means of livelihood. The literally insular nature of British society as a whole has led to a blurring of ethnic distinctions within the Traveller population, particularly as more recent influxes of 'foreign' Gypsies from elsewhere have been much more limited than in a number of other countries. There is also an ideological dimension which tends to confuse the issue: in reaction against misguided preoccupations in the past with questions of 'purity of blood', it has become none too fashionable or respectable in Britain to identify or speak of different categories within the travelling community. Indeed, one detects a good deal of suspicion on the part of some social anthropologists in regard to any emphasis on the Indian origin of Gypsies, and accusations of exoticism, romanticism or escapism are quick to fly.

What guidance can we expect from the Gypsies themselves, self-ascription being an important mechanism in establishing ethnic identity? Who is considered to be 'us' and who is considered to be 'them'? In their eyes the most basic division is between themselves and the *gadžo* (plural *gadžé*),[6] which is the most widespread name for non-Gypsies in dialects of the Romani language. (In Spain the Gypsies' term is *payo*. With Scottish Travellers, the equivalent word is generally *flattie*, while in Ireland, it is *buffer* – neither being Romani.) There is, however, no single Romani word corresponding to 'Gypsy'. An English Gypsy may call himself a *Romanichal* (Gypsy man), a word also used in the USA, Canada and Australia by Gypsies stemming from English Gypsy immigrants. On the Continent, the old-established Gypsies have a variety of names for themselves, such as *calé* (= blacks) in Spain and southern France and *kaale* in Finland, *Sinti* in Germany, and *manouches* in France. In many countries there are numerous representatives from a more recent wave of Gypsy migration, originating in eastern Europe a hundred and more years ago, who call themselves *Rom* or *Roma* and whose speech is much influenced by the impact of their ancestors' long stay in Rumanian-speaking lands – hence their designation as Vlach (= Wallachian) Rom. (The word *Rom* itself has nothing to do with Rumania but means, literally, 'man' or 'husband'.) These Vlach Rom are subdivided into several different tribes: Kalderash, Lovara, Ćurara, etc. At this point a simple 'them and us' dichotomy breaks down. Each Gypsy grouping tends to look upon itself as being the authentic Gypsies. It is clear enough where each of them stands in relation to the *gadžé*. But then there are the others, often in the same country, who are on the borderline between them and the *gadžé*. They recognize that these people are not *gadžé*, because they have a number of things in common with themselves, but somehow they are not the same either. The distinctions are important to Gypsies in matters concerning social relations, marriage and so on, and

[6] The conventions adopted in transcribing Romani are set out on p. 14 below. The word given the form *gadžo* here was introduced into nineteenth-century English literature as *gorgio*, in the writings of George Borrow; many other spellings have been adopted at one time or another, including *gaujo* and *gadjo*.

yet the classifications are seldom clear-cut and unambivalent. The attitudes of Gypsy groups to each other are a contributory factor in the unending debate among outsiders over who should and should not be designated a 'true Gypsy'; they also render it unprofitable to speak in geographical terms of, say, '*French* Gypsies' and make it difficult and misleading to generalize about '*the* Gypsies'.

A final word about awareness of being part of a larger entity. The rise of Gypsy national organizations from the 1960s onwards – in self-defence, to pursue recognition of Gypsy rights and to struggle against policies of rejection and assimilation – has led to international ties which run counter to the fragmented Gypsy order, with its emphasis on difference and distinction. There is the beginning of a new awareness of the historical and cultural ties that Gypsies share.

Perhaps the English term 'people', loose and ambiguous as it is ('a body of persons composing a community, tribe, race, or nation' – *OED*), can just about be stretched to cover this rich mosaic of ethnic fragments which nowadays make up the populations that outsiders call 'Gypsies'. To return to the original question, however, to what extent are they a 'people of Europe'? There are plenty of Gypsies outside Europe – some descended from forebears who never migrated beyond Asia, and many more who themselves emigrated from Europe or are descended from Gypsies who did so. For all except the first category, the long association and intermingling with other peoples in Europe have indelibly marked their language, their ancestry, their culture and their society. After so many centuries, they have every claim to be considered 'of Europe'. They are indeed among the continent's few pan-Europeans.

It is time now to turn to examine their origins. In so doing, shall we then perhaps find more unity – racial, ethnic, linguistic – among the Gypsies' ancestors than has emerged from the diversity of their twentieth-century descendants?

1

Origins

For something like half their history, there are few written records we can usefully turn to in following the Gypsies' trail. Then, once historical references do begin to accumulate, they invariably come from outsiders, and may have been written in ignorance, prejudice and incomprehension.

'The true history of the Gypsy race is in the study of their language', declared one great scholar. Indubitably, the study of Romani can reveal a great deal about the origin and evolution of the language itself. How far that can be equated with the origin and evolution of Romani-speakers is a more speculative matter, and the equivalence cannot be taken for granted. None the less, in seeking to fill the initial void, we now have to turn to philological analysis, in order to test how far linguistic inference can make good what history has failed to record.

The linguistic evidence

The first recorded specimens of Romani – gathered, most likely, in some Sussex ale-house – were relatively late in appearing, being published in England in 1547. These scraps were not recognized for what they were until several centuries later, for they had been tucked away in Andrew Borde's *Fyrst Boke of the Introduction of Knowledge* (completed in 1542) as a sample of 'Egipt speche' – that is, Egyptian (see plate 2). By Borde's day, the language had already had as much time to develop since the Gypsies left their homeland as separates

The .xxxviii. Chapiter treateth of Egipt, and of theyr money and of theyr speche.

Egipt is a countrey ioyned to Jury. The countrey is plentyfull of wyne, corne and hony. Therbe many great wyldernes, in the which be many great wylde beastes. In ye which wyldernes lyuid many holy fathers as it apperith in vitas patru. The people of the coũtry be swarte and doth go disgisid in theyr apparell contrary to other nations, they be lyght fyngerd and vse pyckyng they haue litle maner. Ab euyl loggyng & yet they be pleasant daũsers. Therbe fewe or none of the Egipcians yt doth dwell in egipt for egipt is replenyshed now wt infidel alyons. Ther money is brasse and golde. Yf there be any man yt wyl learne parte of theyr speche Englyshe and Egipt speche foloweth.

Good morow — Lachi tyrdyues
How farre is it to the next towne — Cater mylaʒ barforas

B.iiii.

You be welcome to the towne — Maytta ʒ ves barforas
Wyl you drynke some wyne — Mole pis lauenis
I wyl go with you — A baua tols
Syt you downe and drynke — Hystle lee pee
Drinke drynke for godsake — pepe de ualle
Mayde geue me bread and wyne —
A chae da mano; la boue — Da mai masse
Geue me flesche —
Mayde come hyther harke a worde —
A chae a worde pusse —
Geue me aples and peeres — Da mai pabala ambrell
Much good do it you — Iche misto
Goodnyght — Lachi a tut

The .xxxix. Chapiter treateth of the naturall dysposicion of ye Iues, and of Iury & of theyr money and of theyr speche.

I am an Hebrycyon, some call me a Iew
To Iesu Chryst I was neuer trew
I should kepe Moses olde lawe
I feare at length I shall proue a dawe
Many thynges of Moyses lawes do ȳ not kepe
I beleue not the prophetes, I lye to longe a slepe. Iu

B.v.

Plate 2 Two pages from The Fyrst Boke of the Introduction of Knowledge: the earliest Romani specimens.

modern English from Anglo-Saxon, and Romani was far from being a unitary language. Even Borde's few phrases of 'Egipt speche' show borrowings from Greek and Rumanian. Today, after an evolution extending back for more than a thousand years, with no written models to foster uniformity, there is no single standard of Romani speech. Instead, we have a multiplicity of dialects (in Europe alone, something like 60 or more), obviously related to each other to an important degree, but often mutually unintelligible.

In quoting Romani examples to illustrate the history of the language, I propose to draw particularly on the three finest studies of individual dialects that have ever been written. The first is Alexandre Paspati's *Études sur les Tchinghianés*, published in Constantinople in 1870, which opens with the dictum already quoted: 'La véritable histoire de la race Tchinghianée est dans l'étude de leur idiome'. Then comes John Sampson's monument of patient scholarship, *The Dialect of the Gypsies of Wales*, published in 1926. The third in the trio was written by two Swedes, O. Gjerdman and E. Ljungberg: *The Language of the Swedish Coppersmith Gipsy Johan Dimitri Taikon* (1963).

Conveniently, these three works allow us to examine Romani at three geographical extremes of its European dispersion. They also represent three major types of Romani-speaker. Paspati began to gather his material in the 1850s from nomad Gypsies on the outskirts of Constantinople and in the European part of the Ottoman Empire. He was no secluded scholar: he himself stressed that the language of the Tchinghianés had to be studied in the tent, and that is precisely what he did, becoming in the process a sympathetic friend to the Gypsies. The result was a book of enduring value, even if its phonetics and its etymologies were at times erratic. Its interest is enhanced by the importance of the region of Paspati's investigations as a lengthy and formative stopping place in the original westward migration which first brought Romani-speakers to Europe. A shorthand phrase for the dialect he recorded is 'Greek Romani'.

John Sampson's material was collected over a period of three decades, from 1894 onwards. He was Librarian of Liverpool University and also, at heart, a poet, a romantic and a rebel. He was admitted by the Gypsies as one of their own, and in Wales he lovingly recorded a beautifully constructed dialect which had been preserved in a state far purer than any Romani heard in England at that time. The Gypsies who spoke it had inherited it from ancestors whose presence in Wales can be traced back almost to the seventeenth century: they represent, therefore, a Gypsy population long established in a single country.

The Coppersmith (i.e. Kalderash) dialect recorded by Gjerdman and Ljungberg in the 1940s, on the other hand, was spoken by a first-generation settler in Sweden who had lived and travelled in Norway, Finland, Russia, the Balkans, Poland, Germany and France. Taikon thus exemplified the migratory tendencies of one of the great tribes of Vlach Rom who sprang to prominence in the latter part of the nineteenth century when they came westwards from the Balkans, the Russian steppes and the Hungarian plains, causing almost as much stir as their forefathers who had penetrated western Europe centuries before.

It is time to say something about the phonetic transcription of Romani, for a comparison of the works of Paspati, Sampson, and Gjerdman and Ljungberg immediately brings one up against problems in this area. The trouble arises because, Romani having for long been the language of an unlettered people, there has been no single convention for writing it down. Often transcribers have used the phonetic conventions of their mother-tongue, and languages vary considerably in the consistency between their orthography and their pronunciation. A strictly phonetic alphabet, like that of the International Phonetic Association, in which each symbol indicates a particular sound and none other, would leave no room for ambiguity. But while such an alphabet serves its purpose admirably in a technical work, it uses many more letters than the 26 of the Roman alphabet, and for the more general reader unfamiliar letter-shapes are likely to be somewhat bewildering. I propose to adopt a compromise, in which letters whose approximate sound value is unlikely to be seriously confused by the reader of English are left alone, but a few diacritics and special combinations of letters are used for certain sounds which are variously transcribed in European languages and within English itself. The conventions which will be used here for these special cases are shown in the last column below.

Sound in English word	Paspati	Sampson	Gjerdman/ Ljungberg	
*ch*urch	tch	č	tš	ć
*j*u*dg*e	dj	ǰ	dž	dź
*sh*e	sh	š	š	ś
trea*s*ure	z	ž	ž	ź
in*k-h*orn	kh, k	k′	kh	kh
to*p-h*ole	ph, p	p′	ph	ph
an*t-h*ill	th, t	t′	th	th
lo*ch* (Scottish pronunciation)	kh	χ	x	x

(The conventions in the last column conform with those adopted at a World Romany Congress in 1990, except for *dź*, where the congress opted for a special letter-shape.)[1] The final points to make on phonetic transcription of Romani are that, where it seems necessary, long vowels will be indicated by a macron over the vowel (*ā*, etc) and stress will be shown by an acute accent above the stressed vowel, as in *é*.

Even if it offers no guarantee on the genealogy of the Gypsies themselves, comparative linguistics does give us a wealth of information about the lineage of their dialects. It was first realized some 200 years ago that Romani must be of Indian origin, because of resemblances between its vocabulary and that of some of the Indian languages. The intervening years have added a good measure of clarification, though falling well short of certainty. Since so much has to depend on linguistic deduction, it is as well to pass in review the techniques of comparative linguistics, based on all three main aspects of language – sounds, structure and lexicon.

In establishing affinities between languages, two of the most important clues are community of fundamental vocabulary and similarity of grammatical structure. A third is regularity of

[1] The titles of some of the works cited in footnotes used a different diacritic in conveying these sounds: č, ǰ, š, ž.

sound correspondence – that is, the *consistency* of sound relationships between words which have corresponding meanings
in both languages, so that a given sound in one regularly
becomes another given sound in the other.

It stands to reason that two closely related languages will
have a large number of similar words. Quantity, however, is
not the main consideration: it is important to look particularly
at conservative words of basic significance, least likely to have
been taken over from elsewhere. These conservative elements
of the lexicon include personal pronouns (*I*, *you*, and so on);
verbs expressing basic activities or states (e.g. *drink*, *see*,
sleep); adjectives denoting elementary qualities (e.g. *big* or
hot); or nouns which stand for widely distributed things (e.g.
water or *man*), for parts of the body (e.g. *hair*, *head*, *nose*), or
for close blood relationships (such as *brother*, *father*, *sister*).

As for grammatical features, the accidence or morphology
of a language (that is, the modification of individual words by
inflection or root-vowel changes) is much more conservative
than its syntax (its idiom and sentence construction). When we
meet with resemblances of accidence – e.g. in the declension of
nouns or the conjugation of verbs – it would be far-fetched to
attribute these to chance, and highly unlikely (though not
impossible) that they are the result of borrowing. One cannot
be more categorical than this, since in the last resort there is
nothing that may not be diffused across language boundaries.

If we apply these three tests of evolutionary relationship –
community of basic vocabulary, similarity of grammatical
structure, and regularity of sound correspondence – to Romani
and certain Indic languages, all the findings suggest unity of
origin.

The following table gives a small sample of word community, drawn from the kind of conservative word which is so
important. (At this stage, only Sanskrit and Hindi[2] are quoted
as representing the Indian languages; the question of which
Indic language might be said to have the greatest affinity with
Romani is left for later discussion.)

---

[2] Where *ś* and *ṣ* are roughly equivalent to *sh* in English.

English	Sanskrit	Hindi	Greek Romani	Welsh Romani	Coppersmith Romani
big	vaḍra	barā	baró	bārō	baró
brother	bhrātṛ̥	bhāī	pral, plal	phal	pral
(to) drink	píbati (drinks)	pī-	pī-	pī-	pē-
father	tāta	tāt	dat, dad	dad	dad
hair	vála	bāl	bal	bal	bal
head	śíras	sir	śeró, seró	śērō	śeró
hot, warm	tapta	tattā	tattó	tatō	tató
I	máyā (instr.)	maiṅ	mē	mē	mē
man	mắnuṣa	mānuṣya	manús	manús	manús
nose	nakka	nāk	nak	nakh	nakh
our	asmáka (ours)	hamārā	amaró	amārō	amaró
(to) see	dṛkṣati (sees)	dēkh-	dik-	dikh-	dikh-
sister	bhaginī	bahn	pen, ben	phen	phei
(to) sleep	svápati (sleeps)	sōnā	sov-	sov-	sov-
sun	gharmá (heat)	ghām (heat)	kam	kham	kham
water	paníyá	pānī	paní	pānī	pai
you (sing.)	tuvám	tū	tu	tū	tu

The resemblances between Sanskrit or Hindi and Romani in these examples of basic vocabulary are clear, except perhaps for the words for *brother* and *sister*, to which I shall return later. The list could have been a great deal longer. Each of the three selected Romani dialects contains 500 words or more which are recognizably of Indic origin.

Before following the second and third trail of clues — grammatical apparatus and sound shifts — a wider look at the Indo-Aryan group of languages is needed. Within the great family of tongues known as Indo-European, embracing most of the languages of Europe and stretching as far as central Asia, the easternmost major group goes by the name of Indo-Iranian and is made up of the Indo-Aryan and the Iranian sub-

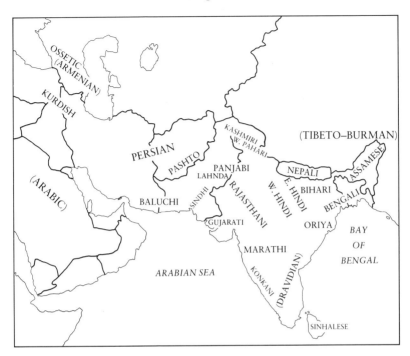

Map 1   Some Indo-Iranian languages.
(Certain non-Indo-Iranian languages in parentheses.)

families. Indo-Aryan, or Indic, developed once some of the
Indo-European speakers (the pastoral nomads known to
history as the Aryans), after generations of eastward migration
from the Eurasian steppes, penetrated the north of the Indian
subcontinent in the second millennium BC, or perhaps earlier.
The oldest recorded form of Indo-Aryan is found in the sacred
texts called Vedas, and from one of the dialects underlying
Vedic Sanskrit there evolved Classical Sanskrit, with a vast
literature. This first period is referred to as Old Indo-Aryan.
Classical Sanskrit became an artificially preserved language,
written according to the book: in it we find no dialects, limited
chronological development, and no geographical divergences.
The Middle Indo-Aryan period started when variant popular
forms, which reduced some of Sanskrit's complexities, began
to develop by about the sixth century BC. These Prakrits
(Prakrit = 'natural', 'unrefined'), which do show evidence of

dialectal differences, seem to have superseded Sanskrit in every-day life as early as the fifth century BC. Sanskrit, however, continued to play a prestigious role similar to that of Latin in Europe and even now is still one of the official languages of India. Prakrit in its turn began (around the sixth century AD) to be overtaken by the most advanced development of Middle Indo-Aryan: Apabhraṃśa ('falling down'). This successor was still a language in Prakrit dress, regulated according to the external model of Sanskrit; sound changes there had been, but changes in grammatical categories and syntax were more limited. We know little about the details of the transition from Middle Indo-Aryan towards the oldest forms of the modern languages classified as New Indo-Aryan, a transition which took place during the centuries leading up to AD 1000, when grammatical innovation was becoming widespread and local differences were growing more and more pronounced. This means that, throughout the very period which is particularly important for establishing the origin and closer affinities of Romani, there is a pall of obscurity over what was happening.

The extensive restructuring of Indo-Aryan which charac-terized the modern speech has led to the great range of spoken forms – several hundred of them – which have emerged as the chief languages of India, Pakistan, Bangladesh, Nepal and Sri Lanka and are now used by well over 650 million people. These include particularly:

Dardic group: Kashmiri
North-Western group: Sindhi, Lahnda (or Western Panjabi)
Northern group: West Pahari, Nepali
Central group: Panjabi, Rajasthani, Gujarati, West Hindi
Mediate group: East Hindi
Eastern group: Bihari, Oriya, Bengali, Assamese
Southern group: Marathi, Konkani (Goanese), Sinhalese.

Alternative groupings are also used, and the number of languages within each is considerably greater than in this list. The risk with any classification is that it may create an im-pression of neatly bounded and self-contained linguistic areas, whereas the facts are quite different. Even today, the spoken languages of India are reminiscent of the situation that prevailed in the Romance or Slavonic world during the Middle Ages, when the various languages and dialects formed a continuum, merging imperceptibly one with another, without any hard and fast geographical boundaries between them. Such boundaries had to await the rise of modern states and of standard national languages (though a continuum often still exists at local level, in rural speech on either side of a frontier).

A number of the languages spoken on the Indian subcontinent do not belong to the Indo-European family. The most important of these are the Dravidian tongues of southern and central India and Sri Lanka (e.g. Telugu and Tamil), which are survivors from the India into which the Aryan newcomers advanced. There have been suggestions that Romani may have branched off from the main Indo-Aryan migration before it entered the subcontinent. However, Sanskrit contains lexical borrowings from Dravidian, which once extended much further north, and a few of these are found in Romani. It follows that the separation between Romani and other Indo-Aryan tongues occurred within Indian territory.

The affinities between the accidence of Romani and of Sanskrit are immediately visible if one compares, say, their verb endings, or the declension of nouns, or the suffixes which are added to adjectives, comparatives, adverbs and participles. It is also clear that Romani has, more recently, shared with other modern Indic languages a number of sound changes which separate Prakrit from Sanskrit. This relationship with the modern tongues is further demonstrated by numerous features of word formation and grammatical apparatus – the way in which personal pronouns and the interrogative pronoun (*kon?*, 'who?') have developed; the -*o* and -*i* endings for masculine and feminine forms; the creation of abstract nouns by adding the suffix -*ben* or -*pen* (e.g. Welsh Romani *taćo*, 'true' and *taćiben*, 'truth'; Greek Romani *ćor-*, 'to steal', *ćoribé*, 'theft'); the replacement of the genitive case by a construction on the lines of 'the paternal horse' (i.e. adding an adjectival ending to the noun for 'father' to express 'the father's horse': in Kalderash, *dadésko gras*): All these characteristics, and others besides, confirm the affinity with several of the modern

Indic languages, and show that Romani must date from post-Sanskritic times.

The tantalizing question is whether one can go further, so as to narrow the search and identify more closely the region or the people from which the Romani-speaking migrants came, by tying Romani firmly to one of the language groups shown on p. 18. Unfortunately, at this point linguistics begins to let us down. Although it is possible to go a long way in reconstructing a proto-language (a hypothetical ancestor of all Gypsy dialects),[3] just as linguistic palaeontologists have done in so many other situations, the fact remains that not enough is yet known of the emergence of the modern Indian vernaculars to take the quest beyond rather general comparisons of shared evolutionary features which do not permit enough fine-tuning to identify a particular language with certainty as Romani's closest relation.

The hunt for such a language has caused a debate to rage ever since the link of Romani with India was discovered some two centuries ago. No-one has ever proffered a candidate from the Mediate, Eastern or Southern branches, but at some time or other the remainder have all been prayed in aid. For the most part the arguments have been based on phonology, either by establishing features in the sound system which are preserved by Romani and another Indic language but are reduced or lost elsewhere, or, conversely and more conclusively, by identifying sound shifts that are shared with another language. Occasionally other factors are invoked too, such as comparisons of paradigms of verbs and pronouns.

For much of the twentieth century there have been two main schools of thought. In the one camp were the proponents of a North-Western or a Dardic origin for Romani: John Sampson was one of these and he argued that Romani originated in the north-west provinces, the departure from there occurring at least as early as the end of the ninth century AD. In the other

---

[3] Two independently conducted attempts in that direction are: T. Kaufman, 'Explorations in protoGypsy phonology and classification', an unpublished paper read at the sixth South Asian Languages Analysis Roundtable, Austin, Texas, 25–26 May 1984; and B. Higgie, 'Proto-Romanes Phonology', Ph.D. dissertation, University of Texas at Austin, 1984.

camp, most notably represented by Sir Ralph Turner, formerly head of the London School of Oriental and African Studies,[4] were those who sought to show that Romani belonged originally to the Central group (now typified by Hindi), with which it shares its earliest innovations. As to the exact connections within the group, Turner pointed out that, at the remote period at which Romani must have been severed from it, the difference between the dialects which were to become, say, Hindi and Rajasthani was too small for us to recover their traces today. But he was confident enough to exclude as close relations 'the ancestors of Sinhalese, Marathi, Sindhi, Lahnda, Panjabi, Dardic, and West Pahari, and probably Gujarati and Bengali'. Romani does show some Dardic or North-Western phonological and lexical features, but Turner explained these as later accretions, the result of a migration, probably before 250 BC, out of the Central area into the north-west. Such a migration would also account for the fact that Romani preserved a number of sounds which were to be radically modified in the Central group but not in the linguistically more conservative north-west. The sojourn in these new surroundings, so the argument goes on, lasted several centuries until the Gypsy diaspora eventually took place at some time before the ninth century AD.[5] Turner's case was cogently argued, his evidence seemed solid, and his position tended to be the one adopted, explicitly or implicitly, in subsequent general works on Gypsies, even if the dates quoted by some adherents did fluctuate.

More recently this measure of consensus has fallen apart. Indeed, as if to emphasize the diversity of the interpretations which may be drawn from the one set of data, it has been suggested by Terrence Kaufman, an American linguist, that

[4] See R. L. Turner, 'The position of Romani in Indo-Aryan', *JGLS*(3), 5 (1926), pp. 145–89; J. Sampson, 'Notes on Professor R. L. Turner's "The position of Romani in Indo-Aryan"', *JGLS*(3), 6 (1927), pp. 57–68; R. L. Turner, '"The position of Romani in Indo-Aryan": A reply to Dr J. Sampson', *JGLS*(3), 6 (1927), pp. 129–38.

[5] A comprehensive survey of the linguistic debate is I. Hancock's 'The development of Romani linguistics', in *Languages and Cultures: Studies in Honor of Edgar C. Polomé*, eds M. A. Jazayery and W. Winter (Berlin, 1988), pp. 183–223.

the phonological facts are best explained by postulating that
protoGypsy moved on into Iranian-speaking territories before
300 BC – perhaps as a result of the inroads of Alexander the
Great into north-western India in 327–326 BC.[6]

Physical anthropology

Historical linguistics cannot determine the racial and ethnic
origin of the early Romani-speakers. There is no inherent or
necessary link between language and race: there are indeed
many well-attested cases of whole ethnic groups switching
language through time. So there can be no assurance that
groups of people are racially related simply because they speak
related languages. One has to consider at this point how far
physical anthropology may be able to plug the gaps left by
linguistics. Up to the Second World War, physical anthropology
meant the comparative study of anatomical characteristics in
different human populations and individuals. It meant particularly the measurement of the body and its parts, notably
the skull.

The results of the most extended comparative anthropometric survey of Gypsies attempted by a physical anthropolog-
ist – Professor Eugène Pittard – were published in 1932.[7]
Pittard concentrated on Gypsies in the Balkans, in the hope
that this would provide data on what he called 'les vrais
Tziganes'. By dint of applying tape and callipers to many more
Gypsies than had ever been surveyed before, he reached the
conclusion that the typical Gypsy population was slightly taller
than the European average, with legs comparatively long in
relation to the torso; their heads tended strongly towards
dolichocephalic ('long-headed', i.e. relatively long and narrow)
skulls, with black hair, smallish ears, wide eyes with heavily

---

[6] Kaufman, 'Explorations in protoGypsy', p. 42. Higgie ('Proto-Romanes
Phonology', pp. 19, 141) indicates an even earlier date – something like the
sixth century BC. Reservations about such datings were set out in A. M.
Fraser, 'Looking into the seeds of time', *Tsiganologische Studien* (1992),
no. 1.

[7] E. Pittard, *Les Tziganes ou Bohémiens* (Geneva, 1932).

pigmented irises, and long, narrow, straight noses. Pittard awarded them

a highly honourable place in human aesthetics. Very fine men and very beautiful women are often found among them. Their swarthy complexion [*teint légèrement basané*], jet-black hair, straight well-formed nose, white teeth, dark-brown wide-open eyes, whether lively or languid in expression, the general suppleness of their deportment, and the harmony of their movements, place them high above many European peoples as regards physical beauty.

After measuring hundreds of men and women and recording four dimensions of the body and limbs, five of the head, five of the face, and ten of the features, Pittard was left with two major problems. The first was that his findings not infrequently conflicted with indices recorded by his predecessors (who examined much smaller cohorts): this made him stress the need to take the data from 'les vrais Tziganes', as free as possible from admixture with other strains (and in that respect he regarded nomadic life as a preservative of racial purity). Faced with the other problem, he had to concede defeat: the data on the many Indian ethnic groups were too sparse or unreliable to allow him to draw any conclusion as to the origin of the Gypsies, and he himself pointed out that the diversity in some of the Gypsy data might indicate a complex origin.

In general terms, it has to be said that much of the earlier work on supposed racial types, based largely on the measurement of skulls, has been shown to be inaccurate and lacking in statistical validity. Indeed, it now appears to be accepted that cranial structures are only imperfectly determined by hereditary factors, and that too much reliance should not be placed upon arguments based on skull formation to indicate long-term continuity of a human group. Work in this area in regard to Gypsies subsequent to Pittard's,[8] though interesting, has produced no greater certainty. New techniques and indicators

[8] E.g. B. Ély, 'Les Crânes tsiganes des collections du Musée de l'Homme', *Bulletins de la Société d'Anthropologie de Paris* (1967), pp. 177–92; and R. Reyment, 'Les Voyageurs suédois: aspects physiques et linguistiques', *Études Tsiganes* (1981), no. 4, pp. 1–14.

are, however, constantly being developed. The study of blood groups – with their precisely understood genetics – has come to provide an alternative means of classification of the living and has to a great extent supplanted direct body observations. More recently this approach has been extended to include other hereditary biochemical characteristics. The science of population genetics, for which blood groups have provided the bulk of the data, has sometimes proved able to trace migration and invasion routes of man. At first sight, blood-type studies would appear to hold out some promise of success in the case of Gypsies too.

From the 1940s onwards, a number of investigations found that the blood groups of various samples of Gypsy population in Europe produced a B gene frequency well above European levels. The ABO distributions seemed to give strong support to the hypothesis of Indian origin (the B gene being more than twice as frequent on the subcontinent as in Europe, though the pattern varies from one part to another). The Gypsies' rhesus frequencies, though not differing so much from European values, were also consistent with an Indian origin. Then some further studies of Gypsies – in Sweden, Britain and Slovenia – produced results which, while differing significantly from the patterns in the surrounding populations, also deviated from the patterns given by earlier studies of Gypsies. In effect, this line of biological investigation[9] bumps up against the same kind of problem as Pittard encountered. The researcher may have had difficulty in defining the Gypsy sample, and in any case Gypsies have undergone racial admixture and the gene pool of any particular cohort may be very mixed: it would have taken only about one marriage per hundred on average to be with a non-Gypsy since they left India to bring their present proportion of non-Indic ancestors to over one half. Moreover, small and isolated groups diverge genetically from each other, owing to random genetic change. Promising work continues in

[9] Well summarized in regard to Gypsies in R. C. Gropper, 'What does blood tell?', *GLS/NAC Newsletter*, 4 (1981), nos 2, 3 and 4. A straightforward introduction to blood group studies generally is A. E. Mourant's *Blood Relations: Blood Groups and Anthropology* (Oxford, 1983).

this field,[10] but before it can be expected to add materially to the state of our knowledge the conclusion reached in regard to Gypsies by Mourant in 1983 remains valid: 'There is a need for considerable further research on this interesting group of populations, with particular reference to those factors which differ in frequency between Europe and the north Indian region.'[11]

In short, physical anthropology and population genetics, in their present state of theory and application, are suggestive but not conclusive. They lead us rather less far than did historical linguistics, except that they do tend to confirm – in a way that linguistics cannot – the Indian link between language and original speaker and to indicate that the origin of both is to be sought in the Indian subcontinent, even if no combination of linguistics, physical anthropology and genetics gives us any clue as to the historical circumstances which brought about the Romani-speakers' migration and diffusion, or why there should have been an exodus at all.

Ethnic parallels

There is, however, at least one ethnic inference to be afforded by the language. It lies in the Gypsies' widespread name for men of their own race – in European Romani, *rom*; in Armenian Romani, *lom*; and in Syrian and Persian Romani, *dom*. All of these can be shown (given the regular sound changes in Armenian and European Romani) to be in exact phonetic correspondence with Sanskrit *ḍōmba* and Modern

---

[10] For a current investigation of blood groups and other genetic markers (e.g. fingerprints, taste sensitivity) which shows marked differences between Gypsies in Hungary and other Hungarians and a considerable similarity between Gypsies and Indians, see T. Tauszik, 'Human- and medical-genetic examinations on the Gypsy population in Hungary', *GLS/NAC Newsletter*, 9 (1986), no. 4. Recent data from Slovakia and India are compared in V. Bhalla, 'Marker genes as guides to the kinship of populations: a plea for linguistic-cum-anthropogenetic approach to the problem of "Roma" ancestry', in *Romani Language and Culture*, eds S. Balić et al. (Sarajevo, 1989), pp. 155–63.

[11] Mourant, *Blood Relations*, p. 98.

Indian *ḍom* or *dum*, which refer to a particular conglomerate
of tribes. There are references to Doms as musicians as far
back as the sixth century. In Sanskrit the word took on the
sense of 'man of low caste living by singing and music'. In
modern Indian tongues the corresponding words have a
variety of similar meanings: e.g. 'caste of wandering musicians'
(Sindhi); 'menial' (Lahnda); 'strolling musician' (Panjabi);
'low-caste black-skinned fellow' (West Pahari). The name
could preserve for us the original caste and status of the
ancestors of the Asiatic and European Gypsies, though it fails
to connect Romani with any particular Indian dialect. The
Doms, like other migrant tribes of India, may well have been
of Dravidian origin. They still exist as vagrant tribes, with a
wide variety of trades and activities – basket-maker, scavenger,
bard, musician, smith and metal-worker. It is a plausible
enough hypothesis to think that Doms made up at least the
bulk of the group or groups which emigrated. As for reasons
for the emigration, we can but guess: perhaps famine, or war.

Such a link with the Doms does not satisfy everyone, and
some look around for other parallels. For almost a century and
a half there have been suggestions that the Banjara – a mixed
race of roving traders forming one of what used to be called
the 'criminal and wandering tribes' of India – are close relations to the Gypsies.[12] Many of them are now in central and
southern India, and often use the dialect of the region in which
they dwell. It has to be said that their own language, Banjari
or Lamani,[13] bears little similarity to Romani.

Then again, some Gypsies who in modern times have themselves studied the problem of origins have been attracted by
alternative hypotheses[14] which would make their ancestors
kshatriyas – the warriors who formed the second rank among

[12] The earliest such suggestion appears to be in G. de Longpérier, 'L'Inde
et ses mystères', *Musée universel*, 1 (1857), pp. 330–6. A recent refutation
of these theories is L. Mroz, 'Les Lohar, les Banjara et le problème de
l'origine des Tsiganes', *Études Tsiganes* (1990), no. 1, pp. 3–14.
[13] G. A. Grierson, *Linguistic Survey of India*, vol. 9, part III (Delhi,
1907), pp. 255–325; R. L. Trail, *The Grammar of Lamani* (Norman, OK,
1970).
[14] A representative example can be found in J. Kochanowski, 'Roma –
History of their Indian origin', *Roma*, 4 (1979), no. 4, pp. 16–32.

*Plate 3   Banjara basket-maker of New Delhi, 1969. © Bruce Dale /
National Geographic Society, Washington, DC.*

the four castes of Hindu society – rather than a motley crew of
minstrels and low-caste vagrants; and they have received support from Indian writers[15] in supposing that the Gypsies may
descend from Jat and Rajput warriors.[16] Such a mixture would
already be one way of accounting for the range of physical
types evident among the modern Gypsy populations; but for
good measure these warriors are credited with a large number
of camp followers – Banjara and others – who served as
blacksmiths, soothsayers, entertainers and so on, the social
distinctions between the warriors and their camp followers
gradually blurring. Such theories are not infrequently seasoned
with a liberal measure of subjectiveness. The refinement which
would superimpose on a wave of Jats in the eighth century a
second layer of warriors in the twelfth century, after the battle
of Taraīn in 1192 when the Rajputs were defeated by the
Turko-Afghan Ghaznavids, will hardly endear itself to the
more sceptical reader.

So long, however, as it remains impossible to narrow the
options of time and place, there will still be plenty of room for
dispute as to exactly who, in terms of caste, occupation and
ethnic origin, left the Indian subcontinent a thousand years or
more ago, and whether or not they left as a single group.
Some, like Sampson, have claimed on linguistic grounds that
the Gypsies, on first entering Persian territory, must have been
a single race speaking a single language. Others, like Turner,
have produced contrary linguistic evidence and argued that the
morphological, lexical and phonological differences between
European, Armenian and Asiatic Romani might be more easily
explained if there had been more than one exodus or if there
was already some differentiation within the language at the
time of the exodus. This latter standpoint appears the more
persuasive; none the less it need not preclude the possibility
that the various migrant groups preserved contact or came

[15] Notably W. R. Rishi, Introduction to *Multilingual Romani Dictionary*
(Chandigarh, 1974); Introduction to *Romani Punjabi English Dictionary*
(Patiala, 1981); 'Roma – a study', *Roma*, 7 (1983), no. 2, pp. 1–10; and
'History of Romano movement, their language and culture', in *Romani
Language and Culture*, pp. 1–10.
[16] The Jat hypothesis is discussed further in the next chapter, at pp. 35–6
below.

again into contact with each other and thus exerted a certain amount of mutual linguistic influence.

Lexicostatistics

The debate might be cut short if only there were some technique which permitted developments in language prehistory to be given an absolute dating, in the same way that the constant rate of breakdown of Carbon-14 in organic substances has allowed radiocarbon dating to be so successful in other fields. A method was indeed developed in the 1950s by an American linguist, Morris Swadesh, which claimed to permit the approximate dating of language splits in terms of real time. It is generally referred to as glottochronology or lexicostatistics,[17] and is based on the general observation that the greater the time-depth separating the members of a language family from the point at which they diverged from their common ancestor, the greater the differentiation between them. The fundamental assumption is adopted that basic vocabulary (unlike phonology and structure) is one sector of language where change takes place at a relatively constant rate. The general importance of such basic vocabulary in analysing language relationships has already been discussed (p. 15 above). What Swadesh did was to seek to make this traditional approach precise by choosing a list of 200 items, later reduced to 100, which could be used, not just in assessing relationships, but also in calculating elapsed time.

The procedure followed by the glottochronologists is to identify the words in the two languages under consideration which correspond most closely to each meaning in the diagnostic list and then to note the pairs which can be considered as cognates – that is, to be retained from the same original word in the common ancestor language. In the other cases the original word has been lost or changed its meaning in one or

---

[17] Two explanations of the technique by Swadesh are: 'Lexico-statistic dating of prehistoric ethnic contacts', *Proceedings of the American Philosophical Society*, 96 (1952), pp. 452–63; and *The Origin and Diversification of Language*, ed. J. Sherzer (London, 1972), esp. pp. 271–84.

other (or both) of the languages. The number of cognates is used to measure the minimum time since the two languages separated. A standard retention rate was calculated by striking an average from what had actually happened in 13 pairs of languages. For the 100-item list of core words, the result was an average retention rate of 86 per cent per millennium, and two languages that began to diverge 1,000 years ago will share some 74 per cent cognates (86 per cent of 86 being 74). A formula was produced for calculating the length of separate existence of two languages once their percentage of cognates had been established.

The main defect of this technique is that it does not happen to work very well in the case of some language states which can be dated by other means. The initial hypothesis of a constant retention rate is not substantiated: indeed it is difficult to see any *a priori* reason for assuming that languages do undergo word loss at a constant rate, even in areas of vocabulary which are least permeable to cultural influence. The lessons of sociolinguistics indicate that social factors, which differ between times and places and peoples, are highly relevant to linguistic change. In the case of Romani, for instance, one can think of a number of reasons why it could be open to outside influence, and contrariwise a number of others for its being resistant to innovation. The Gypsies' need to speak the language of the host country and lack of any written standard of their own could make Romani specially vulnerable: generally, it is when individuals speak another language as well as their own native one that convergence occurs most rapidly. On the other hand, the advantage of preserving Romani as a private speech would work in the opposite direction; so too might frequent movement, which would leave Gypsies less subject to acculturation to other societies.

None the less, it has seemed worthwhile to conduct an experiment with the technique, because it offers some quantitative measure of similarities and differences between languages and dialects, and hence the degree of their relationship.[18] In a comparison of Romani with eight representatives of the Dardic,

---

[18] The results, including a table of word comparisons between Romani and selected Indic languages, are set out in more detail in Fraser, 'Looking into the seeds of time'.

North-Western, Northern and Central groups (Kashmiri, Multani, Sindhi, Kotgarhi, West Hindi, Panjabi, Marwari and Gujarati), three come roughly at the top, with some 50 per cent of cognates shared with Romani. These are Hindi, Multani (a dialect of Lahnda) and Kotgarhi (a West Pahari dialect). Slightly behind them follow Panjabi, Marwari (the main dialect of Rajasthani) and Gujarati, while Sindhi lags still further behind. Decisively at the bottom is Kashmiri, with no more than about 33 per cent: this sharp differentiation contrasts oddly with numerous previous suggestions that Romani is of a Dardic type. However, a simple distinction between cognates and non-cognates is too crude to give any weight to the extent to which equivalent words, though cognates, may have drifted apart by phonetic change. If – at the price of introducing an additional degree of speculation – one replaces Swadesh's binary notation with a five-fold one ranging from 4 to 0, in which one point is subtracted for each differing phoneme,[19] Hindi goes into the lead, with Kotgarhi next in line, while Multani is seen to lag much further behind, at about the same level as Panjabi.

Having come thus far, it is impossible to resist calculating the minimum elapsed time on the Swadesh scale since Romani began to diverge from other Indo-Aryan tongues. In relation to the top three (West Hindi, etc.) Swadesh's formula gives a date around 390 BC or earlier. With Kashmiri, on the other hand, one gets something like 1700 BC. These dates seem within the bounds of credibility, although the one for Kashmiri – 1700 BC – is much earlier than anything which the formula produces for divergence of the others from Kashmiri. Apart from that, the date fits comfortably enough with expectations: the Dardic group, of which Kashmiri is a member, must have started to become isolated from the Indo-Aryan mainstream not long after the arrival of the Aryans in north-west India. As for the 390 BC date in relation to Hindi and so on, Turner did say that protoRomani must have migrated out of the Central

[19] This refinement is drawn from the work of Marcel Cortiade, who has used a lexicostatistical method in assessing degrees of affinity between Romani dialects: 'Romany phonetics and orthography', *GLS/NAC Newsletter*, 7 (1984), no. 4; 'Distance between the Romani dialects', *GLS/NAC Newsletter*, 8 (1985), no. 2; and *Romani fonetika thaj lekhipa* (Titograd, 1986).

group before the middle of the third century BC. Indeed Kaufman postulated a final departure from India in the fourth century BC.

So there we have some interesting coincidences. But Turner and others also argued that, after leaving the Central area, protoRomani must have spent a good deal of time in the north-west of the subcontinent. That kind of reunion could be expected to boost the vocabulary shared with the new neighbour-languages. Reacquisitions will upset calculations of time-depth; this could be one factor in the differing results produced in regard to Kashmiri's divergence from Romani as compared with other New Indo-Aryan tongues (Kashmiri having been much influenced by some of the latter). The most valid use of the technique appears to lie, not in seeking to establish the time-depth that separates two languages, but in supporting rigorous comparisons between them through providing concrete data and a standard framework and focusing on a range of concepts expressed by words which are more intrinsically durable than most.

The Romani language and its speakers have been exposed to a multitude of historical, demographic and sociolinguistic influences over the centuries; so too, in their separate ways, have the languages and populations of India. After the lapse of so much time it may be a forlorn hope to seek to prove with any certainty the precise people (or combination of peoples) from which the European Gypsies sprang in the past or which is most closely related to them today. Yet it would be premature to abandon the search. In the linguistic domain we have, fortunately, in works like Grierson's monumental *Linguistic Survey of India*,[20] a cornucopia of raw material for sustained evaluation of Romani – phonological, lexicostatistical, morphological – alongside the modern Indo-Aryan tongues. Such studies may still offer new comparisons on the wide and systematic basis needed to produce fresh insights into the position of Romani in Indo-Aryan and to narrow the current range of apparent options.

[20] G. A. Grierson, *Linguistic Survey of India*, 20 vols (Delhi, 1903–28), which gives, for each major dialect of every language of the subcontinent, a uniform list of 241 words and phrases, as well as a synopsis of grammar and a selection of narrative texts.

2

Early Migrations

Persia

In Persia we begin at last to find a few texts which may be of some assistance in penetrating Gypsy prehistory, though too much weight should not be placed on them: the language will remain the principal support for some time to come.

The Arabian historian Hamza of Ispahan relates (*c*.950) that the Persian monarch Bahram Gur (the 'great hunter' of Omar's *Rubaiyat*, whose reign ended in 438), after deciding that his subjects should work for only half the day and spend the rest of their time eating and drinking together to the sound of music, encountered one day a group which had wine but no music. When he reproached them with neglecting music, they prostrated themselves and said they had tried to obtain the services of a musician but had been unable to find one. The monarch then persuaded the king of India to send him musicians – 12,000 of them – and they were distributed to the various parts of the Persian kingdom, where they multiplied. 'Their descendants', noted Hamza, 'are still there, although in small numbers; they are the Zott.'

Half a century later, another account of the legend is found in the Persian national epic which relates the country's history in 60,000 verses, Firdawsi's *Shah-nameh* ('Book of Kings'), completed in 1010. He too refers to a request made by Bahram Gur to the Indian King Shangul for musicians and entertainers: 'The indigent classes here drink wine without music, a circumstance of which the wealthier cannot approve. Therefore, of

Plate 4   Scene from a 16th-century illustrated Persian manuscript: Shangul of India entertained by Bahram Gur. Reproduced by courtesy of the Director and University Librarian, the John Rylands University Library of Manchester.

those Luri, choose and send to me ten thousand male and female who play upon the lute.' Bahram Gur gave the Luri wheat and cattle and asses and despatched them to the provinces of his kingdom so that they might toil as husbandmen and also make music for the poor. Within a year the Luri had heedlessly consumed all their wheat as well as their cattle; the king rebuked them for their thriftlessness

and then dismissed them, with an order that, taking their asses, they should load them with their chattels, and support themselves by means of their songs, and the strumming of their silken bows; and that each year they should travel over the country, and sing for the amusement of the high and the low. The Luri, agreeably to this mandate, now wander the world, seeking employment, associating with dogs and wolves, and thieving on the road by day and by night.[1]

Too often the assumption has been made, in looking for traces of the Gypsies, that any reference to a migrant group pursuing a Gypsy-like occupation can for that reason be equated with them. This may be one of those occasions; and the Gypsy exodus is difficult to reconcile with the time of Bahram Gur. But the names by which these minstrels are described are significant; as for the chronology, it is perhaps reasonable to draw the conclusion from the prevalence of the Bahram Gur legend that an Indian minstrel element of the kind described there as Zott or Luri must indeed have been established in Persia well before the tenth century – giving some time for the tradition to have won enough acceptance for Hamza of Ispahan to feel able to carry it back to the time of Bahram Gur.

Zotti (plural *Zott*) and *Luli* or *Luri* are still Persian names for 'Gypsy'; in Syria, Palestine and Egypt, *Luri* is found in a variant form *Nuri* (plural *Nawar*). *Zott* is an arabicized version of the Indian tribal name *Jat*. Whether the original Gypsies were identical with the Jats of India (a people strongly

---

[1] The original Persian, with a translation, is given in an essay, remarkable for its time, by J. S. Harriot, 'Observations on the Oriental origin of the Romnichal', *Transactions of the Royal Asiatic Society*, 2 (1830), pp. 518–58.

represented in the Punjab) is a matter which has been debated for a hundred years or more and, as already pointed out (p. 28), the Jat hypothesis still finds adherents. If one were to accept all early references to the Zott[2] as references to the Gypsies, the historical picture of the early Gypsy migrations would soon build up. From chroniclers and geographers we learn of a number of occasions when people were transported away from the Indus valley, westwards to Persia and beyond. Numerous detachments from Sind served in the Persian army at the time of the Arab expansion of the seventh century and, when the tide ran against the King of Kings, they deserted to the Arab side and embraced Islam and settled in Basra. Other colonies of Zott were established elsewhere. Then, once the Arab surge through Asia reached its eastern extremity with the invasion of Sind in the early eighth century, a large number of Jats and other inhabitants of Sind were deported to the banks of the Tigris; on several successive occasions sizeable bands of these were later displaced to colonize northern Syria. The first entry of Gypsies into Christian territories would then be accounted for by an event recorded by the Arab chronicler Tabari, who relates how large numbers of Zott were taken prisoner in 855 when the Byzantines attacked Syria and carried them off with their women, children and buffaloes.

The difficulty is that the name Zott was in the end applied fairly indiscriminately to anyone originating in the valley of the Indus. These records tell us what was happening to segments of population of Indian origin, particularly the Jats. Whether they tell us anything of the original Gypsy ancestors is highly dubious. The fact that the Arabs gave the name Zott to Gypsies probably means no more than that they transferred to them, since they came from India, the name of the Indian people with which they had most frequently come into con-

---

[2] Set out comprehensively in M. J. de Goeje, *Mémoire sur les migrations des Tsiganes à travers l'Asie* (Leiden, 1903). An earlier version of de Goeje's thesis that Gypsies can be identified with the Jats was incorporated, in translation and with a long commentary, in D. MacRitchie, *Accounts of the Gypsies of India* (London, 1886), pp. 1–126. And the Gypsy section of Sir Richard Burton's *The Jew, the Gypsy and El Islam* (London, 1898) was largely concerned with the same identification, which Burton claimed primacy in making.

tact. (Similarly, in Afghanistan, 'Jat' is nowadays a derogatory term applied to a wide range of communities of diverse origin and low social status, although primarily it is taken to refer to a peripatetic people of Indo-Pakistani origin.)[3]

The linguistic evidence back in India lends little support to the Jat hypothesis. Another objection of some weight is the fact that a history of migrations concentrated in the south of Persia does not really match the dispersion routes which can be inferred from the way Romani developed in Persian territory. It has to be said, however, that the linguistic deductions are hampered by the fact that, just as our knowledge of the emerging New Indo-Aryan vernaculars suffers at a crucial stage from paucity of data over several centuries, it is difficult to assess the pace of the widespread linguistic restructuring which probably was taking place while the Gypsies were in Persia. The Arab conquest in 642 entailed for the Persians not only a change of religion but also a change of language: it brought the official use of Persian to an end and led to a catastrophic decline in its employment for literary purposes. It inaugurated an extended period during which Persian absorbed a massive Arabic element, comparable in quantity and character with the Latinate (French and Latin) component in modern English. Not until the second half of the tenth century did Persian, now written in Arabic script, become once more the dominant literary language, and by then it was vastly changed. The earliest texts in the new style date from the ninth century, and that was the formal beginning of Modern Persian. The discontinuity between Middle and Modern Persian is striking, but what the records fail to reveal is how deeply and quickly the Arabic influence managed to penetrate the various regions or the social classes below the top level.

In Persia the Gypsies were intruders: they had to learn the language of their surroundings in order to communicate with the residents. Their linguistic contacts must have been more with the dynamic dialects of peasants than with the fixed idioms of literary gentlemen which are immortalized in dictionaries. The effect of their bilingualism should not be

[3] Cf. A. Rao, 'Note préliminaire sur les *Jat* d'Afghanistan', *Studia Iranica*, 8 (1979), no. 1, pp. 141–9.

exaggerated: the relationship between the purveyors of some commodity or service and their clients is much more superficial than that which exists in fully bilingual communities. None the less, Romani would, once outside India, develop some of its most important and characteristic features.

One can divide the entire family of Romani dialects into three main branches: European, Armenian, and Asiatic (other than Armenian). Turner conveniently labelled them the Rom, Lom and Dom groups, according to their phonetic treatment of the word derived from Sanskrit *ḍōmba*. The non-European varieties of Romani can therefore be called Lomavren (Armenian) and Domari (Asiatic). Sampson showed that European Romani and Lomavren changed the original Sanskrit voiced sounds (i.e. pronounced with vocal cords vibrating) *bh*, *dh*, *gh* and *dźh* to the unvoiced (i.e. pronounced with no vibration of the vocal cords) *ph*, *th*, *kh* and *ćh* (the *h* representing the aspiration of sounds accompanied by a puff of breath: see p. 14), whereas an entirely contrary principle – deaspiration of *bh*, *dh*, *gh* and *dźh* into *b*, *d*, *g* and *dź* – is the hallmark of Asiatic Romani. It may be that the former change (which in Lomavren was less regular than Sampson implied) resulted from the influence of Armenian, many dialects of which possess the unvoiced sounds but not the voiced ones.

Sampson believed that these developments were the after-effects of a parting of the ways which must have taken place on Persian territory, giving rise to the two branches which he called the *ben* (Domari) and the *phen* (European Romani and Lomavren) groups, on the basis of their respective forms for 'sister'. Thus:

Sanskrit	*Domari*	*Lomavren*	*Eur. Romani*	*English*
bhaginī	ben	phen	phen	sister
bhrātṛ	bar	phal	phral[4]	brother

---

[4] *Phral* gives *pal* in English Romani, one of the few Romani words which have firmly entered the English lexicon (where it is first recorded in 1681–2). It illustrates the difficulty there may be in recognizing cognates. Would anyone, in the absence of additional information and merely on the ground of phonetic similarity, suggest that Latin *frater*, Romani *pal*, English *brother* and Slavic *brat* were all cognates? Yet they all go back to proto-Indo-European *bhrater*.

For the time being, it will be convenient to adopt Sampson's designations, though his concept of a unitary *phen* grouping is open to question. The speech of the *ben* Gypsies (Domari) includes the dialects of the Nawar (Palestine and Syria), the Kurbat (northern Syria), and the Karaći (Asia Minor, Transcaucasia and Persia). The Domari dialects declined more extensively than most of the European ones and by the time they were explored they were heavily impregnated with Arabic and the remains were often sparse.[5] We have already observed that, despite Sampson's insistence that both sprang from a single source, some of Domari's dissimilarities from European Romani create doubts about how far we can assume that the parent community was uniform.

Once a parent language does break up into new species, the different fragments may move more or less swiftly along similar or divergent paths. We cannot be sure how rapid the changes were with the *ben* and the *phen* groups, or how early the separation between them took place, or how long each group remained in Persia. Their difference from each other is great enough to point to a relatively early split. The absence of some of the more important Persian loan-words[6] from the dialects of the *ben* Gypsies may indicate that they were the first to leave Persia. How and when they reached Syria is unknown: we hear little specific about them until the nineteenth century, apart from occasional ambiguous references, like that in an Arabic handbook of the fourteenth century, *Mesalek Alabsar* ('Journeys of the Eyes'), written by Al-Umari, an official of the Mameluke chancery, who speaks of several tribes of 'Lors' in Egypt and (particularly) Syria and describes their skill as acrobats.

The number of Persian elements in the dialects of the European Gypsies points to a somewhat prolonged stay. Among

[5] The fullest study is R. A. Stewart Macalister, *The Language of the Nawar or Zutt, the Nomad Smiths of Palestine*, GLS Monograph no. 3 (London, 1914); previously published in *JGLS*(2), 3 (1909– 10), pp. 120–6, 298–317; 5 (1911–12), pp. 289–305.

[6] 'Loan-word' is something of a misnomer, in that the donor language does not get its 'loaned' or 'borrowed' words back. But that is the established term.

them are (in Welsh Romani) *ćakano*, 'star'; *darīav*, 'sea'; *kiś*, 'silk'; *kiśti*, 'belt'; *koro*, 'blind'; *pośúm*, 'wool'; and *veś*, 'forest'. Of these, only the words for 'blind' and 'wool' were found in the Domari speech recorded by Macalister. (Here, and on other occasions, one could lengthen the list of likely or possible borrowings considerably, but at the price of introducing a much greater degree of speculation. For example, Romani *baxt*, 'luck, good fortune', is commonly regarded as an Iranian loan-word from *bakht*, 'fortune, happiness' – recognizable in *baksheesh* – but may well be original. As the Iranian and the Indo-Aryan languages are closely related and share a number of characteristic features, it is not always a simple matter to decide between rival etymons. Similarly, within the Iranian family, it may sometimes be doubtful whether a borrowing was from Persian or Kurdish or Ossetic, or indeed from Armenian which, though no longer considered to be a member of the family, itself contains a vast number of Iranian loan-words.)

As for the time of departure from Persia, a few scholars have argued since the early 1970s that the ancestors of the European Gypsies must have passed through Persia before the first Arab invasions, because of an absence of Arabic words in Romani. This would mean their having left the country before the mid-seventh century – significantly earlier than has commonly been postulated by others. Such an argument, however, runs up against two difficulties. It would be an oversimplification of linguistic process to assume that as soon as the Arabs overpowered Persia their language began to make inroads at all levels to an extent that would immediately have subjected Romani to its influence. In any case there *are* a few Arabic loan-words in European Romani: *berk*, 'breast' (though Romani also kept Indic *ćući*); *xumér*, *xumél*, 'dough', 'breadcrumbs'; *kisí*, 'purse'. Perhaps *lav*, 'word' (as in George Borrow's *Lavengro*) should be added to the list, as being derived from or influenced by Arabic *lafz*, which was taken up both in Persia and (later) in India. Sparse and debatable these may be, but they are perhaps enough to suggest that the ancestors of the European Gypsies cannot have left Persia before the Arab conquest had impregnated the language of the common people with a good number of Semitic words.

Armenia

Armenia, where the *phen* Gypsies appear to have gone after leaving Persia, also came under Arab dominion in the seventh century, though the Armenian language did not become permeated with Arabic as Persian did. The Gypsies' sojourn in Armenia cannot have been brief. The European dialects of Romani contain a number of Armenian loan-words, including *bōv*, 'oven'; *dudúm*, 'melon', 'gourd'; *dźolano*, 'mule'; *kotōr*, 'piece'; *koćo*, 'button'; *mortsī*, 'hide' (= skin); and, possibly, *grai*, 'horse' (?from Armenian *grast*, 'beast of burden'). From Ossetic, spoken to the north of Armenia, probably came *vordón*, 'waggon' – which much later became the Gypsies' word for the horse-drawn caravan so often associated with them now in the popular mind. Not one of these occurs in the *ben* dialects of Asia. Nor indeed are they to be found in the remnants of Lomavren, the dialect of the Gypsies known as Bośa, who, centuries later, are found wandering in Armenia, Turkey, Persia and the southern Caucasus. When the Romani spoken by the Bośa (who called themselves *Lom*) began to be studied in the nineteenth century, it had become a poor thing, much corrupted. Though it was pervaded by Armenian influences, the fact that it shares practically no items of Armenian derivation with European Romani raises the possibility that the division of the *phen* Gypsies occurred before they came fully under the influence of Armenian, or indeed that the innovations common to Lomavren and European Romani occurred independently of each other.[7]

We can only guess as to why there was an exodus from Armenia, but there were plenty of disruptive influences at work. The entry into the Byzantine empire may have been a gradual process, stimulated at first by the disturbed state of the country arising from longstanding Byzantine–Arab rivalry:

[7] There are other linguistic developments which are difficult to reconcile with Sampson's concept of a unitary *phen* grouping which split up only after entering Armenia: cf. J. Bloch, review of *The Dialect of the Gypsies of Wales*, *JGLS*(3), 5 (1926), pp. 134–41, esp. pp. 136–8; R. L. Turner, 'The position of Romani in Indo-Aryan', *JGLS*(3), 5 (1926), pp. 145–89, esp. pp. 177–8, and 'Transference of aspiration in European Gypsy', *Bulletin of the School of Oriental and African Studies*, 22 (1959), pp. 491–8, esp. p. 491.

much of it was harried by Byzantium's soldiery and, in the end, progressively annexed in the early decades of the eleventh century. The Byzantine conquest was short-lived and soon Armenia was being raided by the Seljuks – a clan of that central Asian people, the Turks – until only Cilicia, on the Mediterranean, was left under Armenian rule.

Social cohesion

Having tracked Romani as far as the foothills of Mount Ararat – like Cowper's

> philologists who chase
> A panting syllable through time and space,
> Start it at home, and hunt it in the dark,
> To Gaul, to Greece, and into Noah's ark –

it is prudent to take stock of possible oversimplifications which the linguistic approach to their prehistory may encourage. The danger is that the talk of successive 'splits' in language and separations into different 'bands' risks creating an unconscious image of the Gypsy migration as consisting of hordes of people trooping out of India and, at certain points along their route, neatly breaking into two subdivisions each of which proceeds on its divergent but generally westward way. Such a frame of mind is encouraged by the maps which have sometimes been produced, with arrows showing the probable lines of advance of the early Gypsy migrations. It cannot have been quite like that in practice.

We know nothing for certain about the social organization and culture of the early Gypsies, and can but conjecture. It seems not too fanciful to base such speculation on two assumptions: first, that these Gypsies would have reflected an Indian model of social existence; and secondly, that those of them who did not settle would have shown the special characteristics which can be observed in many peripatetic groups. One feature of Indian social existence, then as now, was the prevalence of ethnic sub-castes or *jatis* (*jati* = 'birth'), which came to have more relevance for the day-to-day working of Hindu society than the main castes (*varnas*). Sub-caste relationships were based on specialization of work. The monoprofessional character of a *jati* leads to economic inter-dependence; it may also give rise to constant territorial move-ment or dispersal, in order to find enough demand for the skills in question, and it is not difficult to find analogies with Gypsies among the peripatetic groups which are particularly profuse in the Indian subcontinent.[8] Another specific feature of a *jati* is endogamy, or marriage customarily inside the group, and this involves maintaining contact within the *jati* but pre-serving a boundary between it and other communities. The Indian model would also indicate a fairly rigid purity and pollution ideology (which could be one important factor in delineating such boundaries).

In the light of this, and of the subsequent evolution of the Gypsies, it seems probable that many in the original groups filled an economic niche by the provision of specialized goods or services, working in relatively small numbers and keep-ing on the move, since they could not afford to swamp the market and needed a wide range of customers. Whether these customers were townspeople, villagers, sedentary cultivators, pastoral nomads, or a combination of these, it is impossible to say. The Gypsies' peripatetic way of life would not have seemed unusual to others: in Iran and neighbouring lands nomadism was widespread, and even in the mid-twentieth century some-thing like a tenth of the total population of Iran remained nomadic, despite sporadic attempts to settle the tribesmen. One essential difference, however, between Gypsies and ordi-nary nomads is that for the former it means moving from place to place in order to sell their products or perform their trades and skills, while for the others it is a question of seasonal moving for pastoral or agricultural reasons. Peripatetic and pastoral nomads may live together in symbiosis: even now a large number of pastoral groups in Turkey, Iran and Baluchistan have at least one peripatetic group attached to

---

[8] Cf. P. K. Misra and K. C. Malhotra (eds), *Nomads in India* (Calcutta, 1982); and J. C. Berland, 'Pārytān: "native" models of peripatetic strategies in Pakistan', *Nomadic Peoples* (1986), nos. 21/22, pp. 189–205.

them, perhaps as vendors of small wares, and sometimes the peripatetics also have sedentary rural customers.

Given the constraints of their life-style, if that is how it was – nomadism, dispersal, minority numbers, and consequently a potential weakening of community ties within the group – how did so many of these early Gypsies maintain their shared social and cultural identity, during an extended period of gradual westward movement? In asking the question, one cannot cease to wonder at their extraordinary tenacity. The Gypsies' diaspora has sometimes been compared with that of the Jews: however, theirs was a diaspora of a people with no priestly caste, no recognized standard for their language, no texts enshrining a corpus of beliefs and code of morality, no appointed custodians of ethnic traditions. In being up-rooted from India and maintaining a mobile existence, a changing identity had become inevitable. Their ethnicity was to be fashioned and remoulded by a multitude of influences, internal and external. They would assimilate innumerable elements which had nothing to do with India, and they would eventually cease to be, in any meaningful way, Indians; their identity, their culture would, however – regardless of all the transformations – remain sharply distinct from that of the *gadźé* who surrounded them and on whom their economic existence depended. They had no promised land as a focus of their dreams and would themselves, in time, forget their Indian antecedents and, indeed, show little interest in their early history, leaving it to *gadźé*, centuries later, to rediscover and pursue obsessively their past and their lineage.

3

Into the Byzantine Empire and the Balkans

Byzantium and Greece

The appetite of the Seljuks for war was overwhelming and the growth of their power was phenomenally fast. Their invasion of Armenia in the middle of the eleventh century dislocated the Armenian people, and it is tempting to suppose that it drove many Gypsies into western Byzantine territory – Constantinople and Thrace – from where they eventually spread throughout the Balkans and the whole of Europe.[1] The Byzantine Empire was now on the brink of rapid decline from the period of greatness when Constantinople ruled the wealthiest realm in the Christian world. In 1071 a Byzantine army was smashed by a force of Seljuks at Manzikert, near Lake Van in Armenia, and much of Anatolia was lost.

The Greek culture of Byzantium survived long after territory was ceded; even in Muslim Anatolia, Greek was not altogether submerged. The Gypsies were exposed to its linguistic influence long before they crossed the Dardanelles, and the impact of Greek on Romani was to be powerful – much more extensive than that of Persian. (Notable too for its historical implications is the *absence* of Turkish elements in European Romani, except for the loan-words which infiltrated much later, in a

---

[1] The analysis of this Byzantine phase of Gypsy history is much eased by a paper of G. C. Soulis, 'The Gypsies in the Byzantine Empire and the Balkans in the late Middle Ages', *Dumbarton Oaks Papers*, no. 15 (1961), pp. 142–65.

limited way, into the speech of Gypsies whose field of activity was confined to the Balkans.)

The earliest reference to the presence of Gypsies in Constantinople comes, most probably, from a Georgian hagiographical text, the *Life of Saint George the Anchorite*, composed at the monastery of Iberon on Mount Athos around 1068.[2] We read there that in 1050 the Emperor Constantine Monomachus was plagued by wild animals which were devouring the game in the imperial park of Philopation in Constantinople. He invoked the help of 'a Samaritan people, descendants of Simon the Magician, who were called Adsincani, and notorious for soothsaying and sorcery', and these Adsincani laid down charmed pieces of meat which killed the ferocious beasts instantly. The name Adsincani used in this text is the Georgian form of the Greek *Atsínganoi* or *Atzínganoi*, the term by which the Byzantines commonly referred to Gypsies. The German *Zigeuner*, French *Tsiganes*, Italian *Zingari*, Hungarian *Czigányok* and similar forms in several other languages all derived from this Byzantine name. The origin of *Atsínganos* has been much debated and is still not free from doubt. The most widely accepted view is that it was a corrupt form of the name of the heretical sect of the *Athínganoi*, applied to the Gypsies because both groups enjoyed a similar reputation for fortune-telling and sorcery. The original, heretical, Athinganoi were severely reduced in numbers, perhaps even wiped out, by persecutions in the ninth century.

The next reference to Athinganoi, here clearly used in the sense of 'Gypsies', comes in the twelfth century, in a commentary by the canonist Theodore Balsamon (who died *c.*1204) on canon LXI of the Council in Trullo (692), which threatened a six-year excommunication for any member of the Church who exploited the public by displaying bears or other animals for amusement or by telling fortunes:

Those who lead around bears are called bearkeepers. They place dyed threads on the head and on the entire body of the animal. Then

---

[2] D. M. Lang (ed.), *Lives and Legends of the Georgian Saints. Selected and translated from the original texts* (London, 1956), p. 154; Latin version in P. Peeters, 'Histoires monastiques géorgiennes', *Analecta Bollandiana*, 36–7 (1917–19), pp. 102–4.

they would cut these threads and offer them along with parts of the animal's hair as amulets, and as cure from diseases and the evil eye. Others, who are called Athinganoi, would have snakes wound around them, and they would tell one person that he was born under an evil star, and the other under a lucky star; and they would also prophesy about forthcoming good and ill fortunes.[3]

Balsamon refers again to these Athinganoi in a commentary on canon LXV of the Council in Trullo. Explaining the nature of ventriloquists, he writes: 'Ventriloquists and wizards are all those who are inspired satanically and pretend to predict the unknown as e.g. the *kritriai*, the Athinganoi, the false prophets, the "hermits" and others.' The message was repeated a century or so later by Athanasius I, Patriarch of Constantinople, in a circular letter to the clergy, instructing them to admonish their flocks not to associate with fortune-tellers, bearkeepers and snake-charmers, and 'especially not to allow the Gypsies [*Adingánous*] to enter their homes, because they teach devilish things'. Some decades later the learned Joseph Bryennius (*c.*1340–*c.*1431), in a treatise on the causes of the misfortunes that had befallen the Byzantine Empire, lamented the fact that people daily associated 'with magicians, soothsayers, *Athingánous* and charmers'.

An interesting variant in the nomenclature appears in a fifteenth-century Byzantine canon which prescribes five years excommunication for 'those who consult the Egyptian women [*Aiguptíssas*] for fortune-telling, or those who bring a soothsayer to their homes to practice sorcery upon them, when they are ill or suffer from some other cause'. That the name *Aiguptíssas* designates the Gypsy women engaged in fortune-telling, and not Egyptians, is proved by the Slavic version of the canon, where the word is translated as *ciganki*.[4] One cannot always be as sure that other Byzantine writers had Gypsies in mind in referring to Egyptians, though it is tempting to interpret in that sense Nicephorus Gregoras's lengthy description[5]

---

[3] Quotations in this paragraph are from Soulis, 'The Gypsies in the Byzantine Empire', pp. 146–7.

[4] Ibid., pp. 147–8.

[5] Quoted in full, ibid., pp. 148–9.

of a troupe of Egyptian acrobats and jugglers who appeared in Constantinople in the first decades of the fourteenth century and who moved on to travel in Thrace and Macedonia and even reached Spain. None the less it is clear that the legend of Egyptian origin (aided no doubt by Egypt's arcane associations with occultism and divination) was already current in Byzantium by the fifteenth century, if not earlier. The modern Greek name for Gypsies – *Gúphtoi* – must go back to this usage.

Further references to Gypsies, whether as Egyptians or by other names, occur in popular verses, possibly of the fourteenth century, and serve to show that they were also identified by the Byzantines with bearkeeping and sieve-making, and that the names had begun to be used as a contemptuous insult.

A fragmented and impressionistic picture thus begins to emerge of the life and condition of the Gypsies within the framework of Byzantine society. When they first appeared in Byzantium, credulity and superstition were widespread at all levels, including the emperors themselves. It is not surprising that the Gypsies should quickly have exploited this in soothsaying and telling fortunes. They were also prominent as entertainers – bearkeepers, snake-charmers and animal trainers generally, and acrobats and jugglers. We may deduce from the derogatory references in the folk literature that they did not enjoy a good reputation. It is, of course, a one-sided picture: we shall never know what view the Gypsies took of Byzantine society or what kind of treatment they received from it.

By now Byzantium was at its last gasp. At the beginning of the fifteenth century the empire was reduced to Constantinople, Salonica and the Morea or Peloponnese, the southern part of the Greek mainland. The capital was surrounded by the Ottoman Turks, who had already conquered Asia Minor and, since first settling in Europe in 1354, near Gallipoli, had gone on to overpower Bulgaria, take much of Greece and reduce Serbia and Wallachia to vassal status. The Gypsies were settled in all those lands long before the Turkish conquest. They appear to have spread from Thrace in various groups through Macedonia to the Greek mainland and the islands, and north to the territories which much later became Yugoslavia and Rumania. Perhaps some of these migrations had been connected with the constant advances of the Ottoman Turks.

Map 2   Eastern Europe about 1360.

Gypsies were well established in the Peloponnese and a number of the Greek islands during the fourteenth century. In a pamphlet written in 1416 by the Byzantine satirist Mazaris, the *Sojourn of Mazaris in Hades*, there is an imaginary letter, dated 21 September 1415 and addressed from the Peloponnese to one Holobolos of the Underworld, which describes the conditions then existing in the peninsula: 'In the Peloponnese ... live pell-mell numerous nations, of which it is not easy nor very necessary to retrace the boundaries, but every ear can easily distinguish them by their language, and here are the most notable of them: Lacedaemonians, Italians, Peloponnesians, Slavs, Illyrians, Egyptians [*Aigúptioi*], and Jews (and among them are not a few half-castes) in all seven nations.'[6] If we can accept that these 'Egyptians' were in fact Gypsies – and

---

[6] Quoted from ibid., p. 152.

in view of the other contemporary references to their presence in the Peloponnese, that is not too rash an assumption – their numbers must have been considerable for them to rank as one of the principal nations living in the peninsula at that time.

They showed a decided preference for settling in Venetian territories, both in the Peloponnese and in the neighbouring islands, no doubt because the colonies held by Venice, the most successful of the pillagers of the eastern empire, enjoyed relative stability and security, whereas other areas suffered greatly from constant Turkish incursions. A description of a people identifiable as Gypsies, by the Franciscan friar Symon Simeonis who visited Candia (Iraklion) on the island of Crete in 1323, reads as follows:

There also we saw a race outside the city, following the Greeks' rite, and asserting themselves to be of the family of Chaym [Ham]. They rarely or never stop in one place beyond thirty days, but always wandering and fugitive, as though accursed by God, after the thirtieth day remove from field to field with their oblong tents, black and low, like the Arabs', and from cave to cave.[7]

The Ionian islands to the west of the Greek mainland, likewise under Venetian rule, also received substantial influxes of Gypsies. On the island of Zante, Jacques le Saige in 1518 describes smiths with working methods very similar to those of Gypsy smiths on the mainland, suggesting direct migration from the Peloponnese.[8] There exist extensive accounts of a Gypsy settlement on Corfu, starting in the second half of the fourteenth century before the island fell into Venetian hands in 1386. By the time we hear of these Corfiote Gypsies, their annual dues have become sufficient to form an independent fief, the *feudum acinganorum* (which survived right down to the nineteenth century), and their arrival in Corfu must have been considerably earlier. Their numbers were probably

---

[7] Translation from the Latin, quoted from F. H. Groome, *Gypsy Folk-Tales*(London, 1899), p. xix.

[8] J. le Saige, *Voyage de J. Le Saige de Douai à Rome, Venise, Jérusalem, et autres saints lieux* (Douai, 1851), p. 74, quoted in Soulis, 'The Gypsies in the Byzantine Empire', p. 156.

swelled by the presence of Gypsies in the steady stream of poverty-stricken migrants (*homines vageniti*), who were, in the late fourteenth and early fifteenth centuries, pouring across the sea into Corfu from the mainland of Epirus, where Gypsies lived at that time in considerable numbers. The feudal system provided the framework of Venetian rule in Corfu. A Venetian decree of 1470 conferring the fief of the Gypsies on Michael de Hugot[9] indicates that the baron of the fief had wide jurisdiction not only over the Gypsies settled in Corfu but also over those living in the Venetian possessions on the Epirote coast. The office was lucrative, for his serfs had to make many payments, both in money and in kind, to their feudal lord, who had the right to bring to trial and punish any of them in all matters of civil or criminal law, with the sole exception of homicide: these were privileges denied to other feudal barons. Moreover, every foreign Gypsy (*Cinganus forensis*) was obliged to pay a fee on entering or leaving the territory under the jurisdiction of the Venetian governor of Corfu, as well as having to pay the annual dues while resident.

On the Greek mainland, Gypsies were strongly established in the area of the Venetian town of Nauplion, in the eastern part of the Peloponnese, and also in Modon (Methoni), another Venetian colony, on the south-western coast of the peninsula. At Nauplion, they appear to have been an organized group under a military leader, for in a decision of 12 August 1444,[10] the Venetian Council of Forty reinstated one *Johannes cinganus* (John the Gypsy) as *drungarius acinganorum* (a *drungarius* was the commander of a group of soldiers), some time after he had been removed from this office by the Venetian governor. The governor's act was condemned as 'contrary to the privileges granted to the predecessors and progenitors of the said John both by our government and by the nobleman Ottaviano Bono' (governor of Nauplion 1397–1404). If John was himself indeed a Gypsy, this is the first record of any privileges having been extended to a Gypsy leader. If it were some kind of fiefdom – as may be the case, given the arrangements in Corfu – the privileges would have been personal to John. On

---

[9] The full Latin text is given in Soulis, pp. 164–5.
[10] Full Latin text: ibid., p. 164.

*Plate 5   Modon in the Morea with Gypsy settlement. Drawn by
Eberhard Reüwich for Breydenbach's* Peregrinatio, *1486.*

the other hand, if they were extended more generally, one can
only speculate that the Venetians, who were in a difficult
situation in Nauplion because of the frequent Turkish raids,
expected in return to be given military assistance in the event
of attack; perhaps too they hoped the Gypsies would cultivate
the land, which had become depopulated.

The seaport of Modon, where the Gypsy settlement was of
fair size, lay conveniently half-way between Venice and Jaffa
and was a welcome stopping-place for pilgrims journeying by

this most popular route to the Holy Land. Several of the diaries of pilgrims mention the Gypsy quarters which their writers saw there.[11] Lionardo di Niccolò Frescobaldi, who visited Modon in 1384, reports seeing a number of *Romiti* outside the walls of the city, whom he thought to be penitents doing penance for their sins.[12] The testimony of subsequent travellers proves that they were Gypsies. Perhaps it was the Gypsies' acquaintance with pilgrims at places such as Modon that led them later to adopt that guise when they needed a cover-story to facilitate their arrival in western Europe.

A century after Frescobaldi, the eye-witness accounts of this colony at Modon come thick and fast from German and Swiss pilgrims who, by that time, had become aware of Gypsies in their homelands and referred to those in Modon as *Zigeuner*; their comments were coloured by contemporary attitudes to Gypsies in their own countries. Bernhard von Breydenbach, writing of his pilgrimage of 1483, condemns them as 'nothing but traitors and thieves, who say they come from Egypt when they come to German lands'.[13] Breydenbach was accompanied by a draughtsman, Eberhard Reüwich, and it is to him that we owe a drawing of Modon with its Gypsy quarter behind it (see plate 5). Konrad Grünemberg (1486) asserted that all Gypsies had 'their origin thence, and their name there'. Dietrich von Schachten (1491) and Peter Fassbender (1492) spoke of them mainly as smiths. Alexander, Count Palatine by Rhine, described a hill near Modon called Gype, which in 1495 had about 200 huts inhabited by Gypsies: 'some people call this hill and its appurtenances Little Egypt'. The account by Arnold von Harff of Cologne, relating to 1497, is the fullest:

Item, we went out to the outskirts, where dwell many poor black naked people in little houses roofed with reeds, some three hundred

[11] See E. O. Winstedt, 'The Gypsies of Modon and the "Wine of Romeney"', *JGLS*(2), 3 (1909–10), pp. 57–69.

[12] *Viaggio di Lionardo di Niccolò Frescobaldi in Egitto, e in Terra Santa*, ed. G. Manzi (Rome, 1818), pp. 72–3; 'Pilgrimage of Lionardo di Niccolò Frescobaldi to the Holy Land' (trans. T. Bellorini and E. Hoade), in *Publications of the Studium Biblicum Franciscanum* no. 6 (1948), pp. 29–90.

[13] Translated from the German quoted in Winstedt, 'The Gypsies of Modon', p. 60.

households; they are called Gypsies [*Suyginer*]: we call them heathens
from Egypt when they travel in these lands. These people follow all
kinds of trade, such as shoemaking and cobbling and also smithery,
which was very strange to see as the anvil stood on the ground and
the man sat at it like a tailor in this country. By him, also on the
ground, sat his housewife spinning, so that the fire was between
them. Beside them were two small leather sacks like bagpipes, half
buried in the ground by the fire. As the woman sat spinning she
raised one of the sacks from the ground from time to time and
pressed it down again. This forced wind through the earth into the
fire so that the man could work. Item, these people come from a land
called Gyppe, which lies about forty miles from the town of Modon.
This district was taken by the Turkish Emperor within the last sixty
years, but some of the lords and counts would not serve under the
Turkish Emperor and fled to our country, to Rome, to our Holy
Father the Pope, seeking comfort and support from him. Wherefore
he gave them letters of recommendation to the Roman Emperor and
to all princes of the Empire, that they should give them safe conduct
and support, since they were driven out for the Christian faith. They
showed these letters to all princes, but none gave them help. They
perished in misery, leaving the letters to their servants and children,
who to this day wander about these lands and claim to be from Little
Egypt. But this is false, since their parents were born in the land of
Gyppe, called Suginien, which lies not half way from here, Cologne,
to Egypt. Wherefore these vagabonds are knaves and spy out the
land.[14]

The story of the letters of recommendation is somewhat
garbled, but highly relevant to the chapter next to come, concerning the Gypsies' entry into western Europe.

A good deal of speculation has been aroused by Harff's use
of the names Gyppe and, in particular, Little Egypt, which was
claimed by some of the early fifteenth-century Gypsy invaders
of western Europe as their original habitat. But it would seem
that the name was not the source of the legend of Egyptian
origin: rather, it was at first merely derived from that legend
and applied to the camping place of the colony of Gypsies
behind Modon.

By the time that the Swiss Ludwig Tschudi passed through

[14] Translated from the German of *Die Pilgerfahrt des Ritters Arnold von
Harff*, ed. E. von Groote (Cologne, 1860), pp. 67–8.

Modon (1519), he found only 30 Gypsy huts there. The decline of the Gypsy population can be explained by their steady departure in the face of Turkish advances, leading to a sharp reduction in commercial activity and pilgrim traffic, and culminating in the capture of Modon itself in 1500.

The Romani language altered considerably during the Gypsies' long stay in Greek-speaking territories. Its pronunciation evolved: *m* became *v* in the middle of words (e.g. Sanskrit *nā́man*, 'name', is in Hindi *nām* and in European Romani *nav*); the *h* sound was lost at the beginning and in the middle of words, often being replaced later by *v* or *y* (e.g. Sanskrit *hásta*, 'hand'; Hindi *hāth*; European Romani *vast*); and the sound *f* was imported into the language in Greek loan-words (e.g. European Romani *foros*, 'town'). The store of Greek terms which they would carry away with them in their further peregrinations still forms a sizeable part of every European variety of Romani, to say nothing of those which are found only in certain dialects and which seem likely to have been more localized later borrowings. Among the earlier acquisitions, they took over new words for heaven, for week, for Sunday and Friday; the names of the goose, dove, crow, magpie and peacock; of the cherry and raspberry; words for bone and broth, lead and copper, room and chair, doll and cradle; key, baton and tongs; saw, nail and plank; kettle, dish and soap; road, town and mansion. *Petalo*, 'horseshoe', and *paramisus*, 'tale', were two important borrowings, one for work, one for pleasure. They took the word for 'left' (*zeravō*) but not for 'right'; the word for 'more' (*komí*), but not for 'less'. Their term for 'king', *kralis*, was derived from Greek, which in turn had borrowed it from the Slav languages. They took the Greek numerals for 7, 8 and 9, 30, 40 and 50 (though English and Welsh Romani lost these some five centuries later and had to resort to more roundabout expressions on the pattern of $3 + 4$, 2×4, $4 + 5$, 3×10). They had begun to form some words with Greek suffixes, using *-mos* for abstract nouns, *-os* as an ending for masculine loan-words, and *-men* or *-mé* in forming passive participles. One participle formed in this way, *marimé*, from a Greek verb meaning 'to dirty', has become an expression for a fundamental concept in the Gypsy system of uncleanness taboos. Whether the concept itself was developed in Greek-speaking territory is an entirely different matter. Similarly, the word they acquired for 'court', *kris* (from the same word *krísis*, 'judgement', as gave *crisis* to English), would take on a particularly Gypsy dimension among the Vlach Rom as a description of their mechanism for settling disputes and punishing offences against the Gypsy moral code. And if they adopted the Greek term for 'frog', it was because their Indic word *beng* (which kept the sense of 'frog' in Syrian Romani) had acquired its present meaning of 'devil', perhaps – as Paspati supposes [15] – from the crude painted representations of St George on horseback slaying the dragon, which the Gypsies must have met with everywhere when they entered Byzantine territory. These and other importations into the language meant that the Greek contribution to Romani vocabulary in Europe would for long remain more important than any other, apart from the original Indo-Aryan. This must, however, have been the final phase of anything like a single language within Europe: once Romani was carried beyond the Greek-speaking regions, the retreat from a common European dialect began. Though one should not read too much into this, it is interesting to note that if one applies the methods of glottochronology (pp. 29–30 above) to Greek and Welsh Romani and Kalderash, the results imply that the unity of basic vocabulary in European Romani started to break up by AD 1040, with a subsequent split by AD 1200 among those who had moved on into the Balkans.

As well as words, the Gypsies acquired in Byzantium and Greece a familiarity with the Christian world. On the roads and in the ports, they had encountered travellers from all over Europe. They may have learned additional languages. They would certainly have heard of the Holy Land; they had seen that pilgrims were privileged travellers. All this knowledge would be profitable to them one day, when they decided to pursue their migrations into the world of western Christianity.

Serbia, Bulgaria, Wallachia, Moldavia

The course which linguistic differentiation was going to follow had already been determined before the end of the fourteenth

---

[15] A. Paspati, *Études sur les Tchinghianés* (Constantinople, 1870), p. 169.

century, for by then the Gypsies were established widely throughout the Balkan provinces. In Serbia, where the south Slavs under Stefan Dushan had at last achieved an empire, one has to reject the identification as Gypsies of *cingarije* listed among the artisans assigned in Stefan's edict founding the monastery of St Michael and St Gabriel at Prizren in 1348: in this instance the name is deceptive, and simply means 'shoe-makers'.[16] But in 1362 a document of the neighbouring Republic of Ragusa (Dubrovnik) recorded an instruction to a goldsmith, at the petition of two 'Egyptians', Vlachus and Vitanus (*ad petitionem Vlachi et Vitani Egyptiorum*), to return to them the eight silver pieces they had deposited with him. And in 1378 Ivan Shishman, Bulgaria's last tsar, gave over to the Rila monastery (Rilski Manastir) some villages partly inhabited by sedentary Gypsies.

This was a time when the Ottoman advance was steadily eating up the Balkans. Ivan Shishman had been forced to declare himself the vassal of the sultan in 1371, and by then the Turks also held most of Macedonia. In 1389 Serbia in turn was reduced to vassal status; in 1391 Bosnia and Wallachia were obliged to pay annual tributes; in 1396 Bulgaria was annexed outright.

Wallachia and Moldavia have a special – and ignominious – place in Gypsy history, for there the Gypsies were system-atically turned into slaves. The Latin-speaking Vlachs, whose descendants inhabit modern Rumania and Moldova, migrated from Transylvania in the thirteenth and fourteenth centuries to, first, Wallachia ('Land of the Vlachs') and then Moldavia, which became independent principalities. Both were Christian states, generally of the Orthodox faith, though Wallachia sometimes wavered towards Rome. Their periods of true in-dependence were brief, and for much of their existence they were under the control of neighbouring powers. But both devised their own very similar methods for dealing with their Gypsy populations and for ensuring that they could preserve them as a valuable labour force.

---

[16] Cf. F. X. Miklosich, *Über die Mundarten und die Wanderungen der Zigeuner Europas* (*Denkschriften der kaiserlichen Akademie der Wissen-schaften*, Philosophisch-historische Klasse, Vienna), vol. 23 (1874), p. 6.

Already in the earliest references the Gypsies had been reduced to servitude and become the property of the ruling prince or the monasteries. The first mention of Gypsies in Rumanian archives occurs in a document issued in 1385 by Voivode (Prince) Dan I, lord of all Wallachia, in favour of the monastery of the Virgin Mary at Tismana: in this the Voivode confirmed the grant of 40 families of Gypsies (*atsingani*) made during the reign (1364–1377) of his uncle Voivode Vladislav to the monastery of St Anthony at Voditza, a dependency of the Tismana monastery. In the year 1388 the monastery of Cozia received from the subsequent Wallachian prince, Mircea the Old, a donation of 300 families. In Moldavia a document of 1428 records a gift of 31 tents of *tsigani* and 13 tents of Tartars by Alexander the Good to the monastery of Bistriţa. A considerable number of later Rumanian documents in Slavic from the fourteenth and fifteenth centuries all confirm the widespread subjection of Gypsies to slavery in these Danubian principalities from an early stage after their arrival.

Gypsies had in fact acquired an economic importance which made the rulers reluctant to let them leave. The principalities had lost the affluence they once enjoyed from being on important trade routes. First the churches and monasteries, then the boyars (estate-owners) found that Gypsies were invaluable to them. Impoverished peasants were selling their land and could be turned into serfs to work the soil, but the Gypsies had filled a niche between peasant and master and were valued as artisans who specialized in certain trades – blacksmith, locksmith, tinsmith, etc. Since they were peripatetic they could not be relied upon to be readily available. To prevent them from escaping they were turned into slaves of the boyars, as they had been of the Church; and to make the controls all-embracing it was declared that every Gypsy without a master was the property of the state.[17]

The Gypsies of the Crown paid an annual tribute but were not obliged to remain in the one spot; they were in fact often hounded from place to place. In summer they lived in tents, and in winter in underground cabins or shelters which they

---

[17] Cf. P. N. Panaitescu, 'The Gypsies in Walachia and Moldavia: a chapter of economic history', *JGLS*(3), 20 (1941), pp. 58–72.

dug in the forest near the villages. The slaves owned by the monasteries and boyars were absolutely at the disposal of their masters and possessed no personal rights. They and their children were chattels who could be sold, exchanged or given away; a Rumanian man or woman who married such a Gypsy became a slave too. Some lived in villages and besides farming their masters' land also worked as barbers, tailors, bakers, masons and domestic servants; the women were employed in fishing and housework, for bleaching linen and for making clothes and embroidery. Their liberty would not be restored fully in Moldo-Wallachia until 1856.[18]

[18] Cf. M. Kogălniceanu, *Esquisse sur l'histoire... des Cigains* (Berlin, 1837).

4

The Great Trick

By the end of the fourteenth century the Kingdom of Hungary was left as the major European power face to face with the Ottomans. The kingdom extended well beyond present Hungarian boundaries and included Transylvania and much of what became, in the twentieth century, Yugoslavia and Czechoslovakia. It is none too clear when Gypsies first appeared within those domains. Agram (Zagreb) was part of Hungary then and, over a lengthy period of 80 years or more, beginning in 1382, court records of Agram refer to a series of litigious butchers with the name Cigan or Cygan, Chickan or Czyganychyn.[1] Elsewhere, from the 1370s, the Hungarian name for Gypsy, *cigány*, occurs in archives both as a family name and in the name of villages.[2] Better still, a letter of 1260 from Ottokar II of Bohemia to Pope Adrian IV about his victory over Bela IV of Hungary appeared to include *Cingari* among the peoples making up Bela's army.[3]

At first, so many occurrences of the word *cygan* or *cigány* or *cingari* heighten the passion of the chase. Then caution begins to creep in. The geographical names which look so much like valuable clues are restricted to a very limited zone in north-western Transylvania and the neighbouring territory – and it

---

[1] L. Wiener, 'Ismaelites', *JGLS*(2), 4 (1910), pp. 83–100.

[2] See J. Vekerdi, 'Earliest archival evidence on Gypsies in Hungary', *JGLS*(4), 1 (1977), no. 3, pp. 170–2.

[3] Quoted by F. Predari, *Origine e Vicende dei Zingari* (Milan, 1841), p. 63.

is precisely there that a noble family Zygan is to be found, with antecedents going right back to the original Hungarian invasion in the ninth century.[4] As for the personal names based on *cygan*, confined to Croatia, none of the references is really persuasive: the people concerned are too settled in their ways and trades, and too fond of resorting to litigation. One suspects that this is another red herring, but whether or not connected with the noble Zygan family-name it is impossible to say. As for King Ottokar, the Gypsy soldiers in the defeated army fade away when a better reading of his letter replaces *Cingarorum* by *Bulgarorum*.

Once the improbabilities are eliminated, the first accounts of Gypsies in Hungary are of fairly late date.[5] In 1416 the southeast Transylvanian town of Brassó (formerly Kronstadt; now Rumanian Braşov) provided 'lord Emaus of Egypt and his 120 companions' with food and money. We learn nothing more of Emaus or of the direction in which he and his company then turned – if westwards, they would be the harbingers of the events of the following year, when there was a dramatic turn-around in Gypsy history and a new era began with a series of widely attested arrivals in central and western Europe, in which Gypsies appear as organized pilgrim groups, claiming, and obtaining, subsidies. When this happened, from 1417 onwards, there was such a stir that it is tempting to assume that Gypsies came as a new phenomenon to Europe west of the Balkans.

It is unlikely that their influx was quite so abrupt and

---

[4] See J. Vekerdi, 'La parola "Zingaro" nei nomi medievali', *Lacio Drom* (1985), no. 3, p. 31.

[5] Two articles still fundamental for early Gypsy history in Europe, though they have been modified and amplified by later research, are: P. Bataillard, 'Beginning of the immigration of the Gypsies into western Europe in the fifteenth century', *JGLS*(1), 1 (1888–9), pp. 185–212, 260–86, 324–45; 2 (1890), pp. 27–53; and E. O. Winstedt, 'Some records of the Gypsies in Germany, 1407–1792', *JGLS*(3), 11 (1932), pp. 97–111; 12 (1933), pp. 123–41, 189–96; 13 (1934), pp. 98–116. A useful corrective to some common misconceptions is: R. Gelsenbach, 'Quellen zur Geschichte der Roma und ihrer Interpretation, dargestellt an Beispielen aus dem 15. Jahrhundert', *Giessener Hefte für Tsiganologie* (1985), 1/85, pp. 8– 16; 2 + 3/85, pp. 3–11.

concentrated. The accounts of the town of Hildesheim in Lower Saxony, for example, record a donation made in 1407 to 'the Tartars in the Town Clerk's Office, when their letters were examined'. The north German term 'Tartars' clearly refers to Gypsies in later entries, and may also have done so here. Similarly, the accounts of Basle in Switzerland register the giving of alms to a *Heiden* in 1414, 'through God's will'. 'Heathen' was a word much used later in reference to Gypsies in German- and Dutch-speaking lands, being almost as common a designation as *Zigeuner*. Less reliably as regards dates, various western chroniclers place Gypsies in Hesse in 1414, and in Meissen and Bohemia in 1416.

The scantiness of the evidence is not necessarily an argument against some Gypsy infiltration of the west, perhaps briefly, at various periods prior to 1417: so long as their numbers were small and they did not make themselves conspicuous, they could have escaped official notice. Virtually nothing, however, in their previous history – made up of a snippet here and a glimpse there – has prepared us for what did happen in 1417 and the immediately following years. In the Romani of the Gypsies of Spain, the expression *o xonxanó baró*, 'the great trick', refers to a certain method of relieving some gullible dupe of a large sum of money. In the entire chronicle of Gypsy history, the greatest trick of all was the one played on western Europe in the early fifteenth century.

Suddenly, we find Gypsies behaving in an unprecedented manner. They are no longer unobtrusive, but almost court attention. They are no uncoordinated rabble, but move in an apparently purposeful way under leaders with impressive titles. And at first they are not hounded or harried, but treated with a measure of consideration. It was as if some unsung genius, stimulated perhaps by all the pressures in the Balkans, had realized the potential advantages to be drawn from the religious environment of the time and had devised a strategy for exploiting it and enhancing the prospects of survival.

Today it is difficult to understand the attitude of the people in the Middle Ages towards penitents, because we have lost their acute consciousness of sin and the certainty of its punishment. Outside the Church – the community of all believers –

there lurked only paganism; and the devil and hell, conceived in a most material form, lay in wait for those who strayed from the path of grace. For Gypsies the important point was that, even after pilgrimages had suffered some decline in repute, it was still considered a duty to entertain the pilgrim and help him on his journey. Thus charitable persons could share in the blessings that descended upon the pilgrim, and pilgrims were instruments for winning grace. Rulers might encourage them by granting them letters of recommendation. Charlemagne had in his time imposed it as a legal obligation that pilgrims should be given roof, hearth and fire wherever they travelled. By claiming to be penitents and pilgrims, the Gypsies could ensure that they were received with a warmer welcome than they had enjoyed hitherto. Some had perhaps already tried out the efficacy of letters of protection (if it was Gypsies we saw at Hildesheim – see p. 62), and now, it would seem, certain of them sought to aim as high as they could. For that purpose no name could be more effectively invoked than that of the Emperor Sigismund.

Sigismund (1368–1437) had been king of Hungary since 1387. In 1411 the College of Electors conferred on him the crown of Germany as well, making him *de facto* Holy Roman Emperor (though he was not duly crowned by the Pope until 1433), and soon this mercurial statesman was too much distracted by the affairs of Bohemia and the Empire to give the governing of Hungary and the stemming of the Turkish tide the attention they demanded. From 1414 to 1418 he paid visits to a number of countries, both within and outside the Empire, and also to the town of Constance, which for a time became the hub of the Christian world thanks to the ecumenical council promoted there by Sigismund in an attempt to win prestige as the restorer of the Church's unity by ending the papal schism. Many princes, abbots and bishops settled in the town at the start of the council in 1414, and Sigismund himself was there for much of 1417 and 1418. The council did succeed in re-establishing the unity of the Church, but it failed to arrest the spread of the Bohemian heresies, despite the condemnation of John Hus after Sigismund had repudiated the safe-conduct he had granted.

Plate 6   Gypsy fortune-teller, in Sebastian Münster's Cosmographia universalis, *1550.*

Imperial safe-conducts

It was towards Constance that some Gypsies turned. It appears to have been at Lindau, on Lake Constance, that they obtained the letters they needed – from Sigismund (perhaps willing to see them for the sake of news from his Hungarian kingdom), or from one of his chancery officials, unless, of course, they procured serviceable documents more deviously. The practice of issuing safe-conducts was widespread in the Middle Ages: they were the forerunners of the later passport. Such documents were made out to a specified individual (and his followers), but Gypsies no doubt found it prudent and economical to have copies quickly made. At any rate, Sebastian Münster relates much later in his *Cosmographia universalis* (1550) that he was shown by some Gypsies near Heidelberg a copy of a letter that had been obtained from Emperor Sigismund at Lindau, granting them free passage. The reason quoted for their wanderings in the document shown to Münster was the one that would be adhered to for some years to come, though variants would eventually emerge: we have already seen the version put forward by Arnold von Harff (p. 54). According to Münster,

it was told how their ancestors in Lesser Egypt [*in minori Aegypto*] had formerly abandoned for some years the Christian religion and turned to the error of the pagans and that, after their repentance, a penance had been imposed upon them that, for as many years, some members of their families should wander about the world and expiate in exile the guilt of their sin.[6]

In some of the verbal by-play which took place in this encounter, Münster claimed he was told that their native country was far beyond the Holy Land and Babylon and that to get there they would have to pass through the land inhabited by the pygmies. When Münster replied, 'Then your Lesser Egypt is not in Africa near the Nile but in Asia along the Ganges or the Indus', he was countered with some other piece of facetiousness. Münster also noted that they possessed a language of their own, which he dismissed as Rotwelsch, German thieves' cant.[7]

In 1417 the municipal accounts of Hildesheim, which had intriguingly noted a visit of 'Tartars' a decade before, record – more explicitly this time – the giving of alms to 'the Tartars from Egypt, for the honour of God', but the town also thought it prudent to set a guard over them. These may have been

[6] The Latin text of Münster can be found in D. M. M. Bartlett, 'Münster's *Cosmographia universalis*', *JGLS*(3), 31 (1952), pp. 83–90. The differing German text is given in R. Gronemeyer, *Zigeuner im Spiegel früher Chroniken und Abhandlungen* (Giessen, 1987), which conveniently brings together many of the references to Gypsies in chronicles, etc. (but not municipal archives).

[7] To discuss the multifarious early theories of Gypsy origins is beyond the scope of this book. The task has been excellently done for the period 1461–1841 in L. Piasere, 'De origine Cinganorum', *Études et documents balkaniques et méditerranéens*, 14 (1989), pp. 105–26.

Map 3 *Europe c.1417, showing places visited by Gypsies, 1407–27.*

members of the group described in the earliest contemporary report of the spread of the Gypsies after they had armed themselves with imperial documents – Hermann Cornerus's *Chronica novella*, completed in Latin about 1435. Referring to the closing months of the year 1417, Cornerus, a native of Lübeck, has this to say of their passage through the northern German territories of Holstein, Mecklenburg and Pomerania:

A certain strange, wandering horde of people, not seen hitherto, came out of eastern lands to Alemannia [Swabia], travelling through that entire region into the provinces by the sea. They were also in the coastal towns; starting from Lüneberg and penetrating Prussia they passed through Hamburg, Lübeck, Wismar, Rostock, Stralsund and Greifswald. They travelled in bands and camped at night in the fields outside the towns, for they were excessively given to thievery and feared that in the towns they would be taken prisoner. They numbered about 300 men and women, not including the children and infants, and were very ugly in appearance and black as Tartars; they called themselves *Secani*. They also had chieftains among them, that is a Duke [*Ducem*] and a Count [*Comitem*], who administered justice over them and whose orders they obeyed. They were however great thieves, especially their women, and several of them in various places were seized and put to death. They also carried letters of recommendation from princes and especially from Sigismund, King of the Romans, according to which they were to be admitted and kindly treated by states, princes, fortified places, towns, bishops and prelates to whom they turned. Certain among them were on horseback, while others went on foot. The reason for their wandering and travelling in foreign lands was said to have been their abandoning of the faith and their apostasy after conversion to paganism. They were committed to continue these wanderings in foreign lands for seven years as a penance laid upon them by their bishops.[8]

This important text tells us a good deal about those Gypsies' organization and their reception. They appear frequently to have split up into smaller groups, but they all came under the same chief; they marched in concert and followed each other closely. The exhibited letters of protection, but were treated

---

[8] Translated from the Latin of Hermann Cornerus, *Chronica novella usque ad annum 1435*, in J. G. Eccard, *Corpus historicum medii ævi* (Leipzig, 1723), vol. 2, col. 1225.

with suspicion. For one thing, the Germans found them very ugly, evidently because of the colour of their skin; and they also had the reputation of being light-fingered. Another chronicler of Lübeck, Rufus, relates much the same story, except that he describes the Gypsies as actually being Tartars (a name that would stick in northern Germany and Scandinavia), and puts their number at 400.

The incursion into the Baltic towns met with no more than mixed success. The letters of protection had not been sufficient to ward off savage retribution in cases of pilfering: whether it was the authorities or the townspeople who meted out the rough justice is not clear. Evidently the Gypsies did not find these Hanseatic towns altogether to their taste, for in 1418 all traces of them occur much further south. In June 'the needy people from Little Egypt' were given 4 pounds and 4 shillings for bread and meat by the city of Frankfurt am Main – the earliest reference to 'Little Egypt' as their place of origin. There are also records of Gypsies in Alsace around this time: somewhat dubious as regards Strassburg, but more precise and reliable for Colmar which, according to the earliest chronicle of the town, was visited on 10 August by thirty *Heiden* with women and children; when they left they were replaced by a further hundred. The darkness of their skins is again emphasized; new observations are the silver ear-rings, and the palmistry of the women, who were dressed in rags which looked like blankets. It is in Switzerland that references come thick and fast, though many of the Swiss chroniclers copied and re-copied each other, and all but one of them lived too late to have been an eye-witness. Zürich, Basle, Solothurn and Berne are all credited with visits. The chroniclers represent the Gypsies as an outlandish and very dark people; they had their dukes and counts, and said they came from Little Egypt. (One of the chronicles of Zürich adds that some said they were from Igritz – an interesting amplification, since Igritz is a small town in northern Hungary, near Miskolc.) They related that they had been driven out by the Turks and that they were condemned to do penance in poverty for seven years. They followed the Christian customs as regards baptism and burial. Their clothing was poor but they had a great deal of gold and silver, ate well and drank well and paid well. A discordant

note is struck, however, by Conrad Justinger, the one chronicler who was contemporary with the events. Under the year
1419 (though this may be a mistake for 1418) he speaks of the
arrival in Switzerland of more than 200 baptized *Heiden* who
camped before Berne in the fields until they were banned by
the authorities because their light-fingered ways had exhausted
the patience of the inhabitants.

The Gypsies appear to have quit Switzerland for the time
being in September 1418. Such groups as remained visible in
western Europe during the following years were not numerous;
it seems indeed as though only a nucleus may have remained,
commanded by a few of the leaders. Sometimes the nucleus
stayed together; sometimes it split into smaller detachments.
Thus, in November 1418, according to Mülich's chronicle, a
troop of Gypsies came to Augsburg, consisting of 'two dukes
and with them 50 men and many women and children, and
they said they were from Egypt'.

When next we have a run of sightings, they are in France.
On 22 August 1419, a band of 'Saracens' appeared in the
little town of Châtillon-en-Dombes (today, Châtillon-sur-
Chalaronne), which at that time was a dependency of Savoy.
These Gypsies presented letters from the Duke of Savoy as well
as from the Emperor; the authenticity of the Savoyard document appears to be assured.[9] They were well received and
were given wine and oats and three florins. Two days later,
'Andrew, Duke of Little Egypt', with 120 or more followers,
arrived at St Laurent, near Mâcon, only six leagues away from
Châtillon. The town supplied them with bread and wine; in a
strange phraseology, the archives describe them as 'men of
terrible stature in person, in hair, as well as otherwise'. They
camped in the fields, and both men and women practised
palmistry and sorcery. When the archives go on to talk of
certain of their deceits, the duke is pointedly referred to as
'Andrew, who calls himself Duke of Little Egypt'. Five weeks
later (1 October 1419), we find Gypsies at Sisteron in Provence,
again under the name of 'Saracens'. They were refused admittance but remained for two days encamped in a field 'like

---

[9] Cf. M. Pastore, 'Zingari nello Stato Sabaudo', *Lacio Drom* (1989), nos
3–4, pp. 6–19, esp. p. 7.

soldiers' (no doubt, in tents), and food was sent out for them and their horses.

Three months go by, and then we meet a Duke Andrew and a company of Gypsies once more, this time in the Low Countries. Quite possibly these were the Gypsies who had been in France the previous year. There can, however, be no certainty of this. The Gypsies appear to have had no difficulty in securing copies of their safe-conducts, and whoever happened to be at the head of a particular band could have passed himself off as the leader named in the document; alternatively, of course, one cannot exclude the possibility that two leaders may have borne the same name. In any event, in January 1420 the civic accounts of Brussels show that the band led by 'the Duke of Little Egypt, named Andries' relieved the burghers of a quantity of beer and wine, bread, a cow, four sheep and 25 gold coins. Then, in March 1420, the accounts of Deventer record a donation by order of the aldermen to 'the Lord Andreas, Duke of Little Egypt' (*Hoefscheid Heren Andreas, Hertoch van Cleyn-Egypten*) 'who had been driven out of his country on account of the Christian faith, and had come to our town with 100 persons, men, women and children, and about 40 horses, and had letters from the King of the Romans, containing an invitation to give them alms and to treat them with kindness in all the countries where they might go'. In all, this company received 25 florins in cash, together with bread, beer, herrings and straw; the town also bore the cost of cleaning out the barn in which they slept, and of conducting them eastwards to Goor.

In the same year there are suggestions of Gypsies in Friesland and near Leiden, but these are untrustworthy. More to the point, a duke and a count leading a company of 'Egyptians' appeared at Bruges in Flanders in September 1421. Their names were not recorded; but we are more fortunate in that respect with neighbouring Hainault and Artois. On 30 September 1421 the aldermen of Tournai deliberated over what to do about the 'Egyptians' at their door. The generous outcome was that 'Sir Miquiel, prince of Latinghem in Egypt' was presented with 12 gold coins, bread and a barrel of beer, 'out of pity and compassion, for the sustaining of him and several other men and women of his company who were driven out of their country by the Saracens because they had turned to the Christian faith'. This is the first time we hear of 'Sir Miquiel, prince of Latinghem' – a place-name more reminiscent of Flanders than of Egypt. But a Duke Michael – the name is suspiciously similar – appeared shortly afterwards at nearby Mons, which in fact received two visits in October, the first consisting of 80 people under Duke Andrew, the second of 60 under Duke Michael, said to be his brother. Egyptians returned to Tournai in May of the following year and were lodged in the market-place. 'And these Egyptians', says the chronicler, 'had a king and lords whom they obeyed, and had privileges, so that none could punish them save themselves.' He gives no names, but offers details of stealing, fortune-telling by the women (accompanied by purse-cutting by children), and artful horse-dealing by the men.

The aldermen's accounts in Burgundian Arras provide picturesque details of some 30 'foreigners from the country of Egypt' who arrived on 11 October 1421 led by a count bearing letters from the Emperor; they stayed there for three days, sleeping at night in a field without removing any of their clothing. The men were very dark-skinned, long-haired and heavily bearded, while the women had cloths wound around their heads like turbans, and wore low-cut chemises covered by a coarse sheet fastened at the shoulder; women and children had rings in their ears. All these appurtenances were quite different from contemporary European fashions. The amazed citizens bestowed on them a quantity of beer and coal.

New letters of protection

Ever since their arrival in 1417 the Gypsies had been saying that their pilgrimage was to last seven years. Once five years had elapsed, the old letters were losing their virtue and nearing their time-limit, so that it was becoming opportune to seek an extension. Moreover, Sigismund's writ did not extend outside the Holy Roman Empire and already (as we saw at Châtillon) Gypsies were taking the precaution of displaying letters from other dignitaries as well. The only universal protection would be that of the Pope. The first mention of papal letters in the

hands of Gypsies is ascribed to 16 July 1422 in a Swiss chronicle: on that day Duke Michael of Egypt and his followers are
said to have produced to the citizens of Basle 'good letters of
safe-conduct from the Pope and our Lord the King and from
other lords'. Ominously, the chronicler also noted: 'that did
them no good at all; they were not welcome'. If the date was
accurate, Duke Michael had managed to reach the Vatican
ahead of another Gypsy leader – the Duke Andrea who is said
to have arrived with a band of about 100 at Bologna on 18
July 1422 and stayed a fortnight. According to a Bologna
chronicle, the story Duke Andrea told was that, when he
lapsed from the Christian faith, his lands were confiscated by
the King of Hungary, and when he wished to re-embrace
Christianity he and some 4,000 men were baptized and
ordered by the king to travel about the world for seven years
and to go to the Pope in Rome; then they would be able to
return to their own country. These Gypsies claimed further
that, when they reached Bologna, they had been journeying for
five years, during which time more than half their original
number had died. They invoked a novel decree by which the
King of Hungary purportedly allowed them to thieve during
these seven years, wherever they might go, without being
amenable to justice. Duke Andrea lodged in the king's inn
(*nell' albergo del re*), while his followers settled inside and
outside one of the city gates.

Many people went to see them, on account of the duke's wife who
could tell fortunes and predict what would transpire in a person's
life, as well as what was happening in the present and how many
children they had and whether a wife was good or bad, and other
things. In many cases she told truly. And amongst those who wished
to have their fortunes told, few went to consult without having their
purse stolen, and women had pieces of their dress cut off. The
women of the band wandered about the town, six or eight together;
they entered the houses of the citizens and told idle tales, during
which some of them laid hold of whatever could be taken. In the
same way they visited the shops under the pretext of buying something, but one of them would steal. Many thefts were committed in
this way in Bologna. So it was cried throughout the town that no-one
should go to see them under a penalty of fifty *lire* and excommunication; for they were the most cunning thieves in all the world. It was

even allowed to those who had been robbed by them to rob them in return to the amount of their losses; in consequence of which several men slipped one night into a stable where some of their horses were shut up, and took the finest of them. The strangers, wanting their horse back, agreed to restore a great number of stolen objects. Seeing that there was nothing more to steal there, they went off towards Rome. Note that they were the ugliest brood ever seen in these parts. They were thin and black and ate like pigs. Their women went about in shifts and wore a coarse outer garment across the shoulder, rings in their ears, and a long veil on their head. One of them gave birth to a child in the market-place and, at the end of three days, she went on with the other women.[10]

On 7 August 1422 we find them at Forli, five leagues from Bologna on the road to Rome. Brother Hieronimus, the chronicler of Forli, put their number at 200. Remarkably, some people said they were from India (*aliqui dicebant, quod erant de India*).[11] Presumably, though the matter is not entirely clear, the people who said this were onlookers and not Gypsies, who are not known subsequently to have made such a claim. Notions of India and its geography were extremely vague at that time (as Columbus would show); the name was indeed sometimes used in reference to Ethiopia. After two days these Gypsies left, saying they were going to see the Pope. Then they disappear from view. But periodically, for decades thereafter – in 1427 at Paris and Amiens, in 1429 at Douai, Rotterdam and Utrecht, in 1430 at Middelburg on the island of Walcheren, and elsewhere in later years – Gypsy chieftains can be observed displaying papal letters. They are not always made out to the same person, and they do not all bear the same date. The most vivid account of them is given in the journal of a Frenchman commonly referred to as the *Bourgeois* of Paris, describing a disorderly Gypsy rabble which stayed at La Chapelle near Paris (still in English hands) from 17 August to 8 September 1427. First came a duke and a count and ten men, all on horseback, who said they were good Christians and were from Lower Egypt. They told the familiar tale of

---

[10] Translated from the Italian of L. A. Muratori (ed.), *Rerum Italicarum Scriptores*, vol. 18 (Milan, 1730), p. 611.
[11] Ibid., vol. 19 (Milan, 1731), p. 890.

relapse from the Christian faith after conquest by the Saracens, followed by reconquest by the Emperor and other Christian lords.

The Emperor and the other lords, after much deliberation, said that they should never hold land in their country without the Pope's consent and that they must go to Rome, to the Holy Father. There they all went, old and young, and a hard journey it was for the children. When they got there they made general confession of their sins. The Pope, having heard their confession, after much thought and consultation imposed this penance: that for seven years they should go to and fro about the world without ever sleeping in a bed. He also ordered, it was said, that so as to provide some means for them every bishop and every abbot who bore a crosier should give them, once, ten pounds *tournois*. He gave them letters about this addressed to the prelates of the church, blessed them, and so they departed.[12]

What are we to make of all this: did Pope Martin V grant audience in 1422 to a band of Gypsies, or two successive bands (first Duke Michael's, then Duke Andrea's), and, having listened to their tale, impose on them another seven-year penance, coupled with letters of protection?[13] There is no record of such a remarkable event in the Vatican archives: a search was made in 1932 and discovered nothing. That is not conclusive, since there have been many losses from these archives; but it does increase the possibility that the Gypsies decided not to trouble His Holiness, or were turned away by his entourage, and addressed themselves instead to some skilful forger in order to obtain an impressive papal brief. The manufacture of forgeries, not least false papal bulls and other papal documents, was a flourishing industry in the Middle Ages, and there existed a lively traffic in them.

Having obtained new safe-conducts, by whatever means, the

[12] *Journal d'un Bourgeois de Paris (1405–49)*, ed. A. Tuetey (Paris, 1881); this translation is from J. Shirley's version, *A Parisian Journal, 1405–1449* (Oxford, 1968), pp. 217–18.

[13] Two relevant articles are: R. A. Scott Macfie, 'The Gypsy visit to Rome in 1422', *JGLS*(3), 11 (1932), pp. 111–15; and F. de Vaux de Foletier, 'Le pèlerinage romain des Tsiganes en 1422 et les lettres du Pape Martin V', *Études Tsiganes* (1965), no. 4, pp. 13–19.

Gypsies made sure of having several copies at their disposal. Some were made out in one name, some in another. One such copy still survives, in the form of a French translation of letters granted to Andreu, Duke of Little Egypt, and dated 15 December 1423 (not 1422). In one curious expression, the Pope grants these penitents the remission of one half of their sins – an unorthodox form of absolution unparalleled elsewhere at this time. The copy is thus highly suspect; and the originals must remain suspect too.

In the following year, 1423, yet another major new document of protection emerges, a document transmitted to us by a well-informed contemporary witness, Andreas, a priest of Ratisbon (now Regensburg) in Bavaria. Andreas noted the arrival of Gypsies ('*Cingari*, vulgarly called *Cigäwnär*') in his diary for 1424.

They were near to Ratisbon, and were succeeding each other, sometimes to the number of 30, men, women and children, sometimes less. They pitched their tents in the fields, because they were not allowed to stay in towns; for they cunningly took what did not belong to them. These people were from Hungary, and they said that they had been exiled as a sign or remembrance of the flight of Our Lord into Egypt when he was fleeing from Herod, who sought him to slay him. But the common people said that they were spies in the country.[14]

A number of unusual points arise here: the reference to tents; the explanation of the Gypsies' exile as being related in some way to the flight of the Holy Family; the suspicion of espionage (which was still being quoted in Germany more than five centuries later as a justification for genocide). But most interesting of all, Andreas made a note of the contents of one of the letters from King Sigismund which these Gypsies possessed. It was dated 23 April 1423, and after the preliminaries went on:

Came in person into our presence our faithful Ladislaus *waynoda Ciganorum* [voivode of the Gypsies] with others pertaining to him,

---

[14] Translated from the Latin of Andreas, Presbyter Ratisbonensis, *Diarium sexennale*, which is in A. F. Oefelius, *Rerum boicarum scriptores* (Augsburg, 1763), vol. 1, p. 21.

who presented their very humble supplications to us, here in Zips in our presence . . . In consequence we, being persuaded by their supplication, have thought proper to grant them this privilege: each time that the said voivode Ladislaus and his people shall come into our said possessions, be it free cities or fortified towns, from that time we strictly entrust and order to your present fidelities that you may favour and keep without any hindrance or trouble the said voivode Ladislaus and the Cigani who are subject to him; and by all means preserve them from any impediments and vexations. If any variance or trouble should occur among themselves, then neither you nor any other of you, but the same voivode Ladislaus, should have the power of judging and absolving . . .

This safe-conduct was delivered in Zips in the northern part of the Hungarian kingdom (now in Slovakia), where Sigismund is known to have been staying at the time in question. It appears to have been obtained by Gypsies who were different in background from those who had preceded them westwards. There is no mention of a pilgrimage, no ascription of exotic origin, and Ladislaus, stated to be a subject of Sigismund, bore a name which was current chiefly in Hungary and Poland, whereas his forerunners Andrew and Michael had names which belonged to all Christendom. His own connection with Hungary (if not that of his followers) must have been of some duration. In effect they look like the front-runners of a second wave of immigration; but it is impossible to follow their tracks, as Ladislaus is never seen again.

Andreas, the chronicler, once more noted the presence of Gypsies at Ratisbon in 1426 and, less precisely as regards location, in 1433 (remarking this time that they 'said they were from Egypt'). But for the most part these later groups did not attract much attention and, for some years to come, it will still be the movements of the original migrants that we can most readily register in any detail.

That is certainly the case in Spain, where the earliest known document relating to Gypsies is a safe-conduct of 12 January 1425, valid for three months, which was granted to 'Don Johan de Egipte Menor' in Saragossa by Alfonso V of Aragon. Alfonso, living up to his cognomen 'the Magnanimous', was obviously well disposed towards these newly arrived pilgrims. A few months later he issued another safe-conduct to Count

Tomás of Little Egypt and his followers, and when the inhabitants of Alagón, near Saragossa, stole from the Gypsy count a greyhound and a mastiff, Alfonso immediately ordered their return. Count Tomás carefully preserved the safe-conduct and in 1435 would produce a copy of it when, shortly after having received a donation of 23 florins from Queen Blanche of Navarre, he arrived at the Spanish frontier post of Canfranc at the foot of the Somport Pass. The toll and customs collector of the city of Jaca and of Canfranc demanded payment, but the most honourable and distinguished (*muyt honrado et inclito*) Count of Little Egypt declared that he and his people were making a pilgrimage through the world for the Christian faith, and that King Alfonso had granted him permission to pass at will through his lands with all his company and his family, freely and without the payment of any toll or tax whatsoever. The royal permit is indeed couched in such terms and, in its present home in Huesca, has a guarantee of authenticity attached to it. The Gypsy count avoided paying duties, but he did have to declare what effects he had: they included '5 horses each worth 20 florins; item 5 robes which were of silk; item 4 silver goblets each weighing one mark [*c.* 8 oz] more or less'.

These are the first references we have to leaders with the names Thomas and John. A Count Thomas will soon reappear. He may or may not have been the unnamed count among the Gypsies whom we have already seen exhibiting a papal brief at La Chapelle on the northern outskirts of Paris in August 1427; but there was certainly a Count Thomas at Amiens shortly afterwards, with papal letters made out in his name. The description of the Gypsies at La Chapelle in the journal of the *Bourgeois* of Paris is one of the fullest to have come down from the early years. With their dark skins and silver ear-rings, they were an exotic sight, and they attracted crowds of curious spectators. The garb of the womenfolk was a shift covered by the blanket-like garment previously observed at Arras in 1421 and Bologna in 1422. The home truths (or fabrications) in their fortune-telling sowed discord in not a few marriages. The *Bourgeois* of Paris observed: 'I must say I went there three or four times to talk to them and could never see that I lost a penny, nor did I see them looking into anyone's hands, but everyone said they did.' In the end the Bishop of Paris ordered both the fortune-tellers and those who had had their hands read to be excommunicated, and the Gypsies were obliged to move on. In under three weeks, still in the month of September 1427, there were some 40 of them at Amiens, headed by a Count Thomas who was given 8 *livres parisis* after he had put his people in a favourable light by telling how they had been expelled from their 'very strange and distant' country for refusing to give up the Christian faith. A year and a half later, in March 1429 at Tournai, we meet with an unnamed Count of Little Egypt and a company of about 60, who have every appearance of being the same as those at Amiens. Notices were put up by the aldermen to warn the townspeople to do them no harm and to encourage alms-giving; in addition, the aldermen sent them wine, wheat, beer, herrings and firewood.

Their visits also led to incidental costs. In May 1428 Hildesheim had to pay for the cleaning of a house where the Gypsies had lodged. There were similar expenses in Flanders about this time when Gypsies were put up in the Woolhouse at Bruges; in Deventer in 1429, when the town also bore the cost of escorting them northwards to their next stopping-place; and in 1429/30 in Rotterdam 'for cleaning the school-house, after the duke and his retinue had lain in it'. The Deventer record is the first in the Low Countries to call the Gypsies *Heidens* ('pagans'), the name by which they continued to be known in the Netherlands. Dukes and counts of Little Egypt are also noted in 1429 in Nijmegen, Utrecht and Arnhem, and in 1430 in Middelburg, Zutphen and Leiden. On several of these occasions the archives refer to papal letters. But when a 'Duke of Egypt' again visits Middelburg in 1431, it is a document from Philip of Burgundy – overlord of much of the Low Countries – that he exhibits. The duke who was at Rotterdam in 1429/30 made doubly sure, by producing 'letters from the Pope and from our dear lord of Burgundy'.

It seems reasonable to assume that the Gypsies who came to Metz and Constance in 1430, Tournai in 1431, Hamburg ('Count John of Little Egypt') and Frankfurt am Main in 1434, and Bruges in 1434/5 were part of the original band. It is more uncertain where the Gypsies hailed from who, further to

the east, frequented Saxony (Erfurt 1432, Meiningen 1435):
possibly they were more recent arrivals from Hungary. Those
who stayed for 11 days in Meiningen had a poor reception,
despite entertaining the townspeople with acrobatics in the
market-place. They seemed outlandish to the citizens because
of the darkness of their skins; in the end the priest had them
driven away.

Taking stock

By this time the reconnaissance phase, if that was what it had
been, was drawing to a close. Enough had been discovered
to establish that life in the west held some attraction for
Gypsies in need of a new homeland. So far they had in varying
degrees become familiar with Germany, Switzerland, the Low
Countries, France, Italy and Spain; but as yet there is no sign
of their having penetrated further to the north or east of
Europe, or of having crossed the English Channel or the North
Sea.

Any construction that one puts on the two decades which
started in 1417 involves some stretching suppositions. The
indications are that up to now we have been dealing, not with
a generalized immigration, but on the contrary with fairly
cohesive bands which travelled widely and in detachments,
and in many cases under some form of control by a few
leaders. There was in effect a degree of unity of action and
close connection with each other. They appear to have told the
same tales and shown similar supporting documents, first from
the Emperor and other potentates and afterwards from the
Pope. Their cover-story was at this stage simply one of doing
penance for apostasy: only in Andreas of Ratisbon's diary is
there a hint of the refinement based on failure to succour the
Holy Family on the flight into Egypt, but it has yet to be
elaborated. Some important aspects of their way of life are still
obscure. It is, for instance, surprising that nothing is said, until
well into the sixteenth century, about the Gypsies having their
own language; nor do we hear of any difficulty in their com-
municating with the inhabitants of countries they were visiting
for the first time. Then again, we have only sparse details of

vehicles and shelters. Tents are mentioned but rarely. The original migrants appear to have had few conveyances and to have bivouacked in the open or under makeshift shelters when they could not persuade townspeople to give them lodging.

Most obscure of all are the social and political organization and the communication network underlying these forays. By the end of the century we shall have encountered some two dozen different names of Gypsy leaders: some of these names crop up only once; others, no doubt, were borne by more than one person. Who *were* these 'dukes' and 'counts', finely dressed and well mounted, and what prompted their incursions? Were they simply acting a part? It is indeed possible that sometimes the leader of the company was of Gypsy blood or had acquired a Gypsy wife: we have seen how, at Bologna, Duke Andrea, who lodged at the Albergo del Re, had a wife who was a noted fortune-teller. Certainly the subordinate chiefs may be supposed to have been of Gypsy origin. But some, at least, of the countries of central and eastern Europe took care that Gypsies should not be ruled by Gypsies. Evidence of this has already emerged, and there will be more to come – in Poland, in Lithuania, in Transylvania and elsewhere. At an early stage in Gypsy history, in Greece and the Balkans, we have seen how rulers and law-givers were appointed, and it was to them that the Gypsies paid their taxes. Corfu had a Gypsy fief, whose baron held special privileges in matters of justice (see p. 50). Over a large tract of Europe, the continuance of the Gypsies had become a matter of self-interest for some important personages. Ladislaus, the voivode of the Gypsies who was favoured with a safe-conduct from the Emperor Sigismund in 1423, was presumably one of these. The difference in status continued to be observed once the Gypsies penetrated the west, and the records of their visits from 1417 onwards often make a marked distinction between the treatment given to the duke or count, who was lodged like a man of some quality, and that meted out to his followers who were quartered in meaner surroundings.

An important concomitant of the special role of the Gypsy leaders was the widespread acceptance that Gypsies had the right to manage their own affairs – an immunity stressed in the 1423 safe-conduct given to Ladislaus, and noted even earlier during the passage of a band of Gypsies at Tournai in 1422. This, together with the privileges of chartered begging which flowed from their status as Christian pilgrims, ensured that, for so long as they were accepted at their own valuation, they could look for substantial if intermittent aid, in food, drink and money, and that there was some chance of any misdemeanours not being treated too harshly. It was no permanent solution, however, for the prejudices and economic structure of the countries they passed through meant that people who were not sedentary were seldom assured of a continuing welcome: the guilds regulated crafts and trades, commerce was also tightly controlled, and peasants were not in the habit of employing casual labour, so that what was left for Gypsies as a livelihood was limited to small services and minor trading and entertainment.

As for the stimulus for the westward migration, Timur (Tamerlane) gave Europe a respite from Ottoman pressure in the early years of the fifteenth century by his attack on the Turks in Anatolia, but the Ottoman advance was resumed in 1415 and the ground which had been lost in Greece and the Balkans was recovered and new conquests were made. In 1417 Wallachia was forced to capitulate, though its dynasty, territory and Christian religion were left intact; thereafter Transylvania and south Hungary suffered repeated raids. It has seemed persuasive to link Gypsy migrations before now with Turkish advances, and it is attractive to make the connection once more; but in so doing it has to be remembered that the larger part of Europe's Gypsy population continued to stay in the Ottoman dominions, which would eventually include much of central and southern Hungary as well. If some of them were free to seek out alternative territories and did so, it is unlikely to have been on account of religious concerns, despite all the stress placed on that aspect when they did move westwards. (In any case, the Turkish record towards Christian and Jew was better than that of, say, Spanish Christians towards Jew and Muslim.) Whether in the longer term they would have found themselves worse off under Ottoman rule is debatable: once the conquest was completed, the lot of the subject peoples was often no worse than it had been under the previous rulers. Generally, the Turks left the civilian population free on condition of paying taxes to the conquerors, and that was no novelty for Gypsies; and Muslim society was not usually race- or colour-conscious. The immediate disruption and danger which confronted them from the ebb and flow of warfare was another matter. The invaders carried fire and sword through the land; in many parts of the Balkans they sacked towns, villages and monasteries and converted whole districts into desolate wastes, and it is plausible to assume that many Gypsies were glad to remove themselves from an arena of constant strife. There is, however, a pointer worth reflecting on in Arnold von Harff's rather garbled account of the Gypsy migration after his visit to Modon (p. 54), when he attributed it to the fact that 'some of the lords and counts would not serve under the Turkish Emperor': barons of Gypsy fiefs and the like probably stood to lose a great deal more than their subjects, and the impetus for organizing exploratory expeditions may in the first instance have come from their self-interest.

The emphasis on 'Little Egypt' when the Gypsies were explaining their origins to the startled westerners possibly indicates that the early bands had recent connections with the Peloponnese. They were not the only refugees from those parts. Though many of the nobles stayed behind and embraced Islam, the advance of the Turks into Europe did set others, together with numbers of the priests and people, fleeing in search of a safe haven and, eventually, wandering west and subsisting on charity. Municipal accounts show that some of them travelled in companies under leaders with titles like the Gypsies' and were treated like them. The archives of Bruges, for instance,[15] record payments from the early fifteenth century to a variety of wandering Greeks, including a few counts; and also to a count of Wallachia driven from his land by the Turkish conquest, and to a knight of Hungary; while after the fall of Constantinople in 1453 all sorts of people of varying degree from the old Greek empire are continually appearing, though generally in small numbers. Indeed, observation of early groups of such refugees and the favourable treatment they received could have been one of the factors

---

[15] Cf. E. O. Winstedt, 'Gypsies at Bruges', *JGLS*(3), 15 (1936), pp. 126–34.

which suggested to the Gypsies their westward migration and their pose as pilgrims.

In view of the uncertainties about the point of departure, it is perhaps time to seek to wring a further historical clue out of the Gypsies' language in regard to their movements after leaving Greece. Practically all the western European Romani dialects show the influence of southern Slav languages and many of them also contain traces – though on a much reduced scale – of Rumanian.[16] Not all dialects have the same lexicon of Slav loan-words, but certain borrowings are very wide-spread; for example *boba*, 'bean'; *būinō*, 'proud'; *maćka*, 'cat'; *miźak*, 'wicked'; *puśka*, 'gun'; *skorni*, 'top-boot'; *stanya*, 'stable'; *trūpos*, 'body'. These Welsh Romani forms have their counterparts in most other western dialects (and also that of Finland). Almost as widespread are: *dosta*, 'enough'; *kirćíma*, 'inn'; *lovína*, 'beer'; *smenténa*, 'cream'. *Lovína* was already one of the words picked up by Andrew Borde. Both it and *smenténa* illustrate, however, one of the difficulties in establishing etymons in the linguistic mishmash of the Balkans, where words readily crossed language boundaries: these two could have been borrowed via Rumanian. Some unambiguously Rumanian loan-words in Welsh Romani are: *baurī*, 'snails'; *manć*, 'cheer up'; *mūra*, 'berry'; *vare-*, '-ever' (e.g. *varekái*, 'wherever'); and there are a number of more debatable possibilities. Magyar influences, on the other hand, were not carried so far afield and appear to be the result of later adoptions, limited to dialects which evolved in central European countries. Are we then to conclude that the Gypsies who made their way to the west in the fifteenth century did not tarry long in Hungary but must all have spent a significant time in the southern Slav lands and also – though to a lesser degree – in Vlach-speaking territories (except for some who went by sea direct from Greece to southern Italy, where the dialects show

---

[16] The best conspectus of borrowings in the European dialects (though based on the state of Romani lingustics of more than a century ago) remains F. X. Miklosich's *Über die Mundarten und die Wanderungen der Zigeuner Europas* (Denkschriften der kaiserlichen Akademie der Wissenschaften, Philosophisch-historische Klasse, Vienna, 1872–81), esp. Part 3 ('Die Wanderungen der Zigeuner') in vol. 23 (1874), pp. 1–46.

very little Slav influence)? It would be imprudent to be so dogmatic: given the variations in extent of borrowing from Slav and Rumanian sources, given too the rapid succession of migrations to the west and the intermingling that followed, the modern dialects may very well descend from fusions of the speech of several already differentiated groups, and Gypsies who at first by-passed the linguistic influence of Slav and Rumanian could have been caught up by it somewhat later, at one remove.

5

The Turn of the Tide

From the 1430s onwards, Gypsies – attracted, perhaps, by tales they heard from earlier path-finders – gradually spread out from eastern Europe. The narratives of chroniclers now loom larger as sources. One has to be wary, however, of accounts written long after the events described, perhaps without any personal contact between chronicler and Gypsies, for they are often derivative, blindly replicating material from elsewhere, and such new ingredients as they contain may be coloured by the attitudes and fantasies of the chronicler's own times. Whenever possible it will still be preferable to turn to local and central archives: it is there that the raw material of Gypsy history is to be found, often deposited before external influences have had time to warp attitudes.

The contribution of the German chronicler Aventinus (Johann Thurmaier), written about 1522, is instructive in a number of ways in considering the next phase. In the *Bavarian Chronicle*, under the year 1439, he has the following account:

At this time, that thievish race of men, the dregs and bilge-water of various peoples, who live on the borders of the Turkish empire and of Hungary (we call them *Zigeni*), began to wander through our provinces under their king Zindelo, and by dint of theft, robbery and fortune-telling they seek their sustenance with impunity. They relate falsely that they are from Egypt and are constrained by the gods[1] to

[1] The original Latin is *a superis*, which lends itself to more than one translation: the meaning may have been intended to be 'their rulers'.

exile, and they shamelessly feign to be expiating, by a seven year banishment, the sins of their forefathers who turned away the Blessed Virgin with the child Jesus. I have learned by experience that they use the Wendish language and are traitors and spies. Likewise others, notably the Emperor Maximilian Caesar Augustus, and Albert the father of our princes, testify to this in public edicts: but so deeply does idle superstition, like lethargy, imbue the minds of men that they believe them to be ill done by and suffer them everywhere to lurk about, to thieve, and to cheat.[2]

This one passage spans a century of deterioration in public attitudes towards Gypsies. The degree of venom is entirely of Aventinus's own time. When he wrote, the Holy Roman Empire had for more than two decades been applying penal sanctions against Gypsies. During the reign of Emperor Maximilian I, of whom Aventinus speaks so approvingly, the Imperial Diet had issued three edicts (in 1497, 1498 and 1500) in which Gypsies were accused of espionage and singled out for expulsion. These set the tone for decrees promulgated by princes, dukes and other potentates of the empire. The suspicion of espionage (already mentioned by Andreas of Ratisbon) was primarily a German preoccupation. Gypsies were especially vulnerable to it since they were obliged to acquire, for their own use, intimate knowledge of a country and information about its inhabitants. Aventinus's apparent recognition of a special Gypsy language (unless he was simply indicating that their having learned an outlandish tongue allowed them to be devious) is noteworthy, though he dismisses it as Wendish, a Slavic tongue spoken in east Germany. Also noteworthy is the explanation of Gypsy migrations as a seven-year exile on account of their failure to succour the Holy Family on the flight into Egypt. If it was the Gypsies themselves who thought up this story, as distinct from simply helping to circulate it once it had grown out of their association in the popular mind with Egypt, it could have been an imprudent piece of embroidery. No-one knew that at the time in question the Gypsies had not yet left India, and it offered European

---

[2] Translated from the Latin of Johann Thurmaier, *Annalium Boiorum libri septem* (Ingolstadt, 1554).

populations the same kind of righteous pretext for intolerance as that which fostered the anti-Semitism fed by allegations of Jewish complicity in the Crucifixion and of sacrifice of Christian children at Passover.

Historically, the most intriguing observation of Aventinus is his claim that the general immigration of Gypsies, in Bavaria at least, began in 1439, under a King Zindelo or Zindel. This is the only time that the passage of a King Zindel is recorded. A good deal can, however, be constructed out of a single reference. There is a great temptation to link each sighting of an early band to one of a few named leaders, and – in extreme cases – to trace out neatly on the map of Europe the hypothetical route followed by each one. The supreme example of this can be found in Adriano Colocci's *Gli Zingari* (1889), which contains just such a map, showing itineraries of King Sindel, Duke Mihali, Duke Andrash and Duke Panuel. The differently coloured lines start in Wallachia and begin to part company only in Hungary. Duke Panuel (a name we have yet to meet) is, for no apparent reason, credited with leading the 1417 foray through the Baltic towns and with subsequently visiting Leipzig (1418) and Metz (1430). Dukes Michael and Andrew journey together as far as Switzerland, then Andrew veers to the south, passes through Bologna, Forli and Rome (1422), turns back via Provence to Paris (1427), and is last seen heading in the general direction of England. Duke Michael's band splits up in Switzerland, one detachment going northwards to Strassburg (1418), Augsburg (1419), Münster and Cassel (1424) and Meissen (1426), while the other travels south-west to Lucerne and Sisteron (1419) and Barcelona (1447). Despite what was clearly a lively imagination, the most that even Colocci could make of King Zindel was to put him at the head of the incursions to the region around Ratisbon (1424, 1426, 1433, 1439). Apart from that, and a few other references among those who drew on Aventinus, Zindel disappears without trace.

We shall, however, still encounter dukes and counts bearing a profusion of names, both familiar and new; but at this point, instead of treating western and northern Europe as a whole, it seems best to consider countries one by one; to trace in each the downward evolution in Gypsy fortunes; and then to reassess their position around the middle of the sixteenth century, in the kind of climate which Aventinus had reflected.[3]

Germany, Austria, Switzerland

It was in Germany that attitudes towards Gypsies first began to harden, although the imperial letters of protection kept much of their power for some time. An opportunistic Count Michell even managed to secure a new one, this time from Emperor Frederick III. There can be little doubt about the authenticity of the document, for it was issued at Seefeld in April 1442, and this matches Frederick's known movements on his way to be crowned at Aachen. The following year Count Michell (or Michael) was in Bensberg, near Cologne, at the castle of the Duke of Jülich-Berg; when he left, it was with a safe-conduct drawn up in terms similar to those of the Emperor's, though it was stipulated that the beneficiaries had to behave themselves properly. Both documents use the expression *Czygenier*. During his lifetime the Duke of Jülich-Berg would grant two further safe-conducts, each made out to a Count Dederich (Derrick), the first in 1448, the second in 1454.[4]

The reception accorded to Gypsies was, however, becoming patchy. Whereas in some towns, such as Hamburg (1441–68)

---

[3] Here as elsewhere, the data have to be extracted from a multitude of sources, including a wealth of documentation in specialist periodicals. In this chapter, which incorporates fairly comprehensively the known historical references to Gypsies up to the 1550s, to quote each source would quickly overload the page. Accordingly, citations concentrate on particularly useful wide-ranging surveys. Several of the works quoted in the preceding chapter remain relevant here too. A good general history up to the middle of the nineteenth century, largely structured thematically, is F. de Vaux de Foletier's *Mille ans d'histoire des Tsiganes* (Paris, 1970).

[4] See O. van Kappen, 'Four early safe-conducts for Gypsies', *JGLS*(3), 44 (1965), pp. 107–15. Three books with general accounts of early Gypsy history in German-speaking lands are: H. Arnold, *Die Zigeuner, Herkunft und Leben im deutschen Sprachgebiet* (Olten, 1965), esp. pp. 33–63; H. Mode and S. Wölffling, *Zigeuner, Der Weg eines Volkes in Deutschland* (Leipzig, 1968), esp. pp. 141–66; and R. Gronemeyer and G. A. Rakelmann, *Die Zigeuner, Reisende in Europa* (Cologne, 1988), esp. pp. 23–78.

Plate 7 Gypsy family, by The Master of the Housebook, c.1480.
Bibliothèque Nationale, Paris.

and Hildesheim (1442 and 1454), alms continued to be handed
over with no indication of hostility, in others Gypsies had
become unwelcome. The records of Siegburg, a little to the
north of Bonn, contain frequent entries of gifts to Gypsies,
starting in 1439, but now these were bribes to induce them to
go away. In Frankfurt am Main, from 1449 onwards, Gypsies
were often refused entry or were forcibly ejected; and in
Franconia they were paid to leave Bamberg in 1463. Bavaria
had one of the more bizarre pleas for general expulsion in
1456, when a doctor, Johann Hartlieb, author of a book on
palmistry, urged the Duke to get rid of Gypsies because of
their lack of scientific method in reading palms.

Sometimes the change of attitude at the top is inexplicably
sudden, as when, in March 1472, Friedrich, Count Palatine,

gives Count Bartholomeus of Little Egypt a letter in the usual terms, but then, in December, himself forbids any Gypsy to pass through his territory. Another prince who sought to exclude them, a decade later, was Albrecht Achilles, Margrave of Brandenburg.

The names of the Gypsy nobles keep diversifying. Sometimes it is only with a death that a new name is recorded in Germany: Duke Panuel in 1445 (near Fürstenau in Lower Saxony); Count Petrus in 1453 (near Bautna); Count Antoni in 1552 (at Brötzingen); and all these, like any other nobles, had coats of arms to decorate their tombs – as did the Count Johann who was buried at Pforzheim in 1498. Among the living, a Duke Ernst and a Count Ambrosius were thrown into prison in 1483 at Hohengeroldseck in the Palatinate, for what offence is not known; they managed, however, to talk their way out by stressing their own importance and promising not to take any reprisals for their imprisonment. In Saxony, in 1488, we meet yet another new name, as a Count Nicolaus Caspar of Little Egypt extracts a letter of protection[5] from Johanna, Countess of Leissnigk, by spinning the familiar tale of penance.

In 1497 the legislature of the Holy Roman Empire felt it necessary to intervene. The Diet accused the Gypsies of espionage and resolved to consider how to get rid of them. Next year it ordained that, as spies, they must be expelled; and this decree was renewed in 1500, allowing them until Easter to remove themselves from German lands, after which time it was to be no crime to take violent action against them; in short, they were outlawed. The measures had little effect and did not prevent the issue of new safe-conducts, like the one granted in 1512 by the Polish duke Bogislav X, ruler over western and central Pomerania, to Ludwig von Rothenburg, Count of Little Egypt, to help him on his way to Danzig (Gdánsk) together with his *zyganisch* company. The Diet's re-enactments of 1544 and 1548 served no greater purpose. Finally, a decree of 1551 sought to close the loopholes by declaring any pass carried by

[5] The complete text is given in C. von Weber, 'Zigeuner in Sachsen 1488–1792', in *Mitteilungen aus dem Hauptstaatsarchive zu Dresden* (Leipzig, 1857–61), vol. 2, pp. 282–303.

a Gypsy to be void and banning all such documents in the future. That was the last of the general decrees to emanate from the imperial Diet, but not of the public order regulations which it had been issuing since 1500; and similar ordinances continued to flow forth in individual German territories.[6] Germany included some 300 states. This meant not just that laws proliferated; it also meant that they were often ineffectual because of the laxity of petty princelings and their failure to act together. Only occasionally do we find evidence of attempts to combine forces, as when the Archbishop of Cologne, the Bishop of Münster and the Duke of Cleves-Jülich-Berg appointed 25 patrolmen in 1538 to take proceedings against incendiaries, Anabaptists, Gypsies, etc.; Cleves-Jülich-Berg, which had been so hospitable a century before, was thus able to give a more practical turn than most to its series of laws which, in 1525–58, banned Gypsies from the duchy. How little impact might be had by an imperial decree on its own is shown by what happened at Nuremberg in 1549. A party of Gypsies having appeared at Heydeck, a village some miles to the south, the city council sent orders to the overseer not to take any action against them but to persuade them to go away; it was only when they turned up again the following year that he was given authority to use force if persuasion failed.

Events followed a similar pattern in the Swiss regions which had, officially, long formed a small part of the Holy Roman Empire but were now laboriously consolidating their independence and their confederation. In 1471 the Tagsatzung (Diet) at Lucerne enacted that Gypsies were not to be housed or sheltered within the Swiss Confederation; and the city-state of Geneva, outside the Confederation, expelled a number of 'Saracens' in 1477. In 1510, again at Lucerne, after complaints that they stole and were dangerous, *Zegynen* were banished from the Confederation, under a penalty of hanging if they returned. Despite that, the complaining continued and at a Diet at Berne in 1516 instructions were given to take special care in keeping them out at the frontiers. A few months before, Geneva had also banned all 'Saracens'. These measures still

[6] Cf. R. A. Scott Macfie, 'Gypsy persecutions: a survey of a black chapter in European history', *JGLS*(3), 22 (1943), pp. 65–78.

cannot have had much effect, for in 1525 it was again enacted at Lucerne that Gypsies were to be expelled from the Confederation and should be punished for stealing on the same basis as any other thieves. Two years later this decree in turn had to be renewed; yet at a Diet in Baden in 1530 it was noted that Gypsies were wandering about everywhere, and local authorities were ordered not to let them in and to impress upon them that they would be hanged if they were caught defrauding people. Only two years later the Gypsy question was on the agenda once more, with the usual outcome: when found, they were to be arrested and punished according to law, and at the frontiers they were to be turned back.

Stories of violent resistance on the part of Gypsies are rare: Geneva provides one of the few examples, when conflict broke out in 1532 between a large band and the town officers who were barring their entry. The Gypsies took refuge in a monastery; the citizens would none the less have executed summary justice on them had the authorities not interfered. Some 20 Gypsies were arrested but they sued for mercy and were discharged '*propter Deum*': something of the pilgrim aura evidently still clung to them.

The Swiss chroniclers of the sixteenth century (notably Brennwald, c.1530; Stumpf, 1538; Wurstisen, 1580) contrasted the Gypsy visitors of the early years with (in Stumpf's description) 'the useless rascals who wander about in our day, and of whom even the most worthy is a thief, for they live solely by stealing'.[7] This is one of the first manifestations of the 'who are the true Gypsies?' debate which still persists, with a number of people suggesting that it is little more than romantic exoticism to claim any real connection between present-day Travellers and an original Indian homeland.[8] In the following century other Swiss chroniclers (Guler, 1616; Sprecher, 1617) would develop this contrast to the point of arguing that the original Gypsies had gone home at the end

---

[7] Translated from the German of Johann Stumpf, *Schweytzer Chronik* (Zürich, 1606), fol. 731.

[8] E.g. J. Okely, *The Traveller-Gypsies* (Cambridge, 1983); N. Martinez, *Les Tsiganes* (Paris, 1986).

of their ordained exile and been replaced by a nondescript thieving rabble.[9]

France

Even when the Hundred Years War had come to an end and the English were finally expelled in 1453 from all of France except Calais, much of France lay outside the direct authority of the monarchy, until the series of confiscations which began some 50 years later incorporated the domains of the Dukes of Burgundy, Anjou, Brittany and Bourbon. What is today French territory was thus subject to a wide diversity of political influences.

For the Gypsies, fragmented political power was no disadvantage.[10] At first they fared reasonably well in most parts of France. Nevers was still the capital of an independent fief when the 'noble prince messire Thomas, comte de Gipte la Minor', with some 30 followers, claimed alms from the townspeople in 1436. Nevers had to welcome another noble prince five years later, when Count Philippe arrived with a band of 40. Perhaps it was the same Philippe who was given two florins by the chapter of St Andrew at Grenoble and the same Thomas who turned up at Troyes, in both cases in 1442. Provence, an independent county, was a favoured region for Gypsies, though the hospitality offered there showed signs of falling off: when a duke of Little Egypt presented himself at Arles in 1438 he was given ten florins; some years later two other chiefs, John and George, also obtained alms at Arles, but the sum declined first to six florins, then to four. Alsace and Lorraine, both part of the Holy Roman Empire, seem to have

---

[9] Cf. A. M. Fraser, 'Counterfeit Egyptians', *Tsiganologische Studien* 1990, no. 2, pp. 43–69.

[10] Gypsy history in France up to the Revolution is analysed in F. de Vaux de Foletier, *Les Tsiganes dans l'ancienne France* (Paris, 1961). Also important for the attitude of the French authorities are H. Asséo, 'Le traitement administratif des Bohémiens', in H. Asséo and J.-P. Vittu, *Problèmes socio-culturels en France au XVIIe siècle* (Paris, 1974), pp. 9–87, and J.-P. Liégeois, 'Bohémiens et pouvoirs publics en France du XVe au XIXe siècle', *Études Tsiganes* (1978), no. 4, pp. 10–30.

maintained cordial relations with Gypsies during the fifteenth
century, but subsequently they followed the current which
swept through the rest of the Empire. Colmar not only distributed bread to the 'Saracens' in 1442 and 1444, but also, on
the former occasion, thought it right to attest, through the
mayor and town council, that Duke Andrew of Little Egypt
and his people had departed in friendly fashion. And in 1450
the same authorities granted Count Philip a safe-conduct certifying that he and his company had comported themselves in a
worthy and Christian manner. At Metz, if the journal of Jean
Aubrion is to be trusted, no fewer than 200 'Egyptians'
pitched their tents on the banks of the Moselle in September
1494; two days later they were joined by another 300, commanded by a duke. When the duke's wife gave birth to a
daughter, the baby was baptized in the church of St Julian,
with three godfathers and two godmothers drawn from the
principal families of Metz.[11] The Gypsies had obviously become aware of the advantages – in terms of protection and of
gifts – that could accrue from having *gadźé* godparents for
their children, and there would be plenty of other occasions
when they followed the same practice.

Relations were for a time apparently no less harmonious
within the possessions of the French monarch. In 1447 we find
alms being given, without any sign of dissension, at Romans in
the Dauphiné (to Count Barthélemy) and again at Orleans.
Millau, in southern France, had at least two visits from
Gypsies in 1457 and received them well. The second company
was led by a Count Thomas: the name is familiar, but his safe-
conduct was evidently from the King of France, and his title,
as recorded, was a bizarre hybrid – 'Count of Little Egypt in
Bohemia'. *Bohémien* was gaining ground in France as a word
for 'Gypsy'. Apparently amicable receptions are also recorded
at Bayonne (1483) and at Riscle in Armagnac and Béthune in
Artois (1500). But there were numerous sources of friction.
Sometimes the Church tried to discourage parishioners from
consulting the Saracens, as they were only too eager to do. In
the diocese of Troyes, in 1456–7, there were several instances
when ecclesiastical penalties (measured out in wax candles)

[11] *Journal de Jean Aubrion, bourgeois de Metz* (Metz, 1857), p. 348.

were imposed on those who had had their hands read or resorted to the healing crafts of the Gypsies. Moreover, the French populace had plenty of reason to be wary of large groups of people on the move. The Hundred Years War had produced fearsome bands of vagabonds and companies of soldiers who intimidated peasant, villager and burgher alike. The Gypsies suffered as a result. The company of some 80 'Egyptians or Saracens' which presented itself in 1453 at La Cheppe, near Châlons-sur-Marne in Champagne, was seen to be bearing javelins and other weapons, and the townspeople themselves ran to fetch sticks, pikes, spears and bows. The royal procurator harangued the strangers, remonstrating that they, or people like them, had already been at La Cheppe recently and had left unfavourable memories: they had filched food and money and anything else that could be carried off. This time they would do better to go to one of the neighbouring localities, and the citizens of La Cheppe would feed them and their horses before they went. After some heated exchanges, the Gypsies withdrew, but one of the townspeople pursued them and, in a quarrel, killed one of them with a spear thrust to the stomach. The killer fled the country, having heard that the Gypsies were under the protection of the French king; but from his exile he pleaded self-defence and was granted royal letters of pardon.

There was just as much suspicion to overcome when Gypsies came to Carpentras in the Comtat-Venaissin, a papal enclave near Avignon, on three occasions in 1465. Bohemia featured again in their leader's title: first, 'Duke of the nation of Bohemia'; then 'Count of the Bohemians of Little Egypt' and 'Count of Little Egypt of the country of Bohemia'. There were complaints of thefts and unspecified misdeeds, and the town authorities decided to give the chief a small sum on condition that they went away. Soon the practice of paying the Gypsies to go elsewhere would become something of an institution in the Rhône region.

Up to the early sixteenth century, municipal officers were left largely to their own devices in dealing with Gypsies, and the reactions of those in positions of power were full of contradictions. Occasionally they fell out among themselves: thus, at Angers in 1498, when the Constable gave orders on behalf of the mayor to close the town gates against a crowd of them, a violent argument broke out between him and the town judge's lieutenant, who had granted them permission to stay. Then royal decrees and judicial findings began to leave little room for doubt about the approved course of action. In July 1504, a missive from Louis XII ordered the bailiff of Rouen to seek out and expel Egyptian vagabonds, notwithstanding any safe-conduct they might produce; and in 1510 the Grand Council, in the course of imposing a sentence of exile on seven Gypsies who had appeared in court, extended the banishment to all other Gypsies in the kingdom of France. Even a royal command, however, might apparently be quickly forgotten, for in 1509 the citizens of Rouen, including a priest, were flocking to have their fortunes told by Gypsies, at the peril of their souls; while at the other end of Normandy, in 1508, Gypsies had no inhibitions about naming the pilgrimage centre of Mont-Saint-Michel as their destination, having armed themselves with the authority of the Duchess of Brittany for crossing her duchy to get there.

A century after it had first been conjured up, the papally imposed penance (see p. 74) was still exercising some of its magic, at least among potentates of the Church. In 1528 the vice-rector of the Comtat-Venaissin granted protective letters to a Count Jean-Baptiste Rolland of Little Egypt to help him on his way in visiting holy shrines and in obtaining alms from the faithful; but in 1533 the King's lieutenant-general in neighbouring Languedoc, where Gypsies had begun to proliferate, ordered them all to leave at once by the shortest route. In 1537 Robert de Croy, Bishop and Duke of Cambrésis and prince of the Holy Roman Empire, did the honours for Count Martin of Little Egypt. Finally, however, in 1539 Francis I decided that, whatever the Church might think, it was time to apply special measures throughout his kingdom against 'certain unknown persons who call themselves Bohemians', wandering as they pleased 'under the guise of a simulated religion or of a certain penitence which they claim to be making through the world'. He decreed that 'henceforth none of the said companies and assemblies of the above-mentioned Bohemians may enter, pass or stay in our kingdom nor in the countries which are subject to us'. As yet, the penalties were somewhat vague, though corporal punishment was specified for any failure to comply. Charles IX gave the screw a few more turns in 1561 and ordered his officers to expel all Gypsies within two months under penalty of the galleys and corporal punishment. If any were found or came back after the two months were up, they were to have their hair shaved off (and beards too, in the case of men) and the men were to be delivered up to the galleys, where they would serve three years. Navarre had followed a similar route in 1538 by deciding to get rid of all vagabonds within four days and forbidding Gypsies to enter the kingdom; any who were found after that were to be whipped, and anyone giving them shelter or doing business with them ran the risk of a heavy fine. These measures were renewed several times.

The Gypsies, however, appear not to have been too much troubled in practice by this spate of edicts in France. They did not hide themselves away; and their leaders still called themselves count or – a new vogue – captain, and knew how to wheedle passports and safe-conducts. The well-tried cover-story could still be effective. Francis I himself, five years after his own edict, took under his protection Antoine Moreul, 'his well-loved captain of Little Egypt', and ordered his officials to permit 'the said noble Moreul and his company with all their goods, whether gold, silver, household effects, horses, or whatever else' to travel day and night, on foot and on horseback, to make their pilgrimage to Compostella or elsewhere, and to stay anywhere for three days, or even six if necessary. Moreul's powers of internal discipline within his company were formally reaffirmed. Henry II in his turn was equally obliging to Count Palque in 1553. The day of these strange pilgrims was not entirely over.

Spain and Portugal

Favourable treatment of the kind which Count Thomas had enjoyed at the hands of Alfonso V of Aragon (p. 77) con-

tinued for several decades.[12] At first it is solely in Aragon and
Catalonia that we find traces of Gypsies: a 'duke' and a 'count'
and a multitude of followers at Barcelona in 1447, and several
visitations at Castellón de la Plana in 1460 (Count Martin),
1471 and 1472. During the reign of John II, who succeeded
his brother Alfonso on the throne of Aragon, Gypsy chiefs
benefited from a series of royal safe-conducts: one in 1460 to
Count Martin; three (1460–71) to Count Jacobo, who also
acquired letters from Henry IV of Castile at some point in the
period 1454–70; one to Duke Paulo (1471); one to Count
Miguel (1472); and three to Count Juan (1474–6). These
documents still invoked the papal fiat and confirmed the
powers of Gypsy leaders to administer justice within their
companies. It was even provided in some instances that the
leader should be given armed assistance in case of need, for
outsiders were said to be daily joining the 'Egyptians', so
that trouble and indiscipline were always possible. The safe-
conduct granted in 1476 to Count Juan, described as being on
his way to the shrines of Compostella and Rome, was unusual
in painting a picture of internal strife, for he was said to be the
mortal enemy of Counts Martin, Miguel and Jaime.

The first troop of Gypsies to be met with in Andalusia, in
the Kingdom of Castile, was accorded a magnificent welcome.
This was in November 1462, when the Constable and Chancellor of Castile, Count Miguel Lucas de Iranzo, entertained
Counts Thomas and Martin of Little Egypt at Jaén; they dined
with their wives at his table and they and their company were
given an abundance of bread, wine, meat, fowls, fish, fruit,
barley and straw; when they departed there were farewell gifts

[12] The history of relations between Gypsies and public authorities in
Spain, to the end of the eighteenth century, is the main subject of B. Leblon's
Les Gitans d'Espagne (Paris, 1985). G. Borrow's *The Zincali* (London,
1841) contains much that is still relevant. Two well documented essays on
the fifteenth century are Amalia Lopéz de Meneses, 'La inmigración gitana
en España durante el siglo XV', in *Martínez Ferrando, Archivero. Miscelánea
de Estudios dedicados a su memoria* (Barcelona, 1968), pp. 239–63; and
'Noves dades sobre la immigráció gitana a Espanya al segle XV', in *Estudis
d'Historia Medieval* (Barcelona, 1971), vol. 4, pp. 145–60. A major source
on legislation in the fifteenth to eighteenth centuries is A. Gómez Alfaro's
doctoral thesis, 'El Expediente general de Gitanos' (Madrid, 1988).

of woollen cloth and silk and a substantial sum of money, and Don Miguel courteously accompanied them for half a league of the way. In 1470 he again played the part of generous host, this time in his residence at Andújar, for five or six days to Count Jacobo of Little Egypt and his wife Loysa and 50 others, and a fortnight later to Duke Paulo and his company. Not a few members of the Spanish nobility would in fact remain protectors of the Gypsies and give them valuable succour even in the hardest of times. Their complicity would be given a variety of explanations by those who denounced it later, with a good deal of malicious stress on the seductive qualities of the Gypsy women and on the talents of the men in procuring fine horses for the stables of their friends. Count Jacobo and Duke Paulo, meanwhile, went on to visit Murcia – for the names and titles are the same and presumably it was the same pair – in July 1470 (Jacobo) and January 1471 (Paulo), picking up sums of money amounting to 2,000 *maravedís* (Jacobo) and 1,000 *maravedís* (Paulo) from the city councillors, who on both occasions had to borrow the cash specially.[13]

In the closing decades of the fifteenth century, a familiar pattern of resistance to unlimited alms-giving becomes evident, and increasingly, from the 1470s onwards, the Gypsies were bought off or turned away when they appeared. By now a new wave was arriving in Spain via the Mediterranean, no longer claiming to be from Little Egypt, but calling themselves Greeks and presenting themselves as being in flight from the Turks. Their leaders did not adopt the title of duke or count, but were designated 'master', 'knight' or 'captain', or simply by their forenames. The geographical attributions in the names given to Gypsies were becoming more and more confused: in 1512 they are referred to in repressive legislation in Catalonia as 'Boemians, et sots nom de Boemians grechs, e Egiptians' ('Bohemians, and fools styled Greek Bohemians, and Egyptians').

Once the crowns of Castile and Aragon were united in 1479, Ferdinand and Isabella set about restoring law and order and consolidating the central power after all the years of

---

[13] D. Creades, 'Les premiers Gitans à Murcie', *Études Tsiganes* (1974), nos 2/3, pp. 5–7.

civil war. They did not immediately cancel existing letters of protection and indeed produced a few themselves, such as the one given to Count Felippo of Egypt la menor in 1491; but these were of limited duration, the emphasis on alms had been watered down, and the stress was now on the right to follow legal and honest trades in order to gain a livelihood. On 4 March 1499, seven years after their expulsion of the Jews, and three years before the forced conversion of the Muslims, a decree of the Catholic Kings (the Pragmatic Sanction of Medina del Campo) stated the Gypsies' options bluntly: either they became sedentary and sought masters, or after 60 days they would be banished. King Charles I, who became Emperor Charles V after bribing his way to the throne of the Holy Roman Empire in 1519, renewed these provisions several times and added some refinements of his own: those caught wandering for the third time could be seized and enslaved for ever; and those who did not settle or depart within 60 days were to be sent to the galleys for six years if between the ages of 20 and 50. This last provision reflected the government's difficulties in manning the galley squadrons as they grew in response to the constant warfare between Spain and the Islamic empire in the Mediterranean: such servitude was being extended to all kinds of offenders, both major and minor. The oarsmen spent much of their sentence chained to the galley bench.

In Portugal,[14] nothing is heard of Gypsies until the early sixteenth century, when the first references occur in literary texts — the earliest being, possibly, a brief allusion to a *Grega* ('Greek') in the *Cancioneiro geral*, 1516. More significantly, the *Farsa das Ciganas* of Portugal's chief dramatist, Gil Vicente, performed in the presence of King John III at Evora in 1521, portrays Gypsies at some length and captures the lisping sound that was already a characteristic of Spanish and

---

[14] Cf. F. A. Coelho, *Os Ciganos de Portugal* (Lisbon, 1892), esp. ch. 3; P. d'Azevedo, 'Os Ciganos em Portugal nos secs. XVI e XVII', *Arquivo Histórico Português*, 6 (1908), pp. 460–8, and 7 (1909), pp. 42–52, 81–90, 169–77; O. Nunes, *O Povo Cigano* (Oporto, 1981), esp. Part II, ch. 4; and E. M. Lopes da Costa, 'La minoranza sociale Rom nel Portogallo moderno (secoli XV–XVIII)', *Lacio Drom* (1989), no. 1, pp. 5–23.

Portuguese as spoken by them[15] – in this case by the *Ciganos* of (no doubt) the Alentejo province, which was well suited to their way of life. (It is curious that, from the very beginning, Portuguese fixed upon *Cigano* as the principal word for 'Gypsy', keeping in line with the Italian, German, and central and eastern European usage descended from *atsinganos*, whereas Spanish settled on *Gitano*, derived from 'Egyptian'.) There are only eight characters in Vicente's play, all Gypsies. The four women, who describe themselves as Greeks, beg for alms 'for the love of God; we are Christians, see here the Cross'; they plead for bread, for clothes, for anything and everything, while the four men offer one-sided horse-deals. They sing and dance, and then the women, addressing themselves to members of the audience, insistently offer to read palms, piling on the flattery and promises of good fortune. After a final dance, they take themselves off with the parting gibe that never before did so honoured a company give so small a reward. Since Gypsies were already such recognizable characters, they must have been established in Portugal for some little time. They had been there long enough, at any rate, to attract the hostile attention of the public authorities with, as a consequence, the usual flurry of repressive measures; but those issued during the reign of John III (1526, 1538 and 1557), banishing *Ciganos* and forbidding them to enter the kingdom, were apparently no more effective than similar measures elsewhere. The law of 1538 was aimed at Gypsies and 'all other persons of whatever nation who live like Gypsies, even if they are not'; as those born in Portugal could not be expelled from Portuguese domains, they were to be sent to the African colonies.

The Low Countries

The Dukes of Burgundy forged a powerful state out of the Low Countries and Burgundy. Philip the Good, who ruled from 1419 to 1467, was master of one of the richest lands in

---

[15] Cervantes would also make a feature of this characteristic in his novella, *La Gitanilla* (1613), and his comedy, *Pedro de Urdemalas* (c.1611).

Plate 8   Maker unknown, Franco-Flemish (probably Tournai) The Visit of the Gypsies, c.1490. Wool tapestry, 350.5 × 502.9 cm, The Currier Gallery of Art, Manchester, New Hampshire, Currier Funds, 1937.7.

Plate 9   Scene from Hieronymus Bosch's The Haywain, *c.1500. Museo Nacional del Prado, Madrid.*

Europe. No doubt this made the Low Countries particularly attractive to Gypsies, but by the 1440s unmistakable signs of resistance are apparent. In December 1442 the virtually republican town of Tournai, formerly so generous, refused entry to some who asked for alms and expected to be lodged. The city accounts of Bruges record a donation of 6 *livres parisis* to Gypsies in 1439/40; on the next occasion, in 1445/6, the alms are stated to be 'in order that their people should remain outside'; and in 1451/2 and 1453/4 it was 'because they were forbidden to remain here longer'. The neighbouring town of Damme was adopting a similar policy. Both may have felt they were being favoured with too many visits: the accounts note eight further payments by Bruges up to the end of the century, sometimes as an inducement to go elsewhere; the citizens also thought it worthwhile to maintain a watch over the Woolhouse where the Gypsies were lodged, for fear of fire. Just how much the aldermen of Damme felt they were under pressure can be imagined from the accounts for 1460, when the town was visited seven times in all by Gypsy bands. In that year we read of the arrival of 'a lord from Little Egypt named Count Jehan' who was there for the fifth time. He was obliged to promise 'under threat of certain punishments and under penalty of his life' that 'neither he himself nor any other people from his native country would return to this town within the forthcoming year'. Nevertheless some days later another 'lord from Little Egypt, named Count Nicolao', descended upon them. He got his alms too, 'on condition that he would march past this town with his people without halting or camping'. Scarcely had he left than Count Jehan reappeared; firm restrictions were put on his stay. A similar evolution can be observed elsewhere in the Southern Netherlands – at Lier (near Antwerp), at Mons, at Nimy: to begin with, sizeable gifts are forthcoming, but later there are payments to go away or keep out, or outright expulsions.

When the Low Countries became part of the Spanish-Austrian empire of the Habsburgs in 1504, and particularly when Emperor Charles V took over and the rule of governors-general was instituted, administration became increasingly centralized. In the matter of Gypsies, Charles displayed no more tolerance in the Low Countries than he did in Spain, but he was not entirely in control of the tempo of repression: when he intended to promulgate a law binding on all the provinces, it had to be enacted in each one separately and that gave an opportunity for delaying tactics by those which were opposed to his zeal for unification. The success or otherwise of his efforts can best be examined in the context of the Northern Netherlands, where the movements of Gypsies have been well documented.[16] A scrutiny of events in one or two of the provinces there affords a representative enough picture of what was happening more generally. For this purpose, the two

---

[16] A comprehensive study of public relations with Gypsies in the Northern Netherlands up to the middle of the eighteenth century is O. van

adjacent eastern provinces of Guelders and Overijssel will suffice.

In Overijssel, Deventer had been among the first towns in the Low Countries to see Gypsies, in 1420 and again in 1429 (pp. 70 and 78). This was the start of a regular pattern of visits throughout the remainder of the century. On two such occasions (1438 and 1441) the leader's title had been upgraded to 'King' of Little Egypt or of the *heiden*. On several others the Gypsies were paid to go away (the citizens bearing the cost of ferry tolls across the River Ijssel), and the value of the offerings steadily declined. During the reign of Charles V there was a spate of edicts in the various provinces of the Northern Netherlands, denying Gypsies admittance or the right to stay and extending the ban to any adventurers who had joined their ranks. For example, in February 1537, from Brussels, the Emperor issued a decree addressed to Overijssel, allowing four days for the 'nation of Egypt', and others who followed them and imitated their style of dress, to disappear from all his domains, upon pain of life and property. Similar measures were being promulgated in other provinces from 1524 onwards; and more would follow, with a regularity which showed how little effect they were having in practice.

In the province of Guelders, there is a lengthy interval between the early sightings at Nijmegen and Arnhem in 1429 and Zutphen in 1430 (p. 78) and the next known appearances of Gypsies which, from 1445 up to the end of the century, are mainly at Zutphen. There too, on at least four occasions, the leader is styled 'King'. In the closing years of the century the Gypsies sought to replenish their stock of letters of protection. They succeeded in winning over the wily Charles of Egmont, Duke of Guelders, who had managed to preserve the independence of his province against the domination of the Habsburgs. The Duke was notoriously superstitious and often resorted to fortune-tellers and sorcerers, but perhaps he hesitated to give his whole-hearted support in the safe-conduct which he issued in 1496, for he qualified it with a prohibition on staying for more than three days in any one place. In other respects he

Kappen, *Geschiedenis der Zigeuners in Nederland* (Assen, 1965). For the Southern Netherlands, see the same author's 'Contribution to the history of the Gypsies in Belgium', *JGLS*(3), 48 (1969), pp. 107–20.

subscribed comprehensively to the story he had been told: 'Count Martin Gnougy, born in Little Egypt, has shown us how our most gracious Father the Pope has laid upon him, his family and his company the task of making certain pilgrimages, as a penance, to Rome, to Santiago of Galicia and other holy places', and therefore he was to be suffered to pass without let or hindrance. In 1506 the Duke bestowed a similar favour on Count Wilhem of Little Egypt with his company of 15, but cautiously added: 'and they will behave themselves properly and decently, so that we shall not have to hear of any complaints or persecutions concerning them'. A third safe-conduct which he granted in 1518 was probably the last to be given to the *heidens* in the Netherlands. The document again betrays some reservations, referring to 'Anthonius, a noble, as he alleges, from Lesser Egypt', and is couched more as a recommendation to the authorities of neighbouring states than as a command to the Duke's own officials. These were not the only safe-conducts to be drawn up in Guelders. The town magistrate at Nijmegen had also given one to a Count Anthon some years before, around the turn of the century; but when Gypsies can next be seen at the gates of Nijmegen, in 1536 and 1543, they are promptly chased away. Zutphen adopted similar tactics in 1538 and 1542.

The first general measure directed against Gypsies in Guelders came in 1544, shortly after Charles V had at last succeeded in subjugating the province. Its terms were similar to those of the 1537 Overijssel decree, except that no more than two days grace was allowed. Further ordinances followed in 1548, 1553 and 1560. Meanwhile, Gypsies continued to wander about, apparently more or less as before, though they took the precaution of travelling in smaller bands so as not to attract attention. When the archives do take notice of them now, they are no longer accorded the status of pilgrims and their leaders are stripped of noble titles.

Italy

The data we have in regard to Italy are at first limited to the north; it is only in the middle of the sixteenth century that they take us even as far south as Rome.[17] Italy was no more than a geographical expression in the fifteenth century; in political terms it was a jigsaw made up of five major powers whose coherence and stability were precarious, and a number of lesser states which sought, with varying degrees of success, to keep their independence intact. It is in one of the larger entities, the Duchy of Milan, that Gypsies first reappear in Italy, 35 years after they were last seen heading towards Rome from Forlì (p. 73). When they do enter the archives again it is because of bloody violence: in June 1457, Count Michele of Egypt and his wife and daughter are killed by a Gypsy named Filippo; but the ducal registers fail to tell us why. For most of the fifteenth century the events recorded are more tranquil. In the Duchy of Modena, one of the lesser powers, an account book of the Duke of Ferrara records a payment in 1469 to a *Cingano* for playing a citole (a plucked stringed instrument) – among the earliest associations of Gypsies with music in Europe – and then, more conventionally, we find two safe-conducts issued by lords of Carpi, one in the 1470s to Count Michael of Lower Egypt and his company, another in 1485 to Count Joannes. In Milan, the young Duke Gian Galeazzo II granted a similar document to Count Martino of Little Egypt in 1480.

Relations turned sour, however, by the closing decade of the century. In Piedmont, ruled by the Duke of Savoy, there were four payments in the years 1494–9 to *Saraceni sive Cingari* to stay away from Barge and Cuorgne, to the south and north of Turin. Milan was more direct in its rebuff, and it was there that the first general measures against Gypsies in Italy were adopted. In 1493, under the rule of Ludovico il Moro, two edicts marked the changeover to outright repression in the Italian states, the second of them ordering all Gypsies in the Duchy to leave at once, on the grounds that they had become too numerous and thievish. France's acquisition of Milan

---

[17] On early legislation concerning Gypsies in the Italian states, see M. Zuccon, 'La legislazione sugli Zingari negli stati italiani prima della rivoluzione', *Lacio Drom* (1979), nos 1–2, pp. 1–68; A. Campigotto, 'I bandi bolognesi contro gli Zingari (sec. XVI–XVIII)', *Lacio Drom* (1987), no. 4, pp. 2–27; and A. Arlati, 'Gli Zingari nello stato di Milano', *Lacio Drom* (1989), no. 2, pp. 4–11.

brought stricter penalties. In 1506 two decrees declared Gypsies to be a public menace and again banned them from the Duchy, bracketing them with other beggars as possible carriers of the plague. Among the penalties were three applications of the *tratto di corda* (which involved hoisting the victim by his hands, tied behind his back, so that the entire weight of the body hung from his wrists). The *tratto di corda* featured again in Francis I's decree of 1517 ordering all *Cinguli et Cadegipti* to leave the Duchy within three days; and again in that of 1523 issued by his puppet duke, the last heir of the Sforza dynasty, who added a fine of 25 golden ducats to the physical penalty. Finally, in 1534, in the interval between the French expulsion from Milan and its reversion to Spanish rule, Francesco Sforza proscribed all '*Egiptii* commonly called *Cingali*' on pain of hanging.

From Milan, the legislative mania spread south and east. In the Marquisate of Mantua, the only known 'ban' is not to be found in any statute book , for it occurred in the burlesque macaronic epic, *Baldus* (1517), of the Benedictine monk Teofilo Folengo. It was fortunate that it was fictional, given its savage phraseology, surpassing anything that Milan had at that stage produced: 'he who goes by the name of Cingar, a cheat, an assassin, a street brigand, a thief, a scoundrel who mints fake coins and subtly files down real ones, shall be banned from all the territories of Mantua; but whosoever shall have the mind to kill him shall gain 150 ducats'.[18] It was in Mantua's southern neighbour Modena that the Milanese model was first emulated in practice, with several measures to expel all Gypsies, promulgated in the period 1524–60. Some of the Papal States followed suit: two towns in the Marches of Ancona – Jesi and Senigallia – resorted to a succession of decrees in 1535–53, as did Bologna from 1550 onwards. The ban became general to all the Papal States in 1552, as a result of an edict by the governor, Gerolamo di Rossi, which spoke of scandal, disorder and theft caused by Gypsies who were in the habit of coming to Rome and staying in the grottoes, the vineyards and

---

[18] Cf. A. Campigotto and L. Piasere, 'From Margutte to Cingar: the archeology of an image', in *100 Years of Gypsy Studies*, ed. M. T. Salo (Cheverly, MD, 1990), pp. 15–29.

the surrounding countryside. The senate of the Republic of Venice joined in with a series of ordinances starting in 1540; and the Duchy of Tuscany (Florence) completed the barrage of rejections in 1547.

Hungary and Transylvania

In Hungary the Gypsies met with a greater degree of tolerance than was usual for the time, though a form of bondage was imposed on some of them, especially in Transylvania (where serfdom was not abolished until 1848). So useful were they in metal-working and the manufacture of weapons that they were declared royal servants, for whose settlement and employment on private estates the consent of the King was necessary. Thus, in 1476, before the citizens of Hermannstadt (now Sibiu, Rumania) could have the Gypsies in their suburbs work for them, they needed to secure the permission of King Matthias Corvinus. In 1496 Matthias's successor, Vladislas II, gave a safe-conduct to Tamás Polgár, *vayvodam Pharaonum* (voivode of 'Pharaoh's people' – a designation sometimes used in early Hungarian documents), allowing him to move and settle wher-ever he pleased in the country with his 25 tents of Gypsy smiths; at that time they were in the service of the Bishop of Pécs, supplying him with musket balls, cannon balls and other weaponry.[19] Later in Vladislas's reign the Gypsies' metal-working skills were put to more macabre use after the uprising of the peasants, who were grievously oppressed in Hungary, as they were indeed throughout central Europe. When, in 1514, a great many of them, led by György Dózsa, rose against their lords, the revolt was brutally suppressed by the voivode of Transylvania, János Zápolya, who would himself one day be king. He had the Gypsies in Temesvár (Timişoara) fashion a throne, crown and sceptre of iron. Once these had been made red hot, Zápolya's men set Dózsa upon the throne, pressed the glowing crown on to his head and forced the searing sceptre into his hands; his followers were then compelled to eat his

---

[19] G. Pray (ed.), *Annales Regum Hungariae ab anno Christi CMXCVII ad annum MDLXIV* (Vienna, 1764–70), vol. 4, p. 273.

charred flesh. The Gypsies' connection with Zápolya would turn to their own disadvantage 20 years later, at a time when he was contesting the Hungarian throne, for they came under suspicion by the opposing faction of being in Zápolya's pay for nefarious purposes, and one band was put to death by impaling, after having had a confession of incendiarism (later withdrawn) wrung from them on the rack. When Zápolya at last achieved the title in 1538, one of his earlier royal acts was to grant a request that ancient Gypsy liberties (*antiquis libertatibus*) should be retained.[20]

By the sixteenth century the custom had become established in Hungary (as in Poland and Lithuania) for a chief of the Gypsies to be chosen by the authorities from among their own numbers; he was given the title of *egregius* ('distinguished'). Beneath him, in each county with a Gypsy population, were lesser chiefs who acted as judges in Gypsy matters. Confusingly, these chiefs also used the title of voivode, and then have to be distinguished from the several voivodes who were drawn from the ranks of the Hungarian and Transylvanian nobility (four for Hungary, two for Transylvania) and who had the profitable duty of collecting the taxes from the Gypsies.

Apart from their metal-working skills, the Gypsies were acquiring a reputation as musicians in Hungary.[21] They are first mentioned in this capacity in a laconic entry in an account book, recording a payment in 1489 'to Gypsies who play the lute on the island of the princess' – that is, on Csepel Island, south of Budapest, the princess being Matthias Corvinus's second wife, Beatrice of Aragon. Another royal payment was noted in the accounts of Louis (Lajos) II: in May 1525 two florins were paid to *pharaones* who played the cithara before His Majesty at the royal race-course. Quite possibly, the Gypsies who were 'ordered' for a meeting of the Diet at Hatvan in the same year were also musicians. The names given to instruments in those days were used without much precision, and the Gypsy *cytharedos* requested by a hussar captain in a letter written in Latin to an aristocrat called Tamás

---

[20] E. O. Winstedt, 'Some Transylvanian Gypsy documents of the sixteenth century', *JGLS*(3), 20 (1941), pp. 49–58.
[21] See Bálint Sárosi, *Gypsy Music* (Budapest, 1978), pp. 55ff.

Nádasdy in 1532 may refer to lutenists and ministrels. (The word *cithara* or *kithara* had extended its usage well beyond its classical sense of 'lyre' and would be transformed into the names of instruments as diverse as the guitar, the cittern and the zither.) After Ferdinand of Habsburg became ruler of part of Hungary, a letter from Queen Isabella's court to Vienna in 1543 commented that 'here the most excellent Egyptian musicians play, the descendants of the Pharaohs'. The writer goes on to observe that the Gypsy cimbalom players 'do not pluck the strings with their fingers but hit it with a wooden stick and sing to it with all their might'. (The cimbalom is an instrument shaped like a small piano, with open strings.)

Gypsies adapted readily enough to Ottoman rule when much of Hungary came under Turkish control after Louis II's disastrous defeat at Mohács in 1526. Many became smiths for the Turkish army; others were musicians, barbers, messengers or executioners. Thanks to Ottoman archives, we have some rudimentary statistics of settled male Gypsies in Buda in the mid-sixteenth century: there were reckoned to be 56 of them in 1546, almost three-quarters being Christian (the remainder bearing the forename Abdullah, given to Muslim converts); some 30 years later the identified number would have risen to 90, nearly all Muslim.[22]

Bohemia, Poland-Lithuania and the Ukraine

The presence of Gypsies in these territories in the fifteenth century is sparsely attested. During the reign (1471–1516) of Vladislas II of Bohemia, however – the same Vladislas as ruled in Hungary – Gypsies were sufficiently well established as metal-workers to be entrusted with the making of weapons and other warlike material. As for the vast unified kingdom of Poland-Lithuania, if – for reasons discussed at the beginning of the previous chapter (p. 60) – one discards names of places

---

[22] L. Mészáros, 'A hódoltsági latinok, görögök és cigányok történetéhez. 16. sz.-i oszmán-török szórványadatok' ['On the history of Latins, Greeks and Gypsies under Ottoman rule. Documents from Ottoman archives of the sixteenth century'], *Századok*, 110 (1976), no. 3, pp. 474–89.

and people, like a clutch of family names Cygan or Czygan found in southern Poland between 1419 and 1436, very little emerges until 1501, when a few letters of protection can be traced. In that year Alexander, King of Poland and Grand Duke of Lithuania, granted a safe-conduct to Polgar, *Vojevoda Cyganorum*, no doubt the same man as the Tamás Polgár who had won the protection of the King of Hungary five years before; he also confirmed at Vilno the privileges of Wasili, voivode of the *Cyhany*, giving him the right to judge disputes among his subjects, and conferring on Gypsies 'freedom of movement in our lands...according to the customs of our ancestors, the Grand Dukes of Lithuania of blessed memory ...according to the former laws, customs and ducal edicts'. This charter was, then, not the first of its kind. In 1513 Alexander's brother Sigismund, who succeeded him, had in his service a Gypsy smith, Mixidarius Wanko de Oppavia. In the course of the sixteenth century there were further incursions of Gypsies into Poland, both from Bohemia and from Germany; while it seems to have been from Poland that Gypsies first reached the Ukraine, where they can be observed in Volhynia around 1501.

The earliest decree of expulsion in these territories was issued in 1538 in Moravia (by then part of the Austrian Habsburg domains) and was renewed several times in the ensuing decades; Bohemia (also Habsburg) took similar steps in 1541 (following the outbreak of fires in Prague, blamed on Gypsies) and in 1549; and the Polish Sejm (Diet) introduced the first of a series of repressive laws in 1557.[23]

Scotland and England

The first undoubted record of Gypsies in Britain[24] is contained in the accounts of the Lord High Treasurer of Scotland for

---

[23] Cf. J. Ficowski, *Cyganie na polskich drogach*, 2nd edn (Kraków, 1985), pp. 16–25, and *The Gypsies in Poland* (n.d. [Warsaw, 1990]), pp. 11–13.

[24] The early history of Gypsies in Scotland and England is discussed in, *inter alia*, W. Simson, *A History of the Gipsies* (London, 1865); H. T.

1505: 'Item, the xxij day of Aprile, to the Egiptianis, be the Kingis command, x Franch crounis; summa vij ℔ [£7].'[25] Before this disbursement by James IV at Stirling, all is speculation in regard to Gypsies in Scotland, including the story of 'Saracens' or 'Moors' who infested Galloway in the mid-fifteenth century and whom James II was anxious to disperse. In Scotland as elsewhere, the Gypsies were unquestionably preceded by native castes of nomadic tinkers, pedlars, mountebanks, etc., and it is all too easy to confuse one with another.

Under James IV the royal relationship with the Gypsies appears to have been untroubled. The payment of 10 French crowns in April 1505 was possibly for some sort of entertainment; the King, 32 years old at the time and an extravagant spender, was fond of music, dancers, acrobats, 'guisers' and raconteurs. Alternatively, it may have been a charitable payment to Gypsies in their capacity as pilgrims. Whatever its origin, it was a sizeable sum of money at a time when £1 represented a year's wage for many. Only a few months later James signed a letter at Linlithgow Palace commending Anthonius Gagino, 'ex parva egipto Comes' (Earl of Little Egypt), to his uncle, King John of Denmark: Gagino, he said, had recently reached Scotland with his retinue during a pilgrimage through the Christian world, and now wished to cross to Denmark. As James himself had ambitions to make a pilgrimage to the Holy Land, he was no doubt attracted by this aspect of the Gypsies' story.

The earliest probable mention of Gypsies in England occurs during the reign of Henry VIII in *A Dialogue of Sir Thomas More, Knight*, where More relates, as one who was present, that in 1514, at an inquest into the death of Richard Hunne in the Lollards' Tower, one of the witnesses referred to an 'Egypcyan' woman who had been lodging in Lambeth but had

Crofton, 'Early annals of the Gypsies in England', *JGLS*(1), 1 (1888–9), pp. 5–24, and 'Supplementary annals of the Gypsies in England, before 1700', *JGLS*(2), 1 (1907–8), pp. 31–4; D. MacRitchie, *Scottish Gypsies under the Stewarts* (Edinburgh, 1894); E. O. Winstedt, 'Early British Gypsies', *JGLS* (2), 7 (1913–14), pp. 5–37; and B. Vesey-FitzGerald, *The Gypsies of Britain* (London, 1944).

[25] *Accounts of the Lord High Treasurer of Scotland*, ed. Sir James Balfour Paul (Edinburgh, 1901), vol. 3, p. 136.

recently gone overseas, and who could tell marvellous things simply by looking into a person's hand.[26] Then Edward Hall in his *Chronicles of King Henry the Eighth* (published 1548) describes two ladies at a Court mummery in 1517 as having 'their heades rouled in pleasauntes and typpets lyke the Egipcians, enbroudered with golde' – a reference to the turban-like head-dress already noted on the Continent. (A pleasance was a kind of fine linen, and tippets were narrow slips of cloth.) We know too that the Gypsies had become widely dispersed in England, for between 1513 and 1523 some 'Gypsions' were entertained by the Earl of Surrey at Tendring Hall in Suffolk, and in 1521 one William Cholmeley gave the large sum of 40 shillings to certain 'Egyptions' at Thornbury, near Bristol, while in 1522 the churchwardens of Stratton, in Cornwall, received 20 pence from 'Egypcions' for the use of the Church House. That the pilgrimage story was current in England as well as Scotland is shown by a document dated 17 August 1530, certifying the delivery to a Justice at Hereford of certain Gypsies under suspicion of theft, including 'one Antony Stephen of the countrey of lytyll Egipte as hedde and capytayne of xix persons of men, women and chylderyn', who 'named them selfes pilgrims'.

It may be that the numbers of Gypsies increased significantly in the late 1520s, for William Harrison and Samuel Rid, writing in 1586 and 1612 respectively,[27] identified that as the period when Gypsies invaded England. We lack contemporary documents to support such a contention, but it was shortly afterwards that the first of the repressive measures in England was passed:[28] an Act of 1530 addressed itself to 'dyverse and many outlandysshe [foreign] People callynge themselfes Egyptians', who

[26] Sir Thomas More, *A dyaloge of Syr Thomas More, knt.* (London, 1529), book 3, ch. 15. The point remains valid even though More may well have been giving a distorted account: cf. A. Ogle, *The Case of the Lollards Tower* (Oxford, 1949), p. 95.

[27] W. Harrison, *A Description of England* (prefixed to Holinshed's *Chronicle*, London, 1587), book 2, ch. 10; S. Rid, *The Art of Juggling or Legerdemain* (London, 1612).

[28] On such legislation, see also C. J. Ribton-Turner, *A History of Vagrants and Vagrancy* (London, 1887).

usyng no Crafte nor faicte of Merchaundyce had comen into this Realme and gone from Shire to Shire and Place to Place in greate Company, and used greate subtyll and crafty meanes to deceyve the People, beryng them in Hande [persuading them] that they by Palmestre coulde telle Menne and Womens Fortunes and so many tymes by crafte and subtyltie had deceyved the People of theyr Money and also had comytted many and haynous Felonyes and Robberies to the greate Hurte and Deceyte of the People that they had comen amonge.

To stop further immigration it was therefore enacted that 'from hensforth no suche Psone be suffred to come within this the Kynge's Realme'. If any did, their goods were to be forfeit to the Crown and they were to be ordered to quit the country within 15 days, failing which they would be imprisoned. Gypsies already in England or Wales were to leave within 16 days or go to prison and be dispossessed of their belongings. Half of any goods thus seized could be retained by the enforcing officer, the other half being delivered to the Exchequer. The Act also deprived them of the benefit *per medietatem linguae* contained in a 100-year-old statute, which gave foreigners charged with a felony the right to be heard by a jury comprising equal numbers of Englishmen and men of their own nation. Unfortunately, no case is on record in which such an intriguing right had previously been exercised by Gypsies.

When Paul Fa or Faa was given 15 days to get out in 1537, it was because he was accused of having murdered another Gypsy. This is the first occurrence of the name Faa or Faw, which was to become very familiar in Scotland: that Gypsy Faas were already known there is shown by the fact that when, in 1539, a George Fae and Michael Meche were examined by the Sheriff of Staffordshire, they were found to possess a variety of letters, including one from the King of Scots and a bill from the Abbot of Holyrood. In the same year another official sought Thomas Cromwell's advice about what should be done with some Gypsies whom he had apprehended in Romney Marsh and who produced a patent of the king under his Great Seal in behalf of John Nany, 'knight, of little Egypt, and his company'.

The 1530 Act may not have achieved its aims, but it was

taken seriously enough: in May 1540 a number of Gypsies
were shipped to Norway from Boston, Lincolnshire, and between 1530 and 1554 some 14 other deportations of Gypsies
and their families can be identified, together with injunctions
from the Privy Council to sheriffs, Justices of the Peace, etc. to
exercise vigilance. In 1544, for example, a company of Gypsies
with 17 horses was arrested in Huntingdonshire and sentenced
to deportation; they were shipped (minus the horses, which
were sold off) to Calais, still an English port. They appear to
have belonged to the same band as engaged Henry VIII's
attention even though he was absent in France seeking to
conquer some extra portion of French territory: in September
1544 the Lord Chancellor, in London, requested the king's
ruling on a case involving Gypsies apprehended for robberies
around Huntingdon. The Lord Chancellor, when the arrests
were made, had instructed the Lord Chief Justice that such as
could be proved felons were to be arraigned; and that some
who were reported to be Englishmen 'should be well whipped
like vagabonds and so remitted to their countries' and the rest
sent to London to be conveyed out of the realm. Two were in
fact found guilty of felony, whereupon an offer of £300 was
made for their pardon – a very substantial sum if translated
into present values. The cash had been delivered, and the Lord
Chancellor knew when to temper justice with rationalized
greed: 'the process seemed to be a good example and it would
be hard to attain this money otherwise', he pointed out. 'We
have taken such order that all the lewd people of this sort shall
be despatched out of the realm with all diligence, and doubt
not but that this example will make that neither they nor any
other like them will much covet hereafter to come hither.'
Probably confident of the outcome, he asked to know the
king's pleasure. Henry's finances had come to grief because of
the wars and rumours of war that filled his closing years. With
little delay, back came the answer from France: 'The Egyptians
you wrote for are to be pardoned and the rest banished.'

Despite all these 'good examples', an abortive piece of
further anti-Gypsy legislation in 1545, towards the end of
Henry's reign, bears testimony to continuing official concern.
That concern extended well beyond Gypsies to vagrancy generally, which in Tudor England constituted a pressing problem.

Thomas More took it as the starting point for his analysis of the country's social ills in *Utopia* (1516). Vagabondage had been growing for years as a result of enclosure and the break-up of the old system of farming (which put thousands of labourers out of work), the increase in population, the expansion of the towns, and the after-effects of Henry's dissolution of the monasteries. Its treatment was elevated into a matter of national priority, for, at a time when the able-bodied poor were supposed to have masters, this large and growing unemployed and landless population appeared to the dominant classes to be a major threat. The most draconian Tudor statute against vagrants was that of 1547, in the first year of Edward VI, when the prospect of a lengthy minority of the boy-king brought with it the possibility of faction feuds and made any increase in the size of the vagrant classes seem highly dangerous. Having condemned 'foolish pity and mercy' in its preamble, it provided for able-bodied vagabonds to be branded on the breast with a V and to be made slaves for two years to a master who might put them to use 'by beating, chaining, or otherwise, in such work and labour (how vile soever it be)' as he saw fit. This Act was, however, too severe for effective enforcement – moreover, Parliament had been unable to agree who should receive the benefit of the slaves – and it was repealed two years later and earlier legislation was revived.[29] In the same year of 1549 the young King Edward noted in his journal that 'there was a privy search made through Sussex for all vagabonds, gipsies, conspirators, prophesiers, all players, and such like'; while in Durham some Faws (Baptist, Amy and George Fawe) were accused by another Gypsy, John Roland, of having counterfeited the king's Great Seal, and were found to be in possession of what appeared to be forged documents.

Matters took rather longer to come to such a pass in Scotland, though there were certain local difficulties. In the Council Register for the city of Aberdeen, under the date 8 May 1527, we read that it was proved that the Egyptians had stolen two silver spoons from Thomas Watson's house and that their master, Eken Jaks (Aiken Jacks being, no doubt, a name

---

[29] Cf. C. S. L. Davies, 'Slavery and Protector Somerset; the Vagrancy Act of 1547', *Economic History Review* (1966), pp. 533–49.

borrowed from the people of Aberdeen), was ordered to give back the spoons, or their equivalent, because he was answerable for his company. When Gypsies again come into prominence in the same neighbourhood, in 1539, they were facing similar charges, though this time they were unanimously acquitted by the jury. The two women accused of theft were Barbara Dya Baptista and Helen Andree. Andree was a local surname but Baptista (much used among French Gypsies) is no Scots name, while Dya is probably the Romani word *dya*, 'mother', used to distinguish her from another Barbara Baptista. Speaking up in court on their behalf was George Faw, their 'capitane and forspeikar [spokesman]' – the earliest mention of a Gypsy by that name in Scotland, though Faw itself is an old Scottish surname. George Faw and his brother John were shortly afterwards involved in a brawl, and in February 1540 the City Council ordered them to remove themselves and their company and belongings out of the town. Perhaps the Baptist and George Fawe who were charged with forgery in Durham in 1549 were the same as the Aberdeenshire Faws of 1539–40.

The Aberdeen councillors were out of step with their king and his Council. James V, who came to the throne in 1513 at the age of a year and a half, after his father's death at Flodden Field, had remarkably cordial relations with the Gypsies for much of his reign. In May 1529 'the Egiptianis that dansit before the King in Halyrudhous' received from him a sum of 40 shillings.[30] In March the following year James issued a safe-conduct to 'Count Martin, a native of Lesser Egypt, and the servants forming his train' – who then disappear from view.[31] And on 15 February 1540 he signed a remarkable writ of the Privy Council which granted considerable privileges to John Faw, 'lord and erle of Litill Egipt'. It referred back to letters previously issued under the Great Seal, enjoining all those in authority in the kingdom to assist John Faw in executing justice upon his company 'conforme to the lawis of Egipt' and in punishing all those who rebelled against him. It went on to say that certain members of Faw's company were in fact

[30] Paul (ed.), *Accounts*, vol. 5 (1903), p. 379.
[31] MS Register of the Privy Seal of Scotland, vol. 8, fol. 153.

already in that position, having robbed him and deserted his company: the names of the miscreants were recorded as Sebastiane Lalow, Anteane Donea, Satona Fingo, Nona Finco, Phillip Hatseyggow, Towla Bailzow, Grasta Neyn, Geleyr Bailzow, Bernard Beige, Demeo Matskalla, Not-faw Lawlowr and Martyn Femine. Of these names, only Faw and Bailzow (pronounced 'Bailyow', i.e. Balliol or Baillie) have any Scottish connection; the rest, other than the English name Lalow/ Lawlowr (Lawlor), seem largely foreign, except that Not-faw must be due to a painstaking clerk's copying down too literally the correction of a Gypsy who said: 'Not *Faw*, Lawlor'. According to the writ, John Faw was refusing to go home without these missing members of his band, on the grounds that (in modernized English) he was 'bound and obliged to bring home with him all them of his company that are alive, and a testimonial of them that are dead'. The ringleader of the dissidents, Sebastiane Lalow, was said to have deviously obtained royal letters discharging his followers from their obligations to John Faw. The writ forbade all support for this splinter group and ordered that any royal letters 'sinisterly purchased or to be purchased' should be disregarded: the rebels were to be apprehended and handed over to their rightful leader 'to be punished for their demerits, conform to his laws'. And the masters of all ships were to accept John Faw and his company for passage overseas. For some commentators, this document represents the full sunshine of royal favour; others have suspected that James would by now have been only too glad to be rid of the Gypsies, but that John Faw played for time by pleading a need for taking the whole tribe with him when he left.

In any event, the treaty was short-lived, for little more than a year later (6 June 1541) an Order in Council revoked all letters of protection and other privileges and banished Gypsies from the kingdom within 30 days, on pain of death. The Lords of Council said they understood perfectly 'the gret thiftis and scathis done be the saidis Egiptianis' (the great thefts and hurts done by the said Egyptians). The suggestion that this reversal arose from some incident when James was associating with Gypsies – in one of the solitary roving expeditions which have been attributed to him – smacks more of the folk-tale than of biography or history: the tradition was that the disguised king attempted to take liberties with a Gypsy woman and was smartly hit over the head with a bottle by one of the men and then subjected to further indignities. Though the 1541 Order in Council did not succeed in removing the Gypsies for ever from Scotland, it does seem to have driven the Faws over the border into England for a time, despite the hostile legislation there too. Then comes another bewildering reversal (all the more bewildering in that a letter had been granted only three months after the 1540 writ to one 'John Wanne son and heir of the late John Fall earl of lesser Egypt', and had recognized him as the ruler over all Gypsies in Scotland and given him power to punish them). James V died in 1542 and was succeeded by his infant daughter, Mary. During the regency, in 1553 while Queen Mary was still in France, the 1540 writ which had granted privileges to John Faw was renewed by another issued in her name in favour of 'oure lovit Johne Faw, lord and erle of Litill Egept' and against Sebastiane Lalow and his dissident crew. Not until the 1570s would the ordinances of the Privy Council and the Acts of the Scottish Parliament become uniformly punitive in regard to Gypsies and those leading a similar way of life.

One tantalizing mystery from this period concerns a portrait (see plate 10) which forms part of a sixteenth-century collection of sketches in Arras in northern France,[32] and which bears the caption 'L'Égyptienne quy rendist santé part art de médecine au roy d'Escoce abandonné des médecins' ('the Egyptian woman who by medical art restored health to the King of Scotland, given up by the physicians').[33] So far the identity of the royal patient remains speculative, and no such dramatic cure is known to historians; but either James IV or James V seems the most promising candidate. James V, when he married his first wife, the eldest daughter of François I, was absent for eight and a half months from Scotland in France (1536–7). Some such incident would help to explain the royal

[32] The *Recueil d'Arras* or Arras collection, no. 266 among the MSS in the municipal library of Arras.

[33] See A. M. Fraser and F. de Vaux de Foletier, 'The Gypsy healer and the King of Scots', *JGLS*(3), 51 (1972), pp. 1–8.

Plate 10 The Gypsy healer who cured the King of Scots.
Bibliothèque Municipale, Arras; photograph, Giraudon, Paris.

favour shown to Gypsies in Scotland at a time when most other monarchs were becoming decidedly less tolerant of them.

Scandinavia

It appears to have been from Scotland and England that Gypsies first entered the Scandinavian countries.[34] James IV of Scotland was the son of a Danish princess, Margaret, and it was to her brother, King John of Denmark, that he recommended Anthonius Gagino in 1505. The first Gypsy to be clearly identified in Sweden also bore the name Anthonius: the Stockholm account books record that, on 29 September 1512, a company of some 60 *tatra* ('Tartars'), said to be from Little Egypt, came to the city with a Count Anthonius at their head and were given 20 marks. This tallies with the observation in Olaus Petri's *Swedish Chronicle* that 1512 was the year in which the people called Tartars first landed in Stockholm. *Tattare* remained by far the most widespread designation for Gypsies in Sweden until the seventeenth century, when *zigenare*, under the influence of German, also came into use, first as a synonym and then as a substitute.

Danish tolerance petered out after little more than 30 years. In 1536, and again in 1554, Christian III of Denmark and Norway ordered all Gypsies to leave his kingdom within three months; his son Frederick II renewed the ban in 1561 and stiffened the penalties. The Gypsies who were shipped off from Boston in Lincolnshire to Norway in 1540 were therefore unlikely to have found much of a welcome there. In Sweden, too, relations did not take long to deteriorate. Gustav I, who had established Swedish independence from Denmark in 1523, started off with relatively mild measures, but in the 1540s he

---

[34] A. Etzler, *Zigenarna och deras avkomlingar i Sverige* (Uppsala, 1944) contains a survey of the early history of Gypsies in Sweden, and Scandinavia generally. Other historical material can be found (for Sweden) in A. Heymowski, *Swedish Travellers and their Ancestry* (Uppsala, 1969); (for Norway) in E. Sundt, *Beretning om Fante- eller Landstrygerfolket i Norge* (Christiania, 1850); (for Denmark) in F. Dyrlund, *Tatere og Natmandsfolk i Danmark* (Copenhagen, 1872); and (for Finland) in R. Vehmas, *Suomen Romaaniväestön Ryhmäluonne ja Akkulturoituminen* (Turku, 1961).

began to hunt Gypsies out of the country – a policy that was continued by his successors when he died in 1560, the year in which Archbishop Laurentius Petri Nericius approved articles forbidding priests to have any dealings with Gypsies: they were not even to baptize the children or bury the dead.

Many have held that it was from Sweden that Gypsies originally migrated into Finland, for long a part of the Swedish kingdom. This theory is supported by the possibility that the Finnish word for 'Gypsies', *Mustalainen* ('black', 'swarthy'), was adapted from the Swedish expression *svart Tattare*, 'black Tartars', and more solidly by the fact that the first mention of Gypsies in Finland records that their voyage across the sea was stopped short at the Finnish island of Åland in the year 1559, when they were sent back to Sweden. These rejects may have been preceded by earlier arrivals coming overland via Estonia in 1515, for there is a statement to that effect in a source-book about medieval Finland.[35] What seems clear enough is that when identifiable Gypsies are finally met with on the Finnish mainland in 1584, as prisoners in the fortress of Åbo, they bear unambiguously Swedish names.

Images and stereotypes

After this survey of the surviving traces of the Gypsy expansion in Europe – and of the reactions to it – what is still sadly lacking is any extensive insight into their internal way of life and their customs. The obscurity is not complete, however: we have, for example, begun to learn more about their appearance, if only because of the effect it had on settled society. Their dark skins made them seem ugly and reprehensible; their long hair and ear-rings and outlandish attire were offensive to many. Among the women particularly, there was a recognizably Gypsy style of dress, which fortunately was captured on canvas or on paper by artists in several countries. From Germany we have the etching of the Master of the Housebook, *c.*1480 (see plate 7) and, rather later, the woodcut in Münster's *Cosmographia*, *c.*1550 (see plate 6). From the Low Countries,

[35] E. Aaltonen, review in *JGLS*(3), 42 (1963), pp. 64–7.

Plate 12 *Gypsy dancer. Detail of a Tournai tapestry, c.1500. Gaasbeck Museum, Belgium.*

Plate 11 *Maker unknown, Franco-Flemish (probably Tournai) The Visit of the Gypsies, c.1490 (detail). Wool tapestry, 350.5 × 502.9 cm, The Currier Gallery of Art, Manchester, New Hampshire, Currier Funds, 1937.7.*

where the arts were flourishing under the patronage of the Burgundian dukes, we have in Hieronymus Bosch's *Haywain* (*c*.1500) one of the earliest representations of a Gypsy fortune-teller at work (plate 9), a theme which was also being picked up in several tapestries woven in the Tournai ateliers. The most spectacular example of these shows a procession of Gypsies at the gates of a town or castle, mingling with the gentry (plate 8); the women are dressed in turbans, just as they had been described by the chroniclers; one of the fine ladies is having her hand read (plate 11), while a second is being relieved of her purse by a Gypsy boy. Another of the Tournai tapestries gives the earliest portrayal of Gypsies dancing (see plate 12).

Gypsy attire was becoming a paradigm for the exotic: a number of religious paintings and engravings in the Low Countries (e.g. by Lucas van Leyden) incorporate Gypsy-like figures when the subject requires Oriental, and especially Egyptian, women to be shown. Similar motifs became popular among Italian painters during the first half of the sixteenth century – as evidenced by Giorgione's *Gypsy and Soldier* (*ante* 1510), Titian's *La Zingarella* (*c*.1510), Il Garofalo's picture of the same name (*c*.1525) and Corregio's *Gypsy Madonna* (*c*.1530). These are more stylized treatments, of limited documentary value, but they show a considerable measure of agreement with the others, and with the drawing of the Gypsy healer (plate 10), in regard to the dress of Gypsy women, depicted as wearing a turban (sometimes wound without artificial aid, sometimes with a wicker support) and a chemise covered by a cloak-like blanket, fastened at one shoulder. At the same time the pictorial representations are beginning to fall into fixed patterns: the fortune-telling scene, often with an attendant child as cut-purse, will soon be a set-piece composition, implanting a particular stereotype in the public's mind.[36]

On the stage, Gypsies were also being type-cast. We have seen Gil Vicente's farce of 1521 portraying the women as importunate fortune-tellers and the men as cozening horse-copers. Even earlier, a Gypsy fortune-teller had been intro-

---

[36] This theme is studied and illustrated in J.-P. Cuzin's catalogue *La diseuse de bonne aventure de Caravage* (Paris, 1977).

duced into an anonymous Swiss play written at Lucerne
around 1475,[37] which starts with the farmer telling his wife to
run and make fast the barn doors and bring in the hens, for
the *Heiden* are at hand. A mid-sixteenth century play[38] by
Hans Sachs, employing, as so often with that prolific *Meister-
singer*, satirical caricatures and stock characters, leaves Gypsy
reputations in shreds after associating them with theft, lock-
picking, purse-cutting, horse-stealing, casting of spells, and
general witchcraft and trickery.

The chroniclers who are writing up the early appearances of
the Gypsies – often a century after the event – add new details
which had featured little, if at all, in accounts by contemporary witnesses, but which now become part of the conventional
wisdom. The present chapter started with an extract from
Aventinus. A contemporary of his, one Krantzius (Albert
Krantz), who lived in Hamburg and wrote his *Saxonia* in
1520, gives an equally sharp commentary on the Gypsies' way
of life, purportedly in relation to the original band of 1417,
but drawn no doubt from observations and attitudes a hundred
years later. Like so many others, he stresses the dark hue of
Gypsy skins and the bizarre clothing. He calls them a burden
on the peasants and inveighs against their pilfering, which he
describes as being the task of the women. They speak many
languages, but have no real homeland, since they were born on
the move; the story of the penance is a fabrication and indeed
they practise no religion whatsoever. They live like animals,
from day to day, and wander from province to province; they
return every few years but split up into many separate bands
so as to avoid having the same people come back to any given
place. The women travel with the small children in waggons
drawn by draught-animals; their nobles have packs of hunting
dogs and often exchange horses, but most of the others go
on foot. They honour the duke, the counts and the soldiers.
Whether these last were Gypsies or were *gadźé* engaged to
protect them is not clear; but Krantz does say that they adopt

[37] *Schauspiele des Mittelalters*, ed. F. J. Mone (Karlsruhe, 1846), vol. 2,
pp. 378ff.
[38] *Die 5 elenden wanderer*, in *Hans Sachs' Werke* (Berlin, 1884), vol. 2,
pp. 58–68.

into their companies both men and women who want to join them.[39] The accuracy of this is debatable, for many of these later commentators clearly had difficulty in coming to terms with the concept of native-born 'Egyptians'; but in so far as it was true, mixed marriages would hardly be unknown.

From a variety of sources we have learned something about Gypsy livelihoods: begging and fortune-telling are the ones most commonly mentioned; others are horse-dealing, metal-working, healing, and music and dancing. Theft is also a recurrent theme, though for the most part their crimes do not appear to have gone far beyond the filching of food and clothing, and money too when opportunity offered. Internally, matters of justice and discipline were largely left in their own hands: there is plenty of evidence that the Gypsy people were recognized as constituting an *imperium in imperio* and that when they came into conflict with one another the authorities made little attempt to discover or punish the guilty party but left it to the Gypsies themselves to do whatever was necessary.

The label 'of Little Egypt' was still applied as a routine formula in describing individuals, but now, so many generations after the start of the westward migration, it was a meaningless tag. The Gypsies were becoming more naturalized to particular countries, even if they did not settle down completely; and when, as happened from time to time, their antecedents were investigated in court, they often turned out, despite the label, to have been born (and perhaps christened) in the country of trial and to have married women from not too far away.[40]

European patterns

The emphasis in this chapter has been on the interaction between Gypsies and rulers, nobles, officials and citizens – for that is what the bulk of the available data is concerned with.

---

[39] A. Krantz, *Rerum Germanicarum historici clariss. Saxonia* (Frankfurt am Main, 1580), pp. 354ff.

[40] For such a trial in the Netherlands in 1553, see van Kappen, *Geschiedenis*, pp. 128–30.

Even within that single area, however, the picture is not entirely representative, for the entries in municipal and national archives are strongly biased towards incidents in which some charge to the public purse was incurred, so that one is left wondering about all the other, much more numerous, occasions when the passage of Gypsies did not attract official attention because they obtained their requirements in exchange for goods and services, or perhaps because they were simply moved on or turned away empty-handed.

In considering the relationship which does emerge, it is possible to discern a fairly consistent pattern as Gypsies spread over virtually the whole of Europe. Sporadic signs of resistance or rejection begin to show up relatively soon after their arrival in a country, as some villagers and townspeople tire of alms-giving; and the conflicts have usually become more widespread within 10 or 20 years. The first edicts of generalized application are issued anything from a few decades to a century or more after their first arrival in a country, even if expulsion and repression have not yet quite become universal throughout Europe.

The Gypsy tale of a seven-year pilgrimage, perpetually re-newed, brilliant in concept though it had been, inevitably lost its magic with the passage of time. Whether it was used as a matter of routine or only sporadically is not clear: it certainly comes up frequently in the archives, but these are skewed towards recording alms-giving incidents. What *is* clear is that, when it was deployed, even the most pious burghers found increasing difficulty, after the first few visits, in mustering enthusiasm for succouring these pilgrims. Indeed, the entire religious climate was changing fast. In 1500 Christendom was still divided basically between Roman Catholic in the west and Greek Orthodox in the east, except for Bohemia and Moravia where the Hussites accounted for more than half the population. Within no more than 50 years, almost 40 per cent of the inhabitants of Europe were observing a 'Reformed' theology; and by 1570, out of every ten subjects of the Holy Roman Emperor, seven were Protestants. Papal briefs lost much of their virtue then. The original strategy which had served the Gypsies well had not entirely outlived its usefulness in the middle of the sixteenth century, but the passion for pilgrimages and the status of the pilgrim had suffered a decisive blow. Moreover, begging, which had been looked on kindly by the Church in the days of the Franciscan idealization of poverty, had for some considerable time attracted increasing sanctions from the authorities and now came under strong attack from Luther and others as something to be rooted out of all Christendom.

When the tide did turn, the Gypsies found themselves with no alternative homeland where they might seek refuge, and little prospect of establishing firm roots should they want to. Right from the start they had outraged latent prejudices in the settled populations they moved among. Settled people, on the whole, do not trust nomads; and in a European society where the majority were pressed into a life of piety, serfdom and drudgery, Gypsies represented a blatant negation of all the essential values and premises on which the dominant morality was based. Similar prejudices were built into the rudimentary arrangements that existed for poor relief in sixteenth-century Europe, resting on the assumption that indigenous poor were to be supported by the various parishes, while foreign beggars were to be sent back without mercy to their birthplace or the place where they had formerly lived. This concept left no room for anyone who did not have a parish. In country after country a policy of rejection was now pursued in regard to Gypsies, with no thought given to where they were to go, or how they were to get there, or whether they would be allowed to enter and stay when they did get there.

6

Pressure of the Gyves

For the next 200 years and more – from the mid-sixteenth to the latter part of the eighteenth century – there is a depressing uniformity about the response of most European powers to the presence of Gypsies. They continued to be viewed as criminals simply because of their position in society and, on top of that, the special racial prejudices remained, together with religious hostility towards what was seen as their heathenish practices and sorcery. More generally, they suffered from the tide of repression that was rising everywhere against vagabondage and the 'sturdy beggar'. The authorities could not come to terms with rootless and masterless men, with no fixed domicile and useless as a workforce: in their eyes, that status was in itself an aberration, at odds with the established order, and had to be put right by coercion and pressure of the gyves. Yet when Gypsies offered legitimate services to the settled population, they were at risk from the ill-will attracted by transient traders and artisans who violated local monopolies, or from the abhorrence that occupations such as pedlar or tinker or entertainer aroused among those in power. The passage of time was to bring scant relief. The Age of Enlightenment did generate vast new areas of light – much lucid philosophy and clear-minded literature, and great leaps forward in science and music – but only a little of it penetrated the darkness which encompassed Europe's dealings with Gypsies.

Expulsion, assimilation, extirpation

Had all the anti-Gypsy laws which sprang up been enforced uncompromisingly, even for a few months, the Gypsies would have been eradicated from most of Christian Europe well before the middle of the sixteenth century. This did not happen. The saving feature, as has emerged repeatedly, was that even the most rigorous penal laws were often not carried into effect, perhaps owing to silent opposition on the part of some of the population, and certainly on account of the defective organization of such police forces as existed. The response to this shortfall between intention and administration was much the same everywhere. The laws were made more numerous and the penalties more stringent. It would be tedious to list them in detail. There is in any case no need: if we consider the course of events in a sample of countries, we shall have observed the entire limited gamut of reactions in practically the whole of non-Ottoman Europe over the next two and a half centuries. Sometimes the storm was allowed to abate: this happened gradually in England and Scotland. Mostly it rolled on unceasingly – disjointedly in German lands, but elsewhere, as in France and the Netherlands, with some measure of administrative reinforcement and co-ordination. A few governments – notably those of the Habsburg empire and of Bourbon Spain – were willing in the end to change direction and try a more rational (but no less ruthless) approach after their original failures.[1]

In England, the years 1550 to 1640 represented the peak of state activity against masterless men. In 1554, early in the reign of Philip and Mary, an Act was passed pointing out that 'divers of the said Company [of Egyptians], and such other like Persons...have enterprised to come over again into this Realm, using their old accustomed devilish and naughty Practices and Devices, with such abominable Living as is not in any Christian Realm to be permitted, named or known, and be not duly punished for the same'. The penalties in Henry VIII's Act of 1530 were stiffened: anyone conveying Gypsies into

---

[1] For particular countries, many of the works cited in chs 4 and 5 remain relevant.

the country was to be fined £40, and any Gypsy so transported and staying for a month was to be deemed a felon
and deprived of the privileges of sanctuary and of 'benefit of
clergy'; in other words, ability to read and write was no bar
to proceedings, which, if successful, meant forfeiture of life,
lands and goods. The same fate awaited Gypsies already in
England or Wales who did not leave within 40 days. These
punishments did not apply to children under 14 and could
also be avoided by any Gypsy who chose to abandon 'that
naughty, idle and ungodly Life and Company, and be placed
in the Service of some honest and able Inhabitant ... or
that shall honestly exercise himself in some lawful Work or
Occupation'. All licences, letters and passports previously used
by 'Egyptians' travelling in England or Wales were declared
void.

The first recorded trial under this Act involved a large band
of Gypsies in Dorset during the reign of Elizabeth, in 1559,
and when the Lord Lieutenant wrote to the Privy Council for
instructions he was informed that the Queen thought it 'very
convenient that some sharp example and execution should be
made upon a good number of them', the rest being deported;
similar advice was given in that same year to the Justices of
Assize in Herefordshire. The Gypsies in Dorset were, however,
acquitted on the technical ground that they had not been
'transported and conveyed' into England but had come overland from Scotland, and the Lord Lieutenant confined himself
to despatching them to their birthplace, as the law provided
should be done with vagabonds. (They did not get very far
before falling foul of the authorities again: they were re-
arrested the following month in Gloucestershire and confined in Gloucester Castle and scourged through the town.)
Deportations as a result of the 1554 Act seem in fact to have
been comparatively few.

As time went on, a smaller proportion of the Gypsy population was of overseas origin, and when an Act 'for further
Punishment of Vagabonds, calling themselves Egyptians' was
passed in 1562 it endeavoured to make the position of those
born in England or Wales rather clearer than had Philip and
Mary's legislation. It confirmed that anyone born in England
or Wales would not be compelled to leave the country, but

only to quit their idle and ungodly life and company. At the same time, however, it specified that anyone aged 14 or above who, for a month 'at one Time or at several Times', was found in any company of vagabonds called or calling themselves Egyptians, 'or counterfeiting, transforming or disguising themselves by their Apparel, Speech or other Behaviour, like unto . . . Egyptians', should suffer death and loss of lands and goods. It is probable that the stress on counterfeit Egyptians in legislation from now on arose less from a need to deal with *gadže* who were joining Gypsy bands than from a concern to avoid defence quibbles that someone born in England or Wales (even of Gypsy parents) could not, by definition, be considered an 'Egyptian'.[2] It is noticeable that a number of 'Egyptians' were now finding it politic to ensure that their offspring were baptized and had documents to confirm the place of birth: such baptismal entries, hitherto sparse, begin to be encountered increasingly through England and Wales. And in the ten court cases involving charges of consorting with and counterfeiting Egyptians which can be traced in the hundred years following the 1562 Act, many of the defendants can reasonably be identified as Gypsies.

The Privy Council was energetic, at least in bursts, in following up the new Act with instructions to county officers and justices. In 1569 all were enjoined to make a strict search for Gypsies and vagrants. This was the year in which the disturbed state of the country following the rebellion of the northern Earls against Elizabeth caused much general disaffection, fostered, it was thought, by wandering valiant rogues and beggars. In 1577 the Privy Council took a considerable interest in proceedings against several persons at Aylesbury, apparently English-born Gypsies, for feloniously keeping company with Egyptians and adopting their dress, language, and behaviour. All were found guilty and hanged.[3] In 1579 the Privy Council authorized special Commissioners to try as felons 40 Gypsies apprehended in the county of

[2] Cf. A. M. Fraser, 'Counterfeit Egyptians', *Tsiganologische Studien* 1990, no. 2, pp. 43–69.
[3] The case is studied in detail in T. W. Thompson, 'Consorting with and counterfeiting Egyptians', *JGLS*(3), 2 (1923), pp. 81–93.

Radnor, so as to save the cost of feeding them in prison until the next assizes. There is no shortage of records of others who met similar fates. Only one instance is known, however, of an attempt to implement the provisions of the 1562 Act by returning members of a Gypsy band each to his or her own parish, there to be established in some acceptable occupation. This was in 1596, after a round-up in Yorkshire in which 196 Gypsies and associates – men, women and children – were collected together for trial: 106 'of full age' were condemned to death at York Quarter Sessions. Only nine of them – less than five per cent of the group – had been born overseas and were executed, to loud lamentations on the part of the others. The remainder were spared, and one William Portington was licensed to conduct these 187 to their places of origin. The straggling troop of homeward-led Gypsies must have been one of the more bizarre processions to be seen on the roads of England. Portington was allowed eight months for the job, which appears to have come to its end in Glamorgan.[4] (The Glamorgan and Radnor episodes are the first clear references to Gypsies in Wales, although there had been indications of some on the English side of the border in 1530.)[5]

Elizabeth's Act of 1562 was the last of its kind directed specifically against Gypsies in England and Wales. It remained on the statute book, though latterly not enforced, until repealed in 1783 as being 'a Law of excessive Severity'. The last time that anyone was hanged in England for being a wandering Gypsy appears to have been in the 1650s, when at the Assizes of Bury St Edmunds 13 people were condemned and executed for this infamy.[6] Long before then, however, the

[4] R. O. Jones, 'The mode of disposing of gipsies and vagrants in the reign of Elizabeth', *Archæologia Cambrensis* (4th series), 13 (1882), pp. 226–31; rptd in *JGLS*(2), 2 (1908–9), pp. 334–8.

[5] For completeness, it may be noted that the earliest reference to Gypsies in Ireland occurred in the only Irish Act to mention them, an Act for the punishment of rogues and vagabonds (1634). Included in the classes of people affected were 'Egyptians' and 'counterfeit Egyptians'. It is doubtful, however, whether this actually indicated a Gypsy presence in Ireland at that time: the wording of much of the definition was simply lifted from that of the English Act of 1597 concerning rogues and vagabonds.

[6] J. Hoyland, *A Historical Survey ... of the Gypsies* (York, 1816), pp. 86–7.

evidence is that Gypsies were finding plenty of local officers prepared to tolerate their passage and leave them relatively unmolested. Indeed, they might often secure a hand-out, as seventeenth-century parish constables' account books testify.[7]

They were, of course, also at risk from the legislation dealing with vagabondage, and the distinction between them and the general run of vagrants became particularly blurred in the official mind once they had to be recognized as native-born. Of the 13 enactments relating to vagrancy and the poor passed under Henry VIII and subsequent Tudors, the most comprehensive was the statute of 1572, styled 'An Act for the Punishment of Vagabonds, and for the Relief of the Poor & Impotent', which was also the harshest of Elizabeth's reign. Persons of the age of 14 or above, 'being Rogues, Vagabonds, or sturdy Beggars', were on conviction 'to be grievously whipped, and burnt through the gristle of the right Ear with a hot Iron of the compass of an Inch about', unless some honest person would take them into service for a year. Those offending a second time were to be deemed felons unless taken into service for two years. For a third offence there would be no alternative to being treated as felons (with terminal consequences). Rogues under 14 were to be whipped or put in the stocks. Though Gypsies were not mentioned in the long recital of the punishable classes, many of its descriptions would clearly have applied to them. As for the relief of the poor, the basic device was to order justices of the peace to register all aged and impotent poor who had been born in their districts or resident there for three years and to settle them in convenient habitations, the cost being borne by local citizens; this introduction of a national infrastructure of compulsory contributions, inaugurating the parish poor-rate, represented a major innovation. Beggars' children between the ages of 5 and 14 might be taken by anyone willing to have them in service, females until they were 18 and males until 24 – thus providing the master with servitude which could last as long as 19 years.

The legislation became gradually less oppressive and its penal element diminished, though remaining savage by modern

---

[7] T. W. Thompson, 'Gleanings from constables' accounts and other sources', *JGLS*(3), 7 (1928), pp. 30–47.

Plate 13 Gypsy Encampment, by Francis Wheatley. *Late 18th century. Birmingham City Museum and Art Gallery.*

standards. Parliament continued to pass vagrancy laws, but they added little that was new. The designation of Gypsies, along with a variety of other groups, as rogues and vagabonds – an association first made in an Act of 1597 – was re-enacted from time to time, as in the 1713 statute which specified that it extended to 'all Persons pretending to be Gipsies, or Wandring in the Habit or Form of Counterfeit Egyptians, or pretending to have Skill in Physiognomy, Palmestry, or like Crafty Science, or pretending to tell Fortunes or like Phantastical Imaginations, or using any Subtile Craft, or Unlawful Games or Plays'. This Act instructed the justices to organize periodic searches for rogues, vagabonds and sturdy beggars and to send such people back, after a whipping or spell of hard labour if that seemed desirable, to their place of last settlement or, if no such place existed, to the place of birth. Gypsies were referred to by name in this manner for the last time in England in the Vagrancy Act of 1822, which declared that 'all Persons pretending to be Gipsies' or to tell fortunes, or wandering abroad or lodging under tents or in carts or waggons were to be deemed rogues and vagabonds, for which the penalty was up to six months' imprisonment. When that was replaced by the Vagrant Act of 1824 (much of it still in force, and available for fining and imprisoning the homeless and beggars), the specific reference to Gypsies was at last dropped, though that did not blunt it as an instrument for keeping them on the move; while highways legislation continued to re-enact the provision against Gypsy camping which had been introduced in the Turnpike Roads Act of 1822 (cf. pp. 2–3).

It was the 1713 Act which first employed the form *Gipsy* instead of *Egyptian* in an English statute. But legislators are not linguistic innovators and the abbreviation was already well established at the beginning of the previous century,[8] having by then passed through intermediate forms like *Gipcyan* or *Gipson*. The earliest Scottish instance of the abbreviation occurs in 1598, in a complaint to the Privy Council in which 'certane gipseis' played a minor role.

In Scotland, the number of vagabonds and 'sorners' (people who forcibly quartered themselves upon others) seems greatly

[8] As in 'both in a tune like two gipsies on a horse' in *As You Like It*.

to have increased during the disorders of the reign of Mary Stuart, and in 1574, while her son James VI was still in his minority and the Earl of Morton was regent, an attempt was made to regulate the system 'for the staunching of masterful idle beggars, away-putting of sorners and provision for the poor' in an Act closely modelled on the English statute of 1572. The penalties ran the same gamut from scourging and burning of the right ear to execution, and the dispositions for relief of the poor were also very similar. The description of persons affected did, however, specifically include Gypsies, under the heading of 'the idle people calling themselves Egyptians'. By virtue simply of earning that description they were to be deemed worthy of punishment. Gone for good was any suggestion that they were recognized as forming a separate community, subject to their own laws and justice (p. 118), though for long afterwards, well into the eighteenth century, the bloody conflicts between rival Gypsy clans were regarded with comparative indifference by the other inhabitants of Scotland.

That Gypsies were held to be a special problem throughout Scotland at this time is proved by the two 'charges' issued by the Privy Council in 1573 and 1576, ordering all representatives of the government to seek out 'certain vagabond idle and counterfeit people of diverse nations falsely named Egyptians' and to present them to the Tolbooth in Edinburgh for trial. Any default on the part of an official would lay him open to trial for favouring thieves and murderers. Notwithstanding all this, Gypsies survived in Scotland, and in 1579 (the year in which James VI took government into his own hands) a further statute was enacted, so close to its precursor as to be practically a repetition. By 1597 it was felt necessary to pass yet another Act against strong and idle beggars, vagabonds and Egyptians, in which the temporary servitude assigned to previous offenders and their children was made life-long and the kirk sessions were allotted a role in administration. The last quarter of the sixteenth and the first quarter of the seventeenth century were – in great measure because of the personal influence of James VI – a period more potentially adverse to Gypsies in Scotland, by reason of stern and continuous legislation, than any other before or since. The pinnacle was reached in 1609 with an 'Act anent the Egiptians', confirming an order of the Privy Council made six years before, and which banished them on pain of death and, with a few weeks' grace, made it lawful to condemn and execute them on proof only 'that they are called, known, repute and holden Egyptians'. In practice these terms were not followed to the extreme, even by the Privy Council, and it seems clear that what was being aimed at was the suppression of those Gypsies who in the eyes of the authorities could be said to be living an idle and vagrant life. Once a Gypsy settled and followed some recognized occupation, he would cease to be an offender. A certain Moses Faw put this to the test by seeking permission to stay in the country, being 'sure that the Estates of Parliament had never any purpose or intention that the said Act should receive execution against honest, lawful and true persons'. He claimed to have cut himself off from 'that infamous society', and offered surety of £1,000 for his maintaining that separation. The Privy Council accepted his plea, and Mosie Faw had proved the point. Unfortunately he had difficulty in living up to his protestations. Less than 18 months later, he was charged with 'hanting with Egiptians'. His principal surety, a landed gentleman named David Lindsay, failed to appear or to pay in the £1,000, and was declared an outlaw. After evidence from the Selkirkshire justices that Mosie's revived association had led to a number of robberies, he and three other Faws were hanged for contravening the 1609 Act by 'abiding and remaining within this kingdom, they being Egyptians'.[9]

There were, however, plenty of others who managed to avoid letting the laws interfere too much with their daily lives. Indeed, the authorities were seriously worried about the prevalence of 'resetting' (harbouring or giving 'receipt' to) Gypsies, who had gone to ground for only a brief period in 1609. In 1616 the Privy Council ordered that the terms of the 1609 Act be proclaimed once more at mercat (market) crosses, with due emphasis on the penalties for resetting, so as to mark its concern that 'great numbers of his Majesty's subjects, of whom some outwardly pretend to be famous and unspotted

[9] Cf. D. MacRitchie, *Scottish Gypsies under the Stewarts* (Edinburgh, 1894), pp. 81–4.

gentlemen, have given and give open and avowed protection, reset, supply, and maintenance upon their ground and lands to the said vagabonds, sorners, and condemned thieves and limmers [rogues], and suffer them to remain days, weeks, and months together thereupon without controlment'. Accusations of resetting continued to flow unabated, and the justices were constantly harried to put the law against vagabonds and Egyptians into execution: Privy Council, Parliament and Kirk all kept pressing, as did the Cromwellian regime during the Protectorate. The Gypsies were always at risk, as court records show. The death penalty was carried out on eight men – six of them Faas – in 1624 for being 'Egyptians'. The following week their wives and children were found guilty of the same crime and sentenced to death by drowning, but the Privy Council referred the matter to King James, who decided that banishment would be sufficient. (Though James had become monarch of England as well as Scotland, the released Faas would then have needed only to cross the border into Northumberland or Cumberland to comply.) In 1626 some Gypsies arrested by the Sheriff of Haddington on suspicion of arson did escape the death penalty because they were found to be innocent and in fact to have prevented the spread of the fire: Charles I's clemency extended as far as downgrading their punishment to perpetual banishment. A few years later, in 1630, when the Earl of Cassillis sought directions on what to do with some Gypsies who had been apprehended but not accused of any particular crime, he was told by the Privy Council to put the statute 'to due and full execution' against as many of them as clearly fell within its terms. And in 1636 the Privy Council ordered the provost and baillies of Haddington to despatch another band of Gypsies – the men by hanging and women without children by drowning, while women who did have children were to be whipped and burnt in the cheek.

Apart once more from nineteenth-century highways legislation (cf. p. 137), the last Scottish Act to call for action specifically against Egyptians (along with vagabonds, etc.) was passed in 1661. Subsequent statutes on vagrancy made no special mention of them. The ferocious 1609 Act, however, had by no means fallen into disuse. Towards the end of the seventeenth century, courts were often beginning to insist on some proof of guilt of a particular crime as well as on the

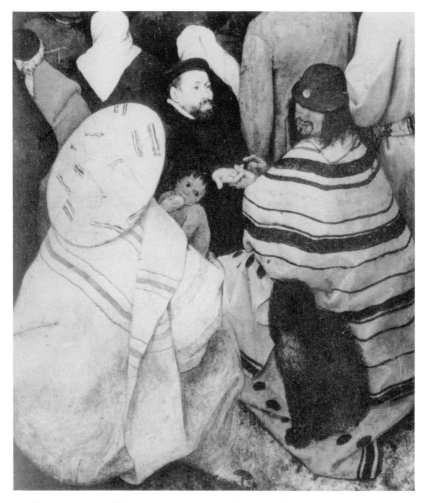

Plate 14   Detail from Pieter Breughel the Elder's Sermon of St John the Baptist, *1565, showing (unusually) a Gypsy man reading a palm. Fine Arts Museum, Budapest.*

habit and repute of being an Egyptian; but not all of them were so scrupulous. The last occasion on which the death penalty was enforced in Scotland for simply being a Gypsy was in 1714,[10] though the fact of being 'called, known, repute and holden Egyptians' appears to have formed part of an

[10] W. Simson, *A History of the Gipsies* (London, 1865), p. 120.

*Plate 15   Gypsies on the move. Engraving by Jacques Callot, 1622.
Photograph, Roger-Viollet, Paris.*

indictment as late as 1770, when two Linlithgow Gypsies were hanged for housebreaking and robbery;[11] and when Jean Gordon, the original of Meg Merrilies in Scott's *Guy Mannering*, presented a petition in 1732 to the Jedburgh Circuit Court, setting forth that she had been indicted as an Egyptian and vagabond and that she was old and infirm and willing to quit Scotland entirely, she was banished accordingly,

[11] Ibid., pp. 133–7.

under pain of imprisonment and scourging should she return. She spent the rest of her life roaming on the English side of the border. Though by now she had lost all her nine sons (one murdered, the others hanged) as well as her husband (transported – see p. 172 below), she retained her spirit to the end: an angry mob ducked her to death in Carlisle about 1746 for making her Jacobite sentiments too obvious, but she was still shouting for Prince Charlie with her dying breath.[12]

On the Continent, events followed a different line of evolution. In France, the climax of repression took longer to build up but, once reached, it was sustained with some measure of effectiveness. To begin with, despite the 1561 ordinance of Charles IX (p. 97), we still find, for the rest of the sixteenth century and beyond, Gypsy companies travelling about without too much manifestation of concern on the part of the authorities. Frequently they covered the same routes, reappearing at intervals in the same places, and often they had trains of horses, mules or donkeys. Such bands, headed by a 'count' or by one or two 'captains', varied considerably in strength, comprising 30, 60, 80 or 100 persons, sometimes more. Incidents of violence were uncommon, though an affray might occasionally break out if local people were obstinate and refused them access, without compensation; usually, however, it was possible to come to some understanding.

Gypsy visitations became such a normal part of life that whenever the representatives of royal authority or the provincial Parlements sought to revive the draconian measures which had been decreed previously, these remained by and large a dead letter. Nothing much seemed to happen, for example, when the Estates of Languedoc, in 1597, ordered office-holders to bar Gypsies from towns and villages and not to issue them with the passports which were required even for internal journeys – an order specifically endorsed with an exhortation from King Henry IV for rigorous observance of the relevant royal edicts. For some time the intended severity of such measures continued to be mitigated by administrative laxity, by widespread connivance, and by the liberality with

---

[12] W. S. Crockett, *The Scott Originals* (Edinburgh, 1912), ch. 6; and A. Gordon, *Hearts upon the Highway* (Galashiels, 1980), pp. 73–4.

Au bout du comte ils treuuent pour desein
Quils sont venus d'Aegipte a ce fertin

Plate 16 *Gypsy camp. Engraving by Jacques Callot, 1622. Collection Grosjean; photograph Giraudon, Paris.*

which passports and documents of safe-conduct were handed out to the captains and their bands. Even Henry IV showed no great consistency: in 1607 he invited Gypsies to his court to dance before him. Gradually, however, from about the middle of the seventeenth century – when Louis XIV was already on the throne but had not yet taken power into his own hands – police action against Gypsies began to be more vigorous and sentences more harsh, though, as usual, there were variations from one part of the country to another. It was also during that period that Gypsies in particular were rounded up for the royal galleys in the Mediterranean. Then, under Louis's personal rule, absolute government reached its apogee and the machinery of centralized administration became more effective and also more uniform. Police regulations issued in 1666 made it clear that male Gypsies were to be arrested and, without legal process, sent in chains to the galleys. Colbert, intent on building up the king's navy, was insistent in his demands, so that ever bigger gangs of them were consigned to Marseilles and Toulon. Matters came to a head with the decree signed by Louis XIV at Versailles on 11 July 1682.[13] This recapitulated previous measures and deplored the fact that the king's predecessors had been unable to banish Gypsies from France, taking as it did so a side-swipe at the noblemen and magistrates 'in most provinces of our kingdom' who had not merely tolerated them but afforded them protection. Then followed a battery of sanctions: men to be sent to the galleys for life; boys not old enough for the galleys to be put into hospices; and women and girls to have their heads shaved and, if they persisted in their vagrant ways, to be scourged and banished from the realm without any need for a trial. These penalties were to be incurred by 'all those who are called *Bohemes* or *Égyptiens*', for no other reason than that. (There was no sign of preoccupation with 'counterfeit Egyptians', apart from the inclusion of 'others in their train' among those affected.) The gentry and justices were forbidden to afford shelter: any lapse would attract removal from office and forfeiture of their domains. The real novelty about this measure was that it was

---

[13] The complete French text is given in F. C. Wellstood, 'Some French edicts against the Gypsies', *JGLS*(2), 5 (1911–12), pp. 313–16.

the first of its kind in France to be widely observed: the network of provincial *intendants* installed by Richelieu during Louis XIII's reign as agents of the central government, with no local roots, keeping a check on local officials and taking over all judicial, policing and financial functions if necessary, had ensured that the Sun King's policies would not easily be circumvented.

The royal decree did have a decided impact, and no other aimed specifically at Gypsies was thought necessary during the remainder of the *ancien régime*, although vagrancy and begging continued to attract legislation. Right up to the time of the Revolution, there are numerous records of Gypsies being hunted down by rural police, many of whom were quick to use their muskets if resisted. But lack of manpower still constituted the weakest link in the flailing administrative attack. Policing of towns was rudimentary; policing of the country was often virtually non-existent. Even after some overdue reforms in the 1760s, the entire police force of provincial France added up to 3,882, of whom 468 were higher administrative officials – this in a country with a population of some 25 millions, the largest in Europe. To cope with major emergencies, such as the arrest of particularly large and dangerous bands of criminals, either the *brigades* (of the rural constabulary) had to amalgamate or the army had to be called in.[14] So far as Gypsies were concerned, a last refuge for groups of significant size appeared to be in the mountains and forests of Alsace and Lorraine, with convenient frontiers nearby. The Basque country and the eastern end of the Pyrenees were also favoured terrain, no doubt partly for similar reasons. Elsewhere, the large Gypsy companies broke up, for they were now too conspicuous. Some families became sedentary, at least for part of the year, while small groups continued their travels off the beaten track. Since France's neighbours were applying similarly repressive legislation, there was not much incentive for Gypsies to leave. Some did, but many preferred to stay in the country they knew: so long as they were circumspect they might hope to fare no worse there. Indeed, France still

[14] Cf. O. H. Hufton, *The Poor of Eighteenth-Century France* (Oxford, 1974), pp. 220–2.

attracted refugees from elsewhere, notably the Netherlands, the Rhineland and Switzerland. More than a quarter of the Gypsies on the French galleys in the mid-eighteenth century had been born outside France.

That is not to say that all was hostility: from time to time there are gestures of sympathy for those making a serious attempt to become less unconventional citizens, even if the *philosophes* declared their disdain for Gypsies' capacity to exploit the superstition of the populace. (Diderot's *Encyclopédie*, the showcase for the whole movement of rationalist humanism, defined them as 'vagabonds who profess to tell fortunes by examining hands. Their talent is to sing, dance and steal.') It was in Lorraine that, on the eve of the Revolution, some degree of perceptiveness broke through. In the north-east corner of that recently incorporated duchy, adjoining the frontier of the Empire, it occurred to a number of administrators and private individuals that if Gypsies had become so importunate and at times dangerous, it might be because all other options were closed to them. They looked for some way of avoiding the costly punitive raids which were having so little success, and in 1786 started negotiations with several Gypsy representatives who explained that, hounded on all sides as they were, their only way of feeding their families was to extract subventions from the local populace when they could; however, they were willing to submit to the French government and accept agricultural work in France or overseas, on condition that they were not confined and not taken in chains to their ultimate destination. The dossier which was put together by these people of Lorraine was sent to the court at Versailles, where consideration was apparently being given to the idea of using Gypsies as colonists in the Americas, notably Guiana, at the time when the project came to an abrupt end on the outbreak of the Revolution.[15] The ensuing change of regime brought with it no alleviation: if anything, matters took a turn for the worse since, in the prevailing atmosphere of highly charged suspicion, the public authorities,

[15] Cf. F. de Vaux de Foletier, *Les Tsiganes dans l'ancienne France* (Paris, 1961), pp. 211–14, and *Les Bohémiens en France au 19e siècle* (Paris, 1981), pp. 92–3.

with stronger armed detachments at their disposal, felt it incumbent on themselves to intensify their raids.

The Netherlands were even more successful than France in implementing a policy of suppression, despite starting with extremely weak central government. When Spain at last accepted the independence of the United Provinces in 1609, the new state was a loose federation of seven little republics with a central States-General of limited jurisdiction. The upheaval of the long revolt against Spain had offered some respite to Gypsies and they were becoming more obtrusive. They thrived especially in the eastern part of the Dutch Republic, notably the provinces of Guelders and Overijssel, where the woods and heaths provided them with good protection.

At first we see a continuation of the classic combination of compulsive law-making coupled with defective implementation. Each of the provinces, as well as the States-General, began regularly to promulgate edicts, of increasing severity, against the Gypsies; but the police were badly organized, and their jurisdiction was restricted to the confines of their own province. One result was that Gypsies tended to camp in remote spots near the provincial borders so that, in case of need, they could quickly flee to the adjacent province. Warning signs brought home to them, all too graphically, the kind of treatment that awaited them if caught (see plate 17); it was clear that nomads could expect little sympathy from the magistrates. They also saw the penalties grow in brutality: probably this was one factor in the rise in the incidence of more serious crime by Gypsies that can be observed in the records towards the close of the seventeenth and at the beginning of the eighteenth century. The prospect of long periods of hard labour, or of ending up on the gallows, as compared with the earlier floggings and brandings, gave them all the more incentive to resist to the end. They lost the battle. The police force was gradually put on a more businesslike footing, and the various provinces overcame their touchiness in regard to their sovereignty in home affairs, to the extent of concluding treaties with each other so as to allow co-ordinated persecution of Gypsies. Intensive *heidenjachten* ('Gypsy hunts') were organized on an ever larger scale, with military

*Plate 17 Dutch warning sign showing the flogging and branding of
a Gypsy, c.1710. The inscription reads: 'Punishment for Gypsies'.
Oil painting on wood, 59 cm h, 40 cm w. Gemeentemuseum,
Roermond (reg. no. 1864).*

assistance. Two bordering German states (the duchy of Cleves, the bishopric of Münster) were persuaded to join in too. The last of the Gypsy hunts was mounted by Gelderland in 1728 in collaboration with Cleves. It was the last, because after that it no longer seemed worthwhile to undertake more. Any Gypsies who had not fled or been wiped out submerged themselves sufficiently to make the authorities satisfied that there were in effect none left to hunt. Many years would go by before other Gypsies could be found venturing back into the Kingdom of the Netherlands.

In their willingness to co-operate with the Dutch Republic, these two German states, Cleves and Münster, were showing, not for the first time (cf. p. 91), a more effective combination than had been usual within the Holy Roman Empire. From the mid-sixteenth century onwards, until it expired in 1806, the Empire meant little more than a loose federation of the princes of Germany, lay and ecclesiastical, under the presidency of the house of Habsburg. But one new piece of constitutional machinery in the early sixteenth century, the concept of *Reichskreise* (Circles of the Empire), had introduced some measure of co-ordination by creating ten regional groupings of member territories to bring them closer together in the field of taxation, law and order, and recruitment for the imperial army. It also helped to swell the tide of regulation. As a result, the decrees we encounter now show a range of jurisdictions: some were applicable to the whole Empire, some to a Circle, some only to an individual state. In sheer volume of anti-Gypsy legislation the Empire matched the rest of Europe taken together. One tally – by no means exhaustive – of its chief measures lists no fewer than 133 in 1551–1774.[16] Breaking these down by half-centuries produces the following sequence: 1551–1600, sixteen; 1601–50, eleven; 1651–1700, thirty; 1701–50, sixty-eight; 1751–74 (24 years), eight. There can be no question of analysing them in detail, but only of examining a few among the more representative.

1577. A public order regulation (*Polizeiordnung*) issued at

---

[16] R. A. Scott Macfie, 'Gypsy persecutions', *JGLS*(3), 22 (1943), pp. 71–3. There is also much relevant material in J. S. Hohmann, *Geschichte der Zigeunerverfolgung in Deutschland* (Frankfurt, 1981), esp. pp. 18–47.

Frankfurt gave renewed force to the earlier legislation of the Diet (p. 90). It forbade all Electoral princes and governments to allow Gypsies to travel or do business in their states or to give them safe-conducts, escorts or passports, and any such documents, current or future, were declared null and void. As was standard practice in such regulations, the stigmatization which went back to the very earliest imperial legislation was reiterated without further discussion, and Gypsies were dismissed as being traitors and spies who explored Christian countries for the benefit of the Turks and other enemies of Christendom. They were immediately to remove themselves from all German countries: any found subsequently could be attacked with impunity.

1652. Elector George I of Saxony, who had headed the organization of German Protestant princes during the Thirty Years War, issued an edict putting Gypsies outside the pale of the law and referring to 'strong bands of people who collect together on horseback or on foot . . . who generally claim to be Gypsies, among whom however a sizeable number of discharged army officers are said to be found, dressed in similar clothing'; not only did these people impose upon villagers, but they also kept game dogs and had the temerity to abuse the Elector's hunting preserves.

1686. Frederick William, the Great Elector of Brandenburg and leading Protestant prince in Germany, decreed that Gypsies were not to be tolerated, and especially not to be allowed any trade or to have lodging or other shelter.

1710. His son Frederick, founder of the Hohenzollern monarchy of Prussia, thought it necessary to go much further and issued what was called a 'sharpened edict against the Gypsies and other vagabond thieving rabble'.

1710. Prince Adolph Frederick of Mecklenburg-Strelitz felt that the sanctions in the principality of Ratzeburg also stood in need of sharpening: henceforth, when no criminal charges could be substantiated against Gypsies captured there, older males not capable of being put to work and women over 25 were to be flogged, branded and expelled in small groups by different routes, and executed if they came back; younger females, and youths not fit for heavy work, were similarly to be ejected; while healthy males faced life confinement with

Plate 18   German sign warning off Gypsies, c.1715. Nördlingen Museum, Bavaria. The inscription reads: 'Punishment for . . . rogues and Gypsies . . .'.

forced labour. Children under 10, however, were to be taken away and handed over to good Christian people to be given a proper upbringing. Mecklenburg-Strelitz was far from being alone among German states in making a practice of forcible removal of young children.

1711. In Frankfurt am Main an ordinance applicable to the various states of the Upper Rhine Circle laid it down that if any of the *Zigeunergesindel* ('Gypsy rabble') remained after four weeks they should 'without further formality be beaten with rods and branded on the back and for evermore be banished from the territories of the entire Circle'. Special signs were to be put up at frontiers showing a Gypsy being flogged, and with the inscription *Zigeuner Straf* ('Gypsy punishment'). Such deterrent signs on the Dutch model, introduced in the Palatinate in 1709, became a popular device and would be seen at crossroads and the like in various parts of Germany for the rest of the century (see plate 18).[17] Anyone defying the prohibitions was to be hanged, and informers were eligible for a share in the accused's effects.

1711. Elector Frederick Augustus I of Saxony (who was also King Augustus II of Poland) authorized the shooting of Gypsies if they resisted arrest. He and the Duke of Saxony – ruler of the duchy which had been partitioned off from the electorate – were concerting action to be taken against Gypsies venturing into their territories.The sanctions adopted were those which had now become standard: flogging, branding and, on a second appearance, death.

1714. In the archbishopric of Mainz it was decreed that all Gypsies and like thievish vagrants were to be executed without trial, simply by reason of their forbidden manner of life; the women and grown children, if not convicted of theft, were to be flogged, branded and banished, or put for life into workhouses. Since they had, it was said, been taking refuge in the forests and terrorizing peasants who refused to lodge them, they should all be hunted down by armed forces and driven from the country or, if they resisted, shot dead. There was an agreement with neighbouring states for rights of passage when escorting captives to places of security. This circular was to be read out repeatedly and 'displayed at places of Gypsy resort, signboard posts, . . . church doors, and . . . publicly printed and published'.

1725. Frederick William I, the second Prussian king and the father of Prussian bureaucracy, had no patience for anyone or anything not contributing to his concept of the state; Gypsies,

---

[17] Cf. R. Andree, 'Old warning-placards for Gypsies', *JGLS*(2), 5 (1911–12), pp. 202–4.

he decreed, both male and female, could be hanged without trial if over 18.

1734. An edict of Ernst Ludwig, Landgrave of Hesse-Darmstadt, outlawed all Gypsies over 14. Hesse-Darmstadt and neighbouring lands, it said, were infested with them, especially in the frontier regions. In summer they dwelt in the woods and fields, and in winter in small villages where they intimidated the inhabitants. Those who did not leave within a month would forfeit life and possessions: anyone could shoot them or take them prisoner, and would receive a reward of six *Reichsthaler* for every live Gypsy brought in and three for a dead Gypsy, as well as keeping their belongings.

1766. Carl Theodor, Count Palatine by Rhine, proclaimed that all kinds of Gypsies, robbers and such like vagabonds were accumulating in his duchy because of the energy with which they were being expelled from Bavaria and other neighbouring lands; they were therefore to be zealously watched, arrested, tortured and punished, and if arrested a second time hanged without further trial on a gibbet. Those professing ignorance of the law should be tortured and, if no particular offence was proved, both men and women were to be beaten, branded on the back with a gallows, and banished.

It is no accident that something like three-quarters of such anti-Gypsy measures identified for 1551–1774 fall within the 100 years following on the Thirty Years War, in which Germany had formed the principal theatre of war. The Peace of Westphalia (1648) enhanced the German princes' powers and presented the hundreds of member states of the Empire with almost full sovereignty. Faced by the widespread devastation created by campaigns in which the armies of both sides, largely made up of mercenary desperadoes, had plundered indiscriminately as they marched, leaving cities, towns, villages and farms ravaged and picked clean, the princes sought to legislate their way towards recovery, or at least towards suppression of some of the major ills confronting the reduced and impoverished population. The loss of life among the subjects of most of them in the Thirty Years War is variously estimated at one-third, one-half and in the worst hit regions 70 per cent, so that the population of Germany dropped from about 20 million to between 12 and 13 million; and subsequent conflicts with France would ensure that parts of Germany continued to serve as battlegrounds and that recovery was further postponed.

To some extent Gypsies had benefited from the chaos of war. They could attach themselves to the marauding armies in one capacity or another; many of them are reported to have accompanied Wallenstein's troops throughout; others followed the Swedish army on the other side. In addition to annihilating millions of people, the war uprooted many thousands, perhaps hundreds of thousands. Once the conflict was over, dispossessed peasants and disbanded soldiers wandered about begging and stealing, and the latter seem to have associated both with *Gauner* ('rogues', 'vagabonds') and with Gypsies. To deal with the vagrant hordes, the princes churned out legislation of the kind we have just seen, unremittingly hostile in intent. In so far, however, as such measures were ever debated – for example, in the assemblies of the *Reichskreise* – dissenting voices were sometimes heard. In the Upper Rhine Circle in 1726, the cathedral chapters of Speyer, Worms and Mainz spoke up against the most extreme penalties which were being considered and pointed out that Gypsies and the like were 'after all human beings and could not dwell between heaven and earth'. The representatives of Nassau-Weilburg, on the other hand, expressed the view that 'the mercy which one wanted perhaps to extend to them in accordance with the precepts of Christianity amounts in practice to the greatest cruelty towards the poor subjects' (who had to bear with them).[18] Alternative proposals, based on providing education and work, fell to the ground because of the absence of suitable institutions. This was the outcome that prevailed time and again. Since the official guardians of the peace appeared ineffectual, a practice grew up of reinforcing them with militia or cavalry and finally of setting up special teams (e.g. four horsemen and a scout on foot) to go bounty-hunting for

---

[18] Cf. H. Arnold, 'Das Vagantenunwesen in der Pfalz während des 18. Jahrhunderts', *Mitteilungen des historischen Vereins der Pfalz*, 55 (1957), pp. 117–52, esp. p. 131.

Gypsies and the like: in the case of the Upper Rhine Circle, such teams were introduced from 1720 onwards.[19]

Ever since Ferdinand I succeeded to the Austrian inheritance and followed his brother Charles V on to the imperial throne in 1558, the Holy Roman Empire had been an Austrian Habsburg empire; and so it would continue until its remains were buried by Napoleon. Attitudes towards Gypsies within the Habsburg family domains (including Bohemia, Moravia and Silesia) for long showed little difference from those elsewhere. Decrees of banishment and penalties of mutilation and execution were the prescribed remedies. Only in 'Royal Hungary' – the western strip that remained under Habsburg rule after the Turks had overrun the rest of Hungary – were there any unusual features. The situation in these frontier lands was very mixed, and decrees for expulsion had an uncertain impact: some lords obeyed, some were more concerned to preserve the skills of Gypsies as smiths, musicians and soldiers. Occasionally the government shared their preoccupation. The Count Palatine (imperial governor) of Hungary, György Thurzó, issued a remarkable safe-conduct in 1616 which had certainly not been presaged by the orders of much more hostile intent to which he had given effect only four years before. This document referred especially to the *voivode* Franciscus and his company, said to be 'performing military services' (so that the authorities had a vested interest in keeping them available), but it contained a general plea for understanding of the Gypsies' plight, couched in ornate Latin prose:

While the birds of the sky have their nests, foxes their earths, wolves their lairs, and lions and bears their dens, and all animals have their own place of habitation, the truly wretched Egyptian race, which we call *Czingaros*, is assuredly to be pitied, although it is not known whether this was caused by the tyranny of the cruel Pharaoh or the dictate of fate. In accordance with their ancient custom they are used to leading a very hard life, in fields and meadows outside the towns, under ragged tents. Thus have old and young, boys and children of

---

[19] Cf. ibid., pp. 133–4; and U. Sibeth, 'Verordnungen gegen Zigeuner in der Landgrafschaft Hessen-Kassel im Zeitalter des Früh-Absolutismus', *Giessener Hefte für Tsiganologie* (1985), no. 4, pp. 3–15, esp. pp. 10–13.

this race learned, unprotected by walls, to bear with rain, cold and intense heat; they have no inherited goods on this earth, they do not seek cities, strongholds, towns or princely dwellings, but wander constantly with no sure resting place, knowing no riches or ambitions, but, day by day and hour by hour, looking in the open air only for food and clothing by the labour of their hands, using anvils, bellows, hammers and tongs.[20]

Thurzó enjoined the authorities to allow such Gypsies to settle in their lands, erect tents and practise their smithery, and to protect them against those who would do them harm. So long as the country remained divided in this way, Gypsies could exploit the political situation in their favour. The position would be altered by the Austrian reconquest of Hungary and Transylvania towards the close of the seventeenth century.

It was there that the first fundamental changes for Gypsies came in Habsburg lands, during the reign (1740–80) of the Empress Maria Theresa. Her father, the Emperor Charles VI, had been relentless in his hostility to Gypsies, and in her earlier years she was content to follow his example, ordering in 1749 that Gypsies, vagrants and foreign beggars be driven out from all her domains. (This did not affect settled Gypsies, some of whom enjoyed considerable favour in high places as musicians. Five of these fortunate ones were Ferencz, János and Latzkó Bakos, László Boromi and László Tinka, who in 1751 obtained *litteras privilegiales* from Count Ferencz Eszterházy of Galantha, proclaiming them to be Free Court Musicians and exempt from taxes.)[21] In 1758–73, however, Maria Theresa sought to apply a series of measures to Hungary (which then included Slovakia) aimed at immobilizing and assimilating Gypsies. In this, as in all her many other innovations, she was guided more by practical considerations than by humanitarianism: Hungary had been ravaged during the conflicts between Habsburg and Turk and was severely underpopulated. In 1758 she decreed that Gypsies were to settle and be subject to taxes and to compulsory service for the

[20] Translated from the Latin in H. M. G. Grellmann, *Historischer Versuch über die Zigeuner* (2nd edn, Göttingen, 1787), pp. 349–50.

[21] B. J. Gilliat-Smith, 'An eighteenth century Hungarian document', *JGLS*(3), 42 (1963), pp. 50–3.

*Plate 19   Hungarian Gypsy band. From an 18th-century oil painting
by unknown artist. Hungarian National Museum, Budapest.*

lord of the manor; they could not own horses and waggons
and would need special permission to leave their villages. (It
was not within her power, however, to legislate away the
resistance displayed by villagers to letting Gypsies put up
houses; and as there was no provision for reimbursement from
the Imperial Exchequer, local communities did not rush to
offer building materials.) In her next decree (1761) she ordered
the name of Gypsy to be dropped, in favour of *Ujmagyar*
('New Hungarian') or similar inventions (e.g. 'New Settler').
Youths of 16 and above were to be called up for military
service if they were fit, and 12- to 16-year-olds to be taught a
craft. Again there was resistance from the general populace:
army officers were reluctant to accept Gypsies as soldiers;
workers were no more enthusiastic about taking them on as
apprentices. The third decree (1767) removed the voivodes'
special jurisdiction over Gypsies, who were made subject to
the ordinary judicial system; they were also forbidden to set
themselves apart in dress, speech or occupation, and each

village was to carry out a census of Gypsies. Maria Theresa's fourth decree (1773) sought to bring their racial identity to an end. Marriage between Gypsies was forbidden; a Gypsy woman marrying a *gadźo* had to produce proof of industrious household service and familiarity with Catholic tenets; in the reverse situation, the male had to prove ability to support a wife and children. Gypsy children over the age of five were to be taken away and brought up in non-Gypsy families. Maria Theresa's son, Joseph II, vigorously continued her policy of forced integration, which no doubt fitted well with his general intention of pressing Hungary into his great machine of a single unified empire. His regulations of 1783, extended to Transylvania, confirmed the previous restrictions and added several more: no changing of names; houses to be numbered; monthly reports on way of life; nomadism forbidden; settled Gypsies allowed to visit fairs only in cases of special need; smithery banned except when certified as necessary by the authorities; numbers of musicians restricted; begging prohibited; Gypsies not to be settlers in their own right, but to be put into the service of others; Gypsy children, from the age of four upwards, to be distributed at least every two years among the neighbouring districts.[22]

Only a few counties and towns appear to have taken the imperial instructions in full seriousness. They had their greatest impact in the Burgenland, in western Hungary (now part of Austria). Elsewhere they must have exercised general pressure towards settlement (and we shall later see the results of that 100 years on), but as for the detail, the 'New Hungarians' gave ample proof of their incorrigibility, refusing to conform in the extinction of their identity or the break-up of the family. Many of those who did settle left their box-like houses empty and lived in shelters of their own construction; children were prone to fleeing back to their parents; and if Gypsies could not legally marry among themselves, it probably did not grieve them too much to continue to follow their own ceremonies and reproduce the race without benefit of clergy, forgoing the pieces of paper required in the Emperor's legislation; there

---

[22] For more detail of all these measures, and their impact in the Austrian Burgenland, see C. Mayerhofer, *Dorfzigeuner* (Vienna, 1987), pp. 23–33.

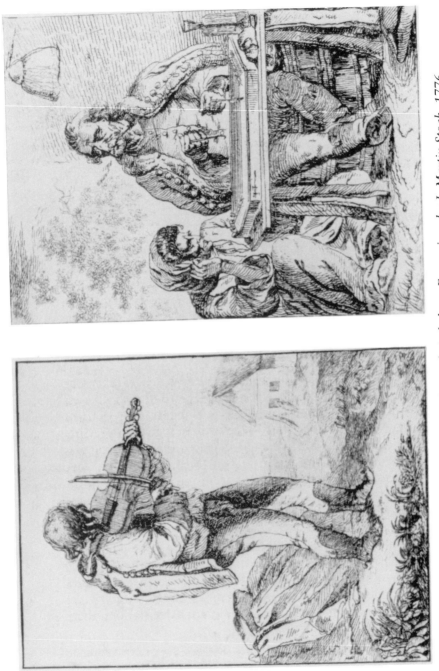

Plate 20 Transylvanian Gypsies, playing violin and cimbalom. Engravings by J. Martin Stock, 1776.

must in any case have been a limited supply of *gadźé* men and women willing to contract legally approved unions with people so overtly despised.

In Prussia, Frederick the Great was not to be outdone in anything by the Habsburgs, prime rivals to the house of Hohenzollern. He experimented with similar ideas and ordered the founding of Gypsy villages. The first settlement, created in 1775, was at Friedrichslohra, near Nordhausen in Saxony; but sequestration succeeded only in making the Gypsies unfit for anything, until in the 1830s most of the adults who remained were taken into the workhouse and the children into care.[23]

If one looks for a single example of a country where both the annihilatory and then the assimilatory approach were pushed to extremes, providing a variety of models for other nations that would reverberate right down to the twentieth century, that country is Spain. In the 1550s the Castilian Cortes, or parliament, can be heard complaining again and again about the plague of godless vagabonds infesting the land. Philip II, son of Charles V and widower of Mary Tudor of England, returned from the Netherlands in 1559 and soon renewed and sharpened the previous anti-Gypsy legislation, extending it also to women going about dressed like Gypsies. The Cortes remained unsatisfied, even after Philip in 1588 placed severe controls on Gypsies' rights to sell goods. Two members produced a report which was scathing in its condemnation of every aspect of Gypsy character and way of life. Their proposal was to separate the men from the women but allow them to marry peasants; and to remove the children and bring them up in orphanages until they reached the age of 10, after which boys would be apprenticed and girls placed in domestic service. The project was shelved, but would re-emerge in the eighteenth century. In the meantime, the Cortes oscillated between banishment and forced sedentarization. Once the Moriscos – the baptized but difficult to assimilate descendants of the Moors – had been taken care of by expulsion in 1609–13, attention focused once again on the Gypsies, much more pernicious in the eyes of many. Passions

[23] Details in R. Pischel, *Beiträge zur Kenntnis der deutschen Zigeuner* (Halle, 1894), esp. pp. 9ff.

were whipped up by a devastating series of published diatribes from priests, legal luminaries and theologians, picking up all the current rumours and accusations (treason, theft, licentious-ness, heresy, stealing of children), and generally adding a few sensational morsels of their own. Their solutions ranged from sending the whole lot to the galleys (Fray Melchor de Huélamo, 1607) to, more commonly, rigorous expulsion. Sancho de Moncada, Professor of Theology at the University of Toledo, in a venomous plea for decisive action addressed to Philip III,[24] joined the latter school but would obviously have preferred something more irreversible; he quoted Scripture as one justification for condemning Gypsies to death, in that Cain had pointed out 'I shall be a vagrant and a wanderer on earth, and anyone who meets me can kill me'. Among the sins he listed was the ability to discourse in a secret language, labelled as *jerigonza* ('jargon'). He no doubt had reservations about the decree which was promulgated in that same year, 1619, for although it ordered all the Gypsies of the kingdom to leave and never return, under pain of death, it also said they might remain if they settled and abandoned the dress, name and language of *Gitanos*, 'in order that, forasmuch as they are not such by nation, this name and manner of life may be for evermore confounded and forgotten'. Moncada had argued against any such half-measure and dismissed the possibility of showing consideration for the women and children: 'there is no law which obliges us to bring up wolf-whelps, to the assured future detriment of the flock'. In 1631 Juan de Quiñones, a judge, added his bit, with all the expertise that came from hanging five Gypsies. He provided stories of sexual immorality and cannibalism. For him, Gypsies were simply the dregs of the population: if their skins were dark, it was because they lived continuously in the open or because they used vegetable dyes; and they reinforced the illusion by dressing differently from others and having a special language.

Faced with all these pressures from Cortes and advisers, Philip IV issued a *premática* (pragmatic sanction) in 1633 which roundly stated that 'those who call themselves *Gitanos*

---

[24] In 'Espulsion de los Gitanos', the second part of the seventh discourse of *Restauracion politica de España* (Madrid, 1619).

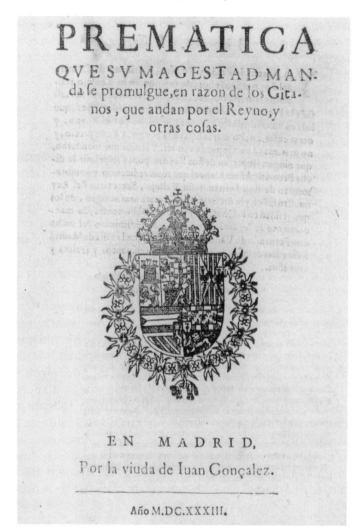

Plate 21   Philip IV of Spain's Pragmatic Sanction of 1633.

are not so by origin or by nature but have adopted this form of
life for such deleterious purposes as are now experienced'.
The country could ill afford further population losses, however, and the aim had now become integration. Gypsies were
forbidden to hold meetings, to dress differently from others or
use their own language, or to live in the *barrios* (districts

in towns) where they had been wont to congregate. Instead, they should mingle with other inhabitants and live like good Christians. The very name of *Gitano* was to disappear; nor were they to be portrayed in dances or other performances. Anyone apprehending a wandering Gypsy could take him as a slave, and reports of marauding Gypsies were to be followed up with organized hunts. This *premática* set the course in the direction of forced assimilation for the next century and a half in Spain. The penalties for contravening it were mainly six years in the galleys in the case of men and flogging and banishment in the case of women. Such were the government's needs in keeping galley crews up to strength in the Mediterranean squadrons that, throughout the seventeenth century, justices were periodically urged to do their bit by speeding up pending cases and by seizing wandering Gypsies; moreover, prisoners were often retained illegally on the galleys long after their sentences had expired.[25]

In 1695 Charles II, the last Spanish monarch of the Habsburg dynasty, placed the coping-stone on the new regime, with a decree[26] stipulating a complete tally by the justices of all Gypsies and their occupations, weapons and livestock. Thereafter, Gypsies might legally live only in places with more than 200 inhabitants, and even then could not dwell together in separate *barrios*; they were prohibited from following any occupation not connected with cultivation and from keeping or using horses or weapons or attending fairs or markets. If they wished to travel anywhere, they needed written permission. Anyone protecting or helping them could be fined 6,000 ducats (if noble) or be sent to the galleys (if plebeian).

When the Bourbons succeeded the Habsburgs in Spain, a

---

[25] Cf. R. Pike, *Penal Servitude in Early Modern Spain* (Madison, WI, 1983), esp. pp. 14–15.

[26] Reproduced in full, along with other basic documentation for the eighteenth century, in M. H. Sanchez Ortega, *Documentación selecta sobre la situación de los gitanos españoles en el siglo XVIII* (Madrid, 1976). A parallel series of eighteenth-century documents is given in M. Torrione, 'Del dialecto caló y sus usuarios: la minoría gitana de España' (doctoral thesis, Perpignan, 1988). An exhaustive analysis of official attitudes in the eighteenth century is A. Gómez Alfaro, 'El Expediente general de Gitanos' (doctoral thesis, Madrid, 1988).

new era of reform set in, one feature of which was a determination to eliminate or reduce antisocial and delinquent groups, or at least to make them more useful to society and the state. The policy applied to Gypsies began to be subject to much tighter central control and to run more uniformly in the entirety of the country – to a degree unknown before in regions like Aragon, Catalonia and Valencia. Under Philip V, founder of the dynasty, a *pragmática* of 1717 reaffirmed his predecessors' constraints and further restricted the legitimate dwelling places for Gypsies to 41 specified towns, scattered all over Spain, with penalties ranging from six to eight years on the galleys for men and 100 lashes plus banishment for women; but his son Ferdinand VI, only ten days after his succession in 1746, was obliged to spread the load by designating another 35 towns (including Seville, Granada, Guadix, Saragossa, Barcelona and Valladolid), the aim being a distribution on the basis of one Gypsy family per 100 inhabitants. Soon, the heaviest urban concentration by far was to be found in Seville.

By now sedentarization had largely been achieved: henceforth only a small proportion of Spanish Gypsies remained nomadic. But their expected submergence had not followed as a matter of course, and the Bishop of Oviedo, governor of the Council of Castile, came up with an answer: all Gypsies should be rounded up throughout Spain in a single, carefully orchestrated night-time raid and be set to forced labour in places of the government's choosing, all their possessions being sold. The women could spin, young boys work in factories, and men and older boys be assigned to the nation's mines and shipyards. Surviving contemporary documents make no bones about talking of the *extinction* of the Gypsies, considered as a race to be incorrigible. Ferdinand VI accepted the bishop's advice, and the raid was carried out at the end of June 1749, with military assistance. According to calculations made at the time, between 9,000 and 12,000 Gypsies were marched off in it. In deciding where to employ them, the government's options had recently altered. The galleys had been abolished in 1748, improvements in naval technology having made them redundant, and the main alternative now lay in transforming the navy yards and arsenals into penal establishments, where

the chained prisoners could perform the heavy labour of construction and maintenance. In addition, the five *presidios*
(garrisons) in North Africa were perennially short of cheap
labour for the building and repair of fortifications, and they
were also now receiving a share of convicts. So too, on a
smaller scale, were the mercury mines at Almadén, as indeed
they had been for some two centuries past, owing to periodic
diversion of prisoners destined for the galleys; but Gypsies
were proportionately in fewer numbers there than on the
galleys. In Almadén, the work was back-breaking and the
threat to health and life from mercury poisoning and other
hazards extremely high; and Gypsies had a high mortality rate
there.

Most of the males seized in the 1749 raid ended up in
naval arsenals: the government was inaugurating a programme of expansion calling for large numbers of unskilled
labourers. Work was beginning on the arsenals at El Ferrol
and Cartagena, while the facilities at La Carraca (Cádiz) were
being extended. Some of the Gypsies would languish there for
16 years, if they survived exhaustion and disease. For others
the internment was of shorter duration. The directors of the
arsenals were soon overwhelmed by the sheer numbers of
workers with low productivity: almost 1,200 had been consigned to La Carraca alone, where huge barracks housed
armies of men who slept without covering on wooden bunks
with their shackles chained to the walls. Moreover, many
of the interned Gypsies were able to prove, with supporting testimony, their irreproachable behaviour in the past.
Ferdinand VI was obliged to issue a further decree in 1749,
recognizing that there might in fact be some good Gypsies,
legally married, bringing up their children properly, and
working diligently; it was grudgingly conceded that these
could be allowed to return to their former homes if, on strict
enquiry, their claims could be substantiated. The government
had seriously misjudged the situation and Ferdinand continued
to retreat. In the end, his half-brother and successor, Charles
III, one of the few able men to sit on the throne of the Catholic
Kings, decided in 1763 that all Gypsies still held captive as a
result of the raid should be set free. This change of direction
met with a good deal of opposition from the king's advisers

and was not implemented until 1765. There followed intense debate, at the end of which two men, Pedro Valiente and Pedro Rodríguez, Count of Campomanes, were given the task of drawing up a report as a basis for future legislation. This crucial document of 1772 pointed out that, while previous laws had striven towards assimilation, national sentiment had worked in the opposite direction, treating the Gypsy as a pariah and allowing him a very restricted field of activity. One of the recommendations was to prohibit the use of the word *Gitano* or even the euphemism 'New Castilian' which had been invented in the seventeenth century; another was to open up all trades to Gypsies. Campomanes and Valiente stressed the role of education and argued that experience had shown only too clearly that legislation which was exclusively penal had little effect on Gypsies, who had to be left at liberty to earn their living peacefully.[27]

In the event, their proposals had a mixed reception from Charles III, and some – notably those on education – were given a much more authoritarian slant. In comparison with the previous three centuries of legislation imbued with a spirit of blood and persecution, the pragmatic sanction which was issued in September 1783 – the same year as Joseph II's regulations relating to Hungary and Transylvania – represented progress of a kind, even if motivated by the utilitarianism common to the European Enlightenment – in this case, a desire to find the most efficient means of transforming what was seen as a horde of idlers into more obviously serviceable citizens. But its aim, backed up by severe penalties, was to stamp out any deviation and to suppress the very name of Gypsy (or New Castilian). Those who were prepared to comply were to be allowed to work at any trade, with certain exceptions, and in any place other than Madrid and the royal residences. The excluded livelihoods were shearing and clipping animals, trading at markets and fairs, and innkeeping in sparsely populated places. (These were all important occupations for Gypsies. Innkeeping, for example, was widespread among

---

[27] The Campomanes–Valiente report is discussed in B. Leblon, *Les Gitans d'Espagne* (Paris, 1985), pp. 67–84, and in Gómez Alfaro, 'El Expediente general', pp. 1085–1119.

Plate 22 Gypsy mule clippers in Spain. Lithograph by Villain.
Bibliothèque Nationale, Paris.

them – and an English traveller, Richard Twiss, had paid
tribute ten years before to the honesty of these innkeepers.)[28]
Those who settled but did not devote themselves to some
worthy employment were to be punished in accordance with
the general laws against vagrants; those who settled and then
committed some crime were to be subject to the same procedures and penalties as anyone else. In so far as there were
special sanctions, they were reserved for those who reverted to
a wandering life with no regular employment: such people
would have their children of 16 or below taken from them and
placed in hospices or houses of instruction, and they themselves would be entered in a special register; anyone on the
register who offended a second time was to be executed, solely
for having returned to his former life.

In practice, the pragmatic sanction was applied effectively –
if with some local variation – only for so long as the central

[28] *Travels through Spain and Portugal in 1772 and 1773* (London, 1775),
pp. 179–80.

pressure was maintained, and that meant during the remaining five years of Charles III's reign, for on his demise the revolutionary situation in France posed many more demanding problems of government;[29] but, by making more realistic the settlement measures of preceding decrees, it ensured that Charles's policy would have a lasting impact. When George Borrow entered Spain at Badajoz in 1836, he heard for the first time, in the broken speech which *caló* now constituted (a hybrid of Romani lexicon and Castilian phonology, morphology and syntax), a proverb which said: *el Crallis ha nicobado la liri de los Calés* ('the king has taken away the law of the Gypsies'). The proverb lamented the destruction of the previous pattern of Gypsy life, and it was to Charles III that it referred.

Transportation

By now, we have observed legislation in a wide stretch of Europe, containing well over half of its population. It has been important to dwell on these measures, because of their impact on the Gypsy way of life, even though, on their own, they give as unbalanced a picture as would a history of England based on the Newgate Calendar. The remaining countries outside the Ottoman empire – such as Portugal, Italy, Switzerland, the southern Netherlands, Denmark, Sweden and Russia – followed much the same path: all attempted banishment or forced settlement in varying degrees. Portugal does, however, merit some special mention for having been the first to use transportation to its overseas colonies as a novel method of expulsion.[30] Colonies needed manpower (the death-rate was high) and colonists needed women. The earliest transportations of Gypsies to the Portuguese African colonies took place in the time of John III, whose decree of 1538 (p. 101)[31]

---

[29] Gómez Alfaro, 'El Expediente general', pp. 1210–1644, examines in detail the implementation of the 1783 pragmatic sanction.

[30] Cf. O. Nunes, *O Povo Cigano* (Oporto, 1981), pp. 74–83.

[31] The texts of this and subsequent measures (up to 1848) are in F. A. Coelho, *Os Ciganos de Portugal* (Lisbon, 1892), pp. 230–66.

adopted this solution to the problem of what to do with those born in Portugal who could not simply be expelled. In 1574 there is the first record of a Portuguese Gypsy being sent, with his wife and children, to Brazil, in commutation of a sentence to the galleys for not having complied with a general expulsion order; he was also the first Gypsy recorded with a Portuguese style of name, Johão de Torres. Then, from 1647, it became the practice to send Gypsy women to Africa (while men went to the galleys). Group deportations to Brazil were first provided for in 1686, at a time when expulsions from Spain were said to be causing a great influx of Gypsies into Portugal: Portuguese-born *Ciganos* who refused to settle were now to be dispatched to the Brazilian province of Maranhão instead of Africa. In 1718 a special round-up of Gypsies was ordered so that they might be distributed to the colonies in India and Africa. By 1760 the Gypsy population in Brazil was large enough for the Governor-General to be complaining vigorously about their disruptive ways, so that King Joseph felt obliged to legislate against them there too.

The use of colonies as dumping-grounds for undesirables being a widespread practice, the Portuguese example was soon followed by other governments, though less whole-heartedly. From the mid-seventeenth century onwards, the Spanish rulers had no scruples about getting rid of Gypsies and other vagabonds by sending them to the army or *presidios* in North Africa, ranging from Ceuta in the west to Oran in the east, but their reservations in regard to America proved insurmountable.[32] Indeed, in 1570 Philip II forbade Gypsies to enter the American colonies and in 1581, reacting to reports that some had secretly gone out there and were cheating the Indians (which, if true, must have been a pinprick as compared with the ruthless exploitation that was the general rule), he ordered his colonial officials to seek them out and ship them back to Spain, where they would be easier to keep under surveillance. In the case of Upper Peru (now Bolivia), the answer came that none had in fact been observed.[33] And when

---

[32] Cf. A. Gómez Alfaro, 'La polémica sobre la deportación de los Gitanos a las colonias de América', *Cuadernos Hispanoamericanos* (Madrid, 1982), no. 386, pp. 319–21, and 'El Expediente general', pp. 1071–84.

[33] 'Gipsies in America, 1581', *JGLS*(2), 6 (1912–13), p. 61.

the proposals in the 1772 report by Campomanes and Valiente were being considered by Charles III and his Council, the American possessions seemed too much at risk from expansionist neighbours to make it safe to saddle them with untrustworthy colonists.

France does not appear to have practised systematic transportation of Gypsies; none the less a good many did go to French colonies in America, whether by commutation of galley service (as was the case with 32 in 1686–9) or by direct deportation to Martinique or Louisiana. Under the Consulate, a plan to transport to Louisiana several hundred Gypsies who had been rounded up as undesirables in the Basque country was averted only by the renewal of war with Britain and the sale of Louisiana to the United States in 1803. (Instead, Bonaparte decreed that they were to be dispersed within France and employed on various public works or in the army or, in the case of women and young children and the older men, locked up in paupers' homes.)

In England, the transportation of vagabonds goes back to Elizabeth's reign, although only later did it come into full spate. The statutory authority was the Vagrancy Act of 1597 (p. 137) which provided that incorrigible or dangerous rogues should be banished overseas. Very early in the reign of James I (1603) an Order in Council sought to transform the general concept of deportation into the narrower one of transportation, by designating approved destinations – Newfoundland, the East and West Indies, France, Germany, Spain and the Low Countries. How the European states in this list reacted on receipt of such exiles is not known; in practice most, if not all, were sent to the American colonies. The whole business was of dubious legality, since many who went were young and poor rather than hardened rogues.[34] For most, forced labour in the colonies was harsher than in England, because with manpower in short supply – until such time as the traffic in black cargoes turned convict workforces into an economic irrelevance – the masters who bought their services from the shippers reduced them to virtual slavery.

In Scotland, idle vagabonds became subject to the threat of

[34] Cf. A. L. Beier, *Masterless Men* (London, 1985), pp. 162–4.

transportation 'into the West Indies or elsewhere' in 1655 by a
Government ordinance during Cromwell's Protectorate, after
the Generals of the military occupation had been appalled by
the 'multitudes of Vagabonds, masterful Beggars, [and] strong
and idle persons' wandering over the country. Within ten years
such possibilities for deportation were being exploited by
ordinary citizens. In November 1665, George Hutcheson, an
Edinburgh merchant, obtained retrospective cover from the
Privy Council for having speculatively rounded up a number of
vagabonds with the intention of sending them to the West
Indies, 'out of a desire', he claimed righteously, 'as well to
promote the Scottish and English plantations in Jamaica
and Barbados for the honour of their country, as to free
the kingdom of the burden of many strong and idle beggars,
Egyptians, common and notorious whores and thieves and
other dissolute and loose persons banished or stigmatized for
gross crimes'. Nothing was said of the profit which he and his
partners stood to gain. Several other similar grants were made
by the Privy Council in subsequent years.[35] In 1715, eight
Border Gypsies – two men and six women – of the names of
Faa, Stirling, Yorstoun, Finnick (Fenwick), Lindsay, Ross and
Robertson were despatched by the Glasgow magistrates to
the Virginia plantations 'for being habite and repute gipsies,
sorners, &c', in fulfilment of the sentence to transportation
which Jedburgh Circuit Court had pronounced on them even
though the evidence on the other charge, of arson, had been
very shaky. One of these, Patrick Faa, also sentenced to
scourging and the pillory and the loss of both ears, was the
husband of Jean Gordon, the formidable woman who became
the prototype of Meg Merrilies.[36]

Early eighteenth-century legislation of Irish parliaments
provided for 'loose and idle vagrants' to be pressed into the
Royal Navy or the plantations in America for up to seven
years, and Irish people had already been sent to the English

---

[35] Cf. F. H. Groome, 'Transportation of Gypsies from Scotland to
America', *JGLS*(1), 2 (1890–1), pp. 60–2, and E. O. Winstedt, 'Early
British Gypsies', *JGLS*(2), 7 (1913–14), pp. 5–37, esp. p. 29.

[36] Cf. G. Douglas, *Diversions of a Country Gentleman* (London, 1902),
pp. 255–67, and Gordon, *Hearts upon the Highway*, pp. 64–9.

plantations under previous vagrancy laws. It is unlikely, however, that Gypsies featured in such consignments: they seem at that time to have been to more than very occasional visitors in Ireland, which had, in the Tinkers, its own indigenous class of itinerants long before Gypsies arrived in the British Isles.

Within the Ottoman empire

Thanks to local archives, central ordinances and police regulations, it is possible, from the fifteenth century on, to construct a history, however one-sided, of the Gypsies within Christendom. In that part of Europe which came under Ottoman rule, their history remained more shadowy. Yet, if their subsequent distribution is anything to go by, the majority of Europe's Gypsy inhabitants (in contrast to little more than a tenth of the continent's total population) were living under the dominion of the Turks at the time when the boundary of the Ottoman empire was at its greatest extent, during the seventeenth century. On similar assumptions, even after the tide of Turkish power began its continuing ebb and the Habsburgs had recovered Hungary and Transylvania and then occupied the Banat of Temesvár and part of Serbia, close on half the Gypsies in Europe remained under Ottoman suzerainty until well into the nineteenth century. (Such Turkish statistics as exist indicate a smaller population, but these concentrated on settled Gypsies and did not condescend to include females.)

One finds within this empire no counterpart to the systematically repressive legislation which Gypsies faced in the rest of Europe. Usually the Ottomans respected the customs and institutions of subject communities, which were ruled with the aid of their own authorities. Some territories enjoyed a large measure of self-government, their dependence being expressed in their annual payment of tribute and the military support which they gave to Turkish expeditions. Among the vassal states, Transylvania, governed by its own aristocracy, was most successful in preserving independence; the Danubian principalities of Wallachia and Moldavia were more vulnerable and provided the Ottoman generals with substantial auxiliary forces and large contributions to the

Plate 23 'Gypsies besieging a house for alms near the village of Gigesti in Wallachia'. Watercolour by Luigi Mayer, c.1794.

Turkish treasury, but they too were allowed a significant degree of self-rule, even though their princes might often be puppets of the sultan or under the protection of neighbouring states. There, the Gypsies' life of slavery (cf. pp. 57–9) went on unreprieved; such new decrees as were issued, like those emanating under Matei Basarab in Wallachia and Vasile Lupu (Basil the Wolf) in Moldavia in the mid-seventeenth century, tended to reinforce rather than attenuate the existing state of affairs, until some modest, and often short-lived, reforms began to be introduced in the latter part of the eighteenth century (forbidding, for example, the disposal of children separately from their parents). Indeed, when a traffic sprang up in the sixteenth century of kidnapping Wallachian Gypsies and selling them off elsewhere, the Grand Vizier addressed a firman (imperial decree) to the officials along the banks of the Danube ordering them to stamp it out.[37]

Among the areas under direct administration, the Ottoman authorities remained chiefly concerned with taxation and the maintenance of law and order, and the governors interfered relatively little with local affairs so long as the levies (in cash, kind and labour) were paid and no threat was posed to the Turkish masters. If a firman did single out Gypsies for special attention, it was usually in the field of administration, public order or taxation. Thus, Süleyman the Magnificent, in a decree of 1530, sought to regulate Gypsy prostitution in the cities of Constantinople, Adrianople, Sofia and Plovdiv; his son, Selim II, ordained in 1574[38] that the Gypsies working in the mines of Bosnia were to elect a chief for each group of 50; while another firman issued in the time of Sultan Ahmed I laid down, for 1604–5, the taxes and fines to be collected from Gypsies (*Kibtian*, i.e. Egyptians) in the western Balkans (more precisely, in what is now southern Albania and north-west Greece). Both the sedentary Gypsies, who had been registered, and the nomad tent-dwellers, who were unregistered, were to pay poll tax at the rate of 180 aspers for each Muslim and 250

---

[37] M. Gaster, 'Rumanian Gypsies in 1560', *JGLS*(3), 12 (1933), p. 61.

[38] Text in T. P. Vukanović, 'Le firman du sultan Sélim II relatif aux Tsiganes, ouvriers dans les mines de Bosnie (1574)', *Études Tsiganes* (1969), no. 3, pp. 8–10.

for each Christian, with appropriate fines for any default. (One asper was then roughly equal to an English halfpenny.) This firman reads as though an appreciable number of nomads were still Christian. Such tribute was normally confined to non-Muslims, but the Muslim Gypsies were obliged to pay because they were considered as schismatics who strayed from the precepts of the law on many points connected with rite and morals. Some of the sedentaries are described as being workers in iron, charcoal-burners and watchmen. Since the firman refers to *ispence* (slave tax), one can infer that there were slaves among these Gypsy subjects; but the majority were free, with most of the rights and obligations of non-Turkish citizens of the Ottoman empire.[39]

In the latter part of the seventeenth century, however, the fiscal screws were tightened. According to Evliya Çelebi,[40] Sultan Mehmed IV even exacted tax from dead Gypsies, until live ones could be found to replace them. Then the levels of taxation were increased sharply, particularly for Muslims: in 1684 a firman addressed to the judges of Thessaloníki, Berrhoia and Genitsa fixed the rates of poll tax and pork tax on Gypsies at 650 aspers for each Muslim and 720 for each Christian. The various imposts were to be collected by the one person 'since the Gypsy race lives separately and is numerically limited, but is free in every respect', and the state officials were enjoined not to interfere in their affairs.[41] Similar rates of taxation, expressed in piastres, were decreed in 1695. At this time there were said to be 45,000 Gypsies altogether in the empire, only 10,000 of whom were Muslims, but those figures also covered Syria, Mesopotamia and Asia Minor. (Ottoman statistics were never very reliable. Two seventeenth-century contemporaries, Sir Paul Rycaut and Evliya Çelebi, suggest differing totals of 15,630 and 11,280 for male Gypsies

[39] Cf. M. Hasluck, 'Firman of A. H. 1013–14 (A. D.1604–5) regarding Gypsies in the Western Balkans', *JGLS*(3), 27 (1948), pp. 1–12.

[40] Evliya Çelebi had little regard for Gypsies, but collected a substantial Romani glossary from the large Gypsy community settled in Komotiní in western Thrace: see V. A. Friedman and R. Dankoff, 'The earliest known text in Balkan (Rumelian) Romani', *JGLS*(5), 1 (1991), pp. 1–20.

[41] G. C. Soulis, 'A note on the taxation of the Balkan Gypsies in the seventeenth century', *JGLS*(3), 38 (1959), pp. 154–6.

of military age on the official register of Rumelia, the Turkish possessions in the Balkans.)[42] Another manifestation of the apparent upsurge of anti-Gypsy feeling can be observed in 1696, when Sultan Mustafa II, in the midst of preparations for a campaign in Hungary, caused police regulations to be issued, aimed at disciplining Gypsies away from disorderly and immoral lives: indeed, the historian Mohammed Ghirai dismissed the women (who certainly fell far short of rigid Mahometan notions of female decorum in dress and demeanour) as prostitutes and the men as pimps.[43]

On the whole, however, they were left pretty much unmolested by western European standards, and the social upheaval and eventual paralysis of administration flowing from the Ottoman occupation no doubt held some compensations for them, and they were unlikely to be concerned about the stunting of cultural and political development under Turkish rule. Despite sporadic attempts (e.g. by the heavy-handed Murad IV in regard to Gypsies in Serbia in the 1630s)[44] to break them of their wandering habits, those who were free must have had considerable liberty of movement: as citizens of the one state, the Balkan people could move about within the empire, and during the four centuries of Ottoman domination there was much internal migration. Gypsy livelihoods did not suffer too much from the constant military forays. The musicians among them were still valued. When the Pasha of Buda organized a festive procession on the occasion of a peace mission of western leaders to his camp in 1584, it was led by three Gypsies dressed in Turkish style, one playing a lute and the others rebecks, to the accompaniment of which they sang songs extolling the Ottoman sultans (see plate 24).[45] And those Gypsies who had specialized in making weapons and ammunition also found plenty of custom among their new

---

[42] W. R. Halliday, *Folklore Studies* (London, 1924), p. 17.

[43] J. G. von Hammer-Purgstall, *Geschichte des osmanischen Reiches* (Budapest, 1827–35), vol. 6, pp. 608–9 and 621.

[44] F. J. Blunt, *The People of Turkey* (London, 1878), vol, 1. pp. 160–1.

[45] F. W. Brepohl, 'Die Zigeuner als Musiker in den türkischen Eroberungskriegen des XVI. Jahrhunderts', *JGLS*(2), 4 (1910–11), pp. 241–4.

*Plate 24   Turkish procession led by Gypsy musicians. Woodcut in
Lewenklaw's* Neuwe Chronika türkischer Nation, *1590.*

lords; they could accompany soldiers into war as weapon-
repairers and musicians. Neither they nor their kinsmen
following less martial pursuits derived any obvious benefit
from the Austrian recovery of territory from the Turks.

Survival of the species

Repressive measures, however inefficiently applied, did in the
end produce enormous changes in the life of the Gypsies in
Europe. To survive, they had to adapt; they also had to make
the most of the loopholes in a system which expressly sought,
by denying them food and shelter, to make honest living
impossible. Some found a degree of security in inaccessible
waste-lands and forests. Some exploited differences in jurisdiction and the spasmodic nature of the authorities' activity,
by making a home in frontier regions. Thus we have found
concentrations near the frontiers between France and Spain,

between German states, and between Lorraine and the Empire; in the Scottish Borders; and in the easternmost parts of the Dutch Republic. Within national boundaries, there were often local demarcations which could be similarly turned to advantage. Many broke up into small groups when it was necessary to avoid attention; conversely, others gathered into larger bands to facilitate self-protection, perhaps ganging up with *gadžé* as they did so, and sometimes resorting to violence. Certain Gypsy brigands gained notoriety in eighteenth-century Germany, large tracts of which were overrun with robber companies of mixed and varying origins. Some of these had a strong Gypsy element: numbering perhaps 50 or 100, armed and defiant, they stole for their sustenance and skirmished with the soldier-police sent to confine them. One of the more noted of these bands, in Hesse-Darmstadt, was led by Johannes la Fortun, commonly known as Hemperla. When at last he was rounded up in 1726 and imprisoned at Giessen along with a number of other Gypsies, all the necessary confessions were extracted by prolonged torture with rack, thumbscrews and Spanish boot (a leg-vice) and sentence was passed. Hemperla and three others were broken on the wheel and decapitated, nine were hanged and thirteen (mostly women) beheaded. A contemporary artist captured the scene of the mass execution and the vast crowds of spectators it attracted (see plate 25).[46] Perhaps the most famous of the Gypsy brigands in Germany was Jakob Reinhardt, known as Hannikel, who was a grandson of one of the men executed at Giessen.[47] Hannikel was hanged in 1787 along with three other Gypsies. There was nothing particularly romantic about him or the murders he was involved in, and it is difficult to believe that, as some have suggested, his career influenced Schiller in the composition of his first drama, *Die Räuber*

[46] There are several accounts of the case, e.g. Simson, *History of the Gypsies*, pp. 79–86; E. M. Hall, 'Gentile cruelty to Gypsies', *JGLS(3)*, 11 (1932), pp. 49–56. All go back to J. B. Weissenbruch, *Ausführliche Relation von der famosen Zigeuner- Diebs- Mord- und Rauber-Bande, welche zu Giessen justificirt worden* (Frankfurt and Leipzig, 1727).

[47] Cf. E. O. Winstedt, 'Hannikel', *JGLS(3)*, 16 (1937), pp. 154–73, and H. Arnold, 'Die Räuberbande des Hannikels', *Pfälzer Heimat*, 8 (1957), pp. 101–3.

Plate 25   *Execution of Gypsies at Giessen (Hesse), 1726. From J. B. Weissenbruch's Ausführliche Relation, 1727.*

('The Robbers', 1781), with its Rousseauistic rejection of a corrupt and corrupting society. Hannikel ranged widely and conducted operations in the Vosges, Lorraine, the Black Forest, Swabia and Switzerland, but his activities centred in the region of Germany bordering on north-eastern Lorraine. It was mountainous and well wooded; but another major reason for that corner being so attractive was the fact that the Landgrave of Hesse-Darmstadt, Ludwig IX, had selected Pirmasens, at its heart, as his residence. Ludwig had a passion for things military, and at Pirmasens he formed a little army into which he recruited a good many Gypsies, allowing their dependants to stay near them. Hannikel's father was one of his drummers. The Landgrave disregarded the prescriptions of the imperial and *Reichskreis* ordinances, and during almost half a century the Gypsy population grew around Pirmasens. They began to move out again in 1790, when a new Landgrave, Ludwig X, showed himself minded to apply the ordinances and even to use the military at Pirmasens to enforce them. The persecution-free oasis turned out to be a mirage, and many of the Gypsies faded away.

Herder, the theoretician of German literature's *Sturm und Drang* and mentor of the young Goethe, had some knowledge of Pirmasens and expressed the view in his *Ideen zur Philosophie der Geschichte der Menschheit* ('Ideas on the Philosophy of the History of Mankind', 1784–91) that this 'abject Indian caste' was useful only for military training, 'which alone can discipline one and all with the greatest rapidity'. Frederick William II of Prussia was of the same opinion and in 1790 ordered that Gypsies should be turned into soldiers. The army had in fact long been, in many parts of Europe, a further escape route which Gypsies might take in the hope of winning tolerance, or opening prison gates, or perhaps gaining preferential treatment. Many were accepted as, or pressed into becoming, soldiers, whether as musicians or as fighting men. Sometimes, as in the French Wars of Religion in the late sixteenth century or in the Thirty Years War, entire bands joined up with campaigning troops, either on their own account or as more regular forces. The editor of the *Mercure françois* observed a number of such soldiers during the Wars of Religion and commented favourably on their military qualities, however unorthodox their life-style ('living like Arabs, taking their own cattle with them').[48] In times of peace they were less popular, as (contrary to Herder's hopes) they did not take kindly to regimental discipline. At one time or another, however, Gypsy soldiers are found serving under the colours of practically every country of Europe, often followed by their wives and children; in Sweden, indeed, during a long period it was rare for a Gypsy not to have seen service as a soldier.

A more devious survival technique, learned early on, was to outflank civil documentary controls. They had been masters at conjuring up safe-conducts. Some became just as adept at procuring false passports needed to meet vagrancy laws which allowed mobility only under licence. The English legislation required a passport of a wide range of itinerants. When such papers were granted, they requested that the holder be permitted to pass unmolested and be given lodgings and relief on his way; normally a fixed term was set on travelling and the papers had to be endorsed by magistrates along the route. Counterfeit passports, however, were cheap and readily available and grew so common that the system became a nonsense.[49] The miscreant forger might be a priest, clerk, scrivener, school-teacher or student. The eight Gypsies who were hanged at Aylesbury in 1577 (p. 133) had been travelling the country with the assistance of counterfeit licences forged by a Cheshire schoolmaster.[50]

The range of travel of Gypsies was nevertheless becoming more restricted, and many now confined themselves to a particular region. In France, for instance, between 1607 and 1637 Captain David de La Grave is reported a score of times at 12 different places in lower Provence, but not elsewhere. It is the same with Pierre de La Grave. (Gypsy surnames in France were by then predominantly French, preferably with an air of nobility.) Captain Jean de La Grave, on the other hand, was venturing some way northwards into the Dauphiné as well as

---

[48] *La Continuation du Mercure François* (1610–12), fol. 317.
[49] Cf. Beier, *Masterless Men*, pp. 142–4.
[50] Cf. F. G. Blair, 'Forged passports of British Gypsies in the sixteenth century', *JGLS*(3), 29 (1950), pp. 131–7.

Provence; and we find people with the same surname, and very probably of the same family, in various other parts of France.[51] Just how many became completely sedentary, and how many of those that did so were then submerged into the general populace, there is no means of knowing. In some countries, however, it is clear that the Gypsy population was settling in large numbers. At the same time its size can also be seen to be growing, even if systematic figures are available only for Hungary and Spain. The censuses which were taken in 1780–3 during the reign of Emperor Joseph II bear witness to the magnitude of the Gypsy population in Hungary (including Croatia and Slovenia but not Transylvania): the tally varied between 30,241 and 43,609, despite the fact that married women had not been included. The main recorded livelihoods were smithery and other manual work; behind these came music.[52] In 1785 some 12,000 Gypsies were identified in Spain, rather more than two-thirds of them being in Andalusia, the poorest region, where Seville, for example, had 600, Jerez 386, Cádiz 332, Málaga 321 and Granada 255.[53] This was at a time when the total population of Spain stood at around 10 million, a quarter of what it is today. It can also be deduced from the censuses instigated by Charles III that, long before his pragmatic sanction of 1783, much of the work of sedentarization had already been accomplished by earlier decrees, in that over 88 per cent of the Gypsies in Spain, Catalonia excluded, were already sedentary. In Catalonia progress was much slower because that region, autonomous until 1716, had contented itself with a policy of expulsion.

Sedentarization did not necessarily mean assimilation, as Spain also proved. But, all over Europe, even Gypsies who remained nomadic were acquiring national characteristics under the social influences of the countries in which their main field of activity lay. In Scotland, for example, the process started fairly early and, by the end of the eighteenth century,

[51] Cf. Vaux de Foletier, *Les Tsiganes dans l'ancienne France*, pp. 69–70.

[52] Cf. J. H. Schwicker, *Die Zigeuner in Ungarn und Siebenbürgen* (Vienna, 1883), pp. 62–70.

[53] Cf. A. Gómez Alfaro, 'Anotaciones a los censos gitanos en Andalucía', *Actas del I Congreso de Historia de Andalucía* (Córdoba, 1978), vol. 1, pp. 239–56.

many Gypsies there had settled to the extent of choosing one locality as a headquarters, where they often established good relations with the local people, and it was not unknown for their children to attend school. They soon became more mixed with the general population and their bands more broken up than Gypsies in a number of other countries. Perhaps it was the 1609 Act which led many of them to assume ordinary forenames and surnames common at that time in Scotland, adopting for preference those of influential families, although two important Scottish Gypsy names – Faa and Baillie – go back further than that. Some became figures of standing in their community. Billy Marshall, a famous chief of the Galloway Gypsies, achieved legendary status.[54] He is said to have been born in 1671, in which case he must have lived to 120, for it is certain that his death took place in 1792. He left a prodigious number of descendants, having been married 17 times. In the course of his long life he was a private in King William's army at the battle of the Boyne and served in a number of Continental campaigns, though inclined to desert when it suited him. In 1723 he appears as a leader of the Levellers in Galloway, concerting operations in the widespread popular revolt against the landed proprietors who were dispossessing tenant farmers and enclosing grazing lands (including those traditionally open to their employees' animals) in order to improve the raising of stock; by the end of the year there were few dykes left standing in Galloway.

The uniformly hostile tone of the legislative texts can too easily disguise the extent to which it proved possible in practice for Gypsies to achieve a tolerable footing with local interests. In Spain, the nationwide round-up in 1749 had evoked testimony of this from some of the Gypsies' home villages. More unusual was the relationship established with the people of Villarejo de Fuentes, a little town 60 miles to the south-east of Madrid: on the evidence of events at a wedding held there in November 1781, the local priest as well as the town officials had been won over, to the point of their joining in uninhibitedly in tumultuous celebrations. After a

---

[54] The fullest account of his exploits is in A. M'Cormick, *The Tinkler-Gypsies* (Dumfries, 1907), esp. chs 1, 2 and 12.

horseback procession to the church, the Gypsy women, in all their finery, danced in front of the priest before thronging inside, throwing sweetmeats around them, to the sound of a guitar. According to the sour report of an observer who denounced the entire affair,[55] the bride was escorted to the church hand-in-hand with one of the town officials, brother of the priest, and there was little sign of devotion during the nuptial mass. The procession away from the church was loudly cheered by the crowd. The formal inquiry which followed the denunciation confirmed its essential details, and the priest was severely reprimanded by his bishop.

Scant glimmerings of light

The official attitude of the ecclesiastical authorities – whether Orthodox, Catholic or Protestant – certainly did not encourage any laxity towards Gypsies, widely held to be irreligious. Not until the nineteenth century would there be much sign of concern for the state of Gypsy souls. In Italy, time and again, diocesan and provincial synods showed suspicion and hostility matching the tone of the laws of the Italian states (including the Papal States), and with few exceptions they revealed little inclination to ease Gypsies' access to sacraments. Much the same held good elsewhere, except in the context of general measures for stamping out the Gypsy way of life. Forced conversion or compulsory religious instruction featured prominently in the grand designs of monarchs such as Emperor Joseph II, and a number of German states sought to remove children from their parents, so as to have them baptized and brought up in sound Christian families; but missionary work was sparse and there was little disinterested attempt to bring Gypsies into the body of the church. Sometimes this was literally true: in the Basque country in France, churches often denied entry to *Cascarots,* as Gypsies were known there, and segregated them into a lean-to from which they might follow the service. That did not mean that lapses were to be tolerated. In Portugal the bishops, in 1635, excommunicated Gypsies

---

[55] Sanchez Ortega, *Documentación*, pp. 232–4.

who did not go to confession during Lent; while Spanish theologians were especially strong on the need for severity. Yet, curiously enough, the Inquisition treated Gypsies relatively mildly, no doubt because such cases as came before the Holy Office – and they were infrequent – turned out to smack less of heresy or witchcraft than of banal trickery and exploitation of public credulity, often involving the bait of buried treasure, or secrets to be revealed by divination, or magic cures or charms, or the casting of spells. At most, the punishment inflicted appears to have been a severe flogging.[56] It is also noticeable that the Gypsies who did attract the inquisitors' attention were not uninstructed in the matter of religion and had generally been baptized and confirmed and married in church. Similarly, when an attempt was made in Lorraine in 1788 to investigate Gypsies' religious practices, they were found not to have any special religion of their own but to seek the Catholic sacraments of baptism, matrimony and extreme unction; if, however, they could not find a priest who would perform a marriage ceremony, the union was effected in front of their chiefs.[57]

Protestant churches were generally no more favourably inclined towards Gypsies and saw as little contradiction in both keeping them at a distance and condemning them as irreligious. Martin Luther, in his preface to a 1528 edition of the *Liber vagatorum,* had warned against the *büeberey* (knavish tricks) of such vagrants and given the seal of his approbation to repression. The Dutch Calvinist theologian Voetius argued against baptizing Gypsies' children[58] (a question much debated in provincial synods in the Netherlands of his day), since he considered the parents incapable of ensuring a Christian upbringing. That issue had been settled in Sweden almost a century before with the Archbishop of Stockholm's prohibition on baptism and burial (p. 123). There were, however, Swedish pastors who chose to disobey, and one who did so in 1573 was told by the Archbishop that he was casting

---

[56] Cf. Leblon, *Gitans d'Espagne*, pp. 163–228.

[57] Vaux de Foletier, *Les Tsiganes dans l'ancienne France*, pp. 213–14.

[58] G. Voetius, *Selectarum disputationum theologicarum* (Utrecht, 1655), vol. 2, pp. 652–9.

pearls before swine. Some 20 years later, the diocesan synod at
Linköping confirmed the ban on any contact with *tattare,* and
found it necessary to reprimand a priest who allowed one of
them to take communion on Easter day.[59] Not until 1686
were priests in Sweden given instructions to christen Gypsy
children if the parents so desired.

In secular fields the pace of progress towards more informed
knowledge of Gypsies was only slightly less laggard. There
were some hints of modest advance on the linguistic front in
the latter part of the sixteenth centry – first when a Dutch
magistrate, Johan van Ewsum, was interested enough to gather
together a collection of Romani words and phrases in the
1560s.[60] It remained unpublished until 1900, however; by
then it had become possible to detect in it traces of the dialectal break-up of Romani in the occasional borrowings from
German and the presence of the main phonetic features that
characterize the German dialects of the language as spoken
by the Sinti. More immediately important was the publication
in 1597 by another Dutchman, Bonaventura Vulcanius, of
71 Romani words with Latin equivalents, contributed by
Joseph Scaliger, a fellow professor at Leiden, and the most
erudite scholar of his time.[61] Probably gathered in the south
of France, this was only the second list ever to have been
printed. As in the case of his English predecessor, Andrew
Borde (p. 10), Scaliger appears to have conducted his research
in some tavern, to judge by the prominence of expressions
connected with drinking. Whether or not under the influence
of such an environment, occasional muddles occurred, as when
he sought to record the Romani for 'you drink'. He must
have been conversing in French and have asked for the Gypsy
equivalent of *tu bois.* Misheard as *du bois,* this produced
the word he transcribed as *kascht,* the Romani for 'wood'.
Infiltration by several other languages is discernible in his
sample – German and Slavonic in the vocabulary, and Spanish
in the phonology. The passages published by Vulcanius were

[59] A. Etzler, *Zigenarna och deras avkomlingar i Sverige* (Uppsala, 1944),
pp. 58–60.
[60] A. Kluyver, 'Un glossaire tsigane du seizième siècle', *JGLS*(2), 4 (1910–
11), pp. 131–42.
[61] *De literis et lingua Getarum sive Gothorum* (Leiden, 1597), pp. 100–9.

ahead of their time in drawing a contrast between Gypsies,
with a language of their own, and *Errones* (used in the modern
sense of 'Travellers'), who were said to be of local origin
and to speak an artificial jargon. But the Gypsies' language
was passed off as Nubian (Coptic), for, following Cornelius
Agrippa (1527), Vulcanius identified Lesser Egypt with Nubia,
an assumption which may have seemed plausible because of
the existence of the Coptic and Ethiopian Churches, but an
error which would lead astray a number of his successors.
Over the next 150 years, a few more lists appeared, with no
greater impact.

Similarly, when the first scholarly treatises devoted to
Gypsies begin to be published, they creak under the inert
mass of what had previously been written and consolidate
the prejudices of earlier generations. Three such discourses
are worth noting. They were produced in quick succession,
apparently independently of each other, by Protestant scholars
not long after the end of the Thirty Years War, at a time when
peace and order were paramount considerations. Each of them
reads rather like the work of a medieval scholiast, and in spirit
they belong to the era when writers went out of their way to
deny their own originality by referring back constantly to
ancient authorities. All provided the intellectual justification
for repression: the only differences were of emphasis.

The first was a dissertation by Jakob Thomasius, read
in 1652 at Leipzig,[62] where he was Professor of Moral
Philosophy. By then any recognition of Gypsies as an ethnic
immigrant group had been receding for 70 years or more.
Thomasius accepted that there had at one time been pilgrims
coming from the east, of Egyptian descent, and he did not
dispute Vulcanius's view on the language still in use. However
inconsistently with that, he argued, as had some of the Swiss
and other chroniclers before him, that the great majority
must have turned back, and that any few remnants had been
submerged in a rabble consisting of the dregs of society who
claimed to be Gypsies simply in the hope of benefiting from
pilgrim status. For Thomasius, these people were capable

---

[62] *Dissertatio philosophica de Cingaris* (Leipzig, 1671); German translation 1702.

of any wickedness, and the only answer was to send them packing to the ends of the earth. The position of Voetius, the Dutch theologian who disapproved of the christening of Gypsy children, was basically similar: the sole aspect of the conventional stereotype that he challenged was the much repeated claim that Gypsies were spies in the service of the Turks. The third in the trio, the German Ahasuerus Fritsch,[63] was a jurist who found all these theories of exotic origin very difficult and was certain only that in his own time Gypsies were nothing more than a thievish company, an idle and conniving mishmash drawn together from various countries. He appropriated Aventinus's remark about having heard them use the Wendish language (p. 86), but equated it with Rotwelsch, as Münster had done a century earlier (p. 65). True to his legal and political background, he was prolix on the subject of why Gypsies should on no account be tolerated and on laws to achieve their suppression.

These were men of standing and influence, and their writings were heeded. The eighteenth century saw even weightier restatements of old themes when encyclopaedias began to be created and to multiply, the prototype being Ephraim Chambers's *Cyclopædia* (1728). One of the main aims of encyclopaedias is to make available up-to-date knowledge on particular subjects, and such information generally carries a special authority; they can therefore be taken as a guide to the development of scholarship and of what is considered to be the objective opinion of the day. On Gypsies, their writers were as superficial and uncritical of their sources as anyone else. Chambers's entry on 'Egyptians' began:

in our statutes, a counterfeit kind of rogues, who, being English, or Welsh people, disguise themselves in uncouth habits, smearing their faces and bodies, and framing to themselves an unknown, canting language, wander up and down; and under pretence of telling fortunes, curing diseases, &c. abuse the common people, trick them of their money, and steal all that is not too hot, or too heavy for them.

---

[63] *Diatribe historica-politica de Zygenorum origine, vita ac moribus* (Jena, 1660); German translation 1662.

Typical of the Continental approach was the article which appeared in 1735 in the monumental *Universal-Lexicon aller Wissenschaften und Künste* ('Universal Dictionary of all Sciences and Arts') brought out by the Leipzig bookseller Johann Zedler. Of its 25 columns, three-quarters set out with relish various penal enactments, after the introductory statement: 'It is certain that the Gypsies have at all times been godless, wicked people who are harried with complete justification'.[64] The opening of the definition in Diderot's *Encyclopédie* (1751) has already been quoted (p. 147). It went on to suggest, as so many others had done previously, that the original Gypsies had left. There were fewer of the modern variety to be seen than 30 years before, perhaps because of the attentions of the police, or because people were now poorer or less gullible. Whatever the reason, 'the trade of Gypsy' had become 'less good'. The men dedicated to the advancement of secular thought and the new open-mindedness of the Enlightenment were clearly in no doubt that this was a matter for rejoicing.

[64] For a study based on the treatment of Gypsies in 54 Dutch encyclopaedias, see W. Willems and L. Lucassen, 'Beeldvorming over Zigeuners in Nederlandse Encyclopedieën (1724–1984) en hun wetenschappelijke bronnen', in *Zigeuners in Nederland*, eds P. Hovens and R. Dahler (Nijmegen/Rijswijk, 1988), pp. 5–52 [English version, 'The Church of knowledge', in *100 Years of Gypsy Studies*, ed. M. T. Salo (Cheverly, MD, 1990), pp. 31–50]; and for a study of German encyclopaedias, R. Gronemeyer, 'Die Zigeuner in den Kathedralen des Wissens', *Giessener Hefte für Tsiganologie* (1986), 1–4/86, pp. 7–29.

7

Forces for Change

A spurt of developments in the last few decades of the eighteenth century laid some foundations for reshaping the ways in which outsiders looked at Gypsies, though even in those countries where a *laissez-faire* philosophy came to hold sway there appeared to be little weakening of the passion for regulating them into conformity. Then, in the wider world, a variety of social, economic and political forces came into play, stirring up new currents of migration, both within European countries and on a global scale, until, by the beginning of the twentieth century, many Gypsies could be seen to occupy a different position on the margins of society.

New perceptions

To an unknown Hungarian scholar goes the credit for making the first attempt at a more rounded analysis of the Gypsy way of life (if only that part of it perceived by the dominant society). This appeared in 1775–6 in a series of over 40 anonymous articles in the *Wiener Anzeigen*, a German-language Hungarian journal.[1] The writer was a man of his time, deferential towards Maria Theresa's policies, but at least he set himself the task of dealing with present-day conditions, instead of picking over stale crumbs of received wisdom. His

---

[1] *Allergnädigst-privilegirte Anzeigen, aus sämmtlich-kaiserlich-königlichen Erbländern* (Vienna), 5 (1775), pp. 159–416; 6 (1776), pp. 7–168, *passim*.

account concentrated on Hungary and Transylvania, for he pointed out that, although all Gypsies had many features in common, there was no longer a homogeneous Gypsy nation or collective culture: particular groups were influenced by the circumstances in the host country. Within the regions he knew, the wandering Gypsies lived in tents but spent the winter in caves excavated in hillsides; the huts of the settled Gypsies were a little more conventionally equipped, but only with a few bare necessities – there were no chairs or beds or artificial lighting, and practically no kitchen utensils beyond an earthenware pot and an iron pan. Their food was mainly meat (including carrion) or simple floury dishes such as noodles. Bread they acquired by begging; and they were passionately fond of alcohol and tobacco. They had only one set of clothing. The women did not spin or sew, but obtained clothes by begging or stealing, and they were much given to adorning themselves with jewellery. Gypsy smiths performed their work sitting cross-legged on the ground, women manipulating the bellows; they were quick and dexterous, but erratic, with constant forays by members of the family to peddle their small wares. Gypsy horse-dealers were skilled riders, and knew how to pass off a sick nag as healthy. The musicians were adept at following the tastes of their audience. In some regions, the flaying of animal carcasses and the making of sieves and wooden implements had become supplementary activities; while the gold-washers of Transylvania and the Banat (who sifted gold-bearing sand in summer and made wooden trays and tubs in winter) formed almost a separate caste, hardworking and independent. The author had no high opinion of Gypsy morality and culture: they showed little evidence of honour and shame, though more than enough of pride; they adopted the religion of their environment, without belief; and he had apparently not come across any special ceremonies or customs. He took the view that their traditional way of life and lack of regular application were contrary to the rules of every organized society. The fault lay in their upbringing: parents loved their children inordinately but failed to educate them and thus, once they were grown up, they had no chance of changing their ways. With proper training, he could foresee a useful future for them in agriculture or hand-crafts;

their ability to withstand hardship also suggested military possibilities. His conclusion was that the wise course was to 'strive as far as possible to turn Gypsies into human beings and Christians and then to keep them within the state as useful subjects', though he warned that this would demand much patience and effort.

The *Wiener Anzeigen* series also gave some recognition to the link between Romani and India; and, in view of the groundswell in the direction of denying all separate identity to Gypsies, this was a matter of more than philological significance. The primacy of the discovery (though tentative and ill-defined) may go to a Hungarian pastor, István Váli, when he was at the University of Leiden around 1753–4. The story is, however, based on a third-hand report in the *Wiener Anzeigen* in 1776, and had probably grown in the telling. It was said to be the practice for the island of Malabar to keep three students at Leiden, and that Váli obtained a glossary of over 1,000 words in questioning the three who were there in his day about their mother tongue. Detecting a similarity with the Romani spoken in Hungary, he confirmed, once he came home, that these words were intelligible to the Gypsies of Raab (Györ). There is no indication that Váli took the investigation any further and no details were provided of the language spoken by his informants. Malabar is a geographical designation which is rather ambiguous in its coverage, but generally refers to the south-west coast of India. The mother tongue of students from there was more likely to have been Dravidian (e.g. Malayalam) than Indo-Aryan. There is no record of an István Váli in the Leiden registers, but they do list three students as 'Ceylonensis' in the early 1750s.[2] (Sri Lanka was then a Dutch colony.) It is possible that Váli visited Leiden from some other Dutch university and met them. But even if it was a long list of Sanskrit or Sinhalese vocabulary that he had been given, his Gypsies, no matter how well preserved their Romani, must have been in much more difficulty than the story suggests in recognizing words in either of these Indic tongues.

---

[2] See I. Hancock, 'The Hungarian student Valyi Istvan and the Indian connection of Romani', *Roma*, no. 36 (1991).

Firmer evidence was provided by the glossary of Romani collected by an Englishman, Jacob Bryant, to all appearances at a fair in Windsor in 1776. When his material was communicated to the Society of Antiquaries of London in 1785,[3] Bryant drew attention to analogies between Romani and the Indo-Iranian languages and also singled out a few loan-words from Greek and Slavonic. His samples are instructive in showing that the dialect of these Gypsies was somewhat anglicized phonetically, although they still had numerals which Anglo-Romani later lost. Another of his claims to distinction is that he affords the earliest identifiable instance of an inquisitive collector being unwittingly fobbed off with an occasional Romani obscenity in place of the word asked for.[4]

Jacob Rüdiger, a German scholar, was also one of the first to make the Indian connection. In 1777, at the instigation of a school inspector in St Petersburg, H. L. C. Bacmeister, he persuaded a Gypsy woman in Halle to translate a passage into her dialect; comparing it with a variety of other languages he discerned resemblances with those of India. Bacmeister convinced him that it was closest to Multani (a dialect of Lahnda or Western Panjabi). Rüdiger's findings were published in 1782.[5]

It now remained only for someone to pull the various strands together. Already engaged on such a work of synthesis was another German, Heinrich Grellmann of Göttingen University, who was drawing heavily on previous writers but

[3] *Archaeologia*, 7 (1785), pp. 387–94. Two months before (ibid., pp. 382–6), William Marsden had given the Society the benefit of more soundly based comparisons between English and Greek Romani and Hindi, Marathi and Bengali.

[4] For example, one of the words Bryant was given for 'father' he recorded as *ming*. This is an old Gypsy pleasantry. The word has now entered the English lexicon: at least, when the *Collins Dictionary of the English Language* first appeared in 1979, it contained the entry '*minge... Brit. taboo slang*. 1. the female genitals... [C20: of obscure origin]'. The editor accepted my assurance that it must come from the Gypsy word *mindź*, which has the same meaning in Romani dialects throughout Europe (although its own derivation is far from clear), and subsequent editions give the etymology as '[C20: from Romany; of obscure origin]'.

[5] *Neuster Zuwachs der teutschen fremden und allgemeinen Sprachkunde* (Leipzig, 1782), Part 1, pp. 37–84.

was at last giving more coherent and analytical form to such evidence as had laboriously been accumulated. His book, *Die Zigeuner*, was published in 1783. Its importance was quickly recognized and it was translated into English, French and Dutch.[6] Grellmann's account of the distribution of Gypsies in Europe was incomplete, but seems well informed so far as it goes. He put the Gypsy population at between 700,000 and 800,000, and said they were particularly profuse in Hungary, Transylvania and all over the Balkan Peninsula. Elsewhere in Europe, they were numerous in Spain, especially in the south, and in Italy, but much less so in France, except for Alsace and Lorraine, and scarce in Switzerland, the Netherlands and most parts of Germany apart from the Rhineland. Though many were settled (and here he mentions tavern-keepers in Spain, slaves in Moldavia and Wallachia, and those living in huts near Hungarian and Transylvanian towns), he reckoned that the majority were still wandering about, tents being their favourite shelter. Even within particular countries, he noted the internal divisions which were growing up – for example, in Transylvania and the Banat, between the gold-washers and the others. (There were similar divisions, though he did not mention them, between the nomadic Gypsies in Transylvania and the sedentaries, whom the former looked down on, as was often the case in other countries too.)

In the ordering of his material, Grellmann set the pattern for subsequent scholars for many years to come. He also extended the currency of various bits of scandal-mongering, such as unrestrained depravity among Gypsy women, and accusations of cannibalism. On the latter, he gave considerable exposure to lurid comments in Hungarian and German newspapers on recent proceedings in Hungary (Hont county, now part of Slovakia) involving over 150 Gypsies, 41 of whom, after confessions extracted under torture, were executed by a variety of means (beheading, hanging, breaking on the wheel, quarter-

[6] H. M. G. Grellmann, *Die Zigeuner. Ein historischer Versuch über die Lebensart und Verfassung, Sitten und Schicksale dieses Volks in Europa, nebst ihrem Ursprung* (Dessau and Leipzig, 1783; 2nd edn Göttingen, 1787). English translation, *Dissertation on the Gipsies* (London, 1787; 2nd edn London, 1807). French translations Metz, 1788 and Paris, 1810. Dutch translation Dordrecht, 1791.

ing) for crimes said to include cannibalism. In his second edition (1787), he redressed the balance somewhat by reporting the subsequent findings of a commission of inquiry set up by an incredulous Emperor Joseph II to examine the case of the remainder of these Gypsies: they were pronounced guilty of no more than theft and were released after a beating. As for the original executions, Grellmann now concluded that at most it was possible that the victims had deserved to die as murderers. The damage from his first edition had already been done, however, and it would take a century and more for suggestions of Gypsy cannibalism to die away.

In the earlier, ethnographic part of his work Grellmann borrowed widely from the articles in the *Wiener Anzeigen*. Those provided some material on the linguistic side too, but here his chief mentor was one Councillor Büttner, who, some years before, had misleadingly indicated a link between Romani and Afghanistan.[7] This time the comparison was drawn with Indo-Aryan, reaching the tentative conclusion that the closest affinity was with the Surat dialect (i.e. Gujarati). However imperfect the details, Grellmann's indubitable achievement was that, by deploying linguistic evidence as it was then understood, he ensured that the general proposition of the Indian origin of the Gypsies' language became widely accepted and that their ethnic identity was restored in the eyes of many. For him, latter-day Gypsies were clearly lineal descendants of the early arrivals; and despite his mistaken belief that the exodus from India was a reaction to Tamerlane's invasion at the end of the fourteenth century, he had pointed future research in a less fanciful direction. On the social plane, just as the writer in the *Wiener Anzeigen* had done, he argued strongly against banishment as a way of dealing with Gypsies, for he too believed that men could be rehabilitated and he shared the widespread view of European statesmen and economists (which Malthus would douse with very cold water a decade and a half later) that larger populations were useful to the nation. It is not surprising, then, that he endorsed the measures adopted by Maria Theresa and her son with whole-

---

[7] In the introduction to his *Vergleichungstafeln der Schriftarten verschiedener Völker* (Göttingen, 1775).

hearted approval. Education was the road leading towards the eradication of non-conformity.

In the literary field, Gypsies were also attracting a new kind of attention, as tastes turned to the romantic and the melodramatic and the emphasis shifted away from the precepts of order, calm and rationality towards the individual, the imaginative and the spontaneous. In 1773 Goethe's stormy tragedy *Götz von Berlichingen* had cast a Gypsy chief in the role of the noble savage, and soon it became a cliché for an author to contrast Gypsy life with the shams of ordinary existence.[8] According to another, darker convention which spread in the nineteenth century, Gypsies were wild outcasts who hinted at the supernatural, the mysterious and the criminal: they could be used, in books for children as well as adults, as a device to help in carrying the plot and explaining away robberies, strange events or occult happenings, or (following a precedent set by Cervantes in *La Gitanilla* and continued in *Moll Flanders*, *Le Mariage de Figaro* and *Wilhelm Meisters Lehrjahre*) in accounting for lost children, stolen from their parents. For the most part, writers were still drawing on their own imagination or on other literary sources, rather than direct observation. Not until the appearance of George Borrow's works, starting with *The Zincali* (1841), and culminating in *Lavengro* (1851) and *The Romany Rye* (1857), did the literary stereotype receive a clear challenge, at the hands of an author who loved to associate with Gypsies, had mastered their tongue, and was able to convey something of their real nature in his writings.

By then it was being discovered that the *facts* about the Gypsies were more intriguing than dubious legend. The Romantic Revival had led to a growing interest in primitive folk culture and a predilection for the exotic and the mysterious, and its later phases were marked by a new attention to

[8] As indeed Fielding had already chosen to do in *Tom Jones* (1749), introducing a company of Gypsies in order to portray an ironic image of the Tory dream of utopian society unsullied by civilization. Four years later, however, when involved in the real-life polemics of the trial of a Gypsy woman and a bawd who were accused of abducting a scullery maid, Elizabeth Canning, Fielding took a much less rosy view of Gypsy nature in his pamphlet *A Clear State of the Case of Elizabeth Canning* (London, 1753).

the collection and imitation of folklore (a word invented only in 1846) and of folk ballads, dance and music. Gypsies could not avoid being drawn into this current of human inquiry and were found to be a mine of folk-tales, songs, customs and superstitions. In the historical field, a French archivist, Paul Bataillard, decisively opened out the early history of Gypsies in Europe, in a long series of articles published over several decades, starting in 1843.

Comparative philology became another manifestation of an increasing preoccupation with national origins, once the way had been prepared by Sir William Jones of the East India Company, only a few years after the publication of Grellmann's book, in establishing the place of Sanskrit in the Indo-European family. This novel science would sweep the study of Romani along at a fast pace. The Gypsies' speech became something of an orchid in the philological garden. It was seen to have the antique beauty of a crumbling ruin and presented the interesting spectacle of a language in various states of decay, succumbing gradually to different forces. The opportunity of studying an oriental tongue in Europe attracted not only romantic amateurs but also some of the foremost scholars of the century. It was not even necessary to scrape acquaintance with Gypsies, as was amply demonstrated by one of the great trail-blazers, August Friedrich Pott, among whose many achievements as Professor of General Philology at Halle was the first scientific work on Romani, *Die Zigeuner in Europa und Asien* ('The Gypsies in Europe and Asia', 1844–5). It was based on the growing corpus of published data about particular dialects and, as Pott explained in his foreword, he produced it without ever having had more personal experience of Gypsies than a fleeting glimpse of a few individuals. The 1860s and 1870s were bountiful years for studies of Romani, many written in German. Towering above all others was Franz Miklosich, at the University of Vienna, who was by then able to speak of having at his disposal 'abundant, almost over-abundant material from all countries where Gypsies live', and who was the first to attempt to trace from their language the route the Gypsies must have taken during their westward migrations.

More manipulative was a new-found interest in Gypsies on the part of churches. Protestant churches in particular, having developed revivalist methods in response to a fast-changing society, were single-minded in pursuit of a world freed from heathenism. The missionary fervour did not overlook the need for regenerating the benighted Gypsies, and moral suasion was tried in place of the more familiar legal coercion. With only a few exceptions, the aim of the religious and philanthropic workers who engaged the Gypsies in earnest discussion and pressed their tracts upon them was to circumscribe and eventually eradicate them and their way of life, by persuading them to settle, reclaiming them from the assumed laxity of their morals, and preparing them for occupations which relied on values of dependence and submissiveness. Such attitudes even penetrated the hymnals: a verse of one children's hymn ran

> I was not born without a home
> Or in some broken shed,
> A gipsy baby taught to roam,
> And steal my daily bread.[9]

In Britain, this dedicated work proved to be of limited consequence, though it did record a few successes. John Baird, a minister of the Church of Scotland, embarked on a venture of improvement in 1830 among the Gypsy colony which inhabited a row of cottages at Kirk Yetholm, little more than a mile from the border with England, where they occupied themselves as smiths or in making brooms or horn spoons and travelled for eight to ten months of the year to peddle their wares. Baird's aim was to keep the children in Yetholm all the year round, under suitable supervision, so that they could attend school and receive religious instruction and in due course be found employment, perhaps as domestic servants; he also hoped to persuade the adults to give up wandering. Eventually a Society for the Reformation of the Gypsies in Scotland was set up, funds were raised, and Baird was able to report some promising results with the children; as for keeping the adults at home, 'the success hitherto has been next to an entire failure', as his 1842 report quaintly phrased it. When the Society broke up in 1859, Baird and his successor continued on their own until elementary education was made both

---

[9] C. O'Brien, *Gipsy Marion* (London, n.d. [c.1895]), p. 4.

free and compulsory in Scotland in 1872; a few years later practically all the Yetholm Gypsies had given up wandering.[10] In England, the most notable sustained effort was provided, from 1827 onwards, by James Crabb, a Methodist preacher, and by the Southampton Committee which he inspired and which engaged agents to make daily visits to Gypsy camps around Southampton and in the New Forest. Crabb wanted reform to be gradual and voluntary. His prayer-meetings, rendered palatable by servings of roast beef and plum pudding, did not fail to attract well-behaved Gypsies; but even the reformed and educated children who were put out to service almost all returned to their old life. Similar ventures in Prussia also failed. Several other missions, often modelled on Crabb's, were attempted in England and followed much the same part-religious, part-educational pattern.[11] They were given a guarded reception: conversion was seen all too clearly to go hand-in-hand with adoption of the ways of settled industrial society. The practical achievements, when measured in terms of lasting 'reformation', appear small, even if by the end of the century a few missionaries were emerging from the Gypsies' own ranks to carry on the good work, such as Cornelius Smith, born in a tent in Cambridgeshire in 1831,[12] and, best known of all, his son Rodney, 'Gipsy Smith', a powerful preacher who could gather several thousand people together and who, from the 1880s onwards, conducted missions at home and abroad;[13] so far as Gypsies were concerned, in his eyes salvation lay in leaving behind most aspects of their way of life.

Musical ascendancies

Sporadically, Gypsies had been associated with music in early reports of their presence in Europe, whether as instrumental-

[10] A. Gordon, *Hearts upon the Highway* (Galashiels, 1980), pp. 43–53.
[11] Cf. D. Mayall, *Gypsy-Travellers in Nineteenth-Century Society* (Cambridge, 1988), esp. pp. 97–129.
[12] C. Smith, *The Life Story of Gipsy Cornelius Smith* (London, 1890).
[13] R. Smith, *Gipsy Smith: His Life and Work* (London, 1901); D. Lazell, *From the Forest I Came* (London, 1970).

ists, singers or dancers. Musical talent could be a powerful factor in winning a measure of tolerance, as it did for the Gypsy patriarch Abram Wood who entered Wales in the early eighteenth century and brought with him, it is said, a violin; and when his sons and grandsons turned to the national instrument, the harp, they were welcomed almost everywhere.[14] Yet Gypsies have no common musical language, no way of making music which is identical to them all. When playing as professional entertainers, rather than for themselves, they turned to the music which was characteristic of their environment, as perpetuators and adapters rather than creators, and with instruments typical of the locality,[15] just as, in their folk-tales, they often borrowed motifs from the folklore of different countries which they traversed and gave them a Gypsy colouring. Their natural performing ability was soon in evidence all over Europe. But during the nineteenth century, in three countries in particular – Hungary, Russia and Spain – Gypsies rose to a position of considerable eminence as professional musicians, to a point where they became almost part of the national identity.

In Hungary, a number of the old-established Gypsies (known to others of their race as *romungre*, or Hungarian Rom) had quickly become serviceable to the Magyars as minstrels. Increasingly sedentary, and decreasingly proficient in Romani, they lost touch with their own music and were drawn into the tradition of the Hungarians living around them, taking and transforming it as beguilingly as it was said they could take and transform a horse so that the original owner would not recognize it. Their ascendancy in music was already evident in the mid-eighteenth century (p. 157), when they became indispensable not only to the folk in the villages but

[14] Cf. J. Sampson, 'The Wood family', *JGLS*(3), 11 (1932), pp. 56–71, and A. O. H. Jarman and E. Jarman, *The Welsh Gypsies: Children of Abram Wood* (Cardiff, 1991), chs 4 and 5.

[15] B. Leblon, in *Musiques Tsiganes et Flamenco* (Paris, 1990), points out, however, that they seemed to prefer instruments which had some affinity with the instrumental pattern in India and other eastern lands. He argues that Gypsy music in different countries has more in common than appears on the surface, and that the common features were often linked with oriental music.

also to the Magyar nobility, and at banquets it became the custom for a Gypsy minstrel to stand by the host's chair, ready to minister to his musical mood. Soon Gypsy bands – led by a virtuoso violinist – were making numerous successful appearances. Individual musicians achieved personal reputations. Untutored, their spontaneous freshness and quickness to adapt ensured a continuing ability to please Hungarian listeners: music-making, rather than smithery, became regarded as the highest of Gypsy occupations. To begin with, the famous musicians and bands came from the north-west of the country (now western Slovakia), the part nearest to Vienna, the centre of European musical life. By the middle of the nineteenth century they were to be found all over: 'Gypsy music' was in high fashion.

The first great name was that of the violinist János Bihari (1764–1827), who came from Pozsony (Bratislava) county and whose orchestra was invited to the top public and private celebrations and banquets throughout the country, and also frequently to Vienna: indeed, at the Congress of Vienna in 1814 he played for the assembled monarchs and statesmen. Bihari and his successors created a musical idiom which became part of Hungarian folk tradition, known as *verbunkos* style (*verbunkos* originally denoting a military music played at recruiting). Liszt was one of Bihari's greatest admirers and wrote of him at length in his *Des Bohémiens et de leur musique en Hongrie* (1859), claiming that he 'carried Gypsy music to its greatest height. It had long been an object of favour and admiration by the Hungarian aristocracy; but now it became an integral part of national representation.'[16] In Paris, Liszt acquired a talented *romungro* protégé of his own, a 12-year-old named Józsi Sáray, and had him educated and given lessons at the Conservatoire, to no avail. Józsi turned into a great dandy and proved wilful and unteachable. As soon as he was brought face to face again with his kith and kin, he threw in his lot with them and preferred to join a Gypsy orchestra rather than engage in concert-room torture. Liszt intended his book to be a prologue to his own *Hungarian Rhapsodies*, in

---

[16] F. Liszt, *The Gipsy in Music*, trans. E. Evans (London, 1926), vol. 2, p. 340.

which he imitated every mannerism of Gypsy performance. He exaggerated the role of the Gypsies, and Bartók, Kodály and others would later point out indignantly that he made the mistake of suggesting that they had created all Magyar music; but he was right in claiming that the best Gypsy musicians became the preservers and representatives of national music in the eyes of the general public.[17] They were inseparable from the Hungarian regeneration movement. Many of the Gypsy groups took part with their instruments in the abortive revolution of 1848–9 which left Hungary subject to absolutist rule from Vienna, and afterwards, once liberty had been lost, their consoling violins acquired even greater following. Their fame spread outside the country and, from the 1850s onwards, international tours to other parts of Europe and to America became frequent. Ferenc Bunkó (1813–89), who had been conductor-in-chief of all the Gypsy musicians taking part in the war of independence, performed several times in Paris and Berlin with his ensemble (see plate 26). During his 1865 tour in Berlin they were invited to the crown prince's to play at a dinner and were given an enthusiastic reception; five days later they played before the king. Liszt and others were to complain, however, that such tours, gratifyingly triumphant though they might be, also blunted originality and engendered decadence.

The Gypsy virtuosos won such respect that even members of the nobility were not ashamed to learn from them or to play with them. And it was now no rarity to find them marrying the daughters of well-to-do citizens and sometimes aristocrats. (Jancsi Rigó married a princess, Rudi Nyári a countess, and Marci Berkes a baroness.) Not all were so grand: plenty of Gypsy bands made their music in taverns and wayside inns and at markets, fairs, folk festivals and weddings, where the pickings were leaner and audiences perhaps less respectful and peaceful.

[17] The Vlach Gypsies in Hungary, more recent arrivals than the *romungre* and uninterested in playing to the *gadźé*, preserved their own folk-song style and repertoire. Cf. A. Hajdu, 'Les Tsiganes de Hongrie et leur musique', *Études Tsiganes* (1958), no. 1, pp. 1–30; K. Kovalcsik, *Vlach Gypsy Folk Songs in Slovakia* (Budapest, 1985); and M. Stewart, 'La fraternité dans le chant: l'expérience des Roms hongrois', in *Tsiganes: Identité, Évolution*, ed. P. Williams (Paris, 1989), pp. 497–513.

Plate 26   Ferenc Bunkó's band, 1854. From a drawing by Varsányi.
Hungarian National Museum, Budapest.

Plate 27   Rural Gypsy band in Hungary, c.1840. From a drawing
by Barabás. Hungarian National Museum, Budapest.

For the Russians, on the other hand, the musical strength of the Gypsies lay in their singing – improvised singing in chorus, in several parts. The first record of these choruses dates from the latter half of the eighteenth century, when Gypsy singers were brought from Moldavia to Moscow by Count Aleksey Orlov. Soon a Gypsy chorus and a good orchestra were indispensable adornements in the home of every important member of the nobility. Orlov's chorus, whose members were entered in the list of serfs belonging to the village of Pushkino near Moscow, was much in vogue and could often be heard at soirées offered by Catherine the Great's favourites. Later they were given their freedom and during the Napoleonic invasion of 1812 every man among them of militia age joined the hussars, and the others are reported to have donated money to the government.[18] After the war it became the fashion among Muscovites to have large dinner parties in out-of-town inns, with Gypsies supplying the entertainment. A similar practice grew up in St Petersburg, but there the inns had to be well out of town, for Gypsies were banned from the city.

In the chorus, the women had the main role; and they also danced. The instrument used to accompany them was usually the seven-stringed Russian guitar. Besides peasant songs of Russian, Ukrainian and Polish origin, it was the sentimental songs of contemporary Russian composers that provided the bulk of their material, but in later years educated musicians collaborated in writing a vast number of romances in a Gypsy-like style. All this 'Gypsy music' became an organic part of nineteenth-century Russian musical culture: the aristocracy and bourgeoisie favoured the choirs as much as the Hungarians favoured their Gypsy musicians, seeing in them the same embodiment of romantic freedom as Liszt saw in the Hungarian Gypsy, though Liszt himself wrote in rather disparaging terms of the luxury and artificiality of the setting in which the Gypsy women of Moscow performed – an opinion which the Bolshevik government came to share six decades

[18] V. Bobri, 'Gypsies and Gypsy choruses of old Russia', *JGLS*(3), 40 (1961), pp. 112–20.

or so later, to the point of prohibiting such activities and encouraging songs and dances with better ethnic credentials.

The relationship of Spanish Gitanos to the music for which they became renowned was similar to that of the Hungarian and Russian performers to their repertoire. It was not originally theirs, but was none the less their creation.[19] From the late fifteenth century they appear in the role of interpreters of Spanish song and dance, which in the process took on a Gypsy allure.[20] Their dances formed a popular part of secular and religious events (such as the annual Corpus Christi processions), so that Philip IV's attempt to put a stop to their performances (p. 164) had but little effect. Some of the Spanish vocal forms were gradually metamorphosed in theme and delivery; and, with the emergence of what came to be known as *flamenco* in the nineteenth century, Andalusian culture felt the full impact of the Gitano style. Flamenco had a long, clandestine gestation during the times of savage repression. At its heart was *cante jondo* ('deep song'), a musical style (or, more accurately, three styles – *tonás*, *siguiriyas* and *soleares*) growing out of an Andalusian foundation but, said Manuel de Falla, compounded with Byzantine liturgical, Arab and Gypsy elements.[21] (Others point also to a Jewish influence.) Its motifs, couched in laconic defiance and compressed ambiguity, were love, loyalty, pride, jealousy, revenge, freedom, persecution, sorrow, death; García Lorca described *cante jondo* as 'the sound of gushing blood'. Originally the singer, improvising dramatically, had no accompaniment other than a rhythmic tapping. Guitar and dance emerged later, enriching and reinforcing the *cante*, and eventually showed greater capacity to continue evolving and to stretch the concept of flamenco. The scale typical of *cante flamenco* is Phrygian in character (i.e. the mode represented by the white keys of the piano, beginning on E), a scale which occurs with great frequency from India through Persia and Turkey to the Balkans:

---

[19] The Gypsy and non-Gypsy contributions are well analysed in A. Alvarez Caballero, *Gitanos, payos y flamencos, en los orígines del flamenco* (Madrid, 1988).

[20] Cf. B. Leblon, 'Identité gitane et flamenco', in *Tsiganes: Identité, Évolution*, pp. 521–7, and *Musiques Tsiganes et Flamenco*.

[21] M. de Falla, *El Cante jondo* (Granada, 1922).

Plate 28   El Jaleo. Oil painting by John Singer Sargent (1856–1925). Isabella Stewart Gardner Museum, Boston.

it would seem, however, to have been by way of the Moors, and not the Gypsies, that it came to the Iberian peninsula.

The obscure prehistory of flamenco comes to an end around the time of Charles III's pragmatic sanction of 1783; this may simply be coincidence, though it is not difficult to accept that it was the new regime of sufferance that allowed *cante jondo* to leave the shadows.[22] The first singer whose name has come down to us was a Gypsy, Tío Luis el de la Juliana, born around 1750 at Jerez de la Frontera. In the first half of the nineteenth century the main centres of development were Cádiz, Jerez and Seville (more precisely, Triana, Seville's former Gypsy quarter, now gentrified), and the known interpreters of flamenco in those times all came from sedentary Gypsy families in that one region of Andalusia. The music had not yet acquired the label of *flamenco*, however: that was a name which had been given to Gypsies themselves before it was applied to the music which was the urban creation of professional entertainers in the *cafés cantantes*. These were springing up from 1847 onwards; the first, El Café de los Lombardos, was inaugurated in Seville.[23] A community of flamenco artists emerged from anonymity and became known by sketchy nicknames. Andalusians participated now, as well as Gypsies; their styles influenced each other, and the repertoire was modulated to take account of public tastes. (More privately, flamenco continued to be performed by Gypsies at family gatherings and celebrations, where the mood of the moment rather than the dictates of a commercial audience could be obeyed.) The art of the professionals became more ambitious and elaborate, though Gypsy song and dance remained its foundation; and from a small corner of southern Spain, this art of long-drawn, descending, ornamented phrases, Scarlatti-like guitar accompaniments and assonant repeating verse-lines spread right across the peninsula and into the wider Hispanic world, to become a generally accepted idiom of popular entertainment.

---

[22] Cf. A. Alvarez Caballero, *Historia del cante flamenco* (Madrid, 1981), pp. 15–17.

[23] J. Blas Vega, *Los Cafés cantantes de Sevilla* (Madrid, 1984), p. 27.

Landscapes and townscapes

Many Gypsies found themselves living in a very different world at the end of the century between 1815 and 1914 from that at its beginning. The industrial and social changes which swept over much of Europe in those years were more intensive than had ever been known before. Britain led the widespread retreat from rural life towards a world where societies of peasants and craftsmen were turned into societies of machine-tenders and book-keepers, but by the end of the century many other European countries were catching up on or overtaking Britain in the race. Even then, however, old and new were still mixed together, and areas such as southern Spain and southern Italy had been but little affected, while Hungary and the Balkans were hardly affected at all. More than three-quarters of those living in the Balkans were still peasants: this was the part of the continent where the classic peasant society persisted longest and still offered an environment probably not too far removed from that which existed at the time of the Gypsies' arrival in Europe.

Even where the trend towards industrialization and urbanism was most pronounced, its impact on the Gypsies was less comprehensive than it might have been. The factors which kept them unassimilated may become clearer if we look again at two of the economically more backward regions where sedentarization had already gone furthest – that is, at Spain and Hungary – and then turn to developments in Britain, the sole country to have created, by the middle of the nineteenth century, a mature industrial society, and one of the very few to have by then a large majority of its population living in urban surroundings.

If *Gitanos bravíos* ('wild [i.e. nomadic] Gypsies') were a minority in southern Spain, the causes are to be found mainly in the pressure of Spanish laws, which had considerable success in reducing mobility. Where they had fallen down was in their attempts to avoid large concentrations of Gypsies. Nor had they scored any conspicuous victories in channelling Gypsies exclusively into activities deemed worthwhile to the state: there were too many loopholes to be exploited in the legal demarcations. In settling, Gypsies formed colonies within

Plate 29   Gypsy caves at the Sacro Monte, Granada, 1862. Drawing by Gustave Doré, in J. C. Davillier, L'Espagne *(Paris, 1874).*

many of the towns, such as the Calle de la Comadre and the Callejón de Lavapies near the horse market in Madrid, or Triana in Seville, or the *barrios* de la Vina and of Santa Madre in Cádiz. In Granada, many had congregated in caves scooped out in the sides of the Sacro Monte, where they plied the hammer and forge in the bowels of the earth; later they would become a tourist attraction, second only to the Alhambra on the other side of the Rio Darro, and some of the caves, complete with baths, electricity and telephones, would house prosperous flamenco singers and dancers. Elsewhere in Granada province, there were (as there still are) even more extensive troglodyte settlements at Purullena and the Barrio de Santiago of Guadix – not solely inhabited by Gypsies, for these subterranean dwellings have the advantage of being cheap to construct or acquire and of being cool in summer and warm in winter. Despite governmental measures like the decrees of Philip IV and Charles II, the Gypsies' love of their own distinctive society ensured the survival of many of the *gitanerías* – and a signal contribution to Andalusian culture.

In Hungary, the extensive degree of settlement likewise owed much to government pressures of the eighteenth century, reinforced by later land reform and reclamation, but again its course had not gone in the desired direction. More recent ventures also foundered, even when undertaken by the man best equipped to make them prevail, Archduke Josef Karl Ludwig (1833–1905). The Archduke was the senior member of that branch of the house of Habsburg which had long been settled in Hungary, a great-grandson of Maria Theresa and a great-nephew of Joseph II. He spent many years on military duties. Less conventionally for a member of his family, he became an enthusiastic student of Romani and of Gypsy ways, having been attracted by the music at an early age. Magyar was his mother tongue, and it was in that language that he produced a comprehensive Romani grammar, based on several European dialects.[24] He spent a substantial amount of his own money in establishing a large Gypsy colony on his estate at Alcsúth, some 40 miles south-west of Budapest, in addition to four smaller colonies elsewhere. He supplied these Gypsies

<hr>

[24] *Czigány Nyelvtan* ['The Gypsy Language'] (Budapest, 1888).

with houses, procured them work on the land, and at Alcsúth opened a special school for the children. The colonists pursued this ordered life for so long as the royal protector's eyes were upon them; later, they almost entirely dispersed.

We know a good deal about the general pattern of Gypsy life in Hungarian territories towards the close of the nineteenth century from a detailed census of Gypsies held in January 1893, supplementing the data which had emerged as a by-product of the national census of 1880.[25] (At that time Hungary was three times its present size and took in Transylvania and Slovakia, as well as less extensive regions in what are now Poland, Austria, Slovenia, Croatia, Serbia, Rumania and Ukraine.) It was reckoned that, of the 274,940 Gypsies who were identified, almost 90 per cent were sedentary, 20,406 being half-settled and only 8,938 fully nomadic. Some 105,000 of the total were in Transylvania, where they represented almost 5 per cent of the entire population and, in the regions where Vlachs predominated, sometimes exceeded 10 per cent. A very high proportion of the nomads spoke Romani, whereas less than half the others did so; of the latter, a quarter had Rumanian as their mother tongue. Both the Romani and the Rumanian speakers were principally in Transylvania.

There were some important gaps in the census figures. Several towns, notably Budapest, did not participate. Moreover, any tally of this kind is likely to underestimate the nomadic element, because of the difficulties for enumerators in tracking it down, a feature that was aggravated by weaknesses in the classification system, allowing those who regularly spent the winter in a particular parish but wandered about in the summer to be put into the permanently settled category. The mid-winter timing of the count must have ensured another bias in favour of 'settled' or 'half-settled'. None the less, the sedentary population was clearly in a decisive majority. It did not follow, however, that they had been absorbed into their

---

[25] The results were published in *A Magyarországban . . . czigányösszeirás eredményei* ['Results of the Gypsy Census in Hungary'], ed. J. Jekelfalussy (Budapest, 1895), with an extensive commentary in both Hungarian and German. Details of the 1880 national census are in J. H. Schwicker, *Die Zigeuner in Ungarn und Siebenbürgen* (Vienna, 1883), pp. 75–89.

surroundings. It was more common for settled Gypsies to be living in an enclave of their own in a town or village: this was particularly true of Slovakia. Schooling patterns also revealed few signs of integration: 70 per cent of those of school age were not attending, and over 90 per cent of Gypsies were found to be illiterate (98 per cent in the case of the nomads). The occupations showed a strong preference for self-employment, and revealed how ineffectual the decrees of Maria Theresa and Joseph II had been in steering Gypsies into or out of certain types of livelihood. Relatively few were engaged in agriculture, the major activity in Hungary; but, philosophically, the editor of the census report, citing the Archduke's experiences, accepted that Gypsies were not suited for such work. Even in occupations of an industrial type, they tended to be found in those where they could nurse some degree of independence: metal-working (notably smithery) was the most important, followed by construction work (e.g. brick-making, clay-working) and wood-working (e.g. trough-making). Dealing was also strongly represented (mainly horse-dealing for men, hawking for women). Musicians were most numerous in the area occupied by present-day Hungary. It was partly the thought of their musical prowess that made the editor of this official publication go well beyond sober statistical commentary to launch into a rhapsodic plea for complete incorporation of Gypsies into the nation, because of the good qualities they had to offer – adaptable physiques, skilful hands, musical talents.

The nature of their accommodation was also revealing. Most of the settled Gypsies occupied dwellings with one or at most two rooms, but some were still in tents, while half the semi-sedentaries lived in temporary huts of earth or straw or in caves which they hollowed out. In winter, many of the nomads rented houses or erected huts. Tents were, however, their principal habitation, and were transported in horse-drawn waggons and carts. There was no mention of living-vans, although primitive caravans had begun to be noted in Balkan countries from the early part of the century.[26] The tent, in

---

[26] E.g. F. C. H. L. Pouqueville, *Voyage dans la Grèce* (Paris, 1820), vol. 2, p. 458, writing of the Muslim Gypsies of Bosnia, said 'one often meets

Plate 30   Gypsy dwellings near Klausenburg (Cluj) in the mid-nineteenth century. From C. Boner's Transylvania, 1865.

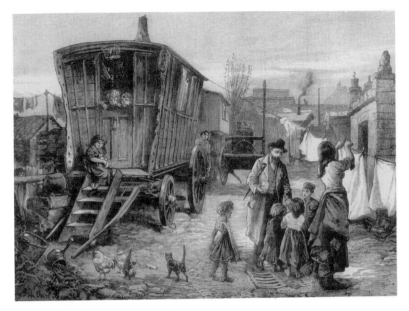

Plate 31   An early Reading waggon in Notting Dale, London, near Latimer Road, with George Smith of Coalville handing out sweets. Illustrated London News, *29 November 1879.*

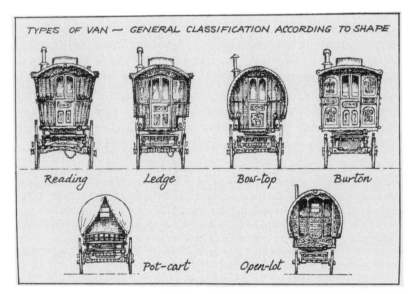

Plate 32   Types of English Gypsy van. Drawing by Denis E. Harvey.

fact, remained the most common habitation of nomad Gypsies all over Europe for much of the nineteenth century, even in freezing Russian winters, although by about mid-century Gypsies in western Europe were gradually transferring to horse-drawn living-waggons which their owners called *vardos*, often still supplementing them with tents and light carts. The most elaborate of these evolved in England, all produced to order by *gadźé* waggon-builders, and by the 1890s Gypsy caravans, never exactly alike despite a standard layout, had reached the summit of their development, at once distinctive, functional and handsome, so much so that they inspired recreational caravanning among the settled population.[27]

In Britain, despite more diffuse types of pressure linked to changes in the wider society, Gypsies showed as little interest in regular wage-labour as did those elsewhere. In the main they were going to stay as they had always tried to be, their earning power based largely on their own efforts and wits and on their capacity to follow a wide variety of itinerant callings. Inevitably, however, as the towns grew and the countryside shrank, many whose field of action was at first predominantly rural would move with their market. More direct stimuli were in any event pushing them in the same direction. The enclosure movement took away many of their traditional camping grounds; and the increased numbers and better organization of the rural police, resulting from the County Police Act of 1839 and its successor of 1856, gave rise to forceful campaigns to remove them from the countryside in Dorset, Norfolk and some other counties. Vagrants and Gypsies were blamed for much of the petty rural crime, even though criminal records show that the violence and theft (including poaching) were usually committed by residents.[28]

with wooden huts covered with tree-bark, set upon wheels, and drawn from place to place by a team of 10 to 12 oxen while the entire family follows its mobile habitation on foot'; and A. Boué, *La Turquie d'Europe* (Paris, 1840), vol. 2, p. 77, after stating that most nomad Gypsies dwelt in tents or temporary huts, added 'exceptionally, one sees Gypsies, especially in Albania, who live in waggons covered with canvas or bark'.

[27] Cf. C. H. Ward-Jackson and D. E. Harvey, *The English Gypsy Caravan* (Newton Abbot, 1972; 2nd edn 1986).

[28] Cf. D. Jones, 'Rural crime and protest', in *The Victorian Countryside*, ed. G. E. Mingay (London, 1981), vol. 2, pp. 566–79.

Gypsies formed only one element in a wide range of peripatetic groups to be found in nineteenth-century Britain, where such people played a much greater part in industrial and social life than they do today.[29] Some members of this community were on the roads in order to obtain employment (such as navvies, following in the track of Victorian public works, builders, agricultural labourers, and itinerant artisans); people like these were on their own, and in other respects conformed to a sedentary model. Then there were tramps on the pad – sometimes alone, sometimes with a female companion – who were generally a seasonal phenomenon, disappearing into city tenements and doss-houses in the winter. There was also a steady immigrant stream from across the Irish Sea, which burst into a flood in the late 1840s following the failure of the potato crops, to the point where some observers fatuously claimed that virtually *all* vagrants were Irish. But for others, travelling was a way of life in itself, and they remained regularly on the move with their families for a sizeable part of each year. They included brush- and basket-makers, horse-dealers, tinkers, cheapjacks, miscellaneous hawkers, travelling potters, fairground people and the like, as well as the Gypsies themselves – in fact the variegated type of population which is today increasingly referred to as Travellers. If that population in the nineteenth century is roughly equated with persons found dwelling in tents, caravans and the open air, we can obtain an idea of its size from the census figures for England and Wales. These (though likely to be underestimates) indicate a fairly steady rise from 1841 (7,659) to 1891 (12,834) and 1901 (12,574). The main concentrations in April 1901 were in four counties around London (Essex, Middlesex, Kent and Surrey), together with Sussex and Hampshire, and in the neighbourhood of other industrial centres in the Midlands (Staffordshire) and the North-West (Lancashire and the West Riding). After those came London itself, Glamorgan and Durham.[30]

---

[29] Two useful studies of wayfaring life in nineteenth-century England are R. Samuel, 'Comers and goers', in *The Victorian City*, eds H. J. Dyos and M. Wolff (London, 1973), vol. 1, pp. 123–60, and Mayall, *Gypsy-Travellers*.

[30] Based on Mayall, *Gypsy-Travellers*, pp. 23–9, which provides a more detailed analysis.

Plate 33 Encampment at Mitcham Common. Illustrated London News, 3 January 1880.

This distribution reflected a pronounced shift over the course of the century in the economic role of Gypsies and in their patterns of livelihood and travel in Britain. In the early 1800s the imperfect supply and demand conditions meant that many of them could serve a very useful function touring the largely inaccessible rural areas, as they had for centuries previously: they supplemented the economic and social life of the village by offering their goods and services to a population which, being distant from shops and towns, was not otherwise catered for. They appeared as purveyors of gossip and news, sellers of cheap wares (often made by themselves), repairers of household goods, seasonal labourers (e.g. for haymaking, pea and fruit picking, hopping); or they could function as itinerant entertainers, enlivening village festivities by their talents in music, song and dance. When these needs began to be increasingly met by other means and as transport and communications improved, they diversified into new crafts or adapted the old ones. Since they relied on settled folk to buy the goods and services which they presented for sale, what they offered and the areas they travelled had to change, and their lives became attuned to new seasonal rhythms in which the more densely populated areas loomed larger.

Around London, the winter months saw many of them migrate inwards. Some moved into houses, some into huts and wooden buildings; others pitched their tents and halted their vans on pieces of common land, perhaps at Wormwood Scrubs, Barnes, Dulwich or Mitcham, or in areas of transition, on brickfields and waste ground of every description, at places like Wandsworth, Battersea and Kensal Green and the shanty town region of the Notting Dale Potteries (where there were estimated to be some 50 families in 1862 – enough to warrant the erection of a mission tent in 1869).[31] Once in the city localities, they were now more likely to be mixing with and living alongside other English and Irish transients. Metropolitan Gypsies earned their living by a variety of means. Hawking and tinkering were their staple occupations, but it would be a mistake, then as now, to think in terms of one livelihood

[31] Descriptions of Gypsy colonies at Wandsworth, Notting Dale and Shoreditch in the 1860s are given in G. Borrow, *Romano Lavo-Lil* (London, 1874), pp. 207–37.

Plate 34 Gypsy fruit-pickers at Send (near Guildford), Surrey, 1910. Smiths, Bucklands, Does, Winmans and Baths are all represented here. Ostrich feathers were much in vogue. Photograph by Fred Shaw.

per family. A man might be, variously, basket-maker, chair-bottomer, knife-grinder, sieve-mender, umbrella-repairer, tinker, horse-dealer, and maker of clothes-pegs and butchers' skewers, sometimes moving around from street to street canvassing for custom, at other times staying at home to make the small articles that formed part of his stock-in-trade until mass production made it simpler to buy stock ready-made. Many of them turned up in force on Fridays for the Caledonian Market. The work unit was family-based. Women played their full part, carrying the hawking basket from door to door and doing the fortune-telling often associated with it; the children's role was to help their parents on their rounds or in manufacturing various items at home.

Some of these colonies – like the Battersea Gypsies who kept close to London – had very limited migration. Indeed, a few of the Battersea group remained encamped all the year round in Donovan's Yard near the South-Western Railway; and at Notting Dale a nucleus of families (most of them Hearnes) remained in continuous occupation. Other cities acquired similarly permanent Gypsyries. In Liverpool, it became the practice of the Everton Gypsies to pitch their tents on a piece of waste ground near Walton Breck; in 1879 they were summoned before the magistrates for having failed to supply themselves with water 'as required by the Public Health Act', but the camp continued to flourish years later. Most of the urban colonies, however, broke up with the onset of spring, and seasonal employment was an essential ingredient of the subsequent migrations, even if, throughout, hawking and tinkering served as mainstays. James Crabb put his readers on the track of the rhythms around London:

Those Christians who wish for opportunities of doing good to the Gipsies in and about London, will find many of them in the suburbs in the months of April, May, and June, when they generally find work in the market gardens. In the months of July and August they move into Sussex and Kent, and are engaged in the harvest. And in the month of September *great numbers* of them are to be found in the hop-districts of Kent, Sussex, and Surrey, where they find employment.[32]

[32] J. Crabb, *The Gipsies' Advocate*, 3rd edn (London, 1832), pp. 136–7.

Mayhew called the September hop-picking the grand
rendezvous for the vagrancy of England and Ireland, and
Gypsies came to it from every part of southern England.
Summer was also a profitable time of year for the fortune-
tellers, in the parks and other resorts for visitors. Fairs and
race-meetings formed a major feature of the Gypsy calendar,
giving some structure to the timing and direction of their
travels, and providing a meeting place for families and friends
as well as allowing them to engage in the serious business of
horse-dealing. Easter Fair at Wanstead Flats was known as the
'Gypsy Fair' from the number who made it their first gathering
of the season; while Epsom was overrun by Gypsies during
Derby week, along with an army of freelance hucksters.
(Crabb solicitously warned his readers: 'The morning would
be the happiest time to visit these Gipsies, as they are too
often, at races, inebriated before night'.) Once the harvests
were in, the movement from town to country was reversed; a
first wave returned to London almost immediately after the
hop-picking, perhaps stocking up *en route* with French and
German baskets in Houndsditch; others began to drift back in
October, and by November the movement was general.

   Thus it was that, in the face of urbanization, industrialization and other European pressures, Gypsies showed themselves
able to maintain their autonomy by exploiting opportunities
created by the dominant system. They resisted temptations to
go over to wage-labour, as so many others were doing. Most –
even when settled – seem to have clung tenaciously to some
ideal of community and independence and self-employment.
In Britain, urbanization did not prove incompatible with maintaining a degree of nomadism, though the distances travelled
now tended to become shorter, reflecting the increased geographical concentration of the clientele: they moved from
village to town where necessary and abandoned old trades in
favour of new activities more suited to the times, but without
compromising their freedom, their ethnic identity or their
occupational and residential flexibility. As the century pro-
gressed, more and more working practices had to change. The
making of articles for hawking became a dwindling trade and
the goods they peddled were increasingly machine-made and
bought from a wholesaler, while the demand for tinkering

and repairing also went into decline when cheap manufactured articles became readily available. Harvest work too was becoming mechanized. A less resilient culture might have succumbed completely; the Gypsies' did not.

Out of bondage

The legal codes which governed Gypsy slaves in Wallachia and Moldavia during the first few decades of the nineteenth century differed but little in substance from the measures applied to them four centuries before.[33] The system had developed over the years into a well-defined classification. On the one hand were the Gypsies of the Crown (in Rumanian: *Tsigani domneśti*);[34] on the other, the slaves owned either by monasteries (*Tsigani mănăstireśti*) or by boyars (*Tsigani boiereśti*). The Gypsies who paid their tribute to the Crown were divided into several classes: *Lingurari* ('spoon-makers'), who made wooden utensils; *Ursari* ('bear-leaders'), who were blacksmiths and tinkers besides training bears to perform tricks; *Rudari* ('miners') or *Aurari* ('goldsmiths', 'gold-washers'), employed in mining and in washing gold; and *Lăieśi* ('members of a horde'), with no fixed occupation and able to roam within the principalities. The *Lăieśi* turned their hands to many things, particularly metal-working, while their women went from house to house telling fortunes and seeking alms (see plate 23). Some of the *Lăieśi* were able to escape and form communities in the Carpathians; under the name of *Netotsi* they acquired a sinister reputation. The real slaves, in the ordinary sense of the term, were the privately owned *Vătraśi* (i.e. those from a *vatră* – a 'hearth', or home), who acted

---

[33] Cf. M. Kogălniceanu, *Esquisse sur l'histoire . . . des Cigains* (Berlin, 1837); A. A. Colocci, *Gli Zingari* (Turin, 1889), esp. pp. 126–46; T. R. Gjorgjević, 'Rumanian Gypsies in Serbia', *JGLS*(3), 8 (1929), pp. 7–25; C. J. Popp Serboianu, *Les Tsiganes* (Paris, 1930), esp. pp. 45–53; G. Potra, *Contribuţiuni la istoricul Ţiganilor din România* (Bucharest, 1939); I. Hancock, *The Pariah Syndrome* (Ann Arbor, 1987), esp. pp. 11–48.

[34] In order to convey the pronunciation of certain Rumanian letters, Rum. ţ is here transliterated as *ts*, and Rum. ş as *ś* (with the same value as in Romani).

as grooms, coachmen, cooks and domestic servants to their owners; some might live in villages as barbers, tailors, cobblers or farriers. It was among the *Vătraśi* that the best musicians were to be found. There were also some *Lăieśi*, mostly smiths and comb-makers, in private hands: these paid their tribute to their owner – monastery or boyar – instead of to the state, the taxes being collected from them in the first instance by a Gypsy 'judge' (*jude*), who passed the money on to a higher official, the Bulibasha, directly responsible to the owner.

Masters could put their Gypsies to death with impunity, and any lapses were often met with fierce punishments. Mihail Kogălniceanu, a Rumanian reformer who campaigned for the emancipation of the Gypsies, described what he had witnessed in Moldavia's capital, Jassy (Iaşi), as a boy:

... human beings wearing chains on their arms and legs, others with iron clamps round their foreheads, and still others with metal collars about their necks. Cruel floggings and other punishments, such as starvation, being hung over smoking fires, solitary confinement, and being thrown naked into the snow or a frozen river, such was the treatment meted out to the wretched Gypsy.

The sanctity of marriage and family ties was likewise made a mockery: the wife was separated from the husband, the daughter wrested from the mother, children torn from the breasts of those who brought them into the world, and sold to different buyers from the four corners of Rumania, like cattle.[35]

In all, Kogălniceanu estimated that Gypsies numbered 200,000 in Wallachia and Moldavia, the privately owned slaves being in the majority and representing some 35,000 families.

It was during the Russian occupation of the Danubian principalities in 1828–34 that some tentative moves in the direction of emancipation began to be made, only to be stifled. Public opinion might be changing, but the owners were not yet ready. The first decisive step was taken by Alexander Ghica, Voivode of Wallachia, who in 1837 liberated 4,000 families of Gypsies of the Crown and settled them in villages, where the boyars were charged with giving them work as peasants. Moldavia followed his example for Gypsies of the Crown in

[35] Kogălniceanu, *Esquisse*, pp. 16–17; also his *Desrobirea Ţiganiloru* (Bucharest, 1891), p. 14.

Plate 35 Poster advertising a slave auction in Wallachia. 'For sale, a prime lot of Gypsy slaves, to be sold by auction at the Monastery of St Elias, 8 May 1852, consisting of 18 men, 10 boys, 7 women and 3 girls: in fine condition.' From I. Hancock, The Pariah Syndrome, *1987.*

1842 and *Tsigani mănăstiresti* in 1844. Ghica's successor, Gheorghe Bibescu, educated in Paris, saw to it in 1847 that Wallachia's church slaves were also freed, though the transition was not always rapid (see plate 35). On the other side of the Carpathians, in Transylvania, the abolition of serfdom which came in 1848 meant that numbers of settled Gypsies who had been tied to villages were free to move, and many of them did, to swell the Gypsy colonies in the towns.

The new generation of Rumanians which was now growing up looked to France for inspiration; their rulers were well aware of the interest which other European countries were taking in these events, and they sought to complete the task. The boyars, however, stubbornly refused to capitulate. Just how deeply entrenched the practice was in Moldavia is shown by the fact that when some of the property of the late Minister of Finance, Aleku Sturza, was auctioned off in 1851 to pay his debts, his chattels included no fewer than 349 Gypsy slaves – men, women and children.[36] It was not until 1855 that Grigore Ghica, Prince of Moldavia, felt strong enough to press for the removal of what he called 'this humiliating vestige of a barbarous society', proposing also that the owners should be recompensed for the loss on their investments. He had his way and the buying and selling of human beings were banned for good; the compensation to be received by the boyars was fixed at eight ducats in respect of *Lingurari* and *Vătraśi* and four for *Lăieśi*, whether male or female, but nothing was to be paid in respect of suckling children and the infirm. Within a matter of weeks, early in 1856, Wallachia took similar steps. Complete legal freedom came in 1864 when, following the Crimean War, a new constitution was framed for the now united (but not yet independent) principalities which had been transformed into Rumania: Gypsies were, at least in principle, deemed to have the rights of Rumanian citizenship. No constitutional measure has ever dispelled the atmosphere of antagonism and prejudice created by their previous status.

Renewed migrations

The latter half of the nineteenth century saw a number of Gypsy tribes spring to international prominence, as some

---

[36] M. Gaster, 'Bill of sale of Gypsy slaves in Moldavia, 1851', *JGLS*(3), 2 (1923), pp. 68–81.

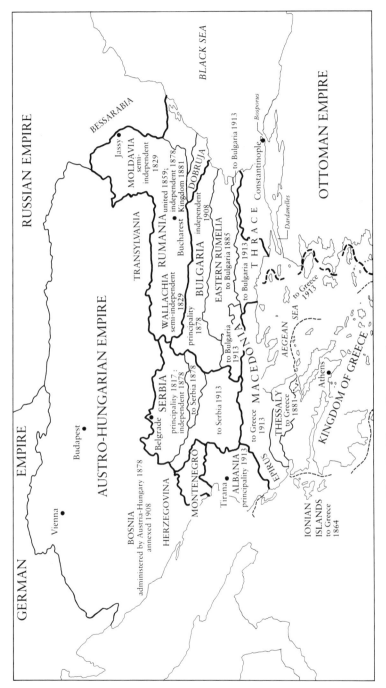

GERMAN EMPIRE

RUSSIAN EMPIRE

BLACK SEA

OTTOMAN EMPIRE

AUSTRO-HUNGARIAN EMPIRE

Vienna

Budapest

BESSARABIA

Jassy

MOLDAVIA
semi-
independent
1829

TRANSYLVANIA

WALLACHIA
semi-independent
1829

RUMANIA
united 1859;
independent 1878;
Kingdom 1881

Bucharest

DOBRUJA

to Bulgaria 1913

BULGARIA
principality
1878

independent
1908

EASTERN RUMELIA
to Bulgaria 1885

T H R A C E

Constantinople

Bosporus

Dardanelles

BOSNIA
administered by Austria-Hungary 1878
annexed 1908

Belgrade

SERBIA
principality 1817;
independent 1878

to Serbia 1878

to Bulgaria
1913

to Serbia 1913

M A C E D O N I A

to Greece
1913

AEGEAN

SEA

to Greece
1913

HERZEGOVINA

MONTENEGRO

to Serbia 1913

Tirana

ALBANIA
principality 1913

EPIRUS

THESSALY
to Greece
1881

Athens

KINGDOM OF GREECE

IONIAN
ISLANDS
to Greece
1864

Map 4 The Balkans in the nineteenth century.

of their members began to move out in all directions from the Balkans and Hungary. Their Romani speech was heavily impregnated by Rumanian influences – hence their dialects have been termed 'Vlach' (or Wallachian) – and they had obviously long been rooted in Rumanian-speaking lands. They called themselves *Rom*. It will be convenient to continue to refer to them, and them alone, by that name, in order to distinguish them from the Gypsies whose ancestors had preceded them westwards centuries before; there are, however, plenty of other groups in central and eastern Europe, not confined to those with Vlach dialects, who would now apply the same designation, *Rom*, to themselves.

The major Rom groupings, with names based on an occupational nomenclature, included Kalderaśa (coppersmiths), Lovara (horse-dealers) and Ćurara (sieve-makers). Also relevant are certain other groups who moved out of the Balkans at about the same time. These were Rumanian-speaking Gypsies whose Romani had for the most part been lost, known by such names as Boyaś (gold-washers), Rudari (miners) and Ursari (bear-leaders).[37]

Subsequent migrations of the Rom had the effect of drawing them apart: the Kalderaśa or Coppersmiths, for example, tended to move towards Russia, Serbia, Bulgaria and Greece, leading to subdivisions based on geographical distinctions, so that some Kalderaśa became labelled in Romani as 'Greeks', others as 'Serbians', others as 'Russians'. Later, there was extensive movement westwards. Once this picked up momentum, it resembled in some ways a re-enactment of what had happened four centuries before, and the reactions of western and northern Europeans – a mixture of curiosity and antagonism – were for the most part similar to those in the fifteenth century. Nowadays, Rom are found in almost every European country, as well as the Americas and elsewhere. They speak closely related dialects of Romani, despite the differences of vocabulary and pronunciation that have crept in, and a Rom who lives in Sweden understands a Rom who lives in Brazil.

---

[37] The designation 'Ursari' can be, however, more of an occupational label and less of a tribal indicator than the others.

In the early 1860s some of the infiltrators were to be seen in Germany and in Poland, where they sought to establish a dominant position among the Gypsies and even to create, in the Kwiek family, a dynasty of 'kings' of Polish Gypsies.[38] From Poland, Kalderaśa and Ćurara went on to Russia and Scandinavia. Some Rom with Austrian passports made their way in 1866 from Berlin to Belgium and then into France, but were soon driven back across the Franco-Belgian frontier.[39] The Coppersmiths who came to France the following year via Germany and Italy had fewer difficulties and were able to travel around in groups of 30, 40 or even 150, in open, four-wheeled, horse-drawn waggons, putting up enormous tents when they stopped for the night. Their stay of four days in February 1868 at Carpentras (to the north-east of Avignon) was long enough to allow a local artist to capture them on canvas (see plate 36). Their ragged clothing contrasted with the mass of gold and silver with which they bedecked themselves. A party of Kalderaśa made an incursion into England in 1868 and pitched their tents on the outskirts of London, where they were none too well regarded by English Gypsies.[40] That was also the year in which the Netherlands began to receive groups of Coppersmiths from central Europe. The Dutch government looked upon them as a completely new phenomenon; and for the general populace they were at first such an exotic novelty that they could charge for entry to their camps and still receive thousands of visitors.[41] Fresh bands of Rom reached France, again from Germany and Italy, in the early 1870s, attracting crowds of curious visitors wherever they went. The earliest mention of Ursari or bear-leaders in the west comes at much the same time as that of the Coppersmiths, with reports from Germany in 1867 and the

[38] Cf. J. Ficowski, *Cyganie na polskich drogach*, 2nd edn (Kraków, 1985), pp. 78–107.

[39] F. de Vaux de Foletier, *Les Bohémiens en France au 19e siècle* (Paris, 1981), has a good chapter on visits from central and east European Gypsies.

[40] T. W. Thompson, 'Foreign Gypsy Coppersmiths in England in 1868', *JGLS*(3), 6 (1927), p. 144.

[41] A valuable account of these incursions is in L. Lucassen, *'En men noemde hen Zigeuners'* (Amsterdam/The Hague, 1990), which covers Gypsy history in the Netherlands from 1750 to 1944.

Plate 36 Hungarian Gypsies at Carpentras in 1868. Painting by Denis Bonnet. Musée Duplessis, Carpentras.

Netherlands in 1868. From 1872 bear-leaders were also to be found on the roads of France. The first came from Serbia and Bosnia with Turkish passports and had names like Galubavich, Lazarovich and Mitrovich; those who followed in subsequent years had similarly Serbian names.

The party of 99 'Greek' Gypsies who arrived by train at Liverpool in 1886 came, according to their passports, from all parts of Greece and European Turkey, and also from Serbia, Bulgaria and Rumania; at least some of them managed to make their way to North America.[42] Some ten years later there were reports of Ursari in southern Scotland and northern England, speaking a jumble of tongues; but in the first decade of the twentieth century it was principally Lovara from Germany who attracted attention in Britain. Late in 1904 a large band with German passports who had been expelled from Holland caused great anxiety to the police and the Home Office until they left for Hamburg after a couple of months in England. A second wave followed in 1906, and from spring to autumn of that year the daily and weekly press joined the police in a campaign against them.[43] Similar events were reported in France, Germany and Switzerland. The biggest stir, however, was caused by the peregrinations of bands of Kalderaśa a few years later. They ranged over several countries of western Europe. In Britain, families with the names Choron, Kirpatsh, Demeter and Maximoff travelled around by train in the period May 1911 to October 1913. They had recently discarded their waggons in France, but they still brought with them their capacious tents, very similar to those which had been painted by Bonnet at Carpentras more than 40 years earlier, and camped in various towns all over the British Isles (see plate 37).[44] They had previously travelled widely in most parts of Europe. While they were in Britain they brought a touch of oriental splendour to drab city waste-grounds.

[42] D. MacRitchie, 'The Greek Gypsies at Liverpool', *Chambers's Journal*, 11 Sep. 1886; A. A. Marchbin, 'Gypsy immigration to Canada', *JGLS*(3), 13 (1934), pp. 134–44.

[43] Cf. C. Holmes, 'The German Gypsy question in Britain, 1904–06', *JGLS*(4), 1 (1978), no. 4, pp. 248–67.

[44] E. O. Winstedt, 'The Gypsy Coppersmiths' invasion of 1911–13', *JGLS*(2), 6 (1912–13), pp. 244–303.

Plate 37 Kalderash tents at Garratt Lane, Wandsworth, London in August 1911. Photograph by Fred Shaw.

The women, with gold coins woven into their hair-plaits and strung around their necks and bosoms, presented a formidable spectacle, quite different from that of their English counterparts in their finery (see plates 38 and 39); and the men, in baggy trousers tucked into top-boots, brightly coloured shirts, and coats and waistcoats with rows of huge buttons of silver (some as large as a hen's egg) were just as resplendent. Much of the men's time was spent in seeking out copper vessels to repair in factories, breweries, hotels, restaurants, and the like: their dexterity and workmanship were widely praised; their grandiose prices were just as widely deprecated.

Few of the new arrivals stayed in Britain. Some were on their way to the Americas; others eventually drifted back to the Continent. In many European countries Rom became an enduring new stratum of Gypsy population. Those who crossed the Atlantic formed an even more important con-

Plate 38 *Kalderash women on the march in England, 1911. Photograph by Fred Shaw.*

Plate 39   *Talaitha Cooper in Paisley shawl and crocheted Gypsy apron, with her daughter Polly, Ascot, August 1912. Photograph by Fred Shaw.*

stituent, for such implantations of Gypsies as had taken place in colonial times in North America seemed to have left few lasting traces. The pace of Gypsy movement to the USA paralleled that of general immigration.[45] Mass migrations to North America from Europe started in 1815, and it was this swelling tide that determined the make-up of today's Gypsy population in the USA. Up to the middle of the century, over half the immigrants were coming from the British Isles, and it was in the 1850s that the arrival of Gypsies (calling themselves 'Romnichels') from Britain reached its highest point. They came in small numbers, as families, and even in the peak period of 1850–62 there were under 400 of them. They appeared to favour Ohio, Pennsylvania and Virginia as their new homes, and engaged in a wide variety of peripatetic trades, including horse-dealing, tinning and basket-making for the men, and fortune-telling and hawking of easily made or cheaply purchased goods for the women; gradually horse-dealing became far and away the preponderant male activity.[46] By the 1870s, the foundations for the present-day Romnichel community had been laid, though new members continued to arrive up to the First World War. Their descendants are still known as Romnichels, for they continued to speak their own dialect and maintain social distance from other Gypsy groups as well as non-Gypsies.

In the 1880s – at a time when the American economy was booming – the general pattern of immigration to the USA changed radically, with a pronounced shift towards the countries of southern and eastern Europe as sources. From then up to 1914 the newcomers came mainly from Austria-Hungary, Italy, Greece, Russia, Rumania and Turkey. Some Gypsy groups joined in. The first appear to have been Rom from Austria-Hungary who landed at New York in 1881, followed by Ludar (Rudari) claiming Bulgarian and Spanish

---

[45] For a detailed analysis, see M. T. Salo and S. Salo, 'Gypsy immigration to the United States', in *Papers from the Sixth and Seventh Annual Meetings, Gypsy Lore Society, North American Chapter* (New York, 1986), pp. 85–96.

[46] Cf. M. T. Salo and S. Salo, 'The Romnichel economic and social organization in urban New England, 1850–1930', *Urban Anthropology*, 11 (1982), pp. 273–313.

nationality in 1882 and a group of Austro-Hungarian musicians in 1883, these last being presumably among the earliest of the so-called 'Hungarian Slovak' Gypsies whose descendants are now referred to generically by American Rom as the *Baśaldé* or 'musicians'. Some came via Cuba, or (from 1900) via Canada, Mexico or South America, where entrance regulations were more lenient. The Ludar were showmen, performers and animal trainers, and most arrived with their trained bears and monkeys; they generally declared Austro-Hungarian or Turkish nationality. (The designation 'Turkish' was at that time much wider in its European coverage, and was also still used to refer to territories which had recently been removed from the Ottoman empire, such as Bosnia-Herzegovina.) Rom tended to bring in more money than the Ludar, and both consistently exceeded the immigrant average. Most of the Rom – who had often embarked at North Sea or English ports – claimed Austro-Hungarian nationality, followed by Russian and Serbian. One of the Serbian groups that stands out in the figures is that which named their birthplace or last residence in Maćva county (to the west of Belgrade) giving rise to the Maćwaya tribal division. Gypsy immigration to the USA direct from Europe virtually ended in 1914 with the First World War and the subsequent tightening of controls, until in the early 1970s Lovara and others began to arrive from the communist countries of eastern Europe.

In all this, Gypsies were to a large extent simply sharing in a much more widespread upheaval. A number of general factors were contributing to the increased tempo of migration in the latter part of the nineteenth century, such as the economic opportunities in western Europe and the United States, improved rail communications, and faster and cheaper sea travel. When one looks at what was happening in North America, the close parallel with general immigration trends – the Romnichels coming at the time of peak immigration from Britain, and the Rom and Ludar with the great wave of immigration from eastern Europe – suggests that, if there were any causes of emigration peculiar to Gypsies, they did not play a major role in their decisions to go. There was, however, distinct unevenness in the readiness of different Gypsy groups to sail to the United States. Romnichels, Rom and Ludar were not the only ones to come; but others were sparsely represented and the resulting pattern of Gypsy population in the USA was far from being a representative cross-section even of those living in the regions of Europe that produced emigrants.

The original upsurge has often been linked with the ending of Gypsy enslavement in Wallachia and Moldavia, but that leaves unexplained the apparent chronology and pattern of the migrations and the social organization of the Rom; while the recorded antecedents of particular Rom, Ursari and Rudari families who came west point to an extensive sojourn in countries other than Moldo-Wallachia and lend no support to the idea that there was a major outflow from Rumania in the 1850s.[47]

These doubts are increased when one considers the evidence of their dialects at the time when they first began to be recorded. The influence of Rumanian is unmistakable; but in differing degrees they also bore clear traces of Hungarian infiltration. This was much more limited in the case of Kalderaśítska than of Lovarítska, which adopted a large number of Magyar words and began to follow the Hungarian stress-accent, while the Ćurari dialect remained somewhere between those two. Non-Rumanian penetration on this scale indicates a fairly protracted exposure to other tongues after the Rom removed themselves from the influence of Rumanian, or during the time when they were under its influence. Similar problems arise with the speech of Rumanian-speaking Gypsy groups outside Rumania who had lost their Romani. The Rudari who became prominent in the latter half of the nineteenth century were by then using a Rumanian which included a strong element of Serbo-Croat vocabulary; while the Boyaś who are in present times found around Pécs in southern Hungary appear to employ an archaic form of Rumanian similar to that spoken centuries ago in the Banat, the ethnically mixed region neighbouring on western Wallachia (later divided among Hungary, Rumania and Yugoslavia).[48]

[47] Cf. A. M. Fraser, 'The Rom migrations', *JGLS*(5), 2 (1992), no. 2.
[48] G. Papp, *A beás cigányok román nyelvjárása: Beás-magyar szótár* ['Rumanian Dialect of Boyash Gypsies: Boyash–Hungarian Dictionary'] (Pécs, 1982).

In considering such developments one needs to look outside Wallachia and Moldavia for a starting point. Rumanian was spoken well beyond the boundaries of those two principalities. It was spoken in the Banat; in the north-eastern part of Serbia; in western Bessarabia; and in much of Transylvania, especially in rural areas to the north of Wallachia. It is easier to assume that the bulk of the Rom had for long been established in such regions (some of them being perhaps descended from the steady trickle of refugees out of Wallachia and Moldavia during the years of oppression) than that they were made up of released slaves flooding from the Danubian principalities for fear that the old order might be re-established.

Conservation and mutation

There is a great temptation to consider the widely distributed Vlach Rom, who in many ways appear more exotic than longer established Gypsies, to be the most faithful custodians of ancient tradition. (Certainly the Rom themselves would argue this to be the case, for they share the characteristic common to most Gypsy groups of being convinced that they themselves are the 'true' Gypsies.) It is, however, never a simple matter to decide how much of the cultural preserve of Gypsies is unique to them. In the field of folklore, for example, they have commonly adapted elements of the culture of the non-Gypsy community with which they are in contact and integrated them into their own songs and tales; in the course of time, that community's heritage may have sunk into oblivion, leaving the Gypsies as the conservators of what they had originally borrowed. On the linguistic front, it is possible, within Romani, to identify the Persian, the Armenian, the Greek and other loan-words and to strip them off, layer by layer, so as to expose the original core. A similar approach is much more difficult in regard to Gypsy cultural tradition and value patterns. This is as true of those who call themselves *le Rom*, 'the Rom', as of all the other groups.

Any Gypsy society is built on an intricate pattern of family relationships. In the case of the Rom, their social institutions, being relatively formal and public within the community, are perhaps more accessible to the observer than those of other groups and hence may win a wider degree of credence as being the norm.[49] In practice, it is extremely risky to extrapolate from the Rom. The first division of their people is that which categorizes them into tribes – most notably Kalderaśa, Maćwaya, Lovara and Ćurara – which the Kalderash generally call a *natsia* ('nation') and the Lovara a *rása* ('race'), both words being, like most Rom organizational terminology, Rumanian loan-words. These 'tribes' have differences in dialect, custom and appearance but recognize each other's right to be considered as Rom, and may intermarry. Each is further divided into *vítsi* (plural of *vitsa*, translatable as 'clan'; but Lovara may use instead the word *tsérha*, literally 'tent'). The *vitsa* is in effect a unit of identification and has its own Romani name, often derived from that of some ancestor (e.g. the Frinkuleśti descend from Frinkulo Mikhailovitch) but sometimes from an animal or a defining characteristic. Such names have their greatest functional significance when two Rom meet for the first time and are trying to place each other. The members of one *vitsa* will perhaps never come together or operate as a group in any way, and the major functional subdivision is the *familia* or extended family which includes married sons and their wives, children and grandchildren; while each residential unit or household within the *familia* (perhaps covering three generations) is known as a *tséra*. Different in kind is the *kumpánia* ('company'), which is not necessarily a kin grouping and may be made up of people from more than one tribe and from several clans or extended families: it is an alliance bound together by economic necessity for work purposes, to exploit a particular territory, and the proceeds are divided equally among its members. The

---

[49] An extensive description of Rom social organization may be found in P. Williams, *Mariage tsigane* (Paris, 1984), dealing with the world of the Rom in general and the Kalderash in Paris in particular. Rom, notably Kalderash and Maćwaya, occupy a prominent place among Gypsies in North America, and there is a growing body of literature about them by North American scholars, e.g. W. Cohn, *The Gypsies* (Reading, MA, 1973); R. C. Gropper, *Gypsies in the City* (Princeton, NJ, 1975); A. Sutherland, *Gypsies, the Hidden Americans* (London, 1975); and M. T. and S. Salo, *The Kalderaš in Eastern Canada* (Ottawa, 1977).

kumpania, composed of a number of households, is often headed by a *rom baró* ('big man') who provides leadership and acts as the link with the *gadźé* (or *gaźé*, as the Rom pronounce it). The *kumpania* is also the basic political unit and its members can make decisions on moral, social, political and economic questions which are considered to be public rather than family matters; to do this they may seek to settle the issue by a *diváno* ('discussion') or, if it is important enough, call for a *kris romani* ('Romany trial') to adjudicate. The *kris* is a formal tribunal made up from different *vitsi*, and is monopolized by men: it consists of a council of elders and one or more judges – all men. Women rarely speak at the *kris*, but can do so if directly involved in the conflict. Its decision is binding on the plaintiffs, who must place their fate in its hands. Its procedure can be protracted and arduous; and among the Lovara, the Kalderash in particular have the reputation of making too much of a meal of the *kris*.

Members of the same *vitsa* are 'relatives', and are expected to give each other aid and protection in time of need. The *vitsa* also has important ritual ties: for example, a man has a special obligation to attend the funeral and *pomána* (death feasts) of members of his *vitsa*. Kinship is thus a powerful force for assistance and co-operation, and often this is strengthened by marriage alliances. The Rom appear increasingly to favour marriage between cousins (though first cousins are in principle felt to be too close), and the partner is preferably from one's own *vitsa* or, failing that, the mother's or grandmother's. But a marriage can also be a new method of creating mutual obligations with members of a *kumpania* with which the family does not already have kinship ties.

Arranging a marriage for one's son is a very important obligation of a father, and he does so with the father of the prospective bride, in collaboration with other male members of their *vitsi*. Negotiations for a betrothal may be long drawn out, and will be a public affair, with interventions from the other Rom present: their society's existence is at stake, and they are looking for a harmonious arrangement founded on reciprocity. In theory, the couple themselves do not participate, but in practice they may be able to influence their parents' choice, and they do have the right to refuse consent to a union. After marriage, the couple usually lives with the man's parents. The new bride's role is then an uneasy one: her duties are to care for her in-laws, perform household duties for them, and produce grandchildren.

One vital consideration is generally the bride-price which the girl's father asks for: it can be high in relation to what most Rom are able to pay. Where it survives (it died out among the Kalderash and Lovara in Poland by the 1950s, for example), this institution of bride-price has a considerable social impact. The number of gold coins to be handed over tends to be fairly stable, but may fluctuate according to the status of the two fathers and the two families and also the girl's own standing (in terms of behaviour, previous history, and capacity as an earner). In exceptional cases where the husband joins his in-laws (perhaps because his parents disapprove of the marriage or because he is an orphan), no bride-price is expected. It is not a commercial transaction, and the money is not spent like other income. It can be regarded as an acknowledgement of reciprocity and of the failure to provide the bride's family with a daughter in return. Sometimes an equal exchange of women between families (usually sister-exchange) is in fact arranged, and dealing with relatives makes that much easier; but such exchanges lead to difficult situations if one of the unions breaks down. Bride-price itself can be a major problem area, and another reason for preferring to acquire a daughter-in-law from close family is that it reduces the chance of chicanery (for example, of the daughter's being taken back by her father without return of the bride-price – not so much for the legitimate purpose of protecting her from ill-treatment, which a father is entitled to do, but as a means of exploiting the system). Divorce and adultery also raise difficult issues. Problems of this kind may require a *kris* before they can be solved: the two parties in dispute then state their grievances and the amount of bride-price to be returned is decided for good.

Not only are many features in these social institutions peculiar to the Rom: they can sometimes also be seen to have evolved within the course of a few generations. It is therefore impossible to generalize from the Rom to Gypsy society as a whole. For instance, among the Coppersmiths who came to

Liverpool in 1911, a man was just as likely to join his bride's extended family on marriage as the other way round.[50] Even in nineteenth-century Transylvania, where one might have looked for fairly close correspondence, the normal rule among nomadic Gypsies (as reported by the main investigator of the day) was for a man to leave his own clan and join that of his wife when he married.[51] Similar rules appear to have had some degree of application among Gypsies elsewhere (including England). As for the bride-price custom, it is far from being universal among Gypsies. For many, the convention in creating a union is or was a form of elopement, whereas for the Rom an elopement represents rejection of parental authority and, even though it may now be on the increase among them too, it is considered a scandalous event. Similarly, the institution of the *kris*, though it used to have its parallels among the Sinti of Germany and Austria, is unknown to many Gypsies, who have no formal or informal central authority for dealing with disputes. Private vengeance may then be the rule for breaches of the code, and a system of justice based on feuding can be found in countries as far apart as England and Finland. In the latter, blood-feuding is accompanied by the important adjunct of institutionalized *avoidance* of violence, in that when one family accepts guilt for an offence it moves away voluntarily and continues to avoid those against whom the offence was committed, while other Gypsies seek to ensure that members of feuding families are kept apart.[52]

Wide divergences like these raise the question, as yet unanswered, of whether such a practice as the bride-price (for which there are counterparts among Indian tribal peoples) is a usage that other Gypsies have allowed to lapse, or whether it permeated the Rom (and a number of neighbouring Gypsy groups) in the course of their lengthy stay in the Balkans. In considering the *kris*, for example, it is not difficult to identify possible influences. In the feudal system of south-east Europe, both before and after the Turkish conquest, the population

[50] Winstedt, 'The Gypsy Coppersmiths' invasion of 1911–13', pp. 260–2.

[51] H. von Wlislocki, *Vom wandernden Zigeunervolke* (Hamburg, 1890), pp. 61–8. (This is, however, a book to be treated with caution.)

[52] M. Grönfors, *Blood Feuding among Finnish Gypsies* (Helsinki, 1977).

was commonly attached to its own chiefs, who were the elders of the village, the most distinguished members of the local community and the heads of its extended families, and who, within their own settlement, helped to collect taxes and transact deals in marketing and contracting; and they also settled minor disputes, following local customary laws. Does that outweigh Indian parallels of a tribal council, presided over by an influential old man, where all disputes are arbitrated and the verdict of the joint deliberation is final? Whichever line of reasoning one cares to follow, it is not easy to reconcile elaborate institutions of the kind so far considered with the idea that the Rom emerged from Moldo-Wallachia after centuries of being treated as chattels, given the scant regard that the slaves' masters paid to marriage and family ties.

If Gypsy customs have, then, become so diversified, is there anything at all in this field that can be identified as some kind of universal or absolute? After eliminating customs which are certainly widespread, but which have analogues in European folklore, perhaps two features in particular stand out as intensely Gypsy and possibly dating from a time before their arrival in Europe. One is a dread of the clinging or haunting presence of the disembodied spirit of someone who has died, which has underlain their funeral rites. That has not, however, prevented the details of those ceremonies from becoming considerably varied, for they may often be linked with observance of other folk-usages or acceptance of other beliefs (as in the case of the association of the *mulo*, meaning 'ghost' as well as 'dead person', with vampirism in many parts of south-eastern Europe). One practice observed by Gypsy groups in different countries, but not everywhere, has been the destruction of the property of the deceased. In England, in the days of 'waggon-time', it was the custom to burn a dead person's living-waggon after the burial, along with the personal belongings and the smashing of all the crockery.[53] Nowadays, when cars or trucks and trailer-caravans have virtually ousted horse

---

[53] Cf. T. W. Thompson, 'English Gypsy death and burial customs', *JGLS*(3), 3 (1924), pp. 5–38 and 60–93; and J. Okely, *The Traveller-Gypsies* (Cambridge, 1983), ch. 12.

Plate 40 The burning of Harriet Bowers's van, in a lane near Garsington, Oxford, 1953. Keystone/Hulton-Deutsch Picture Company.

and waggon, it is the trailer which ought to be broken up or, at a pinch, quietly sold off to some *gadžo*.

Even more pervasive is a dread of contamination, and the taboos which arise from that. It is only in relatively recent times that the full significance of the Gypsies' purity code has been recognized: their pollution beliefs can now be seen as a core element of their cultures, serving to express and reinforce an ethnic boundary and to delineate a fundamental division between Gypsy and *gadžo*.[54] The concept of defilement which is at its root goes by several names in Romani, according to the dialect. The Rom and many other Gypsies from south-eastern Europe use the word *marimé* ('unclean'), drawn from Greek; *moxado* is the Romani form in England and Wales, and *magerdó* that in Poland, both meaning 'stained' (Sanskrit *mrakṣ* = 'smear'); *prastlo* ('dishonoured') or *palećido* ('set apart') are the Sinti expressions. The terminology varies; the code itself, despite differences in its particulars and its observance, shows a considerable degree of consistency. Wherever it is strictly adhered to, the taboo system informs all interaction between male and female and Gypsy and *gadžo*. And for a Gypsy to be declared polluted is the greatest shame a man can suffer, and along with him his household. It is social death, for the condition can be passed on: anything he wears or touches or uses is polluted for others. For a people for whom communal life is of major importance, and where marriages, baptisms, parties, feasts and funerals are frequent social

---

[54] As far back as the 1920s, accounts of uncleanness taboos were published in T. W. Thompson, 'The uncleanness of women among English Gypsies', *JGLS*(3), 1 (1922), pp. 15–43, and 8 (1929), pp. 33–9. Corresponding practices in Poland were analysed in J. Ficowski, 'Supplementary notes on the *mageripen* code among Polish Gypsies', *JGLS*(3), 30 (1951), pp. 123–32. The corpus of recent field studies started with C. Miller, 'Mačwaya Gypsy Marimé' (MA thesis, Seattle, 1968), and subsequently included C. Miller, 'American Rom and the ideology of defilement' and A. Rao, 'Some Mānuš conceptions and attitudes' in *Gypsies, Tinkers and Other Travellers*, ed. F. Rehfisch (London, 1975), pp. 41–54 and 139–67; C. Silverman, 'Pollution and power: Gypsy women in America', in *The American Kalderaš*, ed. M. T. Salo (Hackettstown, NJ, 1981), pp. 55–70; Okely, *The Traveller-Gypsies*; and I. -M. Kaminski, 'The dilemma of power: internal and external leadership. The Gypsy-Roma of Poland', in *The Other Nomads*, ed. A. Rao (Cologne, 1987), pp. 323–56.

occasions, such a sentence is a much feared and very effective punishment. Among the Rom, the only way *marimé* status can be revoked is by convening a *kris*.

The taboos relate to persons, objects, parts of the body, foodstuffs and topics of conversation (and Gypsies have difficulty over sex education in schools); but their overwhelming concern is with the uncleanness of the female and her potential threat to ritual purity. The lower body, particularly of the woman, is considered *marimé* and everything associated with it is potentially defiling – genitalia, bodily functions, clothing touching the lower body, and allusions to sex and pregnancy. Strict washing regulations are enforced, such as separate basins, towels and soaps for the two body zones. A sparklingly clean kitchen sink may still be declared *marimé*: a bowl in which clothing has been washed must not be used for washing face-towels and tablecloths or cooking utensils and crockery, and a woman's clothes have to be washed separately from others. She is more polluted, and hence subject to greater restrictions and isolation, during her most sexual periods – puberty, menstruation, pregnancy, and immediately after childbirth. She then has to be particularly careful about what she touches: in a strict household she may not cook or serve food to men. Before puberty and after menopause, however, the prohibitions are fewer: a young girl may expose her legs by wearing short skirts; older women can associate more freely with men. The sexes are segregated in any public event, and women take second place. But though a woman may have little prestige and be expected always to act modestly and defer to men, one effect of the code is that she has in reserve a potent sanction, for she can defile a man by touching him in public with an article of clothing from her lower body, such as her skirt, and the mere threat of defilement is a powerful weapon.

Marimé regulations pervade all of life, and it is difficult in modern circumstances to honour them to the letter. Fear of the *mulo* and of pollution combine to complicate the task of, say, a travelling house-dwelling Rom seeking to rent accommodation: anything previously occupied by a *gadźo* and with an unknown history is a minefield. Only if a dwelling can be taken over from some other Rom is there much less risk of having to embark, for safety's sake, on elaborate cleansing procedures. *Gadžé* are by definition unclean, being ignorant of the rules of the system and lacking in a proper sense of 'shame': they exist outside the social boundaries, and their places and their prepared food present a constant danger of pollution. The code thus serves to isolate those Gypsies who practise it from any intensive, intimate contact with *gadžé*; and its existence makes all the more understandable the concern, so apparent in their history, to avoid any form of employment that would require such contact.

8

The Approach to Avernus

One effect of the new migrations was to sharpen the attitudes of western European governments in regard to Gypsies, and in some cases to revive notions which were lying dormant. These notions quickly gained ground and, as the twentieth century opened, they were being put ever more rigorously into operation until, during the Nazi era, the gates to the death camps took over the role of the ancients' Avernus as an entrance to hell. In so far as there was felt to be any need for intellectual support for policies of repression, it could readily be found in some of the theories which emerged in the latter part of the nineteenth century – a flourishing time for biological determinism and obsessions with purity of race and stock. The French Count Gobineau's *Essai sur l'inégalité des races humaines* (1853–5) had a marked impact on philosophical and political thought in Europe, most notably in Germany. Its theme was that race was the decisive factor in historical development: there were 'higher' and 'lower' races, and pride of place was assigned to the 'Aryan race' (used loosely as a synonym for those who spoke Indo-European languages), particularly to the Nordic peoples. Gobineau was also convinced of the inferiority of cross-breeds and regarded miscegenation as necessarily disastrous. His ideas were given a further twist by Wagner's son-in-law, the Englishman Houston Stewart Chamberlain, whose principal work, *Die Grundlagen des neunzehnten Jahrhunderts* ('The Foundations of the Nineteenth Century', 1899), exalted the historical role of the Teutons. It needed only a short step further along this line of thought to conclude that it was no longer possible for a people like the Gypsies to throw off the shackles of racial origin. That step was taken when biological doctrines revolutionized criminology, under the stimulus of Cesare Lombroso's *L'uomo delinquente* ('Criminal Man', 1876), which emphasized the atavistic origin of crime. When he came to survey the depravity of inferior peoples, Lombroso had nothing good to say of Gypsies and reinforced the view that some practitioners of crime prevention were already disposed to take of them. They were vain, shameless, improvident, shiftless, noisy, violent and licentious, fond of eating carrion, and suspected of cannibalism. His one begrudging word of praise dismissed their musical arts in Hungary as simply 'a new proof of the genius that, mixed with atavism, is to be found in the criminal'. Even more sweepingly, the movement labelled 'Social Darwinism', which gained a great deal of support after 1890, concluded that the biological factor was the one absolute in *all* spheres of life: the modern state, instead of protecting the weak, should turn its attention to encouraging biologically valuable elements; and the social usefulness or biological capability of the individual became the measure of his or her social worth.

'Combating the Gypsy nuisance'

The resurgence of east-to-west migration did not involve enormous numbers of Gypsies. But it was conspicuous. These newcomers were outlandish in appearance as well as name and could hardly fail to attract attention in official quarters. To begin with, the heightened perceptions led mainly to intensification of measures already in existence. Occasionally, however, they provoked the restoration of an apparatus of aggression which had fallen into disuse. The Netherlands provides a good example of this.[1] After the apparent success of the *heidenjachten* of the eighteenth century (see p. 150), the

---

[1] See L. Lucassen, '*En men noemde hen Zigeuners*' (Amsterdam/The Hague, 1990).

authorities there seemed to forget about Gypsies as a category calling for special treatment: between 1799 and 1868, official Dutch documents remained silent on *Heidens* and *Egyptenaars* despite all the indications that, for at least part of this period, travelling people similar to the Sinti of Germany were active in the Netherlands, mainly as entertainers (musicians, puppeteers, etc.). When Hungarian Coppersmiths and Bosnian bear-leaders began to come in in 1868, the myopia disappeared. Though ragged in appearance, they were well enough endowed with money and had valid travel documents (the main two criteria in the aliens regulations), but central government officials became increasingly uneasy and, borrowing a name for them from German, soon set about dissuading the local authorities, who administered these regulations, from admitting *Zigeuners* or facilitating their stay. The Gypsies of the Sinti variety began to find that the new attitudes were rubbing off on to them too. One reason for Dutch obduracy was that it had become clear that, once the time came for transient Gypsies to leave, neighbouring countries were very reluctant to accept them. There was an infectious vogue for restrictive measures, particularly at German frontiers.

The German states had never ceased to be suspicious of travelling Gypsies. In the mid-nineteenth century their main concern was incomers. In the Grand Duchy of Baden, for instance, a decree of 1855 warned that 'in recent times Gypsies, especially from Alsace, have frequently been entering again and roaming about with their families, purportedly to trade, but mostly for purposes of begging or other illicit pursuits'. Even after the formation of the new German Empire and annexation of Alsace and Lorraine in 1871, the *Länder* that made up the Reich did not abandon their internal frontier controls: each was still responsible for its own policing and for the planning and administration of policy towards Gypsies. Bismarck, the imperial chancellor, took it upon himself in 1886 to draw the attention of *Land* governments to a recent striking growth in 'complaints about the mischief caused by bands of Gypsies travelling about in the Reich and their increasing molestation of the population'. He stressed that in dealing with the problem a fundamental distinction had to be drawn between foreign Gypsies and those who had German citizenship;[2] but by then the larger *Länder* at least had already moved close to that position. In the flurry of decrees stimulated by Bismarck's prompting, the typical policy, in accordance with his prescription, was two-pronged – to exclude or get rid of foreign Gypsies, and to make domestic Gypsies take up a sedentary life if still itinerant. Official documents did not, however, seek to confine themselves to Gypsies in any strict racial sense, for, to avoid problems of definition, phrases like 'Gypsies and persons travelling in the manner of Gypsies' were often used. Preoccupation with foreign Gypsies remained paramount in the early years of the new Reich, and when the imperial chancery called for progress reports in 1889, there was usually most success to report on that front.

Germany appeared to have no difficulty in securing the co-operation of neighbouring states over keeping Gypsies at bay. The directive on *Bekämpfung des Zigeunerunwesens* ('combating the Gypsy nuisance') issued by Prussia's Minister of the Interior in 1906 listed no fewer than nine bilateral agreements: with Austria-Hungary, Belgium, Denmark, France, Italy, Luxembourg, the Netherlands, Russia and Switzerland. By then, however, Prussia was increasingly focusing its attention on domestic Gypsies who had clung to nomadic ways, and was deploying measures against them of a kind foreshadowed by Bismarck. The key was the licence which was needed for the practice of an itinerant trade, and the method was to stifle requests for licences with a host of meticulously applied bureaucratic requirements, including proof of fixed domicile, absence of serious criminal convictions, satisfactory educational provision for children, and proper accounts for tax purposes. The surprising feature was that so many Gypsies did actually succeed in obtaining the necessary papers. The Prussian officials readily accepted the principle of making Gypsies settle – so long as it did not happen locally: that could entail costs for the community, and

---

[2] R. Hehemann, *Die 'Bekämpfung des Zigeunerunwesens' im Wilhelminischen Deutschland und in der Weimarer Republik 1871–1933* (Frankfurt am Main, 1987), pp. 246–50. (This is the most comprehensive work on Gypsy–*gadžo* relations in Germany in the period in question.)

there was a strong incentive to move them on, even at the price of handing out a nomad's licence.[3]

Prussia was a long way from being the German front-runner in such controls. The leading position had been attained by Bavaria, after a slowish start.[4] In the period 1800–1850 Bavarian archives show little evidence of any special preoccupation with Gypsies, who were regarded as simply one subdivision of vagabonds generally. From mid-century there was growing concern with keeping out the foreign variety, and when the requirement for a licence for itinerant traders was introduced in the 1860s, that became the chosen medium of control, as it did elsewhere. The first Bavarian measure directed specifically at Gypsies in the nineteenth century dated from 1885, with a decree calling for strict scrutiny of their papers, whether at the frontier or inland, withdrawal of work permits wherever possible, and close inspection (at Gypsy expense) of any horses for infectious diseases. And even if all those obstacles had been surmounted, Gypsies were still to be kept under close surveillance. The year 1899 saw the setting up in Munich of a clearing house to collate reports of Gypsy appearances and the actions taken against them, and a special register was started. As the data accumulated the inference was drawn that the nature of the Gypsy population was changing: 'genuine' Gypsies were becoming scarce, and the conspicuous bands were those which travelled around in Gypsy fashion under the pretence of dealing in horses or perfumes or being musical entertainers, but actually lived off begging and stealing; mostly they were said to be people from Hungary, or homeless Germans, though there were also Bosnian bear-leaders and Bohemian musicians among them.

This Munich establishment was the source of two major initiatives. The man in charge, Alfred Dillmann, produced a *Zigeuner-Buch* ('Gypsy Book') in 1905 as an aid to police authorities in Bavaria and neighbouring *Länder* in eradicating what he repeatedly called *die Zigeunerplage* ('the Gypsy

---

[3] Cf. W. Günther, *Zur preussischen Zigeunerpolitik seit 1871* (Hanover, 1985), pp. 13–14.

[4] Cf. E. Strauss, 'Die Zigeunerverfolgung in Bayern 1885–1926', *Giessener Hefte für Tsiganologie* (1986), 1–4/86, pp. 31–108.

plague'). In this manual he painstakingly identified no fewer than 3,350 individual Gypsies and other Travellers. Places of origin were given for less than half of them, but of those so identified the majority (some 20 per cent of all entries) came from Austria-Hungary (mostly Bohemia and Austria), and only about a score were said to hail from Bosnia, Croatia, Slovenia, Galicia and Hungary. Two years after the book's publication the number of notifications on the Munich register had grown to more than 6,000. The second initiative was to call a conference in December 1911 with six other *Länder* to co-ordinate action and extend the coverage of the Munich register by drawing on their data-banks too. The outbreak of world war delayed any practical follow-up. After a further conference in 1925, Bavaria pressed ahead in 1926 with a law to make settlement compulsory and authorize sending Gypsies and other *Arbeitsscheue* ('work-shy' people), if not regularly employed, to workhouses for up to two years on grounds of public security; for the latter purpose it no longer mattered whether the Gypsies were nomadic or not. This provision was justified to the Bavarian legislative assembly in the following terms: 'These people are by nature opposed to all work and find it especially difficult to tolerate any restriction of their nomadic life; nothing, therefore, hits them harder than loss of liberty, coupled with forced labour.' In April 1929 the Munich office's catchment area was extended to the whole of Germany, and the German Criminal Police Commission redesignated it the Central Office for Combating the Gypsy Nuisance. All in all, the Weimar Republic had done a good deal of spadework for the regime which would succeed it.

The Bavarian example was influential. Some other police administrations became convinced that they must have Gypsy problems too and that they needed to take similar action. In Switzerland, whose invitation in 1909 to its four neighbours to consider setting up international machinery for information exchange on Gypsies came to nothing, the Justice Department went ahead with a national register based on the Munich model.[5] It was, however, the country's largest charity for

[5] T. Huonker, *Fahrendes Volk – verfolgt und verfemt* (Zürich, 1987), p. 63.

children which inaugurated the most sustained programme for extirpating the travelling life in Switzerland. In 1926 the eminently respectable Pro Juventute foundation decided, in keeping with the theories of eugenics and progress then fashionable, that the children of *Jenische* ('Travellers') should wherever possible be resettled, in order to divert them into the mainstream of society; thus began a system of taking children away from parents without their consent, changing their names, and placing them in foster homes. These institutional-ized abductions continued until 1973, by which time over 600 children had been forcibly removed.[6]

France pursued a different course. There, the decisive changes occurred in the two decades preceding the outbreak of the First World War.[7] In March 1895 a census was taken of all 'nomads, Gypsies and vagabonds' in France. A special commission, set up to analyse the results, reported in 1898: it put the itinerant total at over 400,000, and among them the number of 'nomads travelling in groups and in caravans' was assessed at 25,000. The census had shown the ethnic diver-sity of the itinerant population in France. There was a high proportion of *manouches* (the French equivalent of German Sinti), many of whom had left Alsace-Lorraine at the time of the German annexation, while others bore names which had been appropriated by Gypsies in France centuries before. Most of those recorded had French nationality, although Italian nomads were numerous in Auvergne; some of these were 'Piedmontese Sinti' – basket-makers, hawkers, accordion players. Families from central or eastern Europe were not much in evidence. From 1907 police forces were told to take photographs of 'vagabonds, nomads and Gypsies' wherever possible and to send details to a central registry in Paris. At the same time Parliamentarians were agitating about Gypsy depredations. In the end a law was passed in July 1912, intro-ducing a *carnet anthropométrique* for itinerants of whatever

[6] Ibid., pp. 74–115. W. Haesler, *Enfants de la Grande-route* (Neuchâtel, 1955), found that the social and educational results among the cohort of children whom he studied were unimpressive, but expressed the hope that a change in educational method could bring some improvement.

[7] Cf. F. de Vaux de Foletier, *Les Bohémiens en France au 19e siècle* (Paris, 1981), ch. 10.

Plate 41 A scene from the French census of 1895. Le Petit Journal,
5 May 1895.

nationality. This was an identity document carrying personal
details, photographs, fingerprints and vehicle licence number:
each individual had to have one, and the head of a family
also needed a collective *carnet* covering all members of the
family, a document of about 100 pages, to be stamped in each
commune on arrival and departure. The *carnet* gave rise to
all kinds of harassment, since it opened the way to court
summonses for being out and about while not carrying it (e.g.
because it had been held by the police for checking). Many
communes, however, took to setting up signs at their boundaries simply proclaiming: *Interdit aux nomades* ('prohibited to

nomads'). This control system was to last for almost 60 years in France.

In Britain, there was also pressure for registration towards the end of the nineteenth century, to a large extent stimulated by one man. Gypsies were no longer singled out for special legislative treatment, but were affected by a wide range of more generalized laws, such as those dealing with hawkers, vagrancy, public health, and commons and enclosures. Their position had become all the more vulnerable as urbanization rendered them more obtrusive and their services less needed. No-one claimed to want the assimilation of the 'true Romanies'. Instead, the target was Travellers whose way of life conflicted with the interests of settled society. The fact that, in practical terms, the fate of one group was inextricably bound up with that of the other seems to have been ignored.[8] With blind devotion and single-minded disregard for the well-being of his own family, a philanthropist named George Smith (see plate 31) – 'of Coalville', he liked to add – was pressing from the 1870s for the reform of brickyard children, canal-dwellers and, finally, Gypsies, whom he compared with savages and animals and accused of a total lack of morals. He succeeded in winning much press publicity and his persistence achieved results, in so far as various Moveable Dwellings Bills, of which he was the instigator, came before Parliament in the period 1885–94. Smith wanted all movable dwellings to be registered and to conform with statutory standards and be subject to inspection during day-time, while the children of Gypsies and van-dwellers were to complete a minimum number of school attendances; the underlying aim was social absorption. His Bill collapsed every time he persuaded someone to introduce it and expired along with him in 1895, though most of his objects, other than registration, were incorporated in various Acts by 1936.

In part the opposition to Smith's ideas had arisen on grounds of civil liberties, in part for fear of other school-children being contaminated; but the main force of resistance

---

[8] The pioneering work on this subject was T. Acton, *Gypsy Politics and Social Change* (London, 1974); there is also much relevant material in D. Mayall, *Gypsy-Travellers in Nineteenth-Century Society* (Cambridge, 1988).

came latterly from the Showmen's Guild, formed in 1889 to look after the interests of fairground people and in particular to lobby against the proposals of George Smith of Coalville. Apart from that, there had been no organized body seeking to put forward a view on behalf of those likely to be affected. Although a Gypsy Lore Society was founded in 1888 by a number of *gadže* (whose interest had in large measure been aroused by the writings of George Borrow: see p. 197), contemporary political issues at first received scant attention in the pages of its journal. This Society lasted until 1892, and was then revived in 1907, surviving with a few intermissions up to present times. Having managed to attract to its ranks most of the authorities in Europe and North America on Gypsy lore and language, its primary objective was to gather together scholarly material – in which it had more than a little success. Not until 1908, by which time a run of attempts to pass a Moveable Dwellings Bill was again starting, did the GLS set out to influence opinion as to the way in which Gypsies ought to be treated.[9]

The forgotten holocaust

When the Nazi party was voted into power in Germany in 1933, it inherited a well developed legal apparatus for controlling many of the groups which it deemed to be undesirable. That did not stop its spokesmen from sneering at the soft attitudes prevalent among their predecessors. One of them, Georg Nawrocki, wrote in the *Hamburger Tageblatt* in August 1937: 'It was in keeping with the inner weakness and mendacity of the Weimar Republic that it showed no instinct for tackling the Gypsy question. For it, the Sinti were a criminal concern at best. We, on the other hand, see the Gypsy question as above all a *racial* problem, which must be solved and which is being solved.'[10] Jews and Gypsies were in fact

[9] An account of the early history of the GLS is in A. M. Fraser, 'A rum lot', in *100 Years of Gypsy Studies*, ed. M. T. Salo (Cheverly, MD, 1990), pp. 1–14.
[10] Translated from the German in R. Vossen, *Zigeuner* (Frankfurt am Main, 1983), p. 70.

the only two ethnic groups which would be designated for annihilation by National Socialist ideology.[11]

The new approach meant, however, that guidance was going to be needed in defining precisely those who were covered by the description '*Zigeuner*' and how they were to be distinguished racially from other citizens of the Reich. This need became all the more pressing once the so-called Nuremberg Laws were introduced in 1935 to set out the framework governing eligibility for full citizenship, and especially once the commentaries on them began to treat Gypsies, along with Jews, as a dangerous *Fremdrasse* ('alien race') whose blood was a mortal threat to German racial purity, to be countered by a ban on mingling in marriage or extramarital relations. In 1937 Dr Robert Ritter, a psychologist and psychiatrist who had for some years been conducting research on Gypsies, took over the direction of the newly founded 'Research Centre for Racial Hygiene and Population Biology' in Berlin, an agency of the Reich Department of Health. This became the main centre for work on the identification and classification of Gypsies and the investigation of links between heredity and criminality: through genealogies, fingerprints and anthropometric measurements, Ritter's team sought to establish a comprehensive tally of everyone carrying Gypsy blood and to determine their degree of racial admixture. For this purpose, they travelled to the camping sites, and when Gypsies were interned in concentration camps, they followed them there too. They could also draw on the police records in the Central

---

[11] It was some time after the Second World War before the Nazi treatment of Gypsies began to receive any scholarly attention, but the literature on the subject, mostly in German, is now sizeable. A useful bibliography is G. Tyrnauer, *Gypsies and the Holocaust* (Montreal, 1989). The main work in English is D. Kenrick and G. Puxon, *The Destiny of Europe's Gypsies* (London, 1972), which takes the Nazi period as its focus. Others are B. Müller-Hill, *Murderous Science* (Oxford, 1988), a translation of *Tödliche Wissenschaft* (Reinbeck bei Hamburg, 1984); M. Zimmermann, 'From discrimination to the "Family Camp" at Auschwitz: National Socialist persecution of the Gypsies', *Dachau Review*, 2 (1990), pp. 87–113; S. Milton, 'The context of the Holocaust', *German Studies Review*, 13 (1990), pp. 269–83; and *The Gypsies of Eastern Europe*, eds D. Crowe and J. Kolsti (New York/London, 1991). In French there is C. Bernadac, *L'Holocauste oublié* (Paris, 1979) – an apt title which has been borrowed here.

Plate 42   Robert Ritter and his assistant Eva Justin taking a Gypsy blood sample. Bundesarchiv, Koblenz.

Office which had been transferred from Munich to Berlin and, particularly after the Austrian *Anschluss*, on the data in the similar establishment created in Vienna in 1936 as an international centre. A 1938 decree of Heinrich Himmler, with the title *Bekämpfung der Zigeunerplage* ('Combating the Gypsy Plague'), declared that Gypsies of mixed blood were the most prone to crime and stressed the need for the police to send returns on all Gypsies to the Reich Central Office.[12] In a progress report in January 1940, Ritter felt able to say:

[12] H.-J. Döring, *Die Zigeuner im NS-Staat* (Hamburg, 1964), pp. 58–60.

we have been able to establish that more than 90 per cent of so-called native Gypsies are of mixed blood...Further results of our investigations have allowed us to characterize the Gypsies as being a people of entirely primitive ethnological origins, whose mental backwardness makes them incapable of real social adaptation...The Gypsy question can only be solved when the main body of asocial and good-for-nothing Gypsy individuals of mixed blood is collected together in large labour camps and kept working there, and when the further breeding of this population of mixed blood is stopped once and for all.[13]

The rules for 'racial-biological evaluation' of the Gypsies were further elaborated by Himmler in a decree of August 1941: going back three generations (as compared with two for Jews), the notation system ranged from Z (for *Zigeuner*, denoting 'pure Gypsy') at one extreme, through ZM+, ZM and ZM− (for *Zigeunermischling*, 'part-Gypsy', the plus and minus signs indicating whether Gypsy blood predominated or not), to NZ (*Nicht-Zigeuner*, 'non-Gypsy') at the other extreme. Two Gypsy great-grandparents were enough to debar someone from the 'NZ' category; had the same rules been applied as for Jews, the number so debarred would have been much reduced. The decree also classified (incompletely) the tribes encountered in Germany and distinguished six groups: Sinti (German Gypsies); Rom (descendants of Gypsies who had come from Hungary around 1870); Gelderari (a branch of the Rom), i.e. Kalderash; Lowari (another branch of the Rom); Lalleri (descendants of Gypsies who had come from the former Austro-Hungarian empire around 1900, and in particular from Bohemia, Moravia and Slovakia − in Romani, *lalleri* means 'dumb' people, i.e. speaking a different dialect); and, finally, Balkan Gypsies descended from bear-leaders. In March 1943, Ritter reported to the German Association for Research: 'The registration of Gypsies and part-Gypsies has been completed, roughly as planned, in the Old Reich [pre-war Germany] and in the Ostmark [Austria] despite all the difficulties engendered by the war. Our studies are still in progress in the annexed territories...The number of cases clarified from the racial-

---

[13] Müller-Hill, *Murderous Science*, p. 57.

biological point of view is 21,498 at the present time.' Ten months later, the figure had risen to 23,822.[14]

The scientific establishment welcomed the opportunities offered by the new regime. Professor E. Fischer, Director of the Kaiser Wilhelm Institute of Anthropology, wrote from the heart in the *Deutsche Allgemeine Zeitung* in 1943: 'It is a rare and special good fortune for a theoretical science to flourish at a time when the prevailing ideology welcomes it and its findings can immediately serve the policy of the state.'[15] In practice, however, the air of precision imparted by this scientific infrastructure was unwarranted; fine gradations devised by the theorists who dressed up prejudice as science were not always followed and subjective impressions played an important part, whether in assessments of particular cases referred to Ritter's team, or more especially in the activities of officials at the work-face, who sometimes operated in a considerable muddle when it was a matter of putting the 'race-hygienic' practices into effect.

The method and timing of such measures depended very much on whether the Gypsies concerned were within the (expanded) frontiers of the Reich or in occupied or allied territories. Within the Reich, the principal instrument of control lay in the all-pervasive apparatus created by the unification of police, security and SS organizations in 1936 under the direction of Himmler and his chief lieutenant, Reinhard Heydrich. At first the authorities relied on general provisions which had been adopted in the early years of the Third Reich on eugenic or crime prevention grounds, allowing the sterilization of vagabonds, the deportation of undesirable foreigners and the sending of minor criminals to concentration camps, the first of which had already been established at Dachau, near Munich, in March 1933. From about 1937 onwards, the pressures on 'asocials' (the vague term applied to Gypsies and others who were not part of 'normal society') and then more specifically on Gypsies built up swiftly and remorselessly, with no hostile public reaction, abroad or at home, of the kind which had made the Nazis a little more circumspect in their

[14] Ibid., pp. 59–60.
[15] Ibid., p. 61.

dealings with the Jews, at least in the early days, because of respect for world opinion. In December 1937 the Reich Minister of the Interior issued a basic order on 'preventive crime control by the police' and laid down the rules for dealing with asocial elements: concentration camps were to be the main remedy. In June the following year an express letter from Himmler ordered each police district to transfer a quota of at least 200 such people to concentration camps. In March 1939 special identity papers were issued, coloured brown for the minority of Gypsies considered to be racially pure, brown striped with blue for those of mixed blood, and grey for non-Gypsy vagabonds.

In Austria, incorporated into the Reich in 1938, the bulk of the Gypsy population lived in the Burgenland, the region bordering on (and until 1919 part of) Hungary where Maria Theresa's settlement policy had had its greatest impact. The local Gauleiter, Thobias Portschy, was full of ideas – mainly involving compulsory sterilization, internment and forced labour – for protecting Nordic blood from their threat. It was, however, an order from Berlin in June 1939 which set off the process of rounding up many of the Burgenland's 8,000 Gypsies under the heading of preventive custody. Some went to large concentration camps like Dachau and Buchenwald, or to the newly created women's camp at Ravensbrück and, later, to Mauthausen in Austria itself; others were herded together in work camps. A special Gypsy camp was opened in November 1940 at Lackenbach in the Burgenland – a much larger concern than the one established at Salzburg the year before – and soon over 2,000 prisoners had been consigned there.

Often, however, the Nazis' 'race-hygienic' ambitions outstripped their capacity to implement them. In September 1939 a conference convened by Heydrich decided that all Gypsies still living in the Reich should be removed to Poland, and the following month the order went out to immobilize them and gather them into transit camps in preparation for their deportation; but the state machinery was not yet ready to cope with such a massive undertaking, nor had the scientists been able to take their work far enough. An express letter from Himmler in April 1940 did lead to the deportation of some 2,500 Gypsies from the west and north-west of Germany to

Poland for forced labour, and others followed in the autumn from Austria and Czechoslovakia, to die in the camps and ghettos where they were dumped; but the plan was never fully implemented. As an alternative, the gentlemen of the Reich Security Head Office discussed in 1941 the possibility of taking the German Gypsies out into the Mediterranean and then bombing the ships. Again, the incomplete state of the anthropological investigations was found to be a stumbling-block.

A more sweeping vision was in any case now required, as a result of the German invasion of the USSR in June 1941 and, shortly afterwards, the decision to go for the 'final solution of the Jewish question'. Heydrich, entrusted with that operation, included the Gypsies in his interpretation of the Final Solution. The clearance of the Government General (those parts of Poland which were not incorporated in the Reich but under direct German rule) was given high priority, since transport problems would not be so serious there. At Chelmno, the death camp near a remote Polish village which started operations in December 1941, carbon monoxide from trucks was used to kill Gypsies (eventually some 5,000 of them) rounded up in Poland, including those who had earlier been deported from Germany as well as those who had survived the typhus epidemic in the Lodz ghetto to which they had been brought in their hundreds from Lackenbach only a few months before.[16] Further east, Gypsies in the newly conquered territories – the Baltic republics and White Russia, soon all to be combined into 'Ostland', and the Ukraine – were beginning to suffer the effects of German civilian rule, while in the military zones the *Einsatzgruppen* (SS special action groups), following in the wake of the advancing armies along the 1,000-mile front from the Baltic to the Black Sea, were hard at work on their mission of eradicating Jews, Gypsies, mental patients and other 'undesirable elements', usually by shooting. The turn of the remaining Gypsies in the Reich came in December 1942, when Himmler ordered all those of mixed Gypsy blood to be sent to Auschwitz; this was swiftly followed by a series of

[16] Cf. E. Thurner, *Nationalsozialismus und Zigeuner in Österreich* (Vienna, 1983), pp. 174–9.

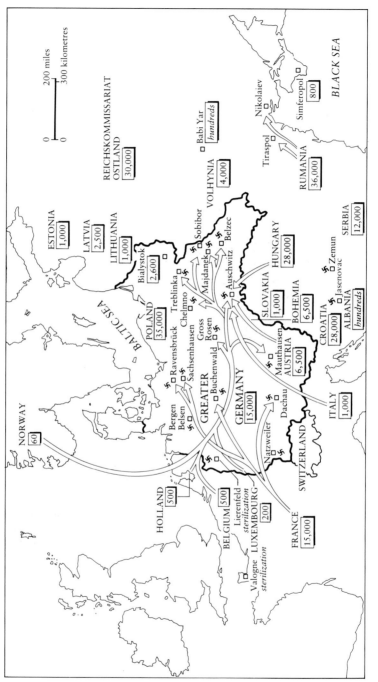

Map 5   Gypsy deportations and massacres, 1939–45.
(After Martin Gilbert, The Macmillan Atlas of the Holocaust, 1982.)

similar decrees applying to occupied territories. Auschwitz-Birkenau had recently been extended; the gas chambers and crematoria, now with a daily capacity of several thousand, had been fully operational for several months and a special Gypsy section was being prepared. Certain categories of Rom and part-Gypsies were exempted from Himmler's Auschwitz decree (for example, those with Aryan spouses and those in the armed forces) but were pressed into 'voluntary' sterilization. Also excluded were racially pure Sinti and Lalleri, who were thought to be less prone to mixed marriages, so that Himmler, perhaps in a desire to preserve a small research sample of what might speculatively be regarded as one variety of early Indo-Germanic life (that at least was the motive attributed to him by Rudolf Höss, the commandant at Auschwitz), was minded to allow them some limited freedom of movement. Ever since October 1942, in fact, nine Gypsy leaders has been under orders to draw up lists of those eligible for such treatment, including part-Gypsies who would be suitable for assimilation with them. This piece of whimsy on the part of the Reichsführer-SS found no favour at all with other leading Nazis; Martin Bormann told him firmly that 'the Führer would not countenance giving back their old freedoms to one section of the Gypsies', and nothing came of any idea of having a Gypsy reservation.

In any case, local criminal police seldom had time for nice distinctions when they saw the opportunity of making their area 'Gypsy free', and in the end no Gypsy could be considered safe from the concentration and death camps. Of these, Auschwitz has acquired immense symbolic significance. It was but one among many (see map 5), but it had the biggest population of Gypsies, from all over Nazi-occupied Europe, and a special enclave of 40 wooden barrack blocks where they were kept in family groups in an attempt to avoid trouble until the final moment came. It was also one of those where experimentation on the inmates was rife, in a perversion of medical science. Soon after the German Gypsies arrived, a new camp doctor, Dr Josef Mengele, took over and was indefatigable in the exercise of his functions, whether making life-or-death 'selections' among the daily new convoys of detainees or subjecting Jews and Gypsies to barbaric suffering. The Gypsy camp at Auschwitz-Birkenau existed for 17 months. Of the 23,000 people squashed in there, 20,078 died; the rest were transferred to other camps. The deaths were caused by starvation, overwork, medical abuse, disease or gas. On 3 August 1944, the Gypsy camp, usually noisy, lay at last silent and deserted: 2,897 women, children and men (including former soldiers of the Wehrmacht) had been driven into the gas chambers during the one night, and there were no Gypsies left. The anthropological records on them survived the war, however, and 20 years later research was still being carried out on this material by a former co-worker of Dr Robert Ritter.

Outside the Reich, the fate of the Gypsies varied widely from country to country,[17] just as the Final Solution did in its application to the Jews. The biggest numerical losses were in Yugoslavia, Rumania, Poland, the USSR and Hungary. In the occupied territories, the Nazis' policy was to intern Gypsies in camps and from there to transport them into Germany and Poland for use as slave labour or (especially from 1943) to be massacred in the death camps. Often there was no need for them to do the gathering and holding themselves. France had already brought in severe restrictions against Gypsies months before the German occupation. After the capitulation the number of internment camps grew, both in the German-administered zone and in Vichy France, and soon there were 30,000 Gypsies and other '*nomades*' guarded by French police and military.[18] Eventually, many of them were deported to concentration camps, notably Buchenwald, Dachau and Ravensbrück; some joined Gypsies from all over Europe in the Natzweiler camp in Alsace where SS doctors were experimenting, largely with Gypsy victims, on the effects of poison gas and typhus.[19] In the Netherlands, Belgium and Luxembourg,

---

[17] There is a summary in chs 6 and 7 of Kenrick and Puxon, *The Destiny of Europe's Gypsies* (revised in the Romani version, *Berša bibahtale*, London, 1988).

[18] Cf. Bernadac, *L'Holocauste oublié*, pp. 43–144.

[19] In France, as in other countries, a number of Gypsies joined underground and partisan movements; for a narrative of clandestine activities of a *kumpania* of Lovara and Ćurara in occupied France, see J. Yoors, *Crossing* (New York, 1971). U. König, *Sinti und Roma unter dem Nationalsozialismus: Verfolgung und Widerstand* (Bochum, 1989) treats the resistance theme more generally.

much of the small Gypsy population was disposed of in similar manner. In Belgium, Lovara and Sinti were affected in equal numbers; catching them was made all the easier by the special register of nomads which Belgium had introduced in 1941.[20] The round-up in the Netherlands, carried out by Dutch police and gendarmerie in May 1944, held greater problems of identification: plans to introduce a Gypsy register in 1937 had been aborted through lack of funds. Once *woonwagenbewoners* (non-Gypsy caravan-dwellers) and those who held passports of allied or neutral countries had been released, 245 Gypsies, mostly Sinti, were sent to Auschwitz; no more than 30 ever came back.[21] Only in one occupied country were extreme measures not enforced: this was Denmark, where the problem lay once more in doubts over ethnic demarcations within the travelling population, simply classified as 'asocial' in its entirety.

There was no room for such niceties in the German protectorate of Bohemia and Moravia, and events there far outstripped in ruthlessness those in nominally independent Slovakia, where the severe discrimination fell short of extermination. Of 8,000 Gypsies in Bohemia and Moravia, only about 600 survived. It was, however, in Yugoslavia that the largest number of Gypsies perished, after the young state had been dismembered among four Axis and pro-Axis powers (Germany, Italy, Hungary, Bulgaria) together with the collaborators in Croatia, which incorporated Bosnia-Herzegovina. Few Gypsies survived the terror in the north once the Croat separatist movement came to power and inaugurated a bloodbath against non-Catholic minorities. So ferocious in its atrocities was the Ustasha (fascist) militia that even the German military authorities were appalled. In occupied Serbia the systematic use of Gypsies as hostages meant that they fell steadily to firing squads (at the rate of 100 for each German killed by partisans, and 50 for each German wounded), while others were dispatched by mobile gassing vans in internment camps. By

[20] J. Gotovitch, 'Quelques données relatives à l'extermination des tsiganes de Belgique', *Cahiers d'histoire de la seconde guerre mondiale*, 4 (1976), pp. 161–80.

[21] B. A. Sijes et al., *Vervolging van Zigeuners in Nederland 1940–1945* (The Hague, 1979); and Lucassen, *'En men noemde hen Zigeuners'*, ch. 6.

August 1942 Serbia was reported to be the first country where the Jewish and Gypsy 'questions' were considered to have been 'solved'. Gypsies were also used as hostages in Greece by the military government, but their deportation to Auschwitz in 1943 was, for once, averted by swift appeals from the Greek Prime Minister and the Archbishop of Athens. Had Britain been occupied, British Gypsies would not have escaped, it seems. In the summer of 1942 the foreign intelligence section of the Security Service of the SS was showing a sinister interest in the numbers living there.

The sovereign states which had chosen to hitch their waggons to Hitler's star all lagged behind Germany in dealing with Gypsies, so long as they remained in charge of their destinies. Italy transported a number of families to islands off the peninsula and left them stranded there. It was only after the Italian capitulation in 1943 that those still living in Wehrmacht-controlled parts of the country were rounded up for forced labour in Germany or sent to concentration camps. In the Italian province of Albania, Gypsy losses were even lighter, for the Italian occupiers and the puppet Albanian government paid scant attention to them; and after the fall of Mussolini the Germans who took over lasted less than a year and, in a precarious military situation, had little time to sort out the ethnic groups there. In Hungary, active persecution of Jews and Gypsies was restricted while the country remained independent. The large operations began in 1944: within a few months of German occupation, some 30,000 Gypsies had been deported, and only a tenth of them ever returned. Rumania's main action was to expel tens of thousands of Gypsies to a dumping ground in the newly formed province of Transnistria, a slice of the Ukraine seized from the USSR; most of them succumbed to typhus. Bulgaria was unique among the satellite and puppet governments of Hitler's Europe in remaining remarkably immune to the plague of racial prejudice. No Bulgarian-born Jews were deported, despite immense pressure from Germany once Bulgaria committed itself to the Axis in 1941. And the Gypsies in Bulgaria and Bulgarian-occupied territories fared better than those in neighbouring lands, though those who joined the partisans in Macedonia were dealt with as summarily as any others. Hitler's Minister to

Sofia remarked sadly of this peasant nation: 'The mentality of the Bulgarian people is lacking in the ideological enlightenment which our people enjoy. Having lived all their lives with Armenians, Greeks and Gypsies, the Bulgarians see no harm in the Jew to justify special measures against him.'[22]

Given the geographically widespread nature of the assault on Europe's Gypsies and the many gaps in the records, it is impossible to be categorical about numbers of casualties; but precise figures are perhaps not important. Tallies of the Gypsy victims who died in Europe during the war range from about a quarter of a million to half a million and more,[23] and there can be no mitigating circumstances in massacre on this scale. Of those who survived, most carried with them indelible physical or mental marks of their experiences. The reason of state which had underlain their treatment soon became an extremely important issue in the context of post-war reparations in Germany (that is, in the Federal Republic, for only a few hundred Sinti stayed in the Soviet zone and subsequently the German Democratic Republic, preferring to preserve their economic independence).[24] If the reason for a Gypsy's victimization was that he was a possible criminal, and not simply that he was a Gypsy, it could be claimed that his fate was 'only' a consequence of ordinary security measures. One line of thought which prevailed for many years in the German courts was that up to late 1942 Gypsies were not being persecuted on racial grounds and that any action taken before then, regardless of whether it was unjustified, merited no compensation. In 1959 the Hamm court of appeal pronounced on the case of a Gypsy, Erik Balasz, who was arrested in Poland in 1940 at the age of 16 and then imprisoned for five years, and whose parents were both murdered: 'It is immaterial whether the claimant was at the time to be regarded as asocial or not. The decisive factor is that the criminal police did regard him as asocial, and for that reason took him into

[22] Cf. Kenrick and Puxon, *The Destiny of Europe's Gypsies*, p. 131.

[23] Vossen, *Zigeuner*, pp. 85–6, in a careful country-by-country analysis, quotes a total of 275,200 deaths as compared with an estimated Gypsy population of 947,500 in 1939 in the countries concerned.

[24] Cf. T. Zülch, 'Und auch heute noch verfolgt?', *Zeitschrift für Kulturaustausch*, 31 (1981), pp. 397–410, esp. p. 399.

protective custody.'[25] Not until December 1963 did a decision of the Federal Court of Justice push the accepted start of racial persecution back to 1938.[26] Even then, however, Gypsy victims who still survived ended up with conspicuously modest amounts of compensation, if they proved themselves tenacious and literate enough to battle their way through the stringent requirements for documentary and medical evidence and successfully established a claim.

[25] 'Compensation claims rejected', *Manchester Guardian*, 30 March 1959, p. 5.
[26] Cf. U. Körber, 'Die Wiedergutmachung und die "Zigeuner"', in *Feinderklärung und Prävention* (Berlin, 1988), pp. 165–75.

9

Modern Times

Frontier crossings

The end of the Second World War left Europe's surviving Gypsy population massively redistributed. Principally this was the result of the large-scale deportations which had taken place, but partly it had been produced by Gypsy flight from one country to another – for example, from Slovenia and Croatia to Italy – in search of a less lethal environment. The return to peace brought further upheaval. Those who were liberated from the camps were often left stranded as displaced or stateless persons, subject to all kinds of red tape and special restrictions. In the post-war years transfers of territory and people between countries introduced a new dimension, as when 15 million Germans were removed from eastern Europe. Not infrequently, families of Sinti who were caught up in this displacement encountered great resistance to being accepted in Germany, and those who did complete the journey were far from being assured of citizenship. More indirectly, the expulsion of more than two million Sudeten Germans contributed to mass migrations *within* the frontiers of Czechoslovakia. Thousands of Gypsies left their isolated settlements in rural Slovakia; some were relocated in the border areas in the west which had been cleared of Germans; more moved to industrial conurbations, often as unskilled factory or construction workers. A different kind of transfer took place in the 1950s from the USSR to Poland, as a stream of expatriates came back from the Polish territories which had been incorporated

into the Soviet Union; among them was a large group of Rom
– mainly Lovara and Kalderash – who had been deported
from that region at the beginning of the war to behind the
Urals. They had great difficulty in reintegrating with the Rom
in Poland, owing to the fact that during the internment their
application of the pollution code had remained orthodox,
whereas in Poland sheer survival had dictated a number of
relaxations.[1]

Subsequently, political turbulence occasioned further dis-
placements: there was a Gypsy element among the 150,000
refugees who fled to the west after the Hungarian uprising
of 1956; and the unrest in Portugal in the 1970s caused an
influx of Gypsies into Spain. For much of the time, however,
the migrations were economic in origin. Some attracted little
notice: in the ranks of the *Gastarbeiter* who went in their
millions to the Federal German Republic from countries
such as Turkey, Yugoslavia, Greece and Spain were Gypsies
who chose to suppress their identity, pursue regular jobs and
send their children to school like anyone else.[2] But, more in
keeping with the past, there also welled up another of those
westward surges out of the Balkans which have punctuated
Gypsy history. This one began in the 1960s and the source
was Yugoslavia, where frontier regulations became more
relaxed than in the rest of eastern Europe. It spread through
the west of the continent but became concentrated in Italy,
Austria, Germany, France and the Netherlands. Some wanted
to emigrate to the USA but very few succeeded. It was a
heterogeneous movement, comprehending both settled and
nomadic Gypsies from a variety of tribal and linguistic groups.
Most conspicuous were those from southern Yugoslavia
known to themselves as *Xoraxané Romá* ('Turkish Gypsies'),
to distinguish them from others, notably from Christian
Gypsies;[3] the collective name disguises, however, a significant
diversity in life-style and (non-Vlach) Romani dialect.

---

[1] Cf. I.-M. Kaminski, 'The dilemma of power: internal and external
leadership. The Gypsy-Roma of Poland', in *The Other Nomads*, ed. A. Rao
(Cologne, 1987), pp. 323–56, esp. pp. 346–8.
[2] Cf. T. Zülch, 'Und auch heute noch verfolgt?', *Zeitschrift für Kulturaustausch*, 31 (1981), pp. 397–410, esp. pp. 401–2.
[3] Cf. M.-T. Rochas, 'Les Tsiganes yougoslaves!!', *Études Tsiganes*, 30

Italy was one of the earliest ports of call, and favourable reports from there led to the arrival of relatives and of more and more Gypsies from a wider area. This in itself ensured that the climate turned towards hostility, and soon other countries were being reconnoitred. Those who had been settled in their country of origin (like the Xoraxané from Kosovo) tended to become peripatetic, while even those who made the opposite switch, from being more or less nomadic in Yugoslavia to becoming urbanized and semi-sedentary, generally still moved on periodically from town to town or from country to country, always on the look-out for new ways of making a living. Many returned to Yugoslavia at regular intervals, taking back the money they had collected, as well as stocks of goods which were sought after in the homeland. Since a high proportion were illiterate and uneducated and often spoke little of the local language, and also because they were Gypsies, any regular work would have been difficult to find. Hawking and the other activities they pursued meant that they could best operate in numerous small units, perhaps travelling quite long distances to towns and villages away from their temporary abode, in order to allow for fallow periods. Some turned to scrap-dealing. With the Xoraxané from Bosnia and Montenegro, copper-working remained open as a livelihood but it now tended to take the form of producing highly ornamented decorative pieces rather than repairing and retinning cooking and eating utensils. Social security benefits became a significant new factor in their economy. These various sources were supplemented by begging and fortune-telling: indeed, for some they were the principal occupation. Begging was a task for the women, often surrounded by their children, or for children alone, especially where legal sanctions were enforced against adult beggars. Some turned to petty crime – shoplifting,

(1984), no. 2, pp. 29–37; L. Piasere, 'In search of new niches: the productive organization of the peripatetic Xoraxané in Italy' (dealing with Gypsies from Kosovo province in the late 1970s), in *The Other Nomads*, pp. 111–32; and W. G. Lockwood, 'East European Gypsies in western Europe: the social and cultural adaptation of the Xoraxané' (dealing with Gypsies from Bosnia-Herzegovina and Montenegro in the mid-1980s), *Nomadic Peoples* (1986), nos 21/22, pp. 63–70.

picking pockets, stealing from vehicles – and again younger children might be drawn in because of their immunity to prosecution. Older established Gypsies did not take kindly to the newcomers and the trouble some of them caused, even though they were generally at pains not to antagonize inhabitants in the locality where they were living.

The type of accommodation varied from place to place. Vehicle-drawn caravans and rough shacks displaced tents, except in emergencies, and when tents were used they were now of the manufactured camping variety. In Italy, the Yugoslavs gravitated for the most part towards small, crude encampments around the periphery of a city. In Germany, many took up residence in slum housing provided by the state. In France there was the possibility of gaining access to sites reserved for Gypsy use, where they might live cheek by jowl alongside French *manouches* and *gitans*; more commonly, it was a question of occupying a shack in some *bidonville* ('shanty-town'), so long as these survived the bulldozers. The Netherlands offered a more considered solution in 1977, when, after several years of uneasy relations with foreign Gypsies living there illegally, the government decided, under parliamentary pressure, to regularize the position of at least some of them – in the end, about 450, among whom were many Xoraxané. Eleven Dutch communities agreed to accept a quota. The Gypsies were provided with semi-permanent, then permanent housing, and special schools were established both for children and (less successfully) for adults.[4] That was, however, regarded as a strictly once-for-all exercise, and the defences against new foreign intruders were strengthened.

Such migrations had considerable repercussions for social organization. These Gypsies, like many before them, quickly adopted the telephone as a means of maintaining a network of contacts, whether in western countries or back in Yugoslavia; but at the same time the new conditions eroded some of the

---

[4] Cf. R. Dahler, 'Zigeuneropvangbeleid Oldenzaal', in *Zigeuners in Nederland*, eds P. Hovens and R. Dahler (Nijmegen/Rijswijk, 1988), pp. 385–415, which gives an account of the reception in Oldenzaal, one of the 11 communities; and W. Willems and L. Lucassen, *Ongewenste Vreemdelingen* (The Hague, 1990).

bonds within the extended family and placed more emphasis on the nuclear family. The leadership structure became less stable too, for ability to cope with the *gadže* and their bureaucratic ways acquired new importance as a qualification, and the former expectation of lengthy tenure of the leader's role began to be undermined by the competitiveness which was another quality the Gypsies were absorbing in their western environment.

Questions of policy

For the bulk of Gypsies, however, horizons after the Second World War were limited by the frontiers of a single country, and it was the national internal policies that mattered to them. There the dividing line lay distinctly between east and west. Most of Europe's Gypsy population came under communist regimes.[5] This should have led – and at times did lead – to some amelioration in their condition, given that the new governments started from the premise that it was the duty of the state to assist underdeveloped groups. Moreover, Marxist-Leninist theory made provision for the existence of different nationalities within a state and also of national minorities (a far more flexible category), and recognized that they could have certain rights. The new communist countries, following policies more designed to further ideological goals than to remedy social injustice, varied in their willingness to apply such principles to Gypsies; in practice, at some stage most demanded their integration, for, while everyone of working age had both the right and also the duty to work, this had to be for a registered co-operative unit or one managed by the state, and entrepreneurial activities were illegal. Any group which did not behave in accordance with the model disturbed the fundamental concept of central planning.

The Soviet Union itself had, over 20 years before, in 1925, recognized Gypsies as a national minority, who could be

[5] *The Gypsies of Eastern Europe*, eds D. Crowe and J. Kolsti (New York/London, 1991), covers post-war developments in Rumania, Czechoslovakia and Hungary.

described as *Tsigan* on identity cards and internal passports. (By 1959 the number who had sought such designation stood at 134,000, although many chose instead to register their children as Russian, Armenian, etc.)[6] A Pan-Russian Gypsy Union was formed in 1926. A number of primary schools opened up which used Romani as a medium of instruction; books and periodicals were printed in Romani; and work began on the creation of a literary language. A State Gypsy Theatre, founded in 1931, was the one Gypsy institution that was not swept away when the government machine was put into reverse later in the 1930s. The post-war period saw no revival of the early policies. A law passed in 1956 outlawed nomadism. It was patchily enforced, however, and some itinerant groups continued to travel from one collective farm to another to provide seasonal labour; others carried on illicit private transactions as street-traders, an occupation which as often as not was connived at.

Poland, starting in the early 1950s, was the first of the new communist states to try to secure integration of nomadic Gypsies by offering housing and employment. (In the sub-Carpathian region in the south, the great majority had long been settled.) Schools enrolled many children and there were attempts to set up co-operative workshops based on traditional skills like coppersmithing; on the whole, however, the kinds of work that were offered – unskilled, poorly paid and physically demanding – held little attraction. Nomads persisted in their migrations and in 1964 the government turned to coercion: Gypsies were forbidden to travel in caravans, they were compulsorily registered, and regulations on meetings and gatherings were strictly applied. Within two years nomadism had greatly diminished, and soon over 80 per cent of Gypsy children were said to be attending school, however intermittently. Settlement brought its own problems: by the 1980s disputes between the new house-dwellers and their neighbours were rife; and hundreds of Gypsies were being expelled from Poland as no longer having citizenship.[7]

---

[6] G. Puxon, *Rom: Europe's Gypsies*, 2nd edn (London, 1975), p. 12.

[7] Cf. J. Ficowski, 'The Gypsies in the Polish People's Republic', *JGLS*(3), 35 (1956), pp. 28–38, and *The Gypsies in Poland* (n.d. [Warsaw, 1990]), pp. 49–53; and Kaminski, 'The dilemma of power', pp. 348–52.

Hungary was also to encounter social difficulties as the increasing visibility of Gypsies in society (and their higher birth-rate) created new tensions and antagonisms. Official and party policies oscillated in regard to recognition of the rapidly growing Gypsy population. For seven years Gypsy orchestras were suppressed as a left-over from decadent times. A Gypsy consultative committee was set up and then abandoned, coupled with a declaration that Gypsies did not constitute a national minority and a reference to the 'phalanx of prejudice' against Gypsies, particularly in rural areas. In 1974 the committee was re-established, to be replaced in 1986 by a more representative Romany Council, followed by a national Gypsy association to link together some 200 local cultural clubs. Some progress was made on housing and employment; as for education, the government at first favoured keeping Gypsy children with others in ordinary Hungarian schools but then, owing to the language problems experienced by those whose mother tongue was a Romani or Rumanian dialect, it began to encourage experimentation with teaching in that mother tongue, either on its own or alongside Hungarian.

It is to Czechoslovakia that one has to turn for the most instructive example of the twists and turns which typified communist regimes' handling of Gypsies.[8] The Czech policy was variously typified by a blend of condescension and impatience, of paternalism and despotism, of benevolent inactivity and strenuous attempts at radical solutions. In the first decade after the communist take-over in 1948, though the announced goal was to integrate the Gypsies, the party and state machinery was occupied with more pressing issues; ideologically, it was assumed that since 'the Gypsies are victims of capitalism', the

---

[8] E. Davidóva, 'The Gypsies in Czechoslovakia', *JGLS*(3), 50 (1971), pp. 40–54; W. Guy, 'Ways of looking at Roms: the case of Czechoslovakia', in *Gypsies, Tinkers and Other Travellers*, ed. F. Rehfisch (London, 1975), pp. 201–29; W. Oschlies, ' "Schwarze" und "Weisse": zur Lage der Zigeuner in der Tschechoslowakei', *Giessener Hefte für Tsiganologie* (1985), 1/85, pp. 24–32; O. Ulč, 'Gypsies in Czechoslovakia: a case of unfinished integration', *Eastern European Politics and Societies*, 2 (1988), pp. 306–33; and D. J. Kostelancik, 'The Gypsies of Czechoslovakia: political and ideological considerations in the development of policy', *Studies in Comparative Communism*, 22 (1989), pp. 307–21.

overthrow of capitalism automatically took care of any Gypsy problem. Despite reports by the media of the usual impressive victories in school attendance, employment and assimilation generally, a turning point came in 1958, when the authorities concluded that the Gypsies' group identity had to be demolished if they were to advance at all, and it was decreed that they were not an ethnic group but people 'maintaining a markedly different demographic structure'. A law was enacted in that year to enforce school attendance and the settlement of nomadic people (who were in practice only a minority of the Gypsy population, and largely confined to the Vlach groups) and also of semi-nomads, by registering them in one place and refusing them employment anywhere else. The law was fairly successful in eliminating full-time nomadism, because the horse-drawn vehicles of the Vlachs were a conspicuous target, and police could raid encampments, kill the horses and burn the waggons. It was singularly ineffective in exercising control over the movement of semi-nomads – many of them travelling back and forth between homes in Slovakia and work-places in Czech districts – for the integration plan was approached with all the enthusiasm accorded to the many other crash programmes of the day, be it the planting of cauliflowers or the promotion of eternal friendship with Outer Mongolia. The local authorities who were supposed to register these Gypsies and provide them with jobs and accommodation generally found it simpler to ignore them.

When the semi-nomads failed to respond to get-together programmes and literacy courses, the government was forced to reassess its position. The provinces were ordered to obtain data about their Gypsy populations and prepare a long-term plan of assimilation. The policy which emerged in 1965 put emphasis on two tasks: full employment of able-bodied Gypsies, and the elimination of Gypsy hamlets and other 'undesirable Gypsy concentrations' (some 1,300 of them in all). There was also to be a campaign against illiteracy and parasitism, and the Academy of Sciences was called in to undertake an analysis of Gypsy life. Integration was conceived as the unconditional surrender of the Gypsies, who were looked on as a primitive, backward and degenerate people. A census held the following year recorded 221,526 of them, predominantly in the east of the country; and by now every eleventh baby born in Czechoslovakia was a Gypsy.

The new 'dispersal and transfer' scheme was founded on regular, planned transplantation from settlements in Slovakia to the Czech lands in the west with a low density of Gypsies, in order to spread them as thinly as possible throughout the Republic. It was bedevilled from the start by inadequate financing, bureaucratic restrictions, hostility of local authorities, and Gypsy failure to abide by the rules; an alarming development was, once again, the emergence of ugly racial bias on a serious scale, particularly in the sphere of housing (including a proposal from a group of workers that Gypsies should be given a one-way ticket to India at state expense). By the end of 1968 the programme had ground to a standstill and unplanned family migrations far out-numbered the planned transfers: the extensive population movement that did take place among Gypsies in post-war Czechoslovakia was largely a typical case of rural-to-urban migration, in search of a securer place in wider society. Then, for a few years, Gypsies were tentatively treated virtually as a national minority and allowed to organize economic co-operatives and form their own sociocultural associations. The latter grew swiftly, attracting not only the poorer Gypsies but also the small and influential intelligentsia which had been regarded as totally assimilated. The 'normalization' which followed the Prague Spring meant that the experiment was short-lived, and in 1973 all Gypsy mass organizations were dissolved on the grounds that they had 'failed to fulfil their integrative function', and a scheme to introduce Romani as a teaching medium in primary schools was dropped. The authorities reverted to assimilation as the only solution. Some of their policies were pursued in stealth, like pressing thousands of Gypsy women to undergo sterilization once they had given birth to a few children. The 1980 census gave some indication of the population explosion: 288,440 Gypsies were counted; even that understimate represented some 2 per cent of the national population (8 per cent in East Slovakia), and these proportions could be expected to increase quickly because of the high birth rate in the much younger Gypsy population. Educationally, some advance was noted from the low base in the 1970 census: for example, only

Plate 43 Gypsies at Pildeşti, Rumania, 1956. Photograph by G. Lükö.

10 per cent of Gypsies over 15 had received no education at all, whereas it had been almost 30 per cent ten years before; and the number of university graduates had risen from 45 to 345.[9]

Rumania and Bulgaria were just as reluctant to confer ethnic group status on Gypsies. Rumania attempted nothing comparable for them, in terms of schooling and cultural support, to what was initially done, on paper if not in practice, for the Hungarian and German minorities; and, as Gypsies became more prominent in industrial wage-labour and in agri-

---

[9] K. Kalibová and Z. Pavlik, 'Demographic specificities of the Romany population in Czechoslovakia', paper at the 7th International Demographic Seminar, Humboldt University, Berlin, 1986.

cultural co-operatives, the long-standing and deeply ingrained popular prejudice against them heightened.[10] Ceauşescu tried to obliterate the Gypsies' culture and force them into squalid ghettos in towns or bleak tented settlements in the countryside. Their valuables – huge old Austro-Hungarian gold coins were their preferred form of savings – were stolen by the Securitate and they were never free from the risk of harassment.

Bulgaria conducted an assimilation campaign lasting for some 30 years. A decree of 1958 prohibited Gypsies from travelling and enjoined councils to channel them into factories and co-operative farms. Some of the old Gypsy quarters were torn down and families accommodated in scattered apartment blocks. From 1969 segregated schools were set up to give thousands of Gypsy children some primary education and direct them towards apprenticeships and technical diplomas; speaking Romani at these schools was forbidden. At the same time the government undermined the ability of Gypsies to preserve their individuality, by closing down and expropriating their newspapers and associations. In the early 1970s, it sought to legislate this large minority (perhaps 3–4 per cent of the total population) out of existence. The designation 'Gypsy' was abolished in identity papers and (as part of more general measures against Muslims) those with Muslim names were obliged to take new Slavonic ones. Newspapers and magazines maintained an information blockade. In the 1980s the state went further and attempted to regulate folk music by prohibiting any Turkish or other foreign bias. The trouble with this was that Gypsy music, though heavily influenced by Turkish music, is in great demand at Bulgarian weddings, baptisms and other celebrations, and could not be ousted from its place. The upshot was that the Gypsies adapted in their own manner to the Bulgarian socialist environment. Economically, their situation became rather better, and they were drawn more extensively into the educational system, even if at the end of it they tended to be left with low-paid jobs; but wherever possible they supplemented wage-labour with free market enterprise, regardless of regulations, just as they con-

---

[10] Cf. S. Beck, 'Tsigani-Gypsies in socialist Romania', *Giessener Hefte für Tsiganologie* (1986), 1–4/86, pp. 109–27.

tinued to find eager audiences for their music, regardless of prohibitions.[11]

In Yugoslavia, questions of ethnic origins were bound to play a major role in the federation formed after the war, given its national, linguistic and cultural complexity, which was mirrored in the diversity of its Gypsy population – the largest in the world – and it was there that a multicultural policy was pushed furthest. In this stronghold for Marxist proponents of a pluralist approach, the Gypsies were in 1981 given nationality (*narodnost*) status on an equal footing constitutionally with such other minorities as Albanians, Hungarians and Turks, and this conferred language and cultural rights, although the new status was far from being applied uniformly by the various Yugoslav republics. The media dropped the word *cigan*, felt to have pejorative overtones, and replaced it with *Rom*, and a few TV and radio stations started regular programmes in Romani. Scores of Gypsy social and cultural associations grew up in the bigger communities, and Gypsies began to participate in regional politics. In 1983, Romani was given a place in a number of primary schools, starting in the predominantly Albanian-populated province of Kosovo. Despite absenteeism and high drop-out rates from school (with the result that only about 20 per cent of adults had completed elementary education), a few hundred Gypsies penetrated the professions and became doctors, lawyers, engineers and so on. The majority, however, continued to live at an economic level well below the average, particularly in the more prosperous northern republics of Croatia and Slovenia to which many families migrated, becoming shanty-dwellers on the outskirts of Zagreb and poorly paid casual and domestic workers in Ljubljana. Yugoslavia was the one communist state which did not seek to force nomadic Gypsies to settle. The pressure to do so came from economic circumstance rather than governmental restriction, and the transition was like a replay of events which, a century before, had led to widespread changes further west. As the living conditions of their clientele and the type of utensils that were used adapted to industrialization, so

[11] Cf. C. Silverman, 'Bulgarian Gypsies: adaptation in a socialist context', *Nomadic Peoples* (1986), nos 21/22, pp. 51–60.

too did nomadic Gypsies in Yugoslavia. Formerly they had camped near villages or on the outskirts of market towns, where they lived for much of the year in tents transported in horse-drawn waggons and gained a living from a peasant society, sometimes as coppersmiths, sometimes as fortune-tellers and beggars of foodstuffs; now, they gradually settled in small market towns or acquired cars or vans to carry their tents and switched to the buying and selling of ready-made goods, new or old, such as used clothing, factory seconds and any consumer commodities which were in short supply.

For the western European countries, the policy pre-occupations after the Second World War had a different focus, reflecting the fact that, with one or two notable exceptions like Spain, their proportion of sedentary Gypsies remained on the whole well below that in the east. As a result, the dominant issue was how to react to peripatetic families, usually living in vehicle-drawn caravans, whose way of life fitted uneasily with the voracious demand for land for development and with general laws on vagrancy, public health, and town and country planning. Nomadism in itself might no longer be expressly prohibited, but legislative systems designed for settled societies could have much the same effect. Travellers were simply evicted or ordered to move on, or perhaps tolerated at places like rubbish tips with no water supply or sanitary facilities. (In Germany, however, legislation in the *Länder* was more single-minded: from 1953 to 1970 Bavaria managed to keep in force regulations subjecting nomads to special controls, with finger-printed documentation, echoing its law of 1926; other *Länder* followed suit.)

In most countries the areas of concern were camping sites and education. Appeals from central bodies to local authorities to set up special sites had very limited effect. The first such circular issued in England, by the Ministry of Housing and Local Government in February 1962, illustrated very well what could be attained by exhortation on its own, unsupported by more direct powers of intervention or assistance. It pointed out that 'the true gypsies, or romanies, have the right to follow their traditional mode of life, and they have a legitimate need for camping sites. . . . Moving people off one unauthorized site and leaving them to find another is no solution, and no answer to the human and social problems involved.' (In practice, though it singled out, but did not define, 'true gypsies', this circular covered all Travellers.) Two years later, only three local authority sites were in operation, taking up to about 50 caravans in all, and at least two of the three had been thought of spontaneously before the circular was issued.[12] In 1965 the Ministry arranged a census of Travellers living in caravans, huts or tents in England and Wales, as a result of which it was concluded that they numbered at least 15,000, or about 3,400 families, now generally recognized to have been a serious underassessment.[13] Scotland carried out a count in 1969 and arrived at an estimate of 2,100 persons or about 450 families.[14] By this time it had been found necessary to pass beyond exhortation and resort to statutory measures in England and Wales, in the form of the Caravan Sites Act of 1968 which, once the relevant part came into force in 1970, made it a duty for local authorities to provide camp-sites for Travellers. Twenty years later, according to Department of Environment figures for July 1990, there were in England 7,357 Traveller caravans on authorized sites (almost a third of them on private ground), while a further 4,610 (39 per cent) had no legal stopping-place. Provision had therefore lagged far behind need, even though, for part of the time, the entire capital cost was covered by central funding in an attempt to speed things up. The government spokesman in a debate in the House of Commons in the same month observed pessimistically: 'The problems will never be solved while we rely on the legislation that we have'. One aspect of the 1968 Act which had a repressive effect was the granting of 'designation orders' to local authorities able to persuade the government that they had enough sites or should not have any at all; they were then empowered to create no-go areas by prosecuting and evicting all families in unapproved places, whether or not those places were owned or controlled by the council. As there

[12] Cf. A. M. Fraser, 'The Travellers. Developments in England and Wales, 1953–63', *JGLS*(3), 43 (1964), pp. 83–112.

[13] Cf. *Gypsies and Other Travellers*, a report by a Ministry of Housing and Local Government Sociological Research Section (London, 1967).

[14] H. Gentleman and S. Swift, *Scotland's Travelling People* (Edinburgh, 1971).

Plate 44   Westway site, London, c.1986. Photograph by Greater
London Council.

are generally no votes to be won in local elections (indeed, often votes to be lost) by providing more, or any, sites for Travellers, designated status became highly prized, to the extent that over 100 local authorities have achieved it.

A linked question was that of schooling, for without security from eviction there could be little continuity in education. Whatever suspicions they might have had in the past, many Gypsies in Britain had become fully aware of an increasing need for some access to school learning, if only because the newer livelihoods required an ability to write estimates and receipts, to read plans and manuals and to hold driving licences and insurance, quite apart from the variety of forms that went with health and employment services and social security. The decentralized nature of British education meant that it was the local education authorities which had the responsibility of providing education for all children residing in their area, whether permanently or temporarily, including Traveller children (though that was formally laid down only in 1981). The existence of over a hundred of these authorities in England and Wales meant that their separate and independent initiatives led to wide disparities in the scale of provision, and the level of commitment ranged from teams of teachers working from resource centres with special educational materials to no provision at all.[15] A good deal of progress was made, however patchily, from the 1970s onwards; none the less a committee of inquiry into the education of children from ethnic minorities found that it had to single out, in its 1985 report, the travelling community as illustrating 'to an extreme degree the experience of prejudice and alienation which faces many other ethnic minority children': it said they had unique difficulty in gaining access to the school system.[16] In 1990 a new specific grant from central government was introduced in support of the education of Travellers, but many of the applications from education authorities were met only in part or not at all.

[15] Cf. T. Acton and D. Kenrick, 'From summer voluntary schemes to European Community bureaucracy: the development of special provision for Traveller education in the United Kingdom since 1967', *European Journal of Intercultural Studies*, 1 (1991), no. 3, pp. 47–62.

[16] Lord Swann, *Education For All* (London, 1985), ch. 16.

The pattern was similar in most other western European countries, in so far as they had any special policies, as distinct from local makeshifts.[17] In France an official working party was set up in 1949 to consider the plight of travelling Gypsies, at a time when many communes simply prohibited them. It recommended abandoning the 'policy of repression and prohibition' and the Minister of the Interior gave his formal blessing to a more positive approach. Twenty years later the *carnet anthropométrique* for itinerants (see p. 255) was at last abolished, to be succeeded by a *carnet de circulation* which had to be checked each month by the police. The pressure on local authorities to establish sites evolved from largely unsuccessful exhortation, via central subsidy, to end with the imposing of a formal obligation to make provision for short-term stays, coupled with freedom to ban camping elsewhere once the obligation was met. By the end of the 1980s sites were scattered unevenly over much of France, particularly in the north-west, with standards ranging from the well-equipped to the very primitive, plus a few housing settlements. On the educational front, voluntary bodies piloted quite a wide assortment of classes and schools, but there was little sign of a coherent central policy.

In Italy, few authorized camps were created, whether by local or central government, and such measures as were taken by way of special classes were private initiatives. These were discontinued, however, once the official emphasis changed towards ensuring access to ordinary classes, with the expressed intention of making supplementary provision for those Gypsy children with learning difficulties – a shift which was not confined to Italy and for which there were respectable arguments so long as the promised back-up was in practice adequate. Belgium was another country which turned away from separate classes, while the provision of sites was left largely to the judgement of local councils, with central financial support, and most of the two dozen or so that did appear were very basic and were designed to regularize caravans which had

---

[17] Cf. J.-P. Liégeois, *School Provision for Gypsy and Traveller Children* (Brussels, 1987), dealing with the member states of the European Communities.

been stationary for decades. The main issue in Spain was hardly what to do about Gypsies who were nomadic, since most lived in poor *barrios* (but nomadism was in any case banned); it was more a question of doing something about the *barrios* and shanty-towns. Less exposed to view was the insidious discrimination that had entered into many wage structures for agricultural day labourers: in 1989 an hour's work in the fields in Murcia was paid at a rate of 300 pesetas for men, 250 for women, and 200 for Gypsies. The government urged municipal authorities to adopt housing programmes to clear the black spots, and some did so; it also subsidized reception classes in schools.

Spain found that there could be a backlash from the rest of the population when Gypsy families moved to new homes or the children started to attend school. It was not alone in that: such reactions were not uncommon, even in the Netherlands and Sweden, two countries which were in certain respects among the most forthcoming. Sweden accepted hundreds of Gypsies expelled from Poland (see p. 276), treated them as refugees and helped them to find both jobs and housing. The Netherlands also arranged homes for a sizeable number of foreign Gypsies (p. 274). As regards domestic Travellers, opinion had been in favour of gathering *woonwagenbewoners* into large groups in a relatively small number of centres. Dutch legislation of 1968 led to experimentation both with such caravan parks and with family units, complemented by special schools and adult education classes. In the late 1970s, however, the policy was reversed as the unsuitability of big camping grounds became more and more apparent; it then proved extremely difficult to replace them with the requisite number of small sites. Similarly, when educational policy veered towards integrating the children into ordinary classes, local reactions often created problems, partly because the existing scholastic level of the Travellers was low, but also as a result of other children closing ranks and the mistrust of their parents.

Statements of good intention and detailed prescription were not lacking in international forums. The Ministers of the Council of Europe, representing the bulk of the European countries outside the then communist bloc, adopted a succession of resolutions and recommendations from 1975 onwards, deprecating the underprivileged situation of nomads in Europe and urging member governments and local authorities to put an end to discrimination, to do something about camping grounds and housing, and to promote education and vocational guidance and health and social welfare. The Council of the European Communities addressed itself to the educational aspects, and its resolution of May 1989 called for 'a global structural approach helping to overcome the major obstacles to the access of gypsy and traveller children to schooling'; this was to be founded on respect for their culture, additional resources, and special training for teachers.[18] The resolution's summary of the current situation in the EC provided some measure of the distance still to be made up in the 12 member states: only 30–40 per cent of half a million and more such children attended school with any regularity; half had never been at all; the proportion going on to secondary school and beyond was tiny; the level of educational skills bore little relationship to the presumed length of schooling; and the illiteracy rate among adults was frequently over 50 per cent, and in some places 80 per cent or more.

The political transformations which 1989 ushered in soon generated new strains and rivalries throughout Europe, lending added significance to the document endorsing the rights of national minorities which was signed the following year by 34 governments at a meeting of the Conference on Security and Co-operation in Europe. After a condemnation of any form of discrimination on ethnic grounds, there came the words: 'In this context they recognize the particular problems of Gypsies.'

These problems had become all the more acute because the collapse of totalitarianism in the east brought a resurgence of feelings which had been held in check since the war; and greater liberty of speech meant increased freedom for expression of prejudice. Serious incidents – houses set on fire, Gypsy families beaten up – began to occur in Hungary, Poland, Czechoslovakia, Rumania and Bulgaria, and have persisted.

[18] 'Resolution of the Council and the Ministers of Education...on school provision for gypsy and traveller children', *Official Journal of the European Communities*, 21 June 1989, 89/C153/02.

There was violence even in places where Gypsies had long been legally settled and seemingly accepted. Private enterprise was no longer a criminal offence, but those Gypsies who were opportunistic enough to identify profitable openings offered by post-revolution free economies earned increased hostility from their trading in scarce commodities. In Rumania particularly, Gypsies fed the resentments of many working people who were suffering from the economic crises, and the newly elected government led the nationalist crusade. When gangs of miners were shipped into Bucharest in June 1990 to put down anti-government dissent, Gypsies were also singled out for special treatment and the miners went on the rampage in their homes for an evening of vicious outrages, before leaving the capital with their President's praise ringing in their ears.

There has been some reversion to nomadism in the east since 1989; and international movement quickened even more once the emergent democracies slackened their border controls and passports became obtainable for the first time in decades. Central and western Europe began to be invaded by emigrants, including tens of thousands of Gypsies from Rumania. As Yugoslavia disintegrated into bitter conflict, Gypsies from there swelled the numbers. In Germany – the prime destination for hordes of asylum seekers – vigilante groups launched defensive action against camps for Gypsies, and pressure mounted for also expelling those who had arrived years before without having official rights of residence, and for amendment of the country's constitution and tightening of its law on asylum. Against this background of heightened tensions over refugees and immigrant workers, 1992 saw the prospect of moves within the European Community towards more standardized policing of entry of non-EC nationals, as a counterpart to the opening of internal borders to free circulation of EC citizens – a freedom which, however, does not necessarily do away with national restrictions on the ability to work or move around, like the French *carnet de circulation*.

Populations and groupings

After so many shakes of the kaleidoscope, it is hardly surprising that today's Gypsy population patterns show a profusion

Plate 45   Arrest of Rumanian Gypsy at refugee centre in Lebach, near Bremen, 1990. Deutsche Presse-Agentur, Hamburg.

of different elements. In surveying the mosaic, how is one to marshal the variety into some kind of order? A good starting point is the basic distinction to be made in most countries between old-established Gypsy groups and those which arrived within the past century or so – like the Rom and, more recently, the Xoraxané – a distinction which manifests itself in all sorts of ways, whether in language, customs or occupations, or in life-style generally. A similar dichotomy is that between Sinti and Roma, designations which are seen as mutually exclusive by Gypsies themselves. A Sinto may use *Roma* to refer to any Gypsies of east European extraction or, indeed, any Gypsies who are not Sinti, while the Roma, in their turn, may just as expansively refer to all west European Gypsies as 'Sinti'. More precisely, the Sinti are Gypsies long resident in German-speaking lands, a fact attested by the strong influence of German on their Romani dialects. They are found in several countries; indeed, a Sinto variety of Romani took root as far east as the Volga, carried there by Gypsies who arrived via Poland in the latter half of the nineteenth century, and during the Second World War it was transplanted further to Kazakhstan. In France, they came to be known as *manouches* (from Romani *manuś*, '[Gypsy] man'). A third major category, distinct from Sinti and Roma, is formed by the Calé of Spain, the Ciganos of Portugal and the *gitans* of southern France, together with cognate groups as far away as Latin America. In western European countries, one can thus often distinguish several strata. In France, one encounters Manouches, Gitans, Rom (mostly Kalderash), Xoraxané, and others. In Italy, the older layers are composed of various Sinti families in the north, together with the Gypsies of the Abruzzi and Calabria in the centre and south who – to judge by the paucity of Slav and German loan-words in their closely related dialects – may well descend from Gypsies who crossed over direct from Greece. Superimposed on these are Xoraxané and other arrivals from Yugoslavia, as well as Kalderaśa, Ćurara, Rudari and similar Danubian tribes.

The situation further east is just as much of a patchwork. In the Balkans, the ethnic and linguistic complexity is particularly significant, given that what took place there has been vital to Gypsy history: from the beginning, the Balkans have contained the densest concentrations and been the *fons et origo* for Europe as a whole. Over the centuries the variegation has become more extreme there than anywhere else.[19] One has to invoke a range of criteria in trying to chart the ramifications among Balkan Gypsies. Nationality is scarcely among them, for many of the Gypsy tribes extend across national borders and there are numerous parallels in internal organization from one country to the next. Dialect and religion (Muslim/Christian) have been two of the more important factors. Occupational specialization, present or past, is another: we

---

[19] For a general conspectus, see W. G. Lockwood, 'Balkan Gypsies: an introduction', in *Papers from the Fourth and Fifth Annual Meetings, Gypsy Lore Society, North American Chapter* (New York, 1985), pp. 91–9; rptd with modifications in *Giessener Hefte für Tsiganologie* (1985), 1/85, pp. 17–23.

have already seen how this had moulded subdivisions among the Rom. The boundary between nomadic and sedentary is also significant, but is by no means sharp or enduring: many sedentary Gypsies move around owing to seasonal occupations, while nomads usually settle down for the winter months.[20] (Nor is there any certain correlation between the nomadic/sedentary dividing line and linguistic conservatism: not a few nomadic groups have dropped Romani, while plenty of sedentaries have maintained it, not least when living in large Gypsy communities.)

On the basis of such distinctions, some 20 principal tribes have been identified for Yugoslavia, and many of these can be further subdivided. Each may have its own territory, possess its own subculture, pursue its own distinctive occupations, speak its own dialect, and conduct marriages within its own group.[21] In Bulgaria, on the eve of the First World War, one investigator was able to list 19 tribes in just the north-eastern portion of the country, using a combination of district, religion, occupation and whether they were nomadic or sedentary; seven of these were tribes of sedentary Muslims, four of sedentary Christians, four of nomad Muslims and four of nomad Christians.[22] Three of them (including the Rudari, then the largest nomadic tribe in north-east Bulgaria) spoke no Romani, while the remaining 16 were equally divided between Vlach and non-Vlach speakers, some of their non-Vlach dialects having claims to be the most primitive in the Balkans. Since then, the tribal distinctions have gradually become less significant as a result of continuing Gypsy national development, coupled with forced sedentarization, cultural assimilation and the governmental refusal to recognize Gypsies as a legitimate ethnic group.

---

[20] For an account of the process of assimilation of *Bijeli* (Serbian Muslim) Gypsies in pre-war Serbia, and their transition from nomadic to sedentary life and gradual blending with the *gadže*, see A. Petrović, 'Contributions to the study of the Serbian Gypsies', *JGLS(3)*, 19 (1940), pp. 87–100.

[21] R. Uhlik, 'Iz ciganske onomastike', *Glasnik Zemaljskog museja u Sarajevu, istorija i etnografija*, new series, 10 (1955), pp. 51–71; 11 (1956), pp. 193–209.

[22] B. J. Gilliat-Smith, 'Report on the Gypsy tribes of north east Bulgaria', *JGLS(2)*, 9 (1915–16), pp. 1–54, 65–109.

Plate 46 *Irish Travellers in the 1970s. Photograph by Janine Wiedel.*

To complicate taxonomy further, there exist, particularly in western Europe, other peripatetic fringe-groups which, by their life-style, have many resemblances to Gypsies and much cultural baggage in common: they travel in families, from generation to generation, and have similar occupations, a similar way of life, similar attitudes towards the surrounding society, similar preferences for in-marriage at a young age. In so far as they have special languages of their own, however, these differ from Romani, though often influenced by it; and any taboo systems are often different too.

In the British Isles, the itinerants in Ireland, who are popularly referred to as Tinkers but now prefer to be called Travellers, form a good example of one such group which already existed at the time of the Gypsies' arrival.[23] Formerly they travelled in rural areas and performed a variety of trades and services, most notably tinsmithing, horse-dealing and peddling, and lived in tents and horse-drawn waggons. Following the Second World War, most of their traditional skills and services became obsolete. No longer able to make a living in the countryside, large numbers migrated to urban areas, especially Dublin, where men signed on the dole and scavenged for scrap metal and second-hand goods, while women begged. More than half of those in Ireland now live in trailer-caravans or prefabricated houses on special camp sites or in publicly provided housing. From the late 1950s, many crossed over to England, particularly the Midlands, where they began to compete with English Gypsies at their own trades. (This was by no means the first such major influx: the Great Hunger had provided a similar stimulus in the 1840s.) The words in their language, 'Gammon' or 'Cant', which developed from the older 'Shelta', are largely drawn from Celtic secret idiom, including syllabic backslang of archaic Irish ('Gammon' itself is derived from 'Ogam', the old Gaelic alphabet); but in construction it is far more English than Irish. In Scotland, too, the tinker was known long before the advent of the Gypsies, and

[23] Cf. S. B. Gmelch, *Tinkers and Travellers* (Dublin, 1975, 2nd edn 1979); J. Wiedel and M. O'Fearadhaigh, *Irish Tinkers* (London, 1976); G. Gmelch, *The Irish Tinkers* (Menlo Park, CA, 1977, 2nd edn 1985); and G. Gmelch and S. B. Gmelch, 'Ireland's travelling people: a comprehensive bibliography', *JGLS*(4), 1 (1977), no. 3, pp. 159–69.

this original population more than held its own with the newcomers. Little is known of the relations between them in the past, but there must have been a good deal of contact, including intermarriage, and the Gypsy stream broadened out. Many Scottish Travellers certainly share some Gypsy taboos (e.g. in regard to washing clothes and dishes in the same basin), while Romani words in their private language, 'the Cant', are pretty universal, alongside words from Gaelic and Scots and also from cant in its old sense (i.e. the secret jargon of the underworld, first recorded in the sixteenth century).[24]

How it was that the similar groups of commercial nomads on the Continent originated is a matter for considerable debate: theories tend to fluctuate between social and economic factors on the one hand and emphasis on Gypsy admixture on the other. It is, however, a futile task to look for precise categorization, particularly if the aim is to rank them in order of 'genuineness'. Geographically most widespread are the *Jenische*.[25] This designation is first attested, tenuously, in 1714, when it was used in regard to a Viennese jargon; 70 years later it had become a label for *Rotwelsch* (German thieves' cant). One popular theory relates it to the Romani root *džan-*, 'to know', giving it the sense of the 'clever' language or people. In Germany, the *Jenische* concentrated particularly in the Rhineland and surrounding regions, their private vocabulary a mixture of Romani, Yiddish, Rotwelsch and German dialect in proportions varying according to locality; they made baskets and sieves and travelled around hawking, knife-grinding and tinsmithing. The *yéniches* of France and Belgium came in from German-speaking lands almost two centuries ago. Their names appear to indicate some relationship with the Sinti of south Germany and Alsace.[26] On the other hand, it has been argued that in Switzerland any contact of the Jenisch with Gypsies must have been very limited in

---

[24] Cf. A. and F. Rehfisch, 'Scottish Travellers or Tinkers', in *Gypsies, Tinkers and Other Travellers*, pp. 271–83; and E. MacColl and P. Seeger, *Till Doomsday in the Afternoon* (Manchester, 1986).

[25] Cf. H. Arnold, *Fahrendes Volk* (Neustadt, 1980); and A. Reyniers and J. Valet, 'Les Jeniš', *Études Tsiganes* (1991), no. 2, pp. 11–35.

[26] Cf. J. Valet, *Les Voyageurs d'Auvergne, nos familles yéniches* (Clermont, 1990).

the past two centuries, but the evidence is inconclusive.[27] A degree of mingling seems probable in whatever country, and is indisputable in some (there is, for example, a good deal of contact and intermarriage between *manouches* and *yéniches* in central France), but in language and pollution code they stand apart. The corresponding group in the Netherlands, known as *woonwagenbewoners* ('caravan-dwellers') or *reizigers* ('travellers'), appears largely to have emerged in the eighteenth century as itinerant pedlars, smiths, knife-grinders, etc., coming mainly from Westphalia, and from peat-diggers who wandered between moorlands in northern Brabant; then, in the nineteenth century, a new stratum was formed from a variety of sources. Mostly they now live in stationary caravans, dealing in scrap, second-hand cars and textiles, or performing casual work.[28]

In Scandinavia, the relationship of similar groups with Gypsies is again uncertain. The *omstreifere* ('wanderers') of Norway may have descended from a union of Gypsies and Germans with native elements; in their special language, *Rodi*, almost a third of the vocabulary was derived from Romani and a tenth from German.[29] Most are now semi-sedentary. Sweden's Travellers have come to be known as *tattare*, for the name originally given to Gypsies was, in the course of the eighteenth century, gradually transferred to itinerant families generally, Gypsies now being called *zigenare*. These *resande* ('travellers', their own preferred designation) also have many Romani words in their vocabularies, as well as dialectal loan-words, and are widely believed to descend partly from Gypsies and partly from settled Swedish families. This has been disputed on the basis of a sample of pedigrees,[30] but even that showed a certain infusion of Gypsy blood.

The *quinquis* of Spain and Portugal – the word is short for *quinquilleros*, 'tinkers' – are a homogeneous, exclusive

---

[27] Cf. S. Golowin, 'Fahrende in der Schweiz', *Giessener Hefte für Tsiganologie* (1985), 2 + 3/85, pp. 40–50; and C. Meyer, *'Unkraut der Landstrasse'* (Zürich, 1988).

[28] Cf. J. H. A. Wernink, *Woonwagenbewoners* (Assen, 1959).

[29] Cf. R. Iversen, *Secret Languages in Norway. Part II: The Rodi (Rotwelsch) in Norway* (Oslo, 1945).

[30] A. Heymowski, *Swedish Travellers and their Ancestry* (Uppsala, 1969).

group with a marked preference for close kin marriage.[31] They are held by some to descend from an isolated branch of early Gypsies, but there is no physical, cultural or linguistic resemblance. Many *quinqui* words date back to Spain's Golden Age. A more plausible theory traces their origins to landless Castilian peasants who turned to nomadism after the rural population had been decimated by a series of prolonged famines and plagues in the sixteenth century. In Spain they remained nomadic until the 1950s – more so than the *gitanos* – travelling in lavishly decorated yellow waggons. Then a succession of laws barring nomadism forced them to become sedentary: many became squatters or shack-dwellers in the shanty-towns that had mushroomed outside Madrid, Barcelona and Bilbao, until these were destroyed and their inhabitants banished to remote areas. Now most live in urban slums and swell the ranks of the unemployed; the word *quinqui* has become almost synonymous with *delincuente* in Castilian, and the people are looked down on by both *gitano* and *payo*.

Given these and many other possibilities of confusion, and the impracticality of hard and fast racial distinctions, it is only to be expected that counting Gypsies will generally turn out to be an exercise in frustration. National censuses often do not make the attempt. Where they do, there are difficulties in defining the target population, whether peripatetic or settled, and then in identifying it or persuading its members to declare themselves in accordance with expectations. (In Yugoslavia, some have objected to calling themselves *Roma*. In a reversal of the trend away from 'Gypsy' and the like, a movement started in Macedonia in 1990 to adopt the name 'Egipcani', and several thousand Gypsies allied themselves to this classification in the 1991 census.) Informed estimates which seek to fill the gaps often show striking discrepancies. Two recent country-by-country analyses[32] led to ranges of 1,988,000–5,621,000 in one and 3,421,750–4,935,500 in the other in respect of Europe's total Gypsy population.

[31] Cf. L. Ignacio, *Los Quinquis* (Barcelona, 1974); and K. Bonilla, 'The Quinquis: Spain's last nomads', *JGLS*(4), 1 (1976), no. 2, pp. 86–92.

[32] R. Vossen, *Zigeuner* (Frankfurt am Main, 1983), pp. 157–62; and J.-P. Liégeois, *Gypsies* (London, 1986), p. 47.

For particular countries, the disparities can be enormous, as when one of these sources quotes figures of *c*.1,000 for the Netherlands and 1,000–8,000 for Sweden, while the other gives 30,000–35,000 and 60,000–100,000 respectively. Part of the differences may be attributed to varying degrees of expansiveness towards including marginal groups (*Jenische, tattare, woonwagenbewoners*, etc.) within the defined population; but even then (as in the case of the higher figures just quoted) the estimates can strain credibility.

The inherent uncertainty is not, however, sufficient excuse for avoiding the question altogether, and some assessment of Gypsy populations is called for here. If one looks at European countries as they existed in the late 1980s, reasonable ranges of magnitude, in descending order (where e.g. '250,000+' represents something between a quarter of and half a million Gypsies), appear to be:

500,000+:	Yugoslavia; Rumania
250,000+:	Hungary; Spain; Bulgaria; former USSR; Czechoslovakia
100,000+:	France
50,000+:	Italy; Germany; UK; Greece
25,000+:	Poland; Albania; Portugal
10,000+:	Austria
1,000+:	Sweden; Finland; Netherlands; Belgium; Switzerland; Denmark
Below 1,000:	Ireland; Cyprus; Norway.

Sometimes a concentration in a single town in a country at the upper end of the scale may far outstrip the entire population in a country in the lower register: Šuto Orizari, a township outside Skopje in Yugoslav Macedonia with some 40,000 Gypsies, mostly Muslim, has the largest single Gypsy community anywhere today, though it is rivalled by Sliven in Bulgaria. As for Europe as a whole, a total of around four million would be compatible with the above ranges. There is no way to be sure, however, and some would argue for much larger figures.[33]

[33] For example, G. Puxon, *Roma: Europe's Gypsies*, 4th edn (London, 1987), p. 13, gives a table which totals 5,991,000, 'including associated sedentary and nomadic groups'.

Turns of speech

In this analysis of groupings, linguistic differences have been an important distinguishing feature. Once one tries to unravel the dialectal complexities of Romani, it is difficult to know where to stop, even if one disregards the Middle East. No language stands still: each year, English acquires about 100 new mainstream words or new meanings for existing words. Romani is especially dynamic. Every Romani speaker, beyond childhood, is bilingual, and in all parts of Europe there have been constant borrowings from the host cultures. New divergences are occurring all the time. With no written standard, there is little to keep the fission of Romani in check, for even though, by word of mouth, the songs and tales for which Gypsies have a talent are handed down from generation to generation, this is living material, constantly altered and creatively rejuvenated. Some of the variants of Romani can no longer be called languages at all and have dwindled to a relatively small vocabulary which can be employed within the context of a national language or dialect – such as the *caló* of the Iberian Peninsula, or Anglo-Romani[34] (as distinct from the archaic language preserved by the Wood family in Wales). Even among those which can legitimately be described as languages, the range of vocabulary is limited, generally no more than a few thousand words. The differences between dialects are often considerable, though much reduced if one concentrates on their central core and disregards the half-integrated loan-words most recently taken over.[35] In the Welsh dialect, some 60 per cent of the vocabulary can be identified as

---

[34] As in the following sentence from a Gypsy girl's account of Appleby horse fair: 'When the little chavvies get up they take the grais down the pani and they wash the grais down, and then they ride the grais up and down the drom'. [*Chavvie* = 'boy'; *grai* = 'horse'; *pani* = 'water' (the River Eden); *drom* = 'road'. At least two of these words are of Indic origin, one is from Greek, and the other, *grai*, is probably from Armenian, if not Indic.]

[35] For a lexicostatistical analysis of a sample, see M. Cortiade, 'Distance between the Romani dialects', *GLS/NAC Newsletter*, 8 (1985), no. 2, pp. 1–4, and 'O kodifikaciji i normalizaciji romskog zajedničkog jezika', in *Romani Language and Culture*, eds S. Balič et al. (Sarajevo, 1989), pp. 205–21.

pre-European in origin; 16 per cent had English roots, 9 per cent Greek, 6 per cent Slavic, and 4 per cent Welsh, the remainder being made up of sprinklings from Rumanian, German and French. The borrowings sometimes took on slightly different meanings, and always were dressed up in Romani suffixes and subjected to Romani grammar.

Franz Miklosich, in 1874, classified European Romani into 13 dialects, primarily on the basis of the sources of such borrowings.[36] Owing to subsequent population movements and new linguistic developments and discoveries, his analysis can no longer serve. Romani has become a network of perhaps more than 60 dialects, falling into a score of groupings.[37] They can be classified in a variety of ways. Phonology by itself is not an adequate touchstone,[38] although sometimes a particular sound-shift may have set one grouping apart. This was the case with certain dialects which, apparently at an early stage in their history, acquired an *h* or *x* sound instead of the original *s* in certain contexts (e.g. *hi* / *hin* / *hum*, 'is' instead of *si* / *isí*). This development – already discernible in van Ewsum's glossary of the 1560s (see p. 187) – is a characteristic of Sinto speech as well as that of the *Kaale* in Finland, and also, in varying degrees, of some dialects in Slovakia and around the Carpathians (east Hungary, Galicia, Transylvania). Since that mutation, however, many further changes have occurred and drawn these dialects away from each other and also created new subdivisions. Within the speech of the Sinti, for example, the dialects of the Sinti *piemontesi* and Sinti *lombardi* of northern Italy have drifted apart, both phonetically and in vocabulary,[39] from the other varieties; and even the latter, though closer together, can be seen to fall into three main categories:[40]

[36] *Über die Mundarten und die Wanderungen der Zigeuner Europas* (*Denkschriften der kaiserlichen Akademie der Wissenschaften*, Philosophisch-historische Klasse, Vienna), vol. 23 (1874), pp. 1–46.

[37] Cf. T. Kaufman, review in *International Journal of the Sociology of Language*, 19 (1979), pp. 131–44, esp. pp. 134–6.

[38] For a classification based on phonology, see J. Kochanowski, *Gypsy Studies*, Part 1 (New Delhi, 1963), pp. 52–118.

[39] Cf. G. Soravia, *Dialetti degli Zingari Italiani* (Pisa, 1977).

[40] Cf. J. Valet, 'Les dialectes du sinto-manouche', in *Tsiganes: Identité, Évolution*, ed. P. Williams (Paris, 1989), pp. 309–14.

– those spoken in Germany, the Netherlands and Alsace;
– those spoken in France; and
– those spoken in Venezia (Italy), Styria (Austria) and Hungary.

Each of these subdivisions is fairly homogeneous, despite lexical differences from country to country, and within them the speaker of one Sinto dialect has no trouble in comprehending the others.

Another primary distinction lies between Vlach and non-Vlach. All the Vlach forms of Romani betray strong Rumanian influence – hence the label. Some have been carried far and wide by the Rom (cf. pp. 226–8), whose main dialects are 'Russian' Kalderash, 'Rumanian' Kalderash, 'Serbian' Kalderash, Lovari, Ćurari and (in the USA) Maćvano. These share an abundance of Rumanian words, representing perhaps two-fifths of their vocabulary, and have taken over certain Rumanian speech habits and constructions (such as the plural ending *-uri / -uria*, used with loan-nouns, and the substitution of Rumanian *mai* for the Romani comparative affix *-der*, e.g. *mai ternó*, 'younger', as compared with Welsh Romani *tarnedér*). Other common features are the use of the ending *-em* in the first person singular of the preterite (cf. Kalderash *kerdem* and Welsh Romani *kedóm*, 'I made'), and the replacement of the sounds *tś* and *dź* by *ś* and *ź* and of the plural definite article, *ē* or *ī*, 'the', by *le* (cf. Kalderash *le gaźé* and Welsh Romani *ī gadźē*).

The non-Vlach dialects generally do not share such close affinities. Over the centuries, they have acquired a great diversity of innovations (not just borrowed words, but also pronunciations and new ways of constructing and manipulating words, phrases and sentences), as might be expected from their wide geographical coverage and long exposure to disparate contact languages. They range right across Europe, from Russia, the Baltic republics and the Ukraine, to Britain and the Iberian Peninsula, and also include the proliferation of non-Vlach dialects in the Balkans, some of which have more recently been carried elsewhere too – for example, the Arliya dialects spoken by thousands of Muslim Gypsies, the Xoraxané. Within that enormous span, however, distinctive features shared by particular dialects may form them into clusters of near relations, as in the Sinto grouping already considered.

So permeated has Romani become by elements from contact languages that many Romani speakers would be hard put to communicate with those elsewhere: a Gypsy from Skopje in Macedonia would make heavy weather of the Romani of, say, a Sinto from northern Italy; and the 'Carpathian' Romani spoken by the house-dwelling Gypsies in northern Hungary is virtually unintelligible to the Vlach tribes in that country. It is indeed debatable whether Romani has not reached a stage where it should be considered as a group of closely related languages rather than as a single language with numerous dialects.

Tradition of change

The great range of ethnic-linguistic diversity is mirrored and crosscut by variations in all aspects of contemporary Gypsies' life, affected by developments in their relationship to the society around them, whether it be population growth and increasing land shortage, sedentarization, having to live close to the *gadžo*, motorized transport, industrialization, or fluctuations in earning opportunities. The demise of Gypsy society has often been forecast: the fact that language, customs, traditions and entire life-style are in constant change and adopt elements from other societies is taken to indicate decline. One group becomes differentiated from another, because the influences come from different sets of *gadžé*; but each is the product of a general tradition of adaptability – social, geographical, and occupational. Some may in the end be submerged; many manage to keep a feeling of radical otherness from the *gadžé* and construct typically Gypsy cultures from what they have absorbed. Old trappings and customs sometimes die away – as when Kalderash women give up the colourful kerchief over their hair, or Lovara women no longer wear picturesque long skirts – but this does not destroy or diminish the feeling of separateness, however much other Kalderash and Lovara may view such lapses as a sign of degeneration, and even if the *gadžo* thinks that the most authentic Gypsies must be the most exotic.

There is always a risk of unwarranted generalization in singling out particular aspects of life among Gypsies and seeking to draw pan-Gypsy inferences. Any statement about 'Gypsy' types of craft or trade, for example, is likely to be open to contradiction, perhaps because some Gypsies have become sober-suited professional people, and certainly because there are no universal principles governing the ways in which Gypsies make their living. Many of the 'traditional' employments may have been picked up far along the road they followed in their history. Much of their phraseology of metal-working, for example, was borrowed from Greek, Rumanian, Slavic or other European languages; and the economic adaptations which became evident in the nineteenth century (cf. ch. 7) were simply part of a centuries-long process, a process which shows no sign of letting up. The old occupational names – Kalderaša, Lovara, Rudari, etc. – have for the most part little meaning now, other than as labels differentiating one group from another. In the regions of Europe with largely industrialized societies, there is dwindling scope for many of the callings to which a good number of Gypsies turned their hand in the past. But while the activities change, what can be said to be old is an underlying propensity for working on their own account, and a generalist repertoire which allows a degree of flexibility suited to their social structure and their desire for independence in organizing their lives. (This is not the same as self-sufficiency, however, for they cannot subsist independently of the wider *gadžo* society and economy.)

Typically, they go out to look for customers, from door to door or enterprise to enterprise, offering a range of goods and services. Sometimes the degree of investment in a livelihood may be such that there is likely to be continuity from generation to generation, as in the case of the circus and fairground families to be found in France and Italy. But where – as is often the case – there is little outlay on tools and equipment, no big stocks, no fixed work-place, they can move all the more easily from place to place, from one source of income to another; there need be no single specialization, and in the course of one lifetime the pattern of activities may alter radically. In many countries Gypsies have steadily shifted away from small-scale trading in new goods and repair services, with a large clientele, towards trade in salvage and construction work, with fewer individual transactions. New livings have emerged or become more widespread, such as – in western Europe – dealing in carpets, textiles, scrap, second-hand cars, furniture, junk and antiques, and contractual building services (e.g. roofing, tarmac-laying). Old ones may continue, such as music and other entertainment, fortune-telling (based on a shrewd assessment of the customer's psychology), or, generally as an ancillary source of income, contract work in horticulture and agriculture. The activity which Travellers in Britain describe as 'calling' can include hawking, fortune-telling, collection of scrap and cast-offs, buying antiques or other resaleable goods, and prospecting for temporary jobs. The pattern varies as they turn to new outlets according to the dictates of opportunity and necessity.

Family values are the important cement in much of Gypsy life, and this is evident in the approach to earning a living too. The children generally start making a contribution once they are old enough. Often poorly educated in the conventional sense, Gypsy children, in going out with adults, seeing and helping them at work, and listening to their advice, may learn to turn their hands to a range of crafts. A wife's income from her rounds is often more regular than the man's, and she may look after the family's daily needs, while the men take care of big outlays – for equipment, a car or lorry or caravan, the expenses of long journeys, feasts and celebrations, or for augmenting any store of valuables, such as gold jewellery. Many Gypsies take pride in their economic flexibility, and look down on the regulated life of *gadže* who subject themselves to the regimentation of wage-labour and its pressures towards conformity. Some prosper; many do not. There are rich Gypsies with Mercedes and expensively equipped trailers, as well as poor Gypsies travelling in modest or miserable circumstances, and downtrodden Gypsies in soulless concrete housing blocks.

It may be helpful to relate these generalities, however

cursorily, to a tiny sample of economic life-histories drawn
from Gypsies who, in the mid-1960s, settled in houses in a
Gypsy hamlet in the south of France, near Grasse.[41] One
concerns Rosette, a widow in her fifties at that time, who came
of a large family of *manouches*, and the other Fernand, a *Sinto
piemonteso* born in 1932.

Rosette's family, in the years when she was growing up after
the First World War, moved from village to village with horse
and living-waggon, putting on silent film shows in places
which the cinema had not reached. They ranged over France,
Germany, Switzerland and Italy, and latterly travelled mainly
in the south-east of France. The films had to be abandoned in
the late 1920s because of competition from talking pictures.
The father then reverted to the knife-grinding and tool-
sharpening which he had learned as a child. When Rosette
married a Kalderash at 18, in 1931, the young couple went to
seek a new life in Corsica, where the husband, soon joined by
others of his family, made a living as a tinner, getting around
in horse and cart. It was there that Rosette started hawking
for the first time, initiated by a Spanish Gypsy woman. Subsequently they pursued a similar life in Algeria and all over
France, eventually replacing the horse with a motor van. They
stayed for a week or so in each place, depending on the
amount of work to be found and also on the tolerance of the
authorities. The men went round hospitals, barracks, hotels,
schools and factories, looking for cooking vessels to repair
or taking special orders for manufacturing them, while the
women helped at the bellows and cleaning the metalwork.
During the Second World War the family groups were dispersed and forced to stop travelling. Rosette's spent the war
living in tents in wretched conditions. When peace came, they
joined up with relatives and took to the roads again, first with
horse and cart, then with a small motor vehicle. Children's
allowances now supplemented their income from tinning.
From 1947 they confined their travels to the Alpes-Maritimes,
where work was plentiful, and rented plots of land for lengthy

---

[41] As described in B. Formoso, *Tsiganes et sédentaires* (Paris, 1986),
which studies this hamlet and its inhabitants in depth. It was set up in 1966
by a local pro-Gypsy association.

periods at Nice and Cannes, living in a big showman's van. The death of her husband in 1956 left Rosette with nine children to look after single-handed. To supplement her widow's pension and children's allowances, she started buying household linen and lace from wholesalers and selling it door to door, coupled with fortune-telling. The older children helped out, and one of her sons collected scrap metal and did some tinning work. When Rosette was sick for several months, the other families in the encampment gave her a share of their earnings. In 1966 she settled in a house in the Gypsy hamlet and continued hawking and fortune-telling as opportunity offered. By now her eldest son, who was finding that there was much less scope for tinning as a result of the spread of stainless steel utensils, worked mainly in collecting scrap and unwanted household articles. Later he moved into second-hand car dealing, supplemented at times by knife-grinding and selling surplus stocks at markets – trades he picked up from other Gypsy families.

Fernand, the *Sinto piemonteso*, was brought up in a family group headed by his maternal grandfather. Like many Sinti in France between the wars, they travelled in horse-drawn waggons and followed a variety of occupations. For the men, who would go out each day with a light cart and knock at doors to see what deals could be done, it was largely a question of horse-trading, basket-making, scrap-collecting, chair-bottoming; and for the women, peddling baskets and haberdashery, and (if the reception seemed favourable) fortune-telling and begging for food and cast-offs. Fernand, who had no schooling, first went out on his own at the age of 13, selling lengths of rope, and soon began looking for scrap metal as well. When he married a second cousin at 17, he started making baskets, which his wife sold along with other small wares; he also did some chair-caning. Then he expanded into scrap and car-breaking (using a cart drawn by a donkey, then a horse, until he bought his first car in 1950), and over the years this became increasingly profitable. With his grandfather and uncles, they travelled in the Alpes-Maritimes and stayed in one locality so long as there was work and they were not moved on. The periods of tolerance reduced as urbanization spread, and by the mid-1950s finding a stopping-place was a major problem. Finally he settled in the Gypsy hamlet. There he switched to buying up clearance stocks and ends of lines from clothing factories, wholesalers and retailers and, helped by his eldest son, sold them at markets and at house doors. The proceeds from the rounds his wife and older daughters were making, together with nine children's allowances, took care of daily subsistence needs. By 1966 he had put enough aside to buy a plot of land, and this was followed by several more. He built a house on one of them and sold it at a profit; then he put up a house on another plot and moved into it himself with his family. Meanwhile his eldest son had taken over the textile trading. Fernand's land and construction deals were not his only money-spinners: from 1973, with Sinti cousins and some Kalderash, he organized a ten-day festival of Gypsy entertainment every summer, involving Gitans, Rom and Manouches; other Gypsies took care of sales of food and drink. The festival always attracted good audiences, to the point where the entertainers could plan to take to the roads again with it.

As these examples indicate (and they could be supplemented by countless others), settling does not in itself transform Gypsies into conventional French citizens, Spaniards, etc. or involve giving up a 'Gypsy' mode of earning a living. It is true that in eastern Europe there has been much greater integration of Gypsies into the national employment structure, often in the unskilled labour force, the area which is currently most affected by lay-offs as unprofitable industries are dispensed with or overhauled. But even in the controlled economies of the former communist countries, Gypsy patterns still showed through. If one looks at what happened in Hungary,[42] one sees market changes driving many of the Vlach semi-nomads away from artisan work into salvage activities (e.g. of feathers and scrap iron) and other forms of dealing which they could carry on with horse and cart – to the point where the authorities, worried by such unorthodoxy, were driven to introduce a licensing system in an attempt to control and limit it. This

[42] Cf. G. Havas, 'Strategien des Beschäftigungswechsels bei verschiedenen Zigeunergemeinschaften in Ungarn', *Giessener Hefte für Tsiganologie* (1984), 2/84, pp. 3–24.

itinerant trading might also be combined with casual seasonal work (e.g. in factories making sugar and preserves) or with forms of employment which left room for a good deal of flexibility (e.g. house repairs and maintenance). Other Gypsies, who lived in Gypsy settlements but had by and large missed out on post-war land collectivization, also found that old livelihoods were being overtaken. They might then accept offers to work long distances away on a mobile basis, perhaps in construction teams which could be moved around from site to site, where they performed basic manual work. This gave them the opportunity to form their own Gypsy squads and to decide whom they were going to work with, and live with in the hostels. It also meant that they could take on secondary employment in the growing private building sector. None the less, their existence is precarious, and their families back in the settlements often have to make ends meet by seeking out such agricultural and domestic work as is sporadically available locally.

Sedentary Gypsies are now in the majority in both east and west, but they can stay in the same place for decades and maintain their specificity. Mobility remains important; and for many in the west, motor vehicles have become essential tools of the trades, making it possible to travel long distances from the one spot in search of customers. Nor are the social habits of formerly nomadic Gypsies necessarily eliminated by sedentarization. They show a liking for staying close to each other, preferably in touch with near relatives; domestic life is concentrated in one room, with little privacy; they take unkindly to the confinements imposed by apartments, which would isolate them and undermine family relationships. It is as if they carry over a style close to that of the encampment, uneasy with solitude, seeking company, and spending a good deal of time outside the house, even when at leisure.

For those who remain on the move, with vehicle-drawn caravans, stopping-places need no longer be at ten-mile intervals as in the days of the horse and *vardo*. This potent symbol of the 'true' Gypsy in *gadźé* eyes has in real life been pushed into a minor place by motorization. Already by 1965 only 6 per cent of families in England and Wales were dependent on such transport, and the percentage has declined

Plate 47   A flash 'Westmorland Star' trailer. B. T. Batsford / Denis E. Harvey.

since then, though the horse still holds an important place in the interests, if not the economy, of many a motorized Gypsy. The new forms of transport and mobile accommodation change the texture of life too. Modern trailer-caravans offer electric light, refrigerators and gas cooking. And for all, sedentary or not, the advent of television, following radio and the cinema, brings the outside world much closer and influences the young particularly, making them less inclined to accept their situation as pariahs and offering new channels for the absorption of *gadže* values. Occasionally, TV may even teach Gypsies about their own past: in the late 1980s in Greece, a programme which linked them to India led to a vogue among some Gypsy girls for dressing up in saris and introducing oriental elements into their dances. Perhaps after 50 years or so these will be seized upon by ethnomusicologists as a cultural remnant from their original homeland.

Pilgrims and Pentecostals

Religion is another sphere where Gypsies reflect the *gadžo* world around them. They have tended to accept the religions of the countries in which they have lived for some time. Thus there are Catholic Gypsies, various types of Protestant and Orthodox Gypsies and, throughout the Islamic world and those parts of south-eastern Europe where the Ottomans most recently ruled, large numbers of Muslim Gypsies. Everywhere they are accused of lacking true piety, just as, originally, they were dubbed 'Heathens', 'Saracens' and 'Tartars'. While this alleged indifference is frequently overstressed, there may be a certain eclecticism in Gypsy religious belief and practice. Muslim Gypsies in Bulgaria think nothing of celebrating St George's Day as much as Orthodox Gypsies, or of dyeing eggs for good luck around Easter.

It was in the guise of pilgrims that Gypsies first came to western Europe. Whether they were punctilious in visiting the shrines which they claimed to be headed for is dubious. As for the sacraments, while baptism became popular among them, they often went their own way in matters of burial and, particularly, marriage. By the nineteenth century, however,

Plate 48   Gypsies at Les-Saintes-Maries-de-la-Mer, 1988.

Gypsy pilgrimages were becoming regular events. Nowadays, there are periodic processions to more than half a dozen French sanctuaries, including Lourdes, and to others in Spain, Portugal, Italy, Belgium and Germany. The best known has long been the gathering on 24 and 25 May each year at Les-Saintes-Maries-de-la-Mer in the Camargue. The 'Saint' Sara who became adopted as a patron never had a place in the Church's calendar of saints; she was the Egyptian servant of Mary Jacobe and Mary Salome, Jesus' aunts, believed to have been carried miraculously to the mouth of the Rhône a few years after the Crucifixion. It was only in the mid-nineteenth century that the presence of Gypsies was noted amongst other pilgrims at Les-Saintes-Maries, and much more recently that they began to dominate the first of the two days. Each year they drape bright new robes around the plaster statue of St Sara, blackened by the smoke of the candles in the crypt;

and on 24 May the church service and the procession to the sea with the statue, escorted by *gardians* on white horses, primarily belongs to them (leaving aside the tourists). The cortège on the following day in honour of the two Marys is more of a Provençal festival, with Gypsy participation. A visit to Les-Saintes-Maries, or any other pilgrimage, is also, however, an important opportunity to renew family and social contacts, to discuss a betrothal, and possibly to conduct a piece of business.

It is perhaps not excessive to see in the post-war surge of missionary and charitable activities on the part of the established churches an element of competition with a potent new movement which started in 1952 in Brittany under the leadership of Clément Le Cossec, a Breton pastor of *gadžé* origins. This religious revival spread out of Brittany to Paris, Bordeaux and other parts of France, and induced a remarkable dissemination of Pentecostalism among Gypsies in Europe and the Americas, giving rise to periodic conventions which brought together masses of Gypsies in the Evangelical equivalent of the Catholic pilgrimages.[43] One reason why the movement was able to make rapid progress was that, whereas the established churches demanded long periods of training for their priests, this one relied on inducting lay preachers (all males) from Gypsy families – the very people who knew where to turn next and who could speak the language of the prospective converts and, radiating assurance, address them in extemporaneous sermons on simple biblical themes. Later, a strategic decision was taken to conduct the missionary work on a tribal basis, using *manouche* preachers to reach *manouches*, *gitans* to approach *gitans*, and so on. (The church

---

[43] Cf. T. Acton, 'The Gypsy Evangelical Church', *Ecumenical Review*, 31 (1979), no. 3, pp. 11–17; C. Le Cossec, ' "Phénomène pentecôtiste" ou réveil religieux', *Études Tsiganes* (1985), no. 1, pp. 19–21; J. Ridholls, *Travelling Home* (Basingstoke, 1986); E. B. L. Sato, 'The social impact of the rise of Pentecostal evangelicalism among American Rom', in *Papers from the Eighth and Ninth Annual Meetings, Gypsy Lore Society, North American Chapter* (New York, 1988), pp. 69–94; K. Wang, 'Le mouvement pentecôtiste chez les Gitans espagnols', in *Tsiganes: Identité, Évolution*, pp. 423–32; and R. Glize, 'L'église évangélique tsigane comme voie possible d'un engagement culturel nouveau', ibid., pp. 433–43.

services tend to be organized on similar lines.) Expeditions were sent abroad and in the 1960s the fire spread to Spain, where the converts became aptly known as the *aleluyas*; progress was also made, but more slowly, within the other countries of western Europe and Greece. The early 1970s saw campaigns in eastern Europe and the Americas; in the USA the pace quickened smartly in the 1980s; in Britain, the annual Evangelical convention can muster thousands of Travellers. In its first three decades, the Gypsy Evangelical Church was said to have converted and baptized some 70,000 Gypsies and to be attracting many more to its meetings; 1,600 Gypsy men had become preachers, 400 of them as pastors. The movement now commands the allegiance of around a third of the Gypsies in France, where the mission has several periodicals and a radio station, a Bible Institute, a mobile school and special classes at camping sites, and something like 50 churches.

Perhaps the disestablished character of such versions of Christianity has something to do with the way that fundamental Evangelical creeds are sweeping communities as diverse as western European and American Gypsies, Australian aborigines and Zairean pygmies. There is apparently also something in the ecstatic aspect of Evangelical faith – the witnessing for Christ – that is highly attractive to people whose traditional manner of life is in some way under threat. By its nature the Gypsy Evangelical Church makes its born-again converts feel elected as special people and brings them closer together in social solidarity. Its baptism by immersion, emotional modes of religious expression, spontaneous testimonies and participatory style of worship, its belief in the necessity of salvation through Christ and the reality of the alternative Hell, its charismatic practices, based on belief in the *chárisma* ('gift of grace') of the Holy Spirit – the laying on of hands and speaking in tongues – all appear to combine to produce a 'heart religion' that appeals to their emotional and psychological needs. Unlike the nineteenth-century missions, its aims are not assimilationist, but its impact on a committed convert's life-style is none the less radical. The fundamentalist approach to the Scriptures puts a premium on literacy and education. The ideal norms ban the use of alcohol, tobacco and drugs, and also gambling, cheating, lying and theft. Pagan ways have to go: bride-price is seen as compatible with the Bible, but fortune-telling is certainly not; the *slavi* or saints' day festivals celebrated by Catholic and Orthodox Gypsies have to be discarded; the traditional funeral practices and the *pomana* (death feasts) of the Rom need to be modified. Whether these new beliefs will continue to spread to the extent they have already in France and Spain, and whether they will prove strong and enduring, we can but wait and see.

Opré Roma!

The Gypsy Evangelical Church presented the first real example in western Europe of a mass pan-Gypsy organization, transcending tribal subdivisions. On the political level, there had been some stirrings towards international pressure-group activity among Gypsies in the 1930s, in Poland and Rumania. A Bucharest congress of 1933, with delegates from much of eastern Europe and beyond, adopted a sweeping and varied programme, largely aimed at social amelioration, and with a strong Eastern Orthodox bias on the spiritual side.[44] Nothing much came of that. After the Second World War the vast new problems which had emerged for Gypsies in advanced industrial societies were, to begin with, addressed largely by *gadźé* organizations concerned with the condition of Gypsy communities. But Gypsies too began to form themselves into religious, political and cultural associations and pressure-groups, both locally and nationally.[45] In Germany, from the 1950s, various Gypsy committees were founded, chiefly at first to further reparation claims; later, the field of activity was broadened, and the Verband deutscher Sinti ('Association of German Sinti') and subsequently the Zentralrat deutscher Sinti und Roma ('Central Council of German Sinti and Roma') came to acquire a good deal of muscle and command of the media. France was the centre of the initial attempts to make

[44] Cf. W. J. Haley, 'The Gypsy conference at Bucharest', *JGLS*(3), 13 (1934), pp. 182–90.
[45] For the position in England, and its various controversies and rivalries, see T. Acton, *Gypsy Politics and Social Change* (London, 1974).

progress on an international front. Some of the creations in the early days were utopian, but in 1965 a body with more realistic goals was founded in Paris, the Comité International Tsigane ('International Gypsy Committee'), which, though seeking to tread a difficult middle path between different tribal groupings and between Catholic, Orthodox, Protestant and Muslim Gypsies, also chose to work closely with the Gypsy Evangelical Church since it was for the most part Gypsy-run. The CIT formed branches in several countries and forged links with independent organizations in others; some of these were large and influential, some had only a nominal existence, some depended on the assistance of benevolently disposed *gadžé*. All of them had as their primary aim, not the adaptation of Gypsies *to* the host society, but the ending of perceived injustice *by* the host society, and were prepared to back this by using *gadžé* methods: demonstrations, lobbying and publicity campaigns. The emphasis was on the need to preserve economic and geographical flexibility, on the right to continue travelling, and on the use of Romani language and Gypsy culture in formal education.

The CIT organized a first World Romany Congress in April 1971 in London, where delegates from some 14 countries adopted the term *Rom* to describe themselves, and also a flag and a simple slogan – *Opré Roma!*, 'Gypsies arise!'. With a change of name, the CIT became the permanent secretariat and executive body of the congress. Five commissions were set up, to deal with social affairs, education, war crimes, language, and culture. The second World Romany Congress, held in Geneva in April 1978, was attended by some 120 delegates and observers from 26 countries. India was strongly represented, and much was made of the Gypsy link with the subcontinent. Delegates to the United Nations, the UN Human Rights Commission and UNESCO were elected. The organization established to carry on the work up to the next congress was called variously the Romani International Union and the Romani Union: under the latter name it obtained consultative status at the UN Social and Economic Commission in 1979. At the third congress, in Göttingen in May 1981, the discussions were dominated by the fate of Gypsies under the Nazis. By now the previous west European bias was diminishing. Yugoslav Gypsies had from the start played a special role in the development of the international movement, but those in other eastern European countries had been more restricted. The collapse of hardline regimes made it feasible to hold the fourth congress on the outskirts of Warsaw in April 1990, and now, of the 250 or so delegates, 75 per cent came from the former communist bloc. At the same time, the upheavals of 1989 had opened up new possibilities for Gypsy intervention in national and local politics. The emerging pattern appeared to be for separate Gypsy parties to be formed and then to strike alliances with major political parties of similar ideology. In Hungary, for example, the Romany Social Democrat party worked with the Hungarian Social Democrats to secure two Gypsy MPs in the April 1990 elections; Czechoslovakia, Rumania and Bulgaria also acquired a few. Sometimes divisions within Gypsy ranks were replicated in a proliferation of Gypsy political parties: in Rumania no fewer than seven were registered.

The fourth World Romany Congress assigned its executive the task of pursuing an ambitious variety of programmes, dealing with reparations, education, culture, public relations, language, and a Gypsy encyclopaedia. This last was conceived of as an encyclopaedia *for*, not *about*, Gypsies, to involve no less than reshaping the world's knowledge from the point of view of the world's Gypsies. Similarly long-term are the efforts being made to elaborate a standard literary language, given that there is as yet little progress towards reconciliation of morphological diversity, no standard vocabulary, and considerable dialectal variation even for quite basic concepts. The bravest attempt so far to produce a standardized Romani[46] was intended for use in Macedonia, Kosovo and adjacent parts of Serbia, with a view to the creation of Romani-language schools in those areas. It was based on the Arliya dialect of Skopje, but drew also on three others spoken in Yugoslavia; despite relatively close affinities within this selection, major problems of reconciliation had to be confronted.[47] The degree

---

[46] Š. Jusuf and K. Kepeski, *Romani gramatika – Romska gramatika* (Skopje, 1980).

[47] Cf. V. A. Friedman, 'Problems in the codification of a standard Romani literary language', in *Papers from the Fourth and Fifth Annual Meetings, Gypsy Lore Society, North American Chapter* (New York, 1985), pp. 56–75.

of compromise involved in going beyond that kind of venture raises the question of whether a single standardized Romani could in fact reach more than an elite, leaving the books, periodicals and newspapers which used it inaccessible to others.

The quest for a standard language is but one aspect of a new-found desire on the part of some Gypsies to bridge the fissures which have opened during the course of their people's long history, and to find one way round the diversification within their own ranks which is the product of prolonged contact with the larger European society. Being a Gypsy does not consist solely in being brought up and living among Gypsies, but also in a relationship with settled people. Much of this book has centred on the issue of whether a small and vulnerable minority had any right to be different; this was repeatedly at the core of the reception they had at the hands of a society which, once having moved beyond outright rejection, looked for their total assimilation. For long, their survival depended on warding off enemies by stratagem rather than force, by staying on the move and keeping out of trouble's way, even though careless of the legislation of their countries of residence. They nursed their autonomy by adapting to the dominant cultures but preserving a social distance intensified by the suspicion with which they were treated by the *gadźé*. Now, in contrast to earlier strategies of remaining inconspicuous and shunning publicity, some seek to find their own road and lay claim to a voice in their affairs, so as to stand solid against the prejudice which half a millennium has done little to overturn. Unity is not likely to come easily.

Bibliography

This bibliography is, with the exception mentioned below, confined to publications cited in the foregoing pages. These are classified under the following headings:
1. Bibliographical works; 2. Periodicals; 3. General studies; 4. Asian background; 5. Particular European countries; 6. Pre-1800 European history; 7. Nineteenth and twentieth centuries; 8. North America; 9. Physical anthropology; 10. Language; 11. Music; 12. Folk-tales; 13. Pollution code; 14. Religion; 15. Other Travellers; 16. Gypsies in art and literature.

The citations represent only a small fraction of the literature. Several additional titles have therefore been included under the first heading to indicate more comprehensive bibliographies.

1 Bibliographical works

Binns, D. *A Gypsy Bibliography* (Manchester, vol. 1 1982, vol. 2 1986, vol. 3 1990, supplement 9 1991).

Black, G. F. *A Gypsy Bibliography* (London, 1914).

German, A. V. *Bibliografiya o tsyganakh: Ukazatel' knig i statei s 1780 g. po 1930 g.* (Moscow, 1930).

Gronemeyer, R. *Zigeuner in Osteuropa. Eine Bibliographie* (Munich, 1983).

Hovens, P. and Hovens, J. *Zigeuners, Woonwagenbewoners en reizenden: een bibliografie* (Rijswijk, 1982).

Hundsalz, A. *Stand der Forschung über Zigeuner und Landfahrer. Eine Literaturanalyse* (Stuttgart, 1978).

Lockwood, W. G. and Salo, S. *Gypsies and Travellers in North America: A bibliography* (Ann Arbor, 1992).

Masson, D. I. *Catalogue of the Romany Collection* [University of Leeds] (Edinburgh, 1962).
Ortega, J. *Los gitanos: guía bibliográfica y estudio preliminar* (Manchester, 1987).
Tyrnauer, G. *Gypsies and the Holocaust: A bibliography and introductory essay* (Montreal, 1989; 2nd edn 1991).

2   Periodicals

Études Tsiganes (since 1955), 2 rue d'Hautpoul, 75019, Paris, France.
Giessener Hefte für Tsiganologie (1984–6), succeeded by *Tsiganologische Studien* (since 1990, on a sporadic basis), c/o Institut für Soziologie, Justus-Liebig-Universität, Karl-Glöckner-Str. 21E, 6300 Giessen, Germany.
Journal of the Gypsy Lore Society (since 1888). There have been some interruptions, and the journal is now in its fifth series: 5607 Greenleaf Road, Cheverly, MD 20785, USA. A *Newsletter of the Gypsy Lore Society, North American Chapter*, published from 1978, became in 1989 the *Newsletter of the Gypsy Lore Society*.
Lacio Drom (since 1965), Centro Studi Zingari, Via dei Barbieri 22, 00186 Roma, Italy.
Roma (since 1974), 3290/15-D, Chandigarh, 160015, India.

3   General studies

Balić, S. et al. (eds). *Romani Language and Culture* (Sarajevo, 1989).
Cohn, W. *The Gypsies* (Reading, MA, 1973).
Colocci, A. A. *Gli Zingari* (Turin, 1889).
Grellmann, H. M. G. *Die Zigeuner. Ein historischer Versuch über die Lebensart und Verfassung, Sitten und Schicksale dieses Volks in Europa, nebst ihrem Ursprung* (Dessau and Leipzig, 1783; 2nd edn Göttingen, 1787). English translation, *Dissertation on the Gipsies* (London, 1787; 2nd edn London, 1807); French translations Metz, 1788 and Paris, 1810; Dutch translation Dordrecht, 1791.
Gronemeyer, R. and Rakelmann, G. A. *Die Zigeuner, Reisende in Europa* (Cologne, 1988).
Hancock, I. *The Pariah Syndrome* (Ann Arbor, 1987).
Hoyland, J. *A Historical Survey . . . of the Gypsies* (York, 1816).
Kenrick, D. and Puxon, G. *The Destiny of Europe's Gypsies*

(London, 1972); Romani version, *Berša bibahtale* (London, 1988).

Kogălniceanu, M. *Esquisse sur l'histoire . . . des Cigains* (Berlin, 1837).

Liégeois, J.-P. *Gypsies* (London, 1986).

Martinez, N. *Les Tsiganes* (Paris, 1986).

Nunes, O. *O Povo Cigano* (Oporto, 1981).

Popp Serboianu, C. J. *Les Tsiganes* (Paris, 1930).

Predari, F. *Origine e vicende dei Zingari* (Milan, 1841).

Rehfisch, F. (ed.). *Gypsies, Tinkers and Other Travellers* (London, 1975).

Salo, M. T. (ed.). *100 Years of Gypsy Studies* (Cheverly, MD, 1990).

Vaux de Foletier, F. de. *Mille ans d'histoire des Tsiganes* (Paris, 1970).

Vossen, R. *Zigeuner* (Frankfurt am Main, 1983).

Williams, P. (ed.). *Tsiganes: Identité, Évolution* (Paris, 1989).

4 Asian background

Berland, J. C. 'Pārytān: "native" models of peripatetic strategies in Pakistan', *Nomadic Peoples* (1986), nos 21/22, pp. 189–205.

Burton, Sir Richard. *The Jew, the Gypsy and El Islam* (London, 1898).

Goeje, M. J. de. *Mémoire sur les migrations des Tsiganes à travers l'Asie* (Leiden, 1903).

Harriot, J. S. 'Observations on the Oriental origin of the Romnichal', *Transactions of the Royal Asiatic Society*, 2 (1830), pp. 518–58.

Kochanowski, J. 'Roma – History of their Indian origin', *Roma*, 4 (1979), no. 4, pp. 16–32.

Longpérier, G. de. 'L'Inde et ses mystères', *Musée universel*, 1 (1857), pp. 330–6.

MacRitchie, D. *Accounts of the Gypsies of India* (London, 1886), pp. 1–126.

Misra, P. K. and Malhotra, K. C. (eds). *Nomads in India* (Calcutta, 1982).

Mroz, L. 'Les Lohar, les Banjara et le problème de l'origine des Tsiganes', *Études Tsiganes* (1990), no. 1, pp. 3–14.

Rao, A. 'Note préliminaire sur les *Jat* d'Afghanistan', *Studia Iranica*, 8 (1979), no. 1, pp. 141–9.

Rishi, W. R. 'Roma – a study', *Roma*, 7 (1983), no. 2, pp. 1–10.

—— 'History of Romano movement, their language and culture', in *Romani Language and Culture*, eds S. Balić et al. (Sarajevo, 1989), pp. 1–10.

5   Particular European countries

Austria
Mayerhofer, C. *Dorfzigeuner* (Vienna, 1987).

Britain
Crabb, J. *The Gipsies' Advocate*, 3rd edn (London, 1832).
Gentleman, H. and Swift, S. *Scotland's Travelling People* (Edinburgh, 1971).
Gordon, A. *Hearts upon the Highway* (Galashiels, 1980).
Gypsies and Other Travellers, report by an MHLG Sociological Research Section (London, 1967).
Jarman, A. O. H. and Jarman, E. *The Welsh Gypsies: Children of Abram Wood* (Cardiff, 1991).
M'Cormick, A. *The Tinkler-Gypsies* (Dumfries, 1907).
MacRitchie, D. *Scottish Gypsies under the Stewarts* (Edinburgh, 1894).
Mayall, D. *Gypsy-Travellers in Nineteenth-Century Society* (Cambridge, 1988).
Okely, J. *The Traveller-Gypsies* (Cambridge, 1983).
Ribton-Turner, C. J. *A History of Vagrants and Vagrancy* (London, 1887).
Simson, W. *A History of the Gipsies* (London, 1865).
Vesey-FitzGerald, B. *The Gypsies of Britain* (London, 1944).
Ward-Jackson, C. H. and Harvey, D. E. *The English Gypsy Caravan* (Newton Abbot, 1972; 2nd edn, 1986).

Denmark
Dyrlund, F. *Tatere og Natmandsfolk i Danmark* (Copenhagen, 1872).

Finland
Grönfors, M. *Blood Feuding among Finnish Gypsies* (Helsinki, 1977).
Vehmas, R. *Suomen Romaaniväestön Ryhmäluonne ja Akkulturoituminen* (Turku, 1961).

France
Vaux de Foletier, F. de. *Les Tsiganes dans l'ancienne France* (Paris, 1961).
—— *Les Bohémiens en France au 19e siècle* (Paris, 1981).

Germany
Arnold, H. *Die Zigeuner, Herkunft und Leben im deutschen Sprachgebiet* (Olten, 1965).

Hohmann, J. S. *Geschichte der Zigeunerverfolgung in Deutschland* (Frankfurt, 1981).
Mode, H. and Wölffling, S. *Zigeuner, Der Weg eines Volkes in Deutschland* (Leipzig, 1968).

Hungary and Transylvania
Jekelfalussy, J. (ed.). *A Magyarországban ... cziganyösszeiras eredményei* ['Results of the Gypsy Census in Hungary'] (Budapest, 1895).
Schwicker, J. H. *Die Zigeuner in Ungarn und Siebenbürgen* (Vienna, 1883).
Wlislocki, H. von. *Vom wandernden Zigeunervolke* (Hamburg, 1890).

The Netherlands
Hovens, P. and Dahler, R. (eds). *Zigeuners in Nederland* (Nijmegen/ Rijswijk, 1988).
Kappen, O. van. *Geschiedenis der Zigeuners in Nederland* (Assen, 1965).
Lucassen, L. *'En men noemde hen Zigeuners'* (Amsterdam/The Hague, 1990).
Willems, W. and Lucassen, L. *Ongewenste Vreemdelingen* (The Hague, 1990).

Norway
Sundt, E. *Beretning om Fante- eller Landstrygerfolket i Norge* (Christiania, 1850).

Poland
Ficowski, J. *Cyganie na polskich drogach*, 2nd edn (Kraków, 1985).
—— *The Gypsies in Poland* (n.d. [Warsaw, 1990]).

Portugal
Coelho, F. A. *Os Ciganos de Portugal* (Lisbon, 1892).

Rumania
Potra, G. *Contribuţiuni la istoricul Ţiganilor din România* (Bucharest, 1939).

Spain
Borrow, G. *The Zincali* (London, 1841).
Leblon, B. *Les Gitans d'Espagne* (Paris, 1985).

Sweden

Etzler, A. *Zigenarna och deras avkomlingar i Sverige* (Uppsala, 1944).

Switzerland

Huonker, T. *Fahrendes Volk – verfolgt und verfemt* (Zürich, 1987).

6   Pre-1800 European history

Aaltonen, E. Review of R. Vehmas's *Suomen Romaaniväestön*, *JGLS*(3), 42 (1963), pp. 64–7.

Allergnädigst-privilegirte Anzeigen, aus sämmtlich-kaiserlich-königlichen Erbländern (Vienna), 5 (1775), pp. 159–416; 6 (1776), pp. 7–168, *passim*.

Andreas, Presbyter Ratisbonensis, *Diarium sexennale*, in A. F. Oefelius, *Rerum boicarum scriptores* (Augsburg, 1763), vol. 1.

Andree, R. 'Old warning-placards for Gypsies', *JGLS*(2), 5 (1911–12), pp. 202–4.

Arlati, A. 'Gli Zingari nello stato di Milano', *Lacio Drom* (1989), no. 2, pp. 4–11.

Arnold, H. 'Das Vagantenunwesen in der Pfalz während des 18. Jahrhunderts', *Mitteilungen des historischen Vereins der Pfalz*, 55 (1957), pp. 117–52.

—— 'Die Räuberbande des Hannikels', *Pfälzer Heimat*, 8 (1957), pp. 101–3.

Asséo, H. 'Le traitement administratif des Bohémiens', in H. Asséo and J.-P. Vittu, *Problèmes socio-culturels en France au XVIIe siècle* (Paris, 1974), pp. 9–87.

Aubrion, J. *Journal de Jean Aubrion, bourgeois de Metz* (Metz, 1857).

Aventinus. See Thurmaier.

Azevedo, P. d'. 'Os Ciganos em Portugal nos secs. XVI e XVII', *Arquivo Histórico Português*, 6 (1908), pp. 460–8; 7 (1909), pp. 42–52, 81–90, 169–77.

Bartlett, D. M. M. 'Münster's *Cosmographia universalis*', *JGLS*(3), 31 (1952), pp. 83–90.

Bataillard, P. 'Beginning of the immigration of the Gypsies into western Europe in the fifteenth century', *JGLS*(1), 1 (1888–9), pp. 185–212, 260–86, 324–45; 2 (1890–1), pp. 27–53.

Beier, A. L. *Masterless Men* (London, 1985).

Bellorini, T. and Hoade, E. (trans.). 'Pilgrimage of Lionardo di Niccolò Frescobaldi to the Holy Land', in *Publications of the Studium Biblicum Franciscanum* no. 6 (1948), pp. 29–90.

Blair, F. G. 'Forged passports of British Gypsies in the sixteenth century', *JGLS*(3), 29 (1950), pp. 131–7.

Blunt, F. J. *The People of Turkey* (London, 1878).

Breydenbach, B. von. *Peregrinatio in terram sanctam* (Mainz, 1486).

Campigotto, A. 'I bandi bolognesi contro gli Zingari (sec. XVI–XVIII)', *Lacio Drom* (1987), no. 4, pp. 2–27.

Chambers, E. *Cyclopædia* (London, 1728).

La Continuation du Mercure François, 1610–12.

Cornerus, H. *Chronica novella usque ad annum 1435*, in J. G. Eccard, *Corpus historicum medii ævi* (Leipzig, 1723), vol. 2.

Creades, D. 'Les premiers Gitans à Murcie', *Études Tsiganes* (1974), nos 2/3, pp. 5–7.

Crofton, H. T. 'Early annals of the Gypsies in England', *JGLS*(1), 1 (1888–9), pp. 5–24.

—— 'Supplementary annals of the Gypsies in England, before 1700', *JGLS*(2), 1 (1907–8), pp. 31–4.

Davies, C. S. L. 'Slavery and Protector Somerset; the Vagrancy Act of 1547', *Economic History Review* (1966), pp. 533–49.

Diderot, D. (ed.). *Encyclopédie* (Paris, 1751–72).

Douglas, G. *Diversions of a Country Gentleman* (London, 1902).

Fielding, H. *A Clear State of the Case of Elizabeth Canning* (London, 1753).

Fraser, A. M. 'Counterfeit Egyptians', *Tsiganologische Studien* (1990), no. 2, pp. 43–69.

Fraser, A. M. and Vaux de Foletier, F. de. 'The Gypsy healer and the King of Scots', *JGLS*(3), 51 (1972), pp. 1–8.

Frescobaldi, N. See Bellorini and Hoade; Manzi.

Fritsch, A. *Diatribe historica-politica de Zygenorum origine, vita ac moribus* (Jena, 1660); German translation 1662.

Gaster, M. 'Rumanian Gypsies in 1560', *JGLS*(3), 12 (1933), p. 61.

Gelsenbach, R. 'Quellen zur Geschichte der Roma und ihrer Interpretation, dargestellt an Beispielen aus dem 15. Jahrhundert', *Giessener Hefte für Tsiganologie* (1985), 1/85, pp. 8–16; 2 + 3/85, pp. 3–11.

Gilliat-Smith, B. J. 'An eighteenth century Hungarian document', *JGLS*(3), 42 (1963), pp. 50–3.

'Gipsies in America, 1581', *JGLS*(2), 6 (1912–13), p. 61.

Gómez Alfaro, A. 'Anotaciones a los censos gitanos en Andalucía', *Actas del I Congreso de Historia de Andalucía* (Córdoba, 1978), vol. 1, pp. 239–56.

—— 'La polémica sobre la deportación de los Gitanos a las colonias de América', *Cuadernos Hispanoamericanos* (Madrid, 1982), no. 386, pp. 319–21.

—— 'El Expediente general de Gitanos' (doctoral thesis, Madrid, 1988).

Gronemeyer, R. 'Die Zigeuner in den Kathedralen des Wissens', *Giessener Hefte für Tsiganologie* (1986), 1–4/86, pp. 7–29.

—— *Zigeuner im Spiegel früher Chroniken und Abhandlungen* (Giessen, 1987).

Groome, F. H. 'Transportation of Gypsies from Scotland to America', *JGLS*(1), 2 (1890–1), pp. 60–2.

Hall, E. *Chronicles of King Henry the Eighth* (London, 1548).

Hall, E. M. 'Gentile cruelty to Gypsies', *JGLS*(3), 11 (1932), pp. 49–56.

Halliday, W. R. *Folklore Studies* (London, 1924).

Hammer-Purgstall, J. G. von. *Geschichte des osmanischen Reiches* (Budapest, 1827–35).

Harff, A. von. *Die Pilgerfahrt des Ritters Arnold von Harff*, ed. E. von Groote (Cologne, 1860).

Harrison, W. *A Description of England* (prefixed to Holinshed's *Chronicle*, London, 1587).

Hasluck, M. 'Firman of A.H. 1013–14 (A.D. 1604–5) regarding Gypsies in the Western Balkans', *JGLS*(3), 27 (1948), pp. 1–12.

Hufton, O. H. *The Poor of Eighteenth-Century France* (Oxford, 1974).

Jones, R. O. 'The mode of disposing of gipsies and vagrants in the reign of Elizabeth', *Archæologia Cambrensis* (4th series), 13 (1882), pp. 226–31; rptd in *JGLS*(2), 2 (1908–9), pp. 334–8.

Kappen, O. van. 'Four early safe-conducts for Gypsies', *JGLS*(3), 44 (1965), pp. 107–15.

—— 'Contribution to the history of the Gypsies in Belgium', *JGLS*(3), 48 (1969), pp. 107–20.

Krantz, A. *Rerum Germanicarum historici clariss. Saxonia* (Frankfurt am Main, 1580).

Lang, D. M. (ed.). *Lives and Legends of the Georgian Saints. Selected and translated from the original texts* (London, 1956).

Le Saige, J. *Voyage de J. Le Saige de Douai à Rome, Venise, Jérusalem, et autres saints lieux* (Douai, 1851).

Lewenklaw von Amelbeurn, H. *Neuwe Chronika türkischer Nation* (Frankfurt am Main, 1590).

Liégeois, J.-P. 'Bohémiens et pouvoirs publics en France du XVe au XIXe siècle', *Études Tsiganes* (1978), no. 4, pp. 10–30.

Lopes da Costa, E. M. 'La minoranza sociale Rom nel Portogallo moderno (secoli XV–XVIII)', *Lacio Drom* (1989), no. 1, pp. 5–23.

Lopéz de Meneses, A. 'La inmigración gitana en España durante el siglo XV', in *Martínez Ferrando, Archivero. Miscelánea de Estudios dedicados a su memoria* (Barcelona, 1968), pp. 239–63.

—— 'Noves dades sobre la immigráció gitana a Espanya al segle XV', in *Estudis d'Historia Medieval* (Barcelona, 1971), vol. 4, pp. 145–60.

Macfie, R. A. S. 'The Gypsy visit to Rome in 1422', *JGLS*(3), 11 (1932), pp. 111–15.

—— 'Gypsy persecutions: a survey of a black chapter in European history', *JGLS*(3), 22 (1943), pp. 65–78.

Manzi, G. (ed.). *Viaggio di Lionardo di Niccolò Frescobaldi in Egitto, e in Terra Santa* (Rome, 1818).

Mészáros, L. 'A hódoltsági latinok, görögök és cigányok történetéhez. 16. sz.-i oszmán-török szórványadatok' ['On the history of Latins, Greeks and Gypsies under Ottoman rule. Documents from Ottoman archives of the sixteenth century'], *Századok* 110 (1976), no. 3, pp. 474–89.

Moncada, S. de. 'Espulsion de los Gitanos', in his *Restauracion politica de España* (Madrid, 1619).

More, Sir Thomas. *A dyaloge of Syr Thomas More, knt.* (London, 1529).

MS Register of the Privy Seal of Scotland, vol. 8.

Münster, S. *Cosmographia universalis* (Basel, 1550).

Muratori, L. A. (ed.). *Rerum Italicarum Scriptores*, vols 18 and 19 (Milan, 1730–1).

Ogle, A. *The Case of the Lollards Tower* (Oxford, 1949).

Panaitescu, P. N. 'The Gypsies in Walachia and Moldavia: a chapter of economic history', *JGLS*(3), 20 (1941), pp. 58–72.

Pastore, M. 'Zingari nello Stato Sabaudo', *Lacio Drom* (1989), nos 3–4, pp. 6–19.

Paul, Sir J. Balfour (ed.). *Accounts of the Lord High Treasurer of Scotland*, vols 3 and 5 (Edinburgh, 1901–3).

Peeters, P. 'Histoires monastiques géorgiennes', *Analecta Bollandiana*, 36–7 (1917–19).

Piasere, L. 'De origine Cinganorum', *Études et documents balkaniques et méditerranéens*, 14 (1989), pp. 105–26.

Pike, R. *Penal Servitude in Early Modern Spain* (Madison, WI, 1983).

Pischel, R. *Beiträge zur Kenntnis der deutschen Zigeuner* (Halle, 1894).

Pray, G. (ed.). *Annales Regum Hungariae ab anno Christi CMXCVII ad annum MDLXIV* (Vienna, 1764–70).

Rid, S. *The Art of Juggling or Legerdemain* (London, 1612).

Sampson, J. 'The Wood family', *JGLS*(3), 11 (1932), pp. 56–71.

Sanchez Ortega, M. H. *Documentación selecta sobre la situación de los gitanos españoles en el siglo XVIII* (Madrid, 1976).

Shirley, J. (trans.). *A Parisian Journal, 1405–1449* (Oxford, 1968).

Sibeth, U. 'Verordnungen gegen Zigeuner in der Landgrafschaft Hessen-Kassel im Zeitalter des Früh-Absolutismus', *Giessener Hefte für Tsiganologie* (1985), no. 4, pp. 3–15.

Soulis, G. C. 'A note on the taxation of the Balkan Gypsies in the seventeenth century', *JGLS*(3), 38 (1959), pp. 154–6.

—— 'The Gypsies in the Byzantine Empire and the Balkans in the late Middle Ages', *Dumbarton Oaks Papers*, no. 15 (1961), pp. 142–65.

Stumpf, J. *Schweytzer Chronik* (Zürich, 1606).

Thomasius, J. *Dissertatio philosophica de Cingaris* (Leipzig, 1671); German translation 1702.

Thompson, T. W. 'Consorting with and counterfeiting Egyptians', *JGLS*(3), 2 (1923), pp. 81–93.

—— 'Gleanings from constables' accounts and other sources', *JGLS*(3), 7 (1928), pp. 30–47.

Thurmaier, J. *Annalium Boiorum libri septem* (Ingolstadt, 1554).

Tuetey, A. (ed.). *Journal d'un Bourgeois de Paris (1405–49)* (Paris, 1881).

Twiss, R. *Travels through Spain and Portugal in 1772 and 1773* (London, 1775).

Vaux de Foletier, F. de. 'Le pèlerinage romain des Tsiganes en 1422 et les lettres du Pape Martin V', *Études Tsiganes* (1965), no. 4, pp. 13–19.

Vekerdi, J. 'Earliest archival evidence on Gypsies in Hungary', *JGLS*(4), 1 (1977), pp. 170–2.

—— 'La parola "Zingaro" nei nomi medievali', *Lacio Drom* (1985), no. 3, p. 31.

Voetius, G. *Selectarum disputationum theologicarum* (Utrecht, 1655).

Von der falschen Betler buberey, Mit einer Vorrede Martini Luther (Wittemberg, 1528).

Vukanović, T. P. 'Le firman du sultan Sélim II relatif aux Tsiganes, ouvriers dans les mines de Bosnie (1574)', *Études Tsiganes* (1969), no. 3, pp. 8–10.

Weber, C. von. 'Zigeuner in Sachsen 1488–1792', in *Mitteilungen aus dem Hauptstaatsarchive zu Dresden* (Leipzig, 1857–61), vol. 2, pp. 282–303.

Weissenbruch, J. B. *Ausführliche Relation von der famosen Zigeuner- Diebs- Mord- und Rauber-Bande, welche zu Giessen justificirt worden* (Frankfurt and Leipzig, 1727).

Wellstood, F. C. 'Some French edicts against the Gypsies', *JGLS*(2), 5 (1911–12), pp. 313–16.

Wiener, L. 'Ismaelites', *JGLS*(2), 4 (1910–11), pp. 83–100.

Winstedt, E. O. 'The Gypsies of Modon and the "Wine of Romeney"', *JGLS*(2), 3 (1909–10), pp. 57–69.

—— 'Early British Gypsies', *JGLS*(2), 7 (1913–14), pp. 5–37.

—— 'Some records of the Gypsies in Germany, 1407–1792', *JGLS*(3), 11 (1932), pp. 97–111; 12 (1933), pp. 123–41, 189–96; 13 (1934), pp. 98–116.

—— 'Gypsies at Bruges', *JGLS*(3), 15 (1936), pp. 126–34.

—— 'Hannikel', *JGLS*(3), 16 (1937), pp. 154–73.

—— 'Some Transylvanian Gypsy documents of the sixteenth century', *JGLS*(3), 20 (1941), pp. 49–58.

Zedler, J. H. (ed.). *Universal-Lexicon aller Wissenschaften und Künste* (Leipzig, 1732–50).

Zuccon, M. 'La legislazione sugli Zingari negli stati italiani prima della rivoluzione', *Lacio Drom* (1979), nos 1–2, pp. 1–68.

7 Nineteenth and twentieth centuries

Acton, T. *Gypsy Politics and Social Change* (London, 1974).

Acton, T. and Kenrick, D. 'From summer voluntary schemes to European Community bureaucracy: the development of special provision for Traveller education in the United Kingdom since 1967', *European Journal of Intercultural Studies*, 1 (1991), no. 3, pp. 47–62.

Beck, S. 'Tsigani-Gypsies in socialist Romania', *Giessener Hefte für Tsiganologie* (1986), 1–4/86, pp. 109–27.

Bernadac, C. *L'Holocauste oublié* (Paris, 1979).

Boner, C. *Transylvania* (London, 1865).

Boué, A. *La Turquie d'Europe* (Paris, 1840).

Chamberlain, H. S. *Die Grundlagen des neunzehnten Jahrhunderts* (Vienna, 1899).

Commission for Racial Equality v Dutton, Court of Appeal, London, 1988.

'Compensation claims rejected', in *Manchester Guardian*, 30 March 1959, p. 5.

Crowe, D. and Kolsti, J. (eds). *The Gypsies of Eastern Europe* (New York/London, 1991).

Dahler, R. 'Zigeuneropvangbeleid Oldenzaal', in *Zigeuners in Nederland*, eds P. Hovens and R. Dahler (Nijmegen/Rijswijk, 1988), pp. 385–415.

Davidóva, E. 'The Gypsies in Czechoslovakia', *JGLS*(3), 50 (1971), pp. 40–54.

Döring, H.-J. *Die Zigeuner im NS-Staat* (Hamburg, 1964).

Ficowski, J. 'The Gypsies in the Polish People's Republic', *JGLS*(3), 35 (1956), pp. 28–38.

Fischer, E. 'Erbe als Schicksal', *Deutsche Allgemeine Zeitung*, 28 March 1943.

Formoso, B. *Tsiganes et sédentaires* (Paris, 1986).

Fraser, A. M. 'References to Gypsies in British highway law', *JGLS*(3), 40 (1961), pp. 137–9.

—— 'The Travellers. Developments in England and Wales, 1953–63', *JGLS*(3), 43 (1964), pp. 83–112.

—— 'A rum lot', in *100 Years of Gypsy Studies*, ed. M. T. Salo (Cheverly, MD, 1990), pp. 1–14.

—— 'The Rom migrations', *JGLS*(5), 2 (1992), no. 2.

Gaster, M. 'Bill of sale of Gypsy slaves in Moldavia, 1851', *JGLS*(3), 2 (1923), pp. 68–81.

Gilliat-Smith B.-J. 'Report on the Gypsy tribes of north east Bulgaria', *JGLS*(2), 9 (1915–16), pp. 1–54, 65–109.

Gjorgjević, T. R. 'Rumanian Gypsies in Serbia', *JGLS*(3), 8 (1929), pp. 7–25.

Gobineau, J.-A. de. *Essai sur l'inégalité des races humaines* (Paris, 1853–5).

Gotovitch, J. 'Quelques données relatives à l'extermination des tsiganes de Belgique', *Cahiers d'histoire de la seconde guerre mondiale*, 4 (1976), pp. 161–80.

Günther, W. *Zur preussischen Zigeunerpolitik seit 1871* (Hanover, 1985).

Guy, W. 'Ways of looking at Roms: the case of Czechoslovakia', in *Gypsies, Tinkers and Other Travellers*, ed. F. Rehfisch (London, 1975), pp. 201–29.

Haley, W. J. 'The Gypsy conference at Bucharest', *JGLS*(3), 13 (1934), pp. 182–90.

Havas, G. 'Strategien des Beschäftigungswechsels bei verschiedenen Zigeunergemeinschaften in Ungarn', *Giessener Hefte für Tsiganologie* (1984), 2/84, pp. 3–24.

Hehemann, R. *Die 'Bekämpfung des Zigeunerunwesens' im Wilhelminischen Deutschland und in der Weimarer Republik 1871–1933* (Frankfurt am Main, 1987).

Holmes, C. 'The German Gypsy question in Britain, 1904–06', *JGLS*(4), 1 (1978), no. 4, pp. 248–67.

Jones, D. 'Rural crime and protest', in *The Victorian Countryside*, ed. G. E. Mingay (London, 1981), vol. 2, pp. 566–79.

Kalibová, K. and Pavlik, Z. 'Demographic specificities of the Romany population in Czechoslovakia', paper at the 7th International Demographic Seminar, Humboldt University, Berlin, 1986.

Kaminski, I.-M. 'The dilemma of power: internal and external leadership. The Gypsy-Roma of Poland', in *The Other Nomads*, ed. A. Rao (Cologne, 1987), pp. 323–56.

Kogălniceanu, M. *Desrobirea Țiganiloru* (Bucharest, 1891).

König, U. *Sinti und Roma unter dem Nationalsozialismus: Verfolgung und Widerstand* (Bochum, 1989).

Körber, U. 'Die Wiedergutmachung und die "Zigeuner"', in *Feinderklärung und Prävention* (Berlin, 1988), pp. 165–75.

Kostelancik, D. J. 'The Gypsies of Czechoslovakia: political and ideological considerations in the development of policy', *Studies in Comparative Communism*, 22 (1989), pp. 307–21.

Liégeois, J.-P. *School Provision for Gypsy and Traveller Children* (Brussels, 1987).

Lockwood, W. G. 'Balkan Gypsies: an introduction', in *Papers from the Fourth and Fifth Annual Meetings, Gypsy Lore Society, North American Chapter* (New York, 1985), pp. 91–9; rptd with modifications in *Giessener Hefte für Tsiganologie* (1985), 1/85, pp. 17–23.

—— 'East European Gypsies in western Europe: the social and cultural adaptation of the Xoraxané', *Nomadic Peoples* (1986), nos 21/22, pp. 63–70.

Lombroso, C. *L'uomo delinquente* (Rome, 1876).

MacRitchie, D. 'The Greek Gypsies at Liverpool', *Chambers's Journal*, 11 Sep. 1886.

Mandla (Sewa Singh) v Dowell Lee, House of Lords, 1983 (2 A.C. 548).

Mills v Cooper, High Court, London, 1967 (2 Q.B. 459).

Milton, S. 'The context of the Holocaust', *German Studies Review*, 13 (1990), pp. 269–83.

Müller-Hill, B. *Murderous Science* (Oxford, 1988), a translation of *Tödliche Wissenschaft* (Reinbeck bei Hamburg, 1984).

Nawrocki, G. '"Cintis" in Hamburg – Großstadtzigeuner ohne Romantik', *Hamburger Tageblatt* no. 223, 18 August 1937.

Oschlies, W. '"Schwarze" und "Weisse": zur Lage der Zigeuner in der Tschechoslowakei', *Giessener Hefte für Tsiganologie* (1985), 1/85, pp. 24–32.

Petrović, A. 'Contributions to the study of the Serbian Gypsies', *JGLS*(3), 19 (1940), pp. 87–100.

Piasere, L. 'In search of new niches: the productive organization of the peripatetic Xoraxané in Italy', in *The Other Nomads*, ed. A. Rao (Cologne, 1987), pp. 111–32.

Pouqueville, F. C. H. L. *Voyage dans la Grèce* (Paris, 1820).

Puxon, G. *Roma: Europe's Gypsies*, 2nd and 4th edns (London, 1975 and 1987).

'Resolution of the Council and the Ministers of Education . . . on school provision for gypsy and traveller children', *Official Journal of the European Communities*, 21 June 1989.

Rochas, M.-T. 'Les Tsiganes yougoslaves!!', *Études Tsiganes*, 30 (1984), no. 2, pp. 29–37.

Samuel, R. 'Comers and goers', in *The Victorian City*, eds H. J. Dyos and M. Wolff (London, 1973), vol. 1, pp. 123–60.

Sijes, B. A. et al. *Vervolging van Zigeuners in Nederland 1940–1945* (The Hague, 1979).

Silverman, C. 'Bulgarian Gypsies: adaptation in a socialist context', *Nomadic Peoples* (1986), nos 21/22, pp. 51–60.

Strauss, E. 'Die Zigeunerverfolgung in Bayern 1885–1926', *Giessener Hefte für Tsiganologie* (1986), 1–4/86, pp. 31–108.

Swann, Lord. *Education For All* (London, 1985).

Thompson T. W. 'English Gypsy death and burial customs', *JGLS(3)*, 3 (1924), pp. 5–38 and 60–93.

—— 'Foreign Gypsy Coppersmiths in England in 1868', *JGLS(3)*, 6 (1927), p. 144.

Thurner, E. *Nationalsozialismus und Zigeuner in Österreich* (Vienna, 1983).

Uhlik, R. 'Iz ciganske onomastike', *Glasnik Zemaljskog museja u Sarajevu, istorija i etnografija*, new series, 10 (1955), pp. 51–71; 11 (1956), pp. 193–209.

Ulč, O. 'Gypsies in Czechoslovakia: a case of unfinished integration', *Eastern European Politics and Societies*, 2 (1988), pp. 306–33.

Willems, W. and Lucassen, L. 'Beeldvorming over Zigeuners in Nederlandse Encyclopedieën (1724–1984) en hun wetenschappelijke bronnen', in *Zigeuners in Nederland*, eds P. Hovens and R. Dahler (Nijmegen/Rijswijk, 1988), pp. 5–52 [English version, 'The Church of knowledge', in *100 Years of Gypsy Studies*, ed. M. T. Salo (Cheverly, MD, 1990), pp. 31–50].

Williams, P. *Mariage tsigane* (Paris, 1984).

Winstedt, E. O. 'The Gypsy Coppersmiths' invasion of 1911–13', *JGLS(2)*, 6 (1912–13), pp. 244–303.

Yoors, J. *Crossing* (New York, 1971).

Zimmermann, M. 'From discrimination to the "Family Camp" at Auschwitz: National Socialist persecution of the Gypsies', *Dachau Review*, 2 (1990), pp. 87–113.

Zülch, T. 'Und auch heute noch verfolgt?', *Zeitschrift für Kulturaustausch*, 31 (1981), pp. 397–410.

8 North America

Gropper, R. C. *Gypsies in the City* (Princeton, NJ, 1975).

Marchbin, A. A. 'Gypsy immigration to Canada', *JGLS*(3), 13 (1934), pp. 134–44.

Salo, M. T. (ed.). *The American Kalderaš* (Hackettstown, NJ, 1981).

Salo, M. T. and Salo, S. *The Kalderaš in Eastern Canada* (Ottawa, 1977).

——— 'The Romnichel economic and social organization in urban New England, 1850–1930', *Urban Anthropology*, 11 (1982), pp. 273–313.

——— 'Gypsy immigration to the United States', in *Papers from the Sixth and Seventh Annual Meetings, Gypsy Lore Society, North American Chapter* (New York, 1986), pp. 85–96.

Sutherland, A. *Gypsies, the Hidden Americans* (London, 1975).

9 Physical anthropology

Bhalla, V. 'Marker genes as guides to the kinship of populations: a plea for linguistic-cum-anthropogenetic approach to the problem of "Roma" ancestry', in *Romani Language and Culture*, eds S. Balić et al. (Sarajevo, 1989), pp. 155–63.

Ély, B. 'Les Crânes tsiganes des collections du Musée de l'Homme', *Bulletins de la Société d'Anthropologie de Paris* (1967), pp. 177–92.

Gropper, R. C. 'What does blood tell?', *GLS / NAC Newsletter*, 4 (1981), nos 2, 3 and 4.

Mourant, A. E. *Blood Relations: Blood Groups and Anthropology* (Oxford, 1983).

Pittard, E. *Les Tziganes ou Bohémiens* (Geneva, 1932).

Reyment, R. 'Les Voyageurs suédois: aspects physiques et linguistiques', *Études Tsiganes* (1981), no. 4, pp. 1–14.

Tauszik, T. 'Human- and medical-genetic examinations on the Gypsy population in Hungary', *GLS/NAC Newsletter*, 9 (1986), no. 4.

10 Language

Bloch, J. Review of J. Sampson's *The Dialect of the Gypsies of Wales*, *JGLS*(3), 5 (1926), pp. 134–41.

Borde, A. *The Fyrst Boke of the Introduction of Knowledge* [lithographic reprint of 2nd edn of 1562/3] (Salzburg, 1979).

Borrow, G. *Romano Lavo-Lil* (London, 1874).

Bryant, J. 'Collections on the Zingara or Gypsey language', *Archaeologia*, 7 (1785), pp. 387–94.

Büttner, J. *Vergleichungstafeln der Schriftarten verschiedener Völker* (Göttingen, 1775).

Cortiade, M. 'Romany phonetics and orthography', *GLS/NAC Newsletter*, 7 (1984), no. 4.

—— 'Distance between the Romani dialects', *GLS/NAC Newsletter*, 8 (1985), no. 2, pp. 1–4.

—— *Romani fonetika thaj lekhipa* (Titograd, 1986).

—— 'O kodifikaciji i normalizaciji romskog zajedničkog jezika', in *Romani Language and Culture*, eds S. Balić et al. (Sarajevo, 1989), pp. 205–21.

Fraser, A. M. 'Looking into the seeds of time', *Tsiganologische Studien* (1992), no. 1.

Friedman, V. A. 'Problems in the codification of a standard Romani literary language', in *Papers from the Fourth and Fifth Annual Meetings, Gypsy Lore Society, North American Chapter* (New York, 1985), pp. 56–75.

Friedman, V. A. and Dankoff, R. 'The earliest known text in Balkan (Rumelian) Romani', *JGLS(5)*, 1 (1991), pp. 1–20.

Gjerdman, O. and Ljungberg, E. *The Language of the Swedish Coppersmith Gipsy Johan Dimitri Taikon* (Uppsala, 1963).

Grierson G. A. *Linguistic Survey of India*, 20 vols (Delhi, 1903–28).

Hancock, I. 'The development of Romani linguistics', in *Languages and Cultures: Studies in Honor of Edgar C. Polomé*, eds M. A. Jazayery and W. Winter (Berlin, 1988), pp. 183–223.

—— 'The Hungarian student Valyi Istvan and the Indian connection of Romani', *Roma*, no. 36 (1991).

Higgie, B. 'Proto-Romanes Phonology', Ph.D. dissertation, University of Texas at Austin, 1984.

Iversen, R. *Secret Languages in Norway. Part II: The Rodi (Rotwelsch) in Norway* (Oslo, 1945).

Josef Karl Ludwig, Archduke. *Czigány Nyelvtan* ['The Gypsy Language'] (Budapest, 1888).

Jusuf, S. and Kepeski, K. *Romani gramatika – Romska gramatika* (Skopje, 1980).

Kaufman, T. Review of W. R. Rishi's *Multilingual Romani Dictionary*, *International Journal of the Sociology of Language*, 19 (1979), pp. 131–44.

—— 'Explorations in protoGypsy phonology and classification', paper at the 6th South Asian Languages Analysis Round-table, Austin, Texas, 25–26 May 1984.

Kluyver, A. 'Un glossaire tsigane du seizième siècle', *JGLS*(2), 4 (1910–11), pp. 131–42.

Kochanowski, J. *Gypsy Studies* (New Delhi, 1963).

Macalister, R. A. Stewart. *The Language of the Nawar or Zutt, the Nomad Smiths of Palestine*, GLS Monograph no. 3 (London, 1914); previously published in *JGLS*(2), 3 (1909–10), pp. 120–6, 298–317; 5 (1911–12), pp. 289–305.

Marsden, W. 'Observations on the language of the . . . Gypsies', *Archaeologia*, 7 (1785), pp. 382–6.

Miklosich, F. X. *Über die Mundarten und die Wanderungen der Zigeuner Europas* (*Denkschriften der kaiserlichen Akademie der Wissenschaften*, Philosophisch-historische Klasse, vols 21–31, Vienna, 1872–81).

Papp, G. *A beás cigányok román nyelvjárása: Beás-magyar szótár* ['Rumanian Dialect of Boyash Gypsies: Boyash–Hungarian Dictionary'] (Pécs, 1982).

Paspati, A. *Études sur les Tchinghianés* (Constantinople, 1870).

Rishi, W. R. *Multilingual Romani Dictionary* (Chandigarh, 1974).

—— *Romani Punjabi English Dictionary* (Patiala, 1981).

Rüdiger, J. C. C. *Neuster Zuwachs der teutschen fremden und allgemeinen Sprachkunde*, Part 1 (Leipzig, 1782).

Sampson, J. *The Dialect of the Gypsies of Wales* (Oxford, 1926).

—— 'Notes on Professor R. L. Turner's "The position of Romani in Indo-Aryan" ', *JGLS*(3), 6 (1927), pp. 57–68.

Soravia, G. *Dialetti degli Zingari Italiani* (Pisa, 1977).

Swadesh, M. 'Lexicostatistic dating of prehistoric ethnic contacts', *Proceedings of the American Philosophical Society*, 96 (1952), pp. 452–63.

—— *The Origin and Diversification of Language*, ed. J. Sherzer (London, 1972).

Torrione, M. 'Del dialecto caló y sus usuarios: la minoría gitana de España' (doctoral thesis, Perpignan, 1988).

Trail, R. L. *The Grammar of Lamani* (Norman, OK, 1970).

Turner, R. L. 'The position of Romani in Indo-Aryan', *JGLS*(3), 5 (1926), pp. 145–89.

—— ' "The position of Romani in Indo-Aryan": A reply to Dr J. Sampson', *JGLS*(3), 6 (1927), pp. 129–38.

—— 'Transference of aspiration in European Gypsy', *Bulletin of the School of Oriental and African Studies*, 22 (1959), pp. 491–8.

Valet, J. 'Les dialectes du sinto-manouche', in *Tsiganes: Identité, Évolution*, ed. P. Williams (Paris, 1989), pp. 309–14.

Vulcanius, B. *De literis et lingua Getarum sive Gothorum* (Leiden, 1597).

11 Music

Alvarez Caballero, A. *Historia del cante flamenco* (Madrid, 1981).
—— *Gitanos, payos y flamencos, en los orígines del flamenco* (Madrid, 1988).
Blas Vega, J. *Los Cafés cantantes de Sevilla* (Madrid, 1984).
Bobri, B. 'Gypsies and Gypsy choruses of old Russia', *JGLS*(3), 40 (1961), pp. 112–20.
Brepohl, F. W. 'Die Zigeuner als Musiker in den türkischen Eroberungskriegen des XVI. Jahrhunderts', *JGLS*(2), 4 (1910–11), pp. 241–4.
Falla, M. de. *El Cante jondo* (Granada, 1922).
Hajdu, A. 'Les Tsiganes de Hongrie et leur musique', *Études Tsiganes* (1958), no. 1, pp. 1–30.
Kovalcsik, K. *Vlach Gypsy Folk Songs in Slovakia* (Budapest, 1985).
Leblon, B. 'Identité gitane et flamenco', in *Tsiganes: Identité, Évolution*, ed. P. Williams (Paris, 1989), pp. 521–7.
—— *Musiques Tsiganes et Flamenco* (Paris, 1990).
Liszt, F. *Des Bohémiens et de leur musique en Hongrie* (Paris, 1859); *The Gipsy in Music*, trans. E. Evans (London, 1926).
Sárosi, B. *Gypsy Music* (Budapest, 1978).
Stewart, M. 'La fraternité dans le chant: l'expérience des Roms hongrois', in *Tsiganes: Identité, Évolution*, ed. P. Williams (Paris, 1989), pp. 497–513.

12 Folk-tales

Groome, F. H. *Gypsy Folk-Tales* (London, 1899).

13 Pollution code

Ficowski, J. 'Supplementary notes on the *mageripen* code among Polish Gypsies', *JGLS*(3), 30 (1951), pp. 123–32.
Miller, C. 'Mačwaya Gypsy Marimé' (MA thesis, Seattle, 1968).
—— 'American Rom and the ideology of defilement', in *Gypsies, Tinkers and Other Travellers*, ed. F. Rehfisch (London, 1975), pp. 41–54.

Rao, A. 'Some Mānuš conceptions and attitudes', in *Gypsies, Tinkers and Other Travellers*, ed. F. Rehfisch (London, 1975), pp. 139–67.

Silverman, C. 'Pollution and power: Gypsy women in America', in *The American Kalderaš*, ed. M. T. Salo (Hackettstown, NJ, 1981), pp. 55–70.

Thompson, T. W. 'The uncleanness of women among English Gypsies', *JGLS*(3), 1 (1922), pp. 15–43; and 8 (1929), pp. 33–9.

14 Religion

Acton, T. 'The Gypsy Evangelical Church', *Ecumenical Review*, 31 (1979), no. 3, pp. 11–17.

Glize, R. 'L'église évangélique tsigane comme voie possible d'un engagement culturel nouveau', in *Tsiganes: Identité, Évolution*, ed. P. Williams (Paris, 1989), pp. 433–43.

Lazell, D. *From the Forest I Came* (London, 1970).

Le Cossec, C. ' "Phénomène pentecôtiste" ou réveil religieux', *Études Tsiganes* (1985), no. 1, pp. 19–21.

Ridholls, J. *Travelling Home* (Basingstoke, 1986).

Sato, E. B. L. 'The social impact of the rise of Pentecostal evangelicalism among American Rom', in *Papers from the Eighth and Ninth Annual Meetings, Gypsy Lore Society, North American Chapter* (New York, 1988), pp. 69–94.

Smith, C. *The Life Story of Gipsy Cornelius Smith* (London, 1890).

Smith, R. *Gipsy Smith: His Life and Work* (London, 1901).

Wang, K. 'Le mouvement pentecôtiste chez les Gitans espagnols', in *Tsiganes: Identité, Évolution*, ed. P. Williams (Paris, 1989), pp. 423–32.

15 Other Travellers

Arnold, H. *Fahrendes Volk* (Neustadt, 1980).

Bonilla, K. 'The Quinquis: Spain's last nomads', *JGLS*(4), 1 (1976), no. 2, pp. 86–92.

Gmelch, G. *The Irish Tinkers* (Menlo Park, CA, 1977; 2nd edn 1985).

Gmelch, G. and Gmelch, S. B. 'Ireland's travelling people: a comprehensive bibliography', *JGLS*(4), 1 (1977), no. 3, pp. 159–69.

Gmelch, S. B. *Tinkers and Travellers* (Dublin, 1975; 2nd edn 1979).

Golowin, S. 'Fahrende in der Schweiz', *Giessener Hefte für Tsiganologie* (1985), 2 + 3/85, pp. 40–50.

Haesler, W. *Enfants de la Grande-route* (Neuchâtel, 1955).

Heymowski, A. *Swedish Travellers and their Ancestry* (Uppsala, 1969).

Ignacio, L. *Los Quinquis* (Barcelona, 1974).

MacColl, E. and Seeger, P. *Till Doomsday in the Afternoon* (Manchester, 1986).

Meyer, C. *'Unkraut der Landstrasse'* (Zürich, 1988).

Rao, A. (ed.). *The Other Nomads* (Cologne/Vienna, 1987).

Rehfisch, A. and Rehfisch, F. 'Scottish Travellers or Tinkers', in *Gypsies, Tinkers and Other Travellers*, ed. F. Rehfisch (London, 1975), pp. 271–83.

Reyniers, A. and Valet, J. 'Les Jeniš', *Études Tsiganes* (1991), no. 2, pp. 11–35.

Valet, J. *Les Voyageurs d'Auvergne, nos familles yéniches* (Clermont, 1990).

Wernink, J. H. A. *Woonwagenbewoners* (Assen, 1959).

Wiedel, J. and O'Fearadhaigh, M. *Irish Tinkers* (London, 1976).

16   Gypsies in art and literature

Beaumarchais, P.-A. C. de. *Le Mariage de Figaro* (1784).

Borrow, G. *Lavengro* (London, 1851).

—— *The Romany Rye* (London, 1857).

Campigotto, A. and Piasere, L. 'From Margutte to Cingar: the archeology of an image', in *100 Years of Gypsy Studies*, ed. M. T. Salo (Cheverly, MD, 1990), pp. 15–29.

Cervantes Saavedra, M. de. *Pedro de Urdemalas* (*c*.1611).

—— *La Gitanilla*, in his *Novelas exemplares* (Madrid, 1613).

Crockett, W. S. *The Scott Originals* (Edinburgh, 1912).

Cuzin, J.-P. *La diseuse de bonne aventure de Caravage* (Paris, 1977).

Defoe, D. *Moll Flanders* (London, 1722).

Fielding, H. *The History of Tom Jones* (London, 1749).

Firdawsi, *Shah-nameh* (1010).

Goethe, J. W. von. *Götz von Berlichingen* (1773).

—— *Wilhelm Meisters Lehrjahre* (1795–6).

Herder, J. G. *Ideen zur Philosophie der Geschichte der Menschheit* (1784–91).

Mone, F. J. (ed.). *Schauspiele des Mittelalters* (Karlsruhe, 1846), vol. 2.

O'Brien, C. *Gipsy Marion* (London, n.d. [*c*.1895]).

Recueil d'Arras ['Arras collection'], municipal library of Arras, MS 266.

Sachs, H. *Die 5 elenden wanderer*, in *Hans Sachs' Werke* (Berlin, 1884), vol. 2, pp. 58–68.

Scott, Sir Walter, *Guy Mannering* (Edinburgh, 1815).

Vicente, G. *Farsa das Ciganas* (1521).

Index